Pharo by Example 5

Based on Pharo by Example
by A.P. Black, S. Ducasse, O. Nierstrasz,
D. Pollet, with D. Cassou and M. Denker

Stéphane Ducasse
Dimitris Chloupis
Nicolai Hess
Dmitri Zagidulin

February 8, 2017
commit 9bfd105

Copyright 2016 by Stéphane Ducasse, Dimitris Chloupis, Nicolai Hess and Dmitri Zagidulin. Copyright 2009 by Andrew P. Black, Stéphane Ducasse, Oscar Nierstrasz, Damien Pollet, Damien Cassou and Marcus Denker. The contents of this book are protected under the Creative Commons Attribution-ShareAlike 3.0 Unported license.

You are **free**:

- to **Share**: to copy, distribute and transmit the work,
- to **Remix**: to adapt the work,

Under the following conditions:

Attribution. You must attribute the work in the manner specified by the author or licensor (but not in any way that suggests that they endorse you or your use of the work).

Share Alike. If you alter, transform, or build upon this work, you may distribute the resulting work only under the same, similar or a compatible license.

For any reuse or distribution, you must make clear to others the license terms of this work. The best way to do this is with a link to this web page: http://creativecommons.org/licenses/by-sa/3.0/

Any of the above conditions can be waived if you get permission from the copyright holder. Nothing in this license impairs or restricts the author's moral rights.

Your fair dealing and other rights are in no way affected by the above. This is a human-readable summary of the Legal Code (the full license):
http://creativecommons.org/licenses/by-sa/3.0/legalcode

[↓] Published by Lulu.com & Square Bracket Associates.
http://squarebracketassociates.org
ISBN 978-1-365-65459-6
First Edition, January 2017.

Book layout and typography based on the sbabook LaTeX class by Damien Pollet.

Contents

	Contents	i
1	**Preface**	**1**
1.1	What is Pharo?	1
1.2	Who should read this book?	2
1.3	A word of advice	3
1.4	An open book	3
1.5	The Pharo community	3
1.6	Examples and exercises	4
1.7	Acknowledgments	4
1.8	Hyper special acknowledgments	4
2	**A quick tour of Pharo**	**7**
2.1	Installing Pharo	7
2.2	Pharo: File components	8
2.3	Launching Pharo	9
2.4	PharoLauncher	10
2.5	The World Menu	11
2.6	Sending messages	13
2.7	Saving, quitting and restarting a Pharo session	15
2.8	Playgrounds and Transcripts	15
2.9	Keyboard shortcuts	16
2.10	The System Browser	19
2.11	Finding classes	22
2.12	Finding methods	25
2.13	Defining a new method	27
2.14	Chapter summary	31
3	**A first application**	**33**
3.1	The Lights Out game	34
3.2	Creating a new Package	34
3.3	Defining the class LOCell	35
3.4	Adding methods to a class	37
3.5	Inspecting an object	39
3.6	Defining the class LOGame	41
3.7	Organizing methods into protocols	46

i

3.8	Finishing the game	47
3.9	Let's try our code	49
3.10	Saving and sharing Pharo code	51
3.11	Chapter summary	56

4 Syntax in a nutshell — 57
4.1	Syntactic elements	57
4.2	Pseudo-variables	60
4.3	Message sends	61
4.4	Method syntax	62
4.5	Block syntax	63
4.6	Conditionals and loops in a nutshell	64
4.7	Primitives and pragmas	66
4.8	Chapter summary	67

5 Understanding message syntax — 69
5.1	Identifying messages	69
5.2	Three types of messages	71
5.3	Message composition	74
5.4	Hints for identifying keyword messages	79
5.5	Expression sequences	81
5.6	Cascaded messages	81
5.7	Chapter summary	82

6 The Pharo object model — 85
6.1	The rules of the model	85
6.2	Everything is an Object	85
6.3	Every object is an instance of a class	86
6.4	Instance structure and behavior	87
6.5	The instance side and the class side	88
6.6	Every class has a superclass	94
6.7	Everything happens by sending messages	97
6.8	Method lookup follows the inheritance chain	99
6.9	Shared variables	105
6.10	Internal object implementation note	109
6.11	Chapter summary	110

7 Some of the key tools of the Pharo environment — 113
7.1	Pharo environment overview	113
7.2	The main code browser	115
7.3	The inspector	128
7.4	The debugger	130
7.5	The process browser	139
7.6	Finding methods	140
7.7	Chapter summary	140

8 Sharing code and source control — 141
- 8.1 Packages: groups of classes and methods — 141
- 8.2 Source control — 148
- 8.3 The File List Browser — 151
- 8.4 In Pharo, you can't lose code — 152
- 8.5 Chapter summary — 153

9 SUnit — 155
- 9.1 Introduction — 155
- 9.2 Why testing is important — 156
- 9.3 What makes a good test? — 157
- 9.4 SUnit by example — 158
- 9.5 The SUnit cookbook — 162
- 9.6 The SUnit framework — 163
- 9.7 Advanced features of SUnit — 166
- 9.8 Continuing after a failure — 168
- 9.9 SUnit implementation — 168
- 9.10 A piece of advices on testing — 171
- 9.11 Chapter summary — 172

10 Basic classes — 175
- 10.1 Object — 175
- 10.2 Numbers — 184
- 10.3 Characters — 188
- 10.4 Strings — 189
- 10.5 Booleans — 190
- 10.6 Chapter summary — 192

11 Collections — 193
- 11.1 Introduction — 193
- 11.2 The varieties of collections — 193
- 11.3 Collection implementations — 196
- 11.4 Examples of key classes — 197
- 11.5 Collection iterators — 209
- 11.6 Some hints for using collections — 213
- 11.7 Chapter summary — 214

12 Streams — 217
- 12.1 Two sequences of elements — 217
- 12.2 Streams vs. collections — 218
- 12.3 Streaming over collections — 219
- 12.4 Using streams for file access — 227
- 12.5 Chapter summary — 229

13 Morphic — 231
- 13.1 The history of Morphic — 231
- 13.2 Manipulating morphs — 233

13.3	Composing morphs	234
13.4	Creating and drawing your own morphs	236
13.5	Interaction and animation	239
13.6	Interactors	242
13.7	Drag-and-drop	243
13.8	A complete example	245
13.9	More about the canvas	250
13.10	Chapter summary	251

14	**Seaside by example**	**253**
14.1	Why do we need Seaside?	253
14.2	Getting started	254
14.3	Seaside components	260
14.4	Rendering HTML	264
14.5	CSS: Cascading style sheets	270
14.6	Managing control flow	272
14.7	A complete tutorial example	278
14.8	A quick look at AJAX	285
14.9	Chapter summary	288

15	**Classes and metaclasses**	**291**
15.1	Rules for classes and metaclasses	291
15.2	Revisiting the Pharo object model	292
15.3	Every class is an instance of a metaclass	293
15.4	The metaclass hierarchy parallels the class hierarchy	295
15.5	Every metaclass inherits from `Class` and `Behavior`	297
15.6	Every metaclass is an instance of `Metaclass`	300
15.7	The metaclass of `Metaclass` is an instance of `Metaclass`	300
15.8	Chapter summary	302

16	**Reflection**	**303**
16.1	Introspection	304
16.2	Browsing code	309
16.3	Classes, method dictionaries and methods	311
16.4	Browsing environments	313
16.5	Accessing the run-time context	315
16.6	Intercepting messages not understood	318
16.7	Objects as method wrappers	322
16.8	Pragmas	325
16.9	Chapter summary	326

17	**Regular expressions in Pharo**	**329**
17.1	Tutorial example — generating a site map	330
17.2	Regex syntax	338
17.3	Regex API	345
17.4	Implementation Notes by Vassili Bykov	351
17.5	Chapter Summary	351

CHAPTER 1

Preface

1.1 What is Pharo?

Pharo is a modern, open-source, dynamically typed language supporting live coding inspired by Smalltalk. Pharo and its ecosystems is composed of the six fundamental elements:

- A dynamically-typed language with a syntax so simple it can fit on a postcard and yet is readable even for someone not familiar with it.
- A live coding environment that allows the coder to modify its code while the code executes, without any need to slow down his or her workflow.
- A powerful IDE providing all the tools to help manage complex code and promote good code design.
- A rich library that creates an environment so powerful that it can be viewed even as a virtual OS, including a very fast JITing VM and full access to OS libraries and features via its FFI.
- A culture where changes and improvements are encouraged and highly valued.
- A community that welcomes coders from any corner of the world with any skill and any programming languages.

Pharo strives to offer a lean, open platform for professional software development, as well as a robust and stable platform for research and development into dynamic languages and environments. Pharo serves as the reference implementation for the Seaside web development framework available at http://www.seaside.st.

Pharo core contains only code that has been contributed under the MIT license. The Pharo project started in March 2008 as a fork of Squeak (a modern implementation of Smalltalk-80), and the first 1.0 beta version was released on July 31, 2009. The current version is Pharo 5.0, released in May 2016. Pharo 6.0 is in alpha development and planned for release in April 2017.

Pharo is highly portable. Pharo can run on OS X, Windows, Linux, Android, iOS, and Raspberry Pi. Its virtual machine is written entirely in a subset of Pharo itself, making it easy to simulate, debug, analyze, and change from within Pharo itself. Pharo is the vehicle for a wide range of innovative projects, from multimedia applications and educational platforms to commercial web development environments.

There is an important principle behind Pharo: Pharo doesn't just copy the past, but it reinvents the essence behind Smalltalk. However we realize that Big Bang style approaches rarely succeed. Pharo instead favors evolutionary and incremental changes. Rather than leaping for the final perfect solution in one big step, a multitude of small changes keeps even the bleeding edge relatively stable while experimenting with important new features and libraries. This facilitates rapid feedback and contributions from the community, on which Pharo depends for its success. Finally Pharo is not read-only, Pharo integrates changes made by the community, daily. Pharo has around 100 contributors, based all over the world. You can have an impact on Pharo too!

1.2 Who should read this book?

The previous revision of this book was based on Pharo 1.4. This revision has been liberally updated to align with Pharo 5.0. Various aspects of Pharo are presented, starting with the basics then proceeding to intermediate topics. Advanced topics are presented in **Deep into Pharo**, a book on the internals of Pharo that is freely available at http://books.pharo.org. In addition for readers interested in web development, a new book **Enterprise Pharo: a Web Perspective** is freely available at http://books.pharo.org.

This book will not teach you how to program. The reader should have some familiarity with programming languages. Some background with object-oriented programming would also be helpful.

This book will introduce the Pharo programming environment, the language and the associated tools. You will be exposed to common idioms and practices, but the focus is on the technology, not on object-oriented design. Wherever possible, we will show you lots of examples.

There are numerous other books on Smalltalk freely available on the web at http://stephane.ducasse.free.fr/FreeBooks.html.

1.3 A word of advice

Do not be frustrated by parts of Pharo that you do not immediately understand. You do not have to know everything! Alan Knight expresses this as follows:

> *Try not to care.* Beginning Smalltalk programmers often have trouble because they think they need to understand all the details of how a thing works before they can use it. This means it takes quite a while before they can master Transcript show: 'Hello World'. One of the great leaps in OO is to be able to answer the question "How does this work?" with "I don't care".

When you don't understand something, simple or complex, do not hesitate for a second to ask us at our mailing lists (pharo-users@lists.pharo.org or pharo-dev@lists.pharo.org), irc and Slack. We love questions and we welcome people of any skill.

1.4 An open book

This book is an open book in the following senses:

- The content of this book is released under the Creative Commons Attribution-ShareAlike (by-sa) license. In short, you are allowed to freely share and adapt this book, as long as you respect the conditions of the license available at the following URL http://creativecommons.org/licenses/by-sa/3.0/.

- This book just describes the core of Pharo. We encourage others to contribute chapters on the parts of Pharo that we have not described. If you would like to participate in this effort, please contact us. We would like to see more books around Pharo!

- It is also possible to contribute directly to this book via Github. Just follow the instructions there and ask any question on the mailing list. You can find the Github repo at https://github.com/SquareBracketAssociates/UpdatedPharoByExample

1.5 The Pharo community

The Pharo community is friendly and active. Here is a short list of resources that you may find useful:

- http://www.pharo.org is the main web site of Pharo.
- On IRC, you can find us on the freenode.net server, channel "pharo".

- SmalltalkHub (http://www.smalltalkhub.com/) is the equivalent of SourceForge/Github for Pharo projects. Many extra packages and projects for Pharo live there.
- Pharo is also active on Slack - a platform for chat based on IRC (http://pharoproject.slack.com), just ask for an invitation on Pharo's website http://pharo.org/community, in the slack section. Everybody is welcomed.

1.6 Examples and exercises

We have tried to provide as many examples as possible. In particular, there are many examples that show a fragment of code which can be evaluated. We use a long arrow to indicate the result you obtain when you select an expression and from its context menu choose **print it**:

```
3 + 4
>>> 7 "if you select 3+4 and 'print it', you will see 7"
```

In case you want to play with these code snippets in Pharo, you can download a plain text file with all the example code from the Resources sidebar of the book's web site: http://books.pharo.org.

1.7 Acknowledgments

We would like to thank Alan Kay, Dan Ingalls and their team for making Squeak, an amazing Smalltalk development environment, that became the open-source project from which Pharo took roots. Pharo also would not be possible without the incredible work of the Squeak developers.

We would also like to thank Hilaire Fernandes and Serge Stinckwich who allowed us to translate parts of their columns on Smalltalk, and Damien Cassou for contributing the chapter on Streams. We especially thank Alexandre Bergel, Orla Greevy, Fabrizio Perin, Lukas Renggli, Jorge Ressia and Erwann Wernli for their detailed reviews.

We thank the University of Bern, Switzerland, for graciously supporting this open-source project and for hosting the web site of this book.

We also thank the Pharo community for their enthusiastic support of this book project, as well as for all the translations of the first edition of **Pharo by Example**.

1.8 Hyper special acknowledgments

We want to thank the original authors of this book! Without this initial version it would have been difficult to make this one. Pharo by Example is a central book to welcome newcomers and it has a great value.

1.8 Hyper special acknowledgments

Thanks to Manfred Kröhnert, Markus Schlager, Werner Kassens, Michael OKeefe, Aryeh Hoffman, Paul MacIntosh, Gaurav Singh, Jigyasa Grover, Craig Allen, Serge Stinckwich, avh-on1, Yuriy Timchuk, zio-pietro for the typos and feedback. Special thanks to Damien Cassou and Cyril Ferlicot for their great help in the book update. Finally we want to thank Inria for its steady and important financial support, and the RMoD team members for the constant energy pushing Pharo forward.

Super special thanks to Damien Pollet for this great book template.

CHAPTER 2

A quick tour of Pharo

This chapter will take you on a high level tour of Pharo, to help you get comfortable with the environment. There will be plenty of opportunities to try things out, so it would be a good idea if you have a computer handy when you read this chapter.

In particular, you will fire up Pharo, learn about the different ways of interacting with the system, and discover some of the basic tools. You will also learn how to define a new method, create an object and send it messages.

Note: Most of the introductory material in this book will work with any Pharo version, so if you already have one installed, you may as well continue to use it. However, since this book is written for Pharo 5.0, if you notice differences between the appearance or behaviour of your system and what is described here, do not be surprised.

2.1 Installing Pharo

Downloading Pharo

Pharo is available as a free download from http://pharo.org/download. Click the button for your operating system to download the appropriate .zip file. For example, the full Pharo 5.0 distribution for OS X will be available at http://files.pharo.org/platform/Pharo5.0-mac.zip.

Once that file is unzipped, it will contain everything you need to run Pharo (this includes the VM, the image, and the sources, as explained below).

Using handy scripts. http://files.pharo.org/get/ offers a collection of scripts

7

to download specific versions of Pharo. This is really handy to automate the process.

To download the latest 50 full system, use the following snippet.

```
wget -O- get.pharo.org/50+vm | bash
```

Installing Pharo

Pharo does not need to install anything in your system, as it's perfectly capable of running standalone. Depending on your platform, download the appropriate zip file, uncompress it in a directory of your choice and now you are ready to launch Pharo. In case of Ubuntu Linux, there is also the extra option of installing Pharo via the Pharo PPA. Pharo can be also installed via the command line.

2.2 Pharo: File components

Pharo consists of four main component files. Although you do not need to deal with them directly for the purposes of this book, it is useful to understand the roles they play.

1. The **virtual machine** (VM) is the only component that is different for each operating system. The VM is the execution engine (similar to a JVM). It takes Pharo bytcode that is generated each time user compiles a piece of code, converts it to machine code and executes it. Pharo comes with the Cog VM a very fast JITing VM. The VM executable is named:

- Pharo.exe for Windows;
- pharo for Linux ; and
- Pharo for OSX (inside a package also named Pharo.app).

The other components below are portable across operating systems, and can be copied and run on any appropriate virtual machine.

2. The **sources** file contains source code for parts of Pharo that don't change frequently. Sources file is important because the image file format stores only objects including compiled methods and their bytecode and not their source code. Typically a new **sources** file is generated once per major release of Pharo. For Pharo 5.0, this file is named PharoV50.sources.

3. The **changes** file logs of all source code modifications (especially all the changes you did while programming) since the .sources file was generated. Each release provides a near empty file named for the release, for example Pharo5.0.changes. This facilitates a per method history for diffs or reverting. It means that even if you did not manage to save the image file on a crash or you just forgot, you can recover your changes from this file. A changes file is always coupled with a image file. They work in pair.

4. The **image** file provides a frozen in time snapshot of a running Pharo system. This is the file where all objects are stored and as such it's a cross platform format. An image file contains the live state of all objects of the system (including classes and compiled methods, since they are objects too) at a given point. An image is a virtual object container. The file is named for the release (like `Pharo5.0.image`) and it is synched with the `Pharo5.0.changes` file.

Image/Change pair

The `.image` and `.changes` files provided by a Pharo release are the starting point for a live environment that you adapt to your needs. As you work in Pharo, these files are modified, so you need to make sure that they are writable. Pay attention to remove the changes and image files from the list of files to be checked by anti-viruses. The `.image` and `.changes` files are intimately linked and should always be kept together, with matching base filenames. Never edit them directly with a text editor, as `.images` holds your live object runtime memory, which indexes into the `.changes` files for the source. It is a good idea to keep a backup copy of the downloaded `.image` and `.changes` files so you can always start from a fresh image and reload your code. However, the most efficient way for backing up code is to use a version control system that will provide an easier and powerful way to back up and track your changes.

Common setup

The four main component files above can be placed in the same directory, but it's a common practice to put the Virtual Machine and sources file in a separate directory where everyone has read-only access to them.

Do whatever works best for your style of working and your operating system.

2.3 Launching Pharo

To start Pharo, do whatever your operating system expects: drag the .image file onto the icon of the virtual machine, or double-click the .image file, or at the command line type the name of the virtual machine followed by the path to the .image file.

- On **OS X**, double click the `Pharo5.0.app` bundle in the unzipped download.
- On **Linux**, double click (or invoke from the command line) the `pharo` executable bash script from the unzipped Pharo folder.
- On **Windows**, enter the unzipped Pharo folder and double click `Pharo.exe`.

In general, Pharo tries to "do the right thing". If you double click on the VM, it looks for an image file in the default location. If you double click on an `.image` file, it tries to find the nearest VM to launch it with.

If you have multiple VMs installed on your machine, the operating system may no longer be able to guess the right one. In this case, it is safer to specify exactly which ones you meant to launch, either by dragging and dropping the image file onto the VM, or specifying the image on the command line (see the next section).

Launching Pharo via the command line

The general pattern for launching Pharo from a terminal is:

```
<Pharo executable> <path to Pharo image>
```

Linux command line. For Linux, assuming that you're in the unzipped `pharo5.0` folder:

```
./pharo shared/Pharo5.0.image
```

OS X command line. For OS X, assuming that you're in the directory with the unzipped `Pharo5.0.app` bundle:

```
Pharo5.0.app/Contents/MacOS/Pharo
    Pharo5.0.app/Contents/Resources/Pharo5.0.image
```

When using a Pharo bundle, you need to right-click on `Pharo5.0.app` and select 'Show Package Contents' to get access to the image. If you need this often, just download a separated image/changes pair and drop that image into the `Pharo5.0.app`.

Windows command line. For Windows, assuming that you're in the unzipped `Pharo5.0` folder:

```
Pharo.exe Pharo5.0.image
```

2.4 PharoLauncher

PharoLauncher is a tool that helps you download and manage Pharo images. It is very useful for getting new versions of Pharo (as well as updates to the existing versions that contain important bug fixes). It also gives you access to images preloaded with specific libraries that make it very easy to use those tools without having to manually install and configure them.

PharoLauncher can be found on SmalltalkHub at http://smalltalkhub.com/#!/~Pharo/PharoLauncher together with installation instructions and download

2.5 The World Menu

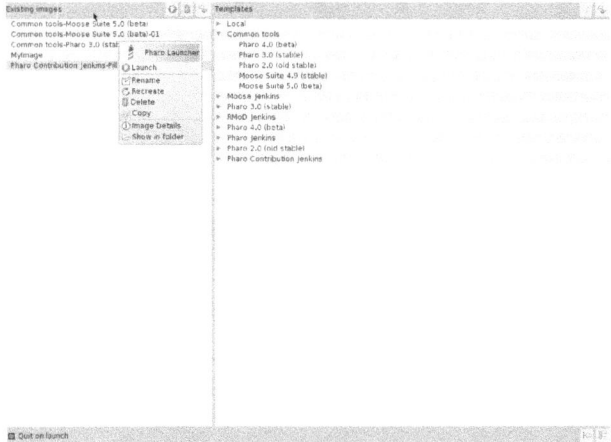

Figure 2.1: PharoLauncher - GUI

links depending on your platform. **PharoLauncher** is basically composed of two columns.

After installing PharoLauncher and opening it (like you would do for any Pharo image), you should get a GUI similar to Figure 2.1.

- The left column lists images that live locally on your machine (usually in a shared system folder). You can launch any local image directly (either by double-clicking, or by selecting it and pressing the Launch button). A right-click context menu provides several useful functions like copying and renaming your images, as well as locating them on the file system.

- The right column lists Templates, which are remote images available for download. To download a remote image, select it and click the Create image button (located on the top right, next to the Refresh template list button).

You can use your own local images with **PharoLauncher**, in addition to working with the images you donwloaded. To do so, simply ensure that your .image and its associated .changes files are placed in a folder (with the same name as your image) in your default image location. You can find the location in the **PharoLauncher** settings.

2.5 The World Menu

Once Pharo is running, you should see a single large window, possibly containing some open playground windows (see Figure 2.2). You might notice a menu bar, but Pharo mainly makes use of context-dependent pop-up menus.

A quick tour of Pharo

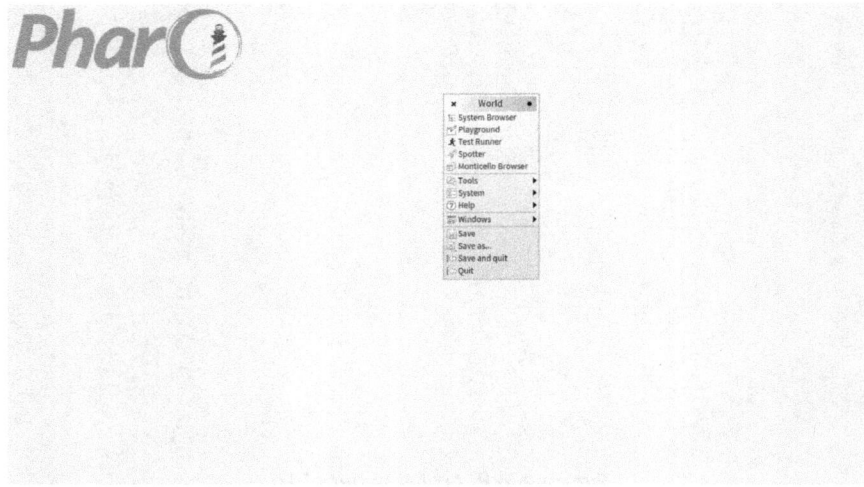

Figure 2.2: Clicking anywhere on the Pharo window background activates the World Menu

Clicking anywhere on the background of the Pharo window will display the **World Menu**, which contains many of the Pharo tools, utilities and settings.

At the top of the **World Menu**, you will see a list of several core tools in Pharo, including the System Browser, the Playground, the Monticello package manager, and others. We will discuss them in more detail in the coming chapters.

Interacting with Pharo

Pharo offers three ways to interact with the system using a mouse or other pointing device.

click (or left-click): this is the most often used mouse button, and is normally equivalent to left-clicking (or clicking a single-mouse button without any modifier key). For example, click on the background of the Pharo window to bring up the World menu (Figure 2.2).

action-click (or right-click): this is the next most used button. It is used to bring up a contextual menu that offers different sets of actions depending on where the mouse is pointing (see Figure 2.3). If you do not have a multi-button mouse, then normally you will configure the control modifier key to action-click with the mouse button.

meta-click: Finally, you may meta-click on any object displayed in the image to activate the "morphic halo", an array of handles that are used to perform operations on the on-screen objects themselves, such as inspecting or resizing them (see Figure 2.4). If you let the mouse linger over a handle, a help balloon

2.6 Sending messages

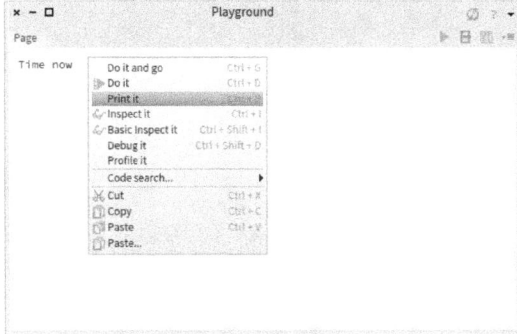

Figure 2.3: Action Click (right click) brings the contextual menu.

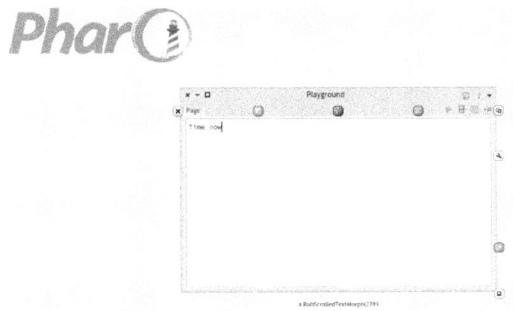

Figure 2.4: Meta-Clicking on a window opens the Halos

will explain its function. In Pharo, how you meta-click depends on your operating system: either you must hold Shift-Ctrl or Shift-Alt (on Windows or Linux) or Shift-Option (on OS X) while clicking.

2.6 Sending messages

In the Pharo window, click on an open space to open the **World Menu**, and then select the **Playground** menu option. The **Playground** tool will open (you may recognize it as the **Workspace** tool, from previous versions of Pharo). We can use **Playground** to quickly execute Pharo code. Enter the following code in it, then right click and select Do it:

```
ProfStef go.
```

This expression will trigger the Pharo tutorial (as shown in Figure 2.6). It is a simple and interactive tutorial that will teach you the basics of Pharo.

Congratulations, you have just sent your first message! Pharo is based on

13

A quick tour of Pharo

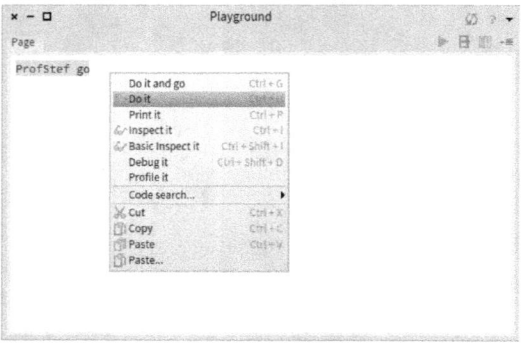

Figure 2.5: Executing an expression is simple with the Do it menu item.

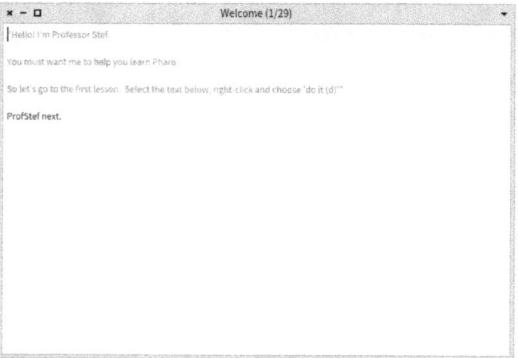

Figure 2.6: PharoTutorial is a simple interactive tutorial to learn about Pharo

the concept of sending messages to objects. The Pharo objects are like your soldiers ready to obey once you send them a message they can understand. We will see how an object can understand a message, later on.

If you talk to Pharoers for a while, you will notice that they generally do not use expressions like *call an operation* or *invoke a method*, as developers do in other programming languages. Instead they will say *send a message*. This reflects the idea that objects are responsible for their own actions and that the method associated with the message is looked up dynamically. When sending a message to an object, the object, and not the sender, selects the appropriate method for responding to your message. In most cases, the method with the same name as the message is executed.

As a user you don't need to understand how each message works, the only thing you need to know is what the available messages are for the objects that interest you. This way an object can hide its complexity, and coding can be kept as simple as possible without losing flexibility.

How to find the available messages for each object is something we will explore later on.

2.7 Saving, quitting and restarting a Pharo session

You can exit Pharo at any point, by closing the Pharo window as you do any other application window. Additionally you can use the **World Menu** and select either `Save and quit` or `Quit`.

In any case, Pharo will display a prompt to ask you about saving your image. If you do save your image and reopen it, you will see that things are *exactly* as you left them. This happens because the image file stores all the objects (edited text, window positions, added methods... of course since they are all objects) that Pharo has loaded into your memory so that nothing is lost on exit.

When you start Pharo for the first time, the Pharo virtual machine loads the image file that you specified. This file contains a snapshot of a large number of objects, including a vast amount of pre-existing code and programming tools (all of which are objects). As you work with Pharo, you will send messages to these objects, you will create new objects, and some of these objects will die and their memory will be reclaimed (garbage-collected).

When you quit Pharo, you will normally save a snapshot that contains all of your objects. If you save normally, you will overwrite your old image file with the new snapshot. Alternatively, you may save the image under a new name.

As mentioned earlier, in addition to the `.image` file, there is also a `.changes` file. This file contains a log of all the changes to the source code that you have made using the standard tools. Most of the time you do not need to worry about this file at all. As we shall see, however, the `.changes` file can be very useful for recovering from errors, or replaying lost changes. More about this later!

It may seem like the image is the key mechanism for storing and managing software projects, but that is not the case. As we shall see soon, there are much better tools for managing code and sharing software developed by teams. Images are very useful, but you should learn to be very cavalier about creating and throwing away images, since versioning tools like `Monticello` offer much better ways to manage versions and share code amongst developers. In addition, if you need to persist objects, you can use several systems such as `Fuel` (a fast object binary serializer), `STON` (a textual object serializer) or a database.

2.8 Playgrounds and Transcripts

Let us start with some exercises:

1. Close all open windows within Pharo.
2. Open a Transcript and a Playground/workspace. (The Transcript can be opened from the `World > Tools > ...` submenu.)
3. Position and resize the transcript and playground windows so that the playground just overlaps the transcript (see Figure 2.7).

You can resize windows by dragging one of the corners. At any time only one window is active; it is in front and has its border highlighted.

About Transcript. The `Transcript` is an object that is often used for logging system messages. It is a kind of *system console*.

About Playground. Playgrounds are useful for typing snippets of code that you would like to experiment with. You can also use playgrounds simply for typing any text that you would like to remember, such as to-do lists or instructions for anyone who will use your image.

Type the following text into the playground:

```
Transcript show: 'hello world'; cr.
```

Try double-clicking at various points on the text you have just typed. Notice how an entire word, entire string, or all of the text is selected, depending on whether you click within a word, at the end of the string, or at the end of the entire expression. In particular, if you place the cursor before the first character or after the last character and double-click, you select the complete paragraph.

Select the text you have typed, right click and select `Do it`. Notice how the text "hello world" appears in the transcript window (See Figure 2.7). Do it again.

2.9 Keyboard shortcuts

If you want to evaluate an expression, you do not always have to right click. Instead, you can use keyboard shortcuts shown in menu items. Even though Pharo may seem like a mouse driven enviroment it contains over 200 shortcuts that allow you operate a variaty of tools, as well as the facility to assign a keyboard shortcut to any of the 80000 methods contained in the Pharo image. To have a look at the available shortcuts go to World Menu > System > Keymap Browser.

Depending on your platform, you may have to press one of the modifier keys which are Control, Alt, and Command. We will use `CMD` in the rest of the book: so each time you see something like `CMD-d`, just replace it with the appropriate modifier key depending on your OS. The corresponding modifier

2.9 Keyboard shortcuts

Figure 2.7: Executing an expresssion: displaying a string in the Transcript.

key in Windows is CTRL, and in Linux is either ALT or CTRL, so each time you see something like CMD-d, just replace it with the appropriate modifier key depending on your OS.

In addition to Do it, you might have noticed Do it and go, Print it, Inspect it and several other options in the context menu. Let's have a quick look at each of these.

Doing vs. printing

Type the expression 3 + 4 into the playground. Now Do it with the keyboard shortcut.

Do not be surprised if you saw nothing happen! What you just did is send the message + with argument 4 to the number 3. Normally the resulting 7 would have been computed and returned to you, but since the playground did not know what to do with this answer, it simply did not show the answer. If you want to see the result, you should Print it instead. Print it actually compiles the expression, executes it, sends the message printString to the result, and displays the resulting string.

Select 3+4 and Print it (CMD-p). This time we see the result we expect.

```
3 + 4
>>> 7
```

We use the notation >>> as a convention in this book to indicate that a particular Pharo expression yields a given result when you Print it.

A quick tour of Pharo

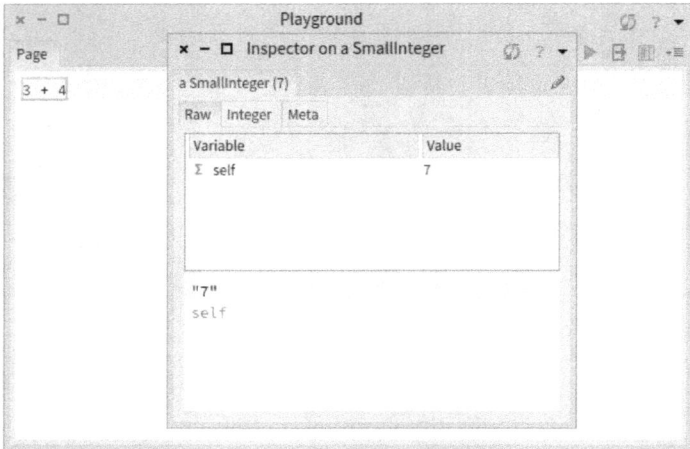

Figure 2.8: Inspecting a simple number using `Inspect`

Inspect

Select or place the cursor on the line of 3+4, and this time `Inspect it` (CMD-i).

Now you should see a new window titled "Inspector on a SmallInteger(7)" as shown in Figure 2.8. The inspector is an extremely useful tool that allows you to browse and interact with any object in the system. The title tells us that 7 is an instance of the class `SmallInteger`. The top panel allows us to browse the instance variables of an object and their values. The bottom panel can be used to write expressions to send messages to the object. Type `self squared` in the bottom panel of the inspector, and `Print it`.

The inspector presents specific tabs that will show different information and views on the object depending on the kind of object you are inspecting. Inspect `Morph new openInWorld` you should get a situation similar to the one of Figure 2.9.

Other operations

Other right-click options that may be used are the following:

- `Do it and go` additionally opens a *navigable* inspector on the side of the playground. It allows us to navigate the object structure. Try with the previous expression `Morph new openInWorld` and navigate the structure.

- `Basic Inspect it` opens the classic inspector that offers a more minimal GUI and live updates of changes to the object.

- `Debug it` opens the debugger on the code.

2.10 The System Browser

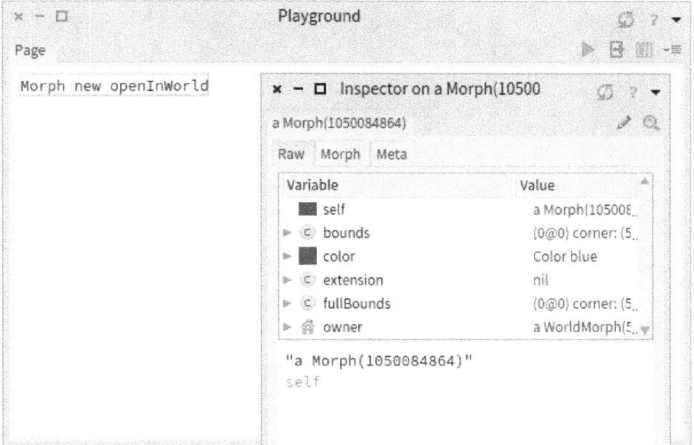

Figure 2.9: Inspecting a Morph using Inspect

- Profile it profiles the code with the Pharo profile tool which shows how much time is spent for each message sent.
- Code search offers several options provided by System Browser, such as browsing the source code of an expression, searching for senders and implementors, and so on.

2.10 The System Browser

The System Browser, also known as "Class Browser", is one of the key tools used for programming. As we shall see, there are several interesting browsers available for Pharo, but this is the basic one you will find in any image. The current implementation of the System Browser is called Nautilus (this is the name of the Jules Verne's submarine).

Opening the System Browser on a given method

This is not the usual way that we open a browser on a method: we use more advanced tools! Now for the sake of this presentation, execute the following snippet:

```
Nautilus openOnMethod: Integer>>#factorial
```

It will open a system browser on the method factorial. We should get a System Browser like in Figure 2.10. The title bar indicates that we are browsing the class Integer and its method factorial. Figure 2.10 shows the different entities displayed by the browser: packages, classes, protocols, methods and method definition.

A quick tour of Pharo

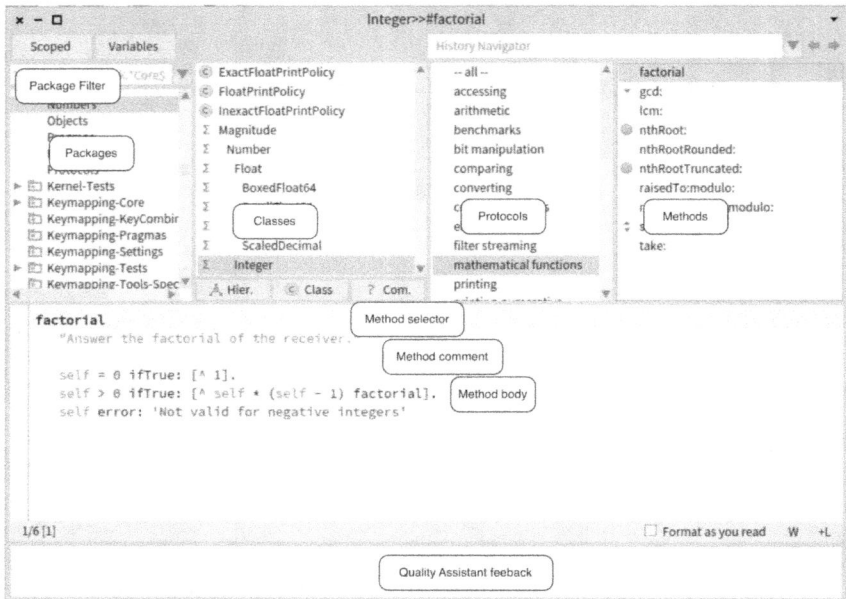

Figure 2.10: The System Browser showing the `factorial` method of class Integer

In Pharo, the default System Browser is Nautilus. However, it is possible to have other System Browsers installed in the Pharo enviroment such as AltBrowser. Each System Browser may have its own GUI that may be very different from the Nautilus GUI. From now on, we will use the terms `Browser`, `System Browser` and (occasionally) `Nautilus` interchangeably.

Navigating using the System Browser

Pharo has **Spotter** (see below) to navigate the system. Now we just want to show you the working flow of the System Browser. Usually with **Spotter** we go directly to the class or the method.

Let us look how to find the `printString` method defined in class `Object`. At the end of the navigation, we will get the situation depicted in 2.11.

Open the Browser by selecting `World > System Browser`. When a new System Browser window first opens, all panes but the leftmost are empty. This first pane lists all known packages, which contain groups of related classes.

Filter packages. Type part of the name of the package in the left most filter. It filters the list of packages to be shown in the list under it. Type 'Kern' for

2.10 The System Browser

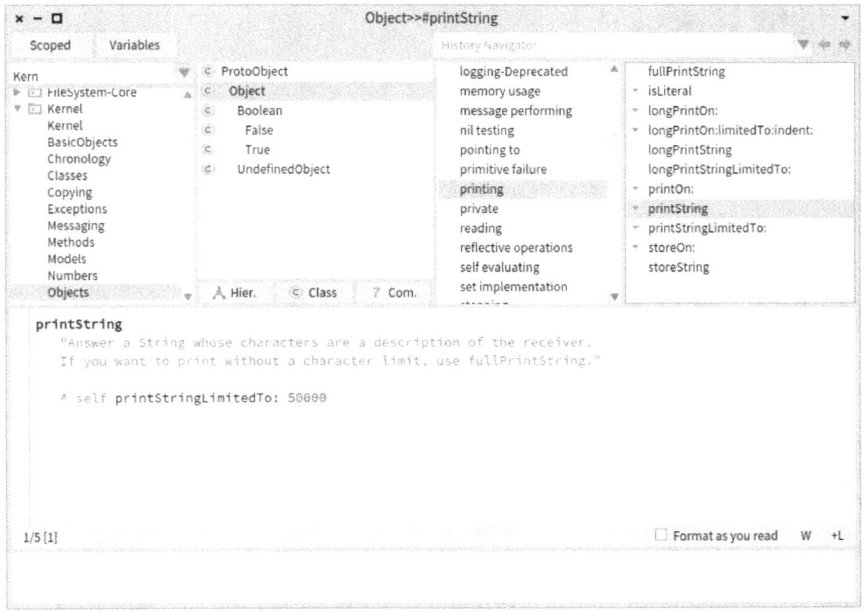

Figure 2.11: The System Browser showing the `printString` method of class `Object`

example.

Expand the `Kernel` package and select the `Objects` element. When we select a package, it causes the second pane to show a list of all of the classes in the selected package. You should see the hierarchy of `ProtoObject`

Select the `Object` class. When a class is selected, the remaining two panes will be populated. The third pane displays the protocols of the currently selected class. These are convenient groupings of related methods. If no protocol is selected you should see all methods in the fourth pane.

Select the `printing` protocol. You may have to scroll down to find it. You can also click on the third pane and type `pr`, to typeahead-find the `printing` protocol. Now select it, and you will see in the fourth pane only methods related to printing.

Select the `printString` method. Now we see in the bottom pane the source code of the `printString` method, shared by all objects in the system (except those that override it).

There are much better way to find a method and we will look at them now.

2.11 Finding classes

There are several ways to find a class in Pharo. The first, as we have just seen above, is to know (or guess) what package it is in, and to navigate to it using the browser.

A second way is to send the browse message to the class, asking it to open a browser on itself. Suppose we want to browse the class Point.

Using the message browse

Type `Point browse` into a playground and `Do it`. A browser will open on the Point class.

Using CMD-b to browse

There is also a keyboard shortcut CMD-b (browse) that you can use in any text pane; select the word and press CMD-b. Use this keyboard shortcut to browse the class Point.

Notice that when the Point class is selected but no protocol or method is selected, instead of the source code of a method, we see a class definition. This is nothing more than an ordinary message that is sent to the parent class, asking it to create a subclass. Here we see that the class Object is being asked to create a subclass named Point with two instance variables, class variables, and to put the class Point in the Kernel-BasicObjects package. If you click on the Comments button at the bottom of the class pane, you can see the class comment in a dedicated pane.

In addition the system supports the following mouse shortcuts

- CMD-Click on a word: open the definition of a class when the word is a class name. You get also the implementors of the message when you click on a selector that is in the body of a method.
- CMD-Shift-Click on a word: open a list browser with all the refs of the class when the word is a class name. You get also the senders of the message when you click on a selector that is in the body of a method.

Using Spotter

The fastest (and probably the coolest) way to find a class is to use **Spotter**. Pressing Shift+Enter opens Spotter, a very powerful tool for finding classes, methods, and many other related actions. Figure 2.12 shows that we look for Point.

Spotter offers several possibilities as shown in Figure 2.12. You can specify to Spotter the kind of *categories* you are interested in. For example, using #class

2.11 Finding classes

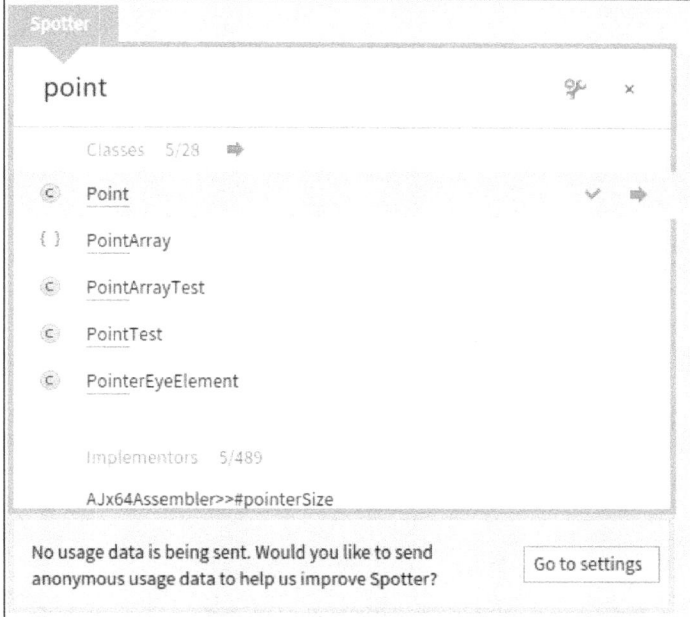

Figure 2.12: Opening Spotter

followed by the word you look for, indicates that you are interested in classes. This is the default so you do not need to type #class.

Figure 2.13 shows how we can ask **Spotter** to show all the implementors of a given messages. We do not have to type the full category name. Other Categories are menu, packages, method (#implementor), examples (#example), pragma (#pragma), senders (#sender), class references (#reference) but also playground code snippets (using #playground).You can just type the beginning of the category to identify it i.e., #ref Point will give all the reference to the class Point.

Spotter can be used even to browse through the OS file system, and has a history category where previous searches are stored for quickly going back to popular searches.

Navigating results

In addition we can use **Spotter** to navigate to our search results similarly to how we use System Browser. Spotter categorizes its search results: for example, classes are under Classes category, methods under the Implementors category, help topics under Help Topics category, etc.

Clicking on the right arrow will take us to our selection and create a tab on top

Figure 2.13: Looking for implementors matching `printString`

that we can click to go back to where we were. Depending on what we click on, we step into our selection and are exposed to more categories.

For example, if our selection is the `Point` class, we will dive inside a group of categories made for instance methods, class methods, super instance methods etc.

The interface is fully controllable through the keyboard. The user can move with Up/Down arrows between items or `Cmd-Shift-Up`/`Cmd-Shift-Down` arrows (note that on Windows and Linux `Cmd` key is the `Alt` key) through categories. At the same time, the search field has the focus, so the user can switch seamlessly between selecting items and refining the search. Pressing `Enter` on a selection opens the System Browser on that specific selected search result.

Using 'Find class' in System Browser

In the SystemBrowser you can also search for a class via its name. For example, suppose that you are looking for some unknown class that represents dates and times.

In the System Browser, click anywhere in the package pane or the class pane, and launch the Class Search window by typing CMD-f CMD-c, or selecting Find class (f,c) from the right-click context menu. Type time in the dialog box and click OK (or press Enter).

A list of classes is displayed, whose names contain the substring time. Choose one (say, Time), and the browser will show it, along with a class comment that suggests other classes that might be useful. If you want to browse one of the others, select its name (in any text pane), and type CMD-b.

Note that if you type the complete (and correctly capitalized) name of a class in the find dialog, the browser will go directly to that class without showing you the list of options.

Using the Finder

You can also open the Finder that is available from the World > Tools... menu, and type part of the name of the class and change the Selectors to Classes in the right combo box. It is less efficient than using **Spotter** or the SystemBrowser as explained above. The Finder is more useful for other types of code searches such as find methods based on examples, as we will show later.

2.12 Finding methods

Sometimes you can guess the name of a method, or at least part of the name of a method, more easily than the name of a class. For example, if you are interested in the current time, you might expect that there would be a method called "now", or containing "now" as a substring. But where might it be? **Spotter** and **Finder** can help you.

Spotter

With **Spotter** you can also find methods. Either by getting a class and navigating or using category such as:

- #implementor a method name will display all the methods that are implemented and have the same name. For example you will get all the do: methods.
- #selector a method name will display all the selectors that matches this name

With Finder

Select World Menu > Tools > Finder. Type now in the top left search box, click Search (or just press the Enter key). You should see a list of results similar to the one in Figure 2.14.

A quick tour of Pharo

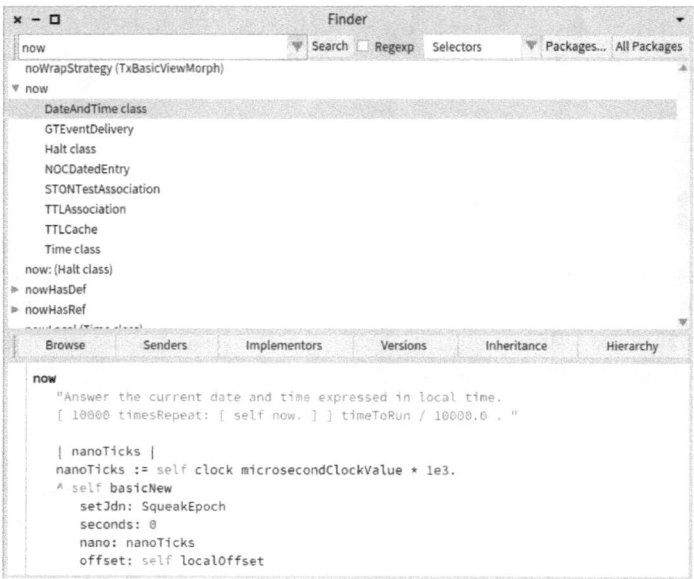

Figure 2.14: The Finder showing all classes defining a method named now.

The Finder will display a list of all the method names that contain the substring "now". To scroll to now itself, move the cursor to the list and type "n"; this type-ahead trick works in all scrolling windows. Expanding the "now" item shows you the classes that implement a method with this name. Selecting any one of them will display the source code for the implementation in the code pane on the bottom.

Finding methods using examples

At other times, you may have a good idea that a method exists, but will have no idea what it might be called. The Finder can still help! For example, suppose that you would like to find a method that turns a string into upper case (for example, transforming 'eureka' into 'EUREKA'). We can give the inputs and expected output of a method and the Finder will try to find it for you.

The **Finder** has a really powerful functionality: you can give the receiver, arguments and expected result and the finder tries to find the corresponding message.

Trying Finder

In the Finder, select the **Examples** mode using the second combo-box (the one that shows Selectors by default).

Type `'eureka' . 'EUREKA'` into the search box and press the Enter key.

The **Finder** will then suggest a method that does what you were looking for, as well as display a list of classes that implement methods with the same name. In this case, it determined that the asUppercase method is the one that performed the operation that fit your example.

Click on the `'eureka' asUppercase --> 'EUREKA'` expression, to show the list of classes that implement that method.

An asterisk at the beginning of a line in the list of classes indicates that this method is the one that was actually used to obtain the requested result. So, the asterisk in front of String lets us know that the method asUppercase defined in the class String was executed and returned the result we wanted. The classes that do not have an asterisk are just other implementors of asUppercase, which share the method name but were *not* used to return the wanted result. So the method Character>>asUppercase was not executed in our example, because 'eureka' is not a Character instance (but is instead a String).

You can also use the Finder to search for methods by arguments and results. For example, if you are looking for a method that will find the greatest common factor of two integers, you might try 25 . 35 . 5 as an example. You can also give the method finder multiple examples to narrow the search space; the help text in the bottom pane explains how.

2.13 Defining a new method

The advent of Test Driven Development (TDD) has changed the way we write code. The idea behind TDD is that we write a test that defines the desired behaviour of our code before we write the code itself. Only then do we write the code that satisfies the test.

Suppose that our assignment is to write a method that "says something loudly and with emphasis". What exactly could that mean? What would be a good name for such a method? How can we make sure that programmers who may have to maintain our method in the future have an unambiguous description of what it should do? We can answer all of these questions by giving an example.

Our goal is to define a new method named shout in the class String. The idea is that this message should turn a string into its uppercase version as shown in the example below:

```
'No panic' shout
>>> 'NO PANIC!'
```

However, before creating the shout method itself, we must first create a test method! In the next section, we can use the "No Panic" example to create our test method.

A quick tour of Pharo

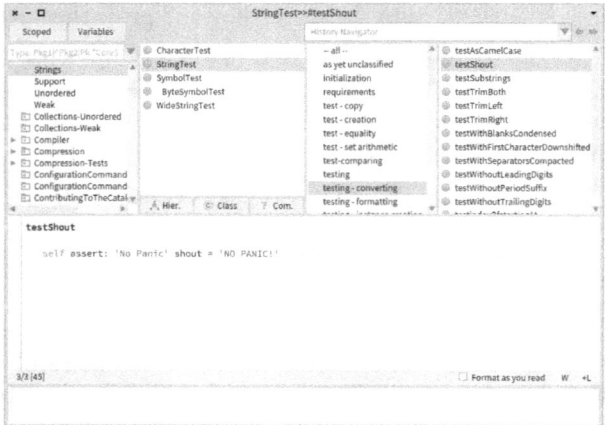

Figure 2.15: Defining a test method in the class StringTest.

Defining a new test method

How do we create a new method in Pharo? First, we have to decide which class the method should belong to. In this case, the shout method that we are testing will go in class String, so the corresponding test will, by convention, go in a class called StringTest.

First, open a browser on the class StringTest, and select an appropriate protocol for our method, in this case 'tests - converting'. The highlighted text in the bottom pane is a template that reminds you what a Pharo method looks like. Delete this template code (remember, you can either click on the beginning or the end of the text, or press CMD-a, to "Select All"), and start typing your method. We can turn our "No Panic" code example into the test method itself:

```
testShout
    self assert: ('No panic' shout = 'NO PANIC!')
```

Once you have typed the text into the browser, notice that the corner is orange. This is a reminder that the pane contains unsaved changes. So, select Accept (s) by right clicking in the bottom pane, or just type CMD-s, to compile and save your method. You should see a situation similar to the one depicted in Figure 2.15.

If this is the first time you have accepted any code in your image, you will likely be prompted to enter your name. Since many people have contributed code to the image, it is important to keep track of everyone who creates or modifies methods. Simply enter your first and last names, without any spaces.

Because there is as yet no method called shout, the automatic code checker (Quality Assitance) in the lower browser pane will inform you, that the mes-

28

2.13 Defining a new method

Figure 2.16: Looking at the error in the debugger.

sage shout is sent but not implemented. This can be quite useful if you have merely made a typing mistake, but in this case, we really do mean shout, since that is the method we are about to create. We confirm this by selecting the first option from the menu of choices.

Running your test method

Run your newly created test: open the **Test Runner** from the World Menu (or press on the circle icon in front of the method name this is faster and cooler).

In the **Test Runner** the leftmost two panes are a bit like the top panes in the System Browser. The left pane contains a list of packages, but it's restricted to those packages that contain test classes.

Select CollectionsTests-Strings package, and the pane to the right will show all of the test classes in it, which includes the class StringTest. Class names are already selected, so click Run Selected to run all these tests.

You should see the upper right pane turn red, which indicates that there was an error in running the tests. The list of tests that gave rise to errors is shown in the bottom right pane. As you can see, the method StringTest>>test-Shout is the culprit. (Note that StringTest>>testShout is the Pharo way of identifying the testShout method of the StringTest class.) If you click on that method in the bottom right pane, the erroneous test will run again, this time in such a way that you see the error happen: MessageNotUnderstood: ByteString>>shout (see Figure 2.16).

A quick tour of Pharo

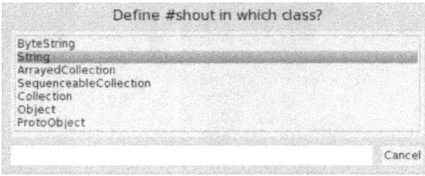

Figure 2.17: Pressing the Create button in the debugger prompts you to select in which class to create the new method.

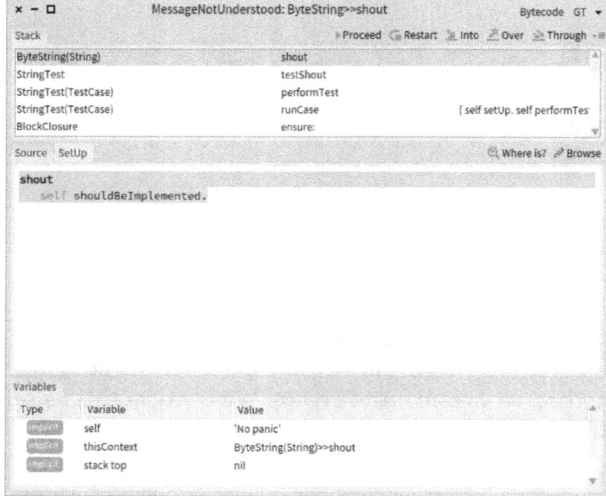

Figure 2.18: The automatically created shout method waiting for a real definition.

The window that opens with the error message is the Pharo debugger. We will look at the debugger and how to use it in Chapter: The Pharo Environment.

Implementing the tested method

The error is, of course, exactly what we expected: running the test generates an error because we haven't yet written a method that tells strings how to shout. Nevertheless, it's good practice to make sure that the test fails because this confirms that we have set up the testing machinery correctly and that the new test is actually being run. Once you have seen the error, you can Abandon the running test, which will close the debugger window.

Coding in the debugger

Instead of pressing Abandon, you can define the missing method using the Create button right in the debugger. This will prompt you to select a class in which to define the new method (see Figure 2.17), then prompt you to select a protocol for that method, and finally take you to a code editor window in the debugger, in which you can edit the code for this new method. Note that since the system cannot implement the method for you, it creates a generic method that is tagged as to be implemented (see Figure 2.18).

Now let's define the method that will make the test succeed! Right inside the debugger edit the shout method with this definition:

```
shout
    ^ self asUppercase,'!'
```

The comma is the string concatenation operation, so the body of this method appends an exclamation mark to an upper-case version of whatever String object the shout message was sent to. The ^ tells Pharo that the expression that follows is the answer to be returned from the method, in this case the new concatenated string.

When you've finished implementing the method, do not forget to compile it using CMD-s and you can press Proceed and continue with the tests. Note that Proceed simply continues on running the test suite, and does not re-run the failed method.

Does this method work? Let's run the tests and see. Click on Run Selected again in the Test Runner, and this time you should see a green bar and text indicating that all of the tests ran with no failures and no errors. When you get to a green bar, it's a good idea to save your work by saving the image (World Menu > Save), and take a break. So, do that right now!

2.14 Chapter summary

This chapter has introduced you to the Pharo environment and shown you how to use some of the major tools, such as the System Browser, Spotter, the Finder, the Debugger, and the Test Runner. You have also seen a little of Pharo's syntax, even though you may not understand it all yet.

- A running Pharo system consists of a *virtual machine*, a .sources file, and .image and .changes files. Only these last two change, as they record a snapshot of the running system.
- When you open a Pharo image, you will find yourself in exactly the same state (i.e., with exactly the same running objects) that you had when you last saved that image.
- You can click on the Pharo background to bring up the **World Menu** and launch various tools.
- A **Playground** is a tool for writing and evaluating snippets of code. You can also use it to store arbitrary text.

- You can use keyboard shortcuts on text in the playground, or any other tool, to evaluate code. The most important of these are Do it (CMD-d), Print it (CMD-p), Inspect it (CMD-i), and Browse it (CMD-b).
- The **System Browser** is the main tool for browsing Pharo code and for developing new code.
- The **Test runner** is a tool for running unit tests, and aids in Test Driven Development.
- The **Debugger** allows you to examine errors and exceptions (such as errors or failures encountered when running tests). You can even create new methods right in the debugger.

CHAPTER 3

A first application

In this chapter, we will develop a simple game: LightsOut (http://en.wikipedia.org/wiki/Lights_Out_(game)). Along the way we will show most of the tools that Pharo programmers use to construct and debug their programs, and show how programs are shared with other developers. We will see the browser, the object inspector, the debugger and the Monticello package browser.

In Pharo you can develop in a traditional way, by defining a class, then its instance variables, then its methods. However, in Pharo your development flow can be much more productive than that! You can define instance variables and methods on the fly. You can also code in the debugger using the exact context of currently executed objects. This chapter will sketch such alternate way and show you how you can be really productive.

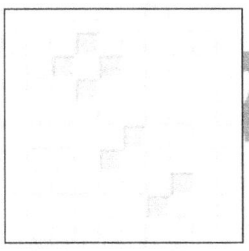

Figure 3.1: The Lights Out game board

A first application

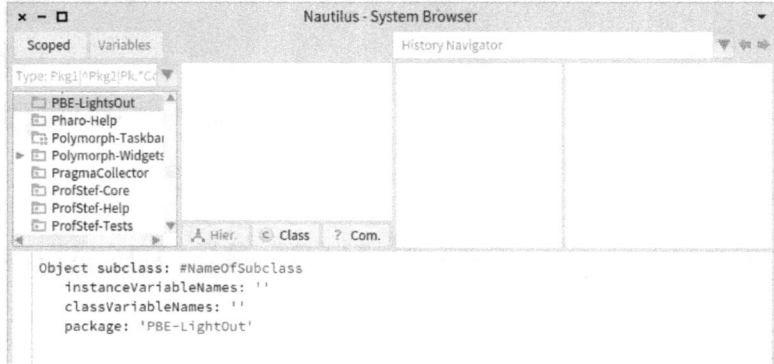

Figure 3.2: Create a Package and class template

3.1 The Lights Out game

To show you how to use Pharo's programming tools, we will build a simple game called **Lights Out**. The game board consists of a rectangular array of light yellow cells. When you click on one of the cells, the four surrounding cells turn blue. Click again, and they toggle back to light yellow. The object of the game is to turn blue as many cells as possible.

Lights Out is made up of two kinds of objects: the game board itself, and 100 individual cell objects. The Pharo code to implement the game will contain two classes: one for the game and one for the cells. We will now show you how to define these classes using the Pharo programming tools.

3.2 Creating a new Package

We have already seen the browser in Chapter : A Quick Tour of Pharo where we learned how to navigate to packages, classes and methods, and saw how to define new methods. Now we will see how to create packages and classes.

From the World menu, open a **System Browser**. Right-click on an existing package in the Package pane and select Add package... from the menu. Type the name of the new package (we use PBE-LightsOut) in the dialog box and click OK (or just press the return key). The new package is created, and positioned alphabetically in the list of packages (see Figure 3.2).

Hints: You can type PBE in the filter to get your package filtered out the other ones (See Figure 3.3).

3.3 Defining the class LOCell

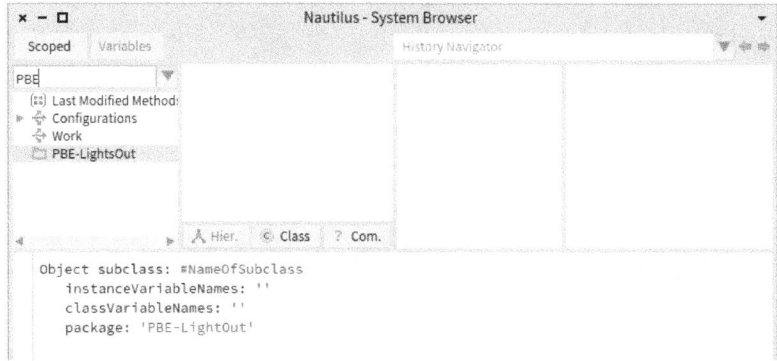

Figure 3.3: Filtering our package to work more efficiently

3.3 Defining the class LOCell

At this point there are, of course, no classes in the new package. However, the main editing pane displays a template to make it easy to create a new class (see Figure 3.3).

This template shows us a Pharo expression that sends a message to a class called Object, asking it to create a subclass called NameOfSubClass. The new class has no variables, and should belong to the category (package) PBE-LightsOut.

Creating a new class

We simply edit the template to create the class that we really want. Modify the class creation template as follows:

- Replace Object with SimpleSwitchMorph.
- Replace NameOfSubClass with LOCell.
- Add mouseAction to the list of instance variables.

You should get the following class definition:

```
SimpleSwitchMorph subclass: #LOCell
    instanceVariableNames: 'mouseAction'
    classVariableNames: ''
    package: 'PBE-LightsOut'
```

This new definition consists of a Pharo expression that sends a message to the existing class SimpleSwitchMorph, asking it to create a subclass called LOCell. (Actually, since LOCell does not exist yet, we passed the symbol #LOCell as an argument, representing the name of the class to create.) We also tell it that instances of the new class should have a mouseAction instance variable, which

35

A first application

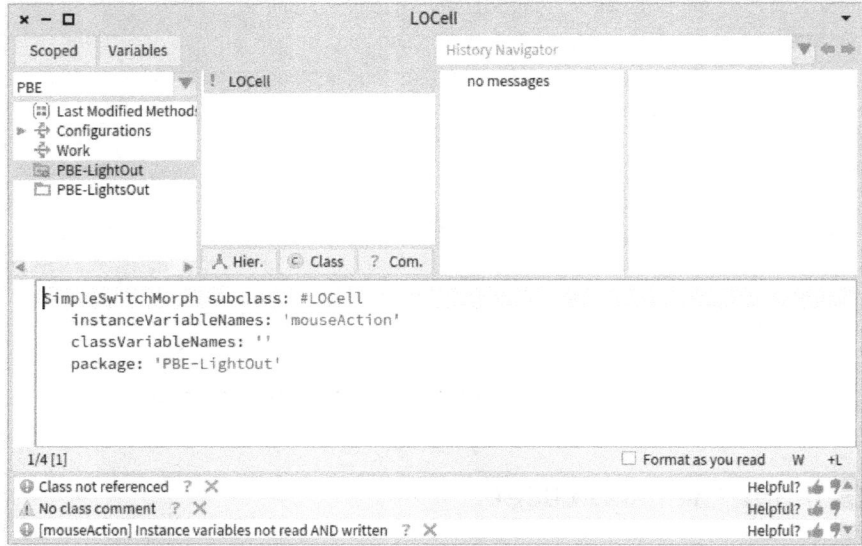

Figure 3.4: The newly-created class LOCell

we will use to define what action the cell should take if the mouse should click on it.

At this point you still have not created anything. Note that the top right of the panel changed to orange. This means that there are unsaved changes. To actually send this subclass message, you must save (accept) the source code. Either right-click and select Accept, or use the shortcut CMD-s (for "Save"). The message will be sent to SimpleSwitchMorph, which will cause the new class to be compiled. You should get the situation depicted in Figure 3.4.

Once the class definition is accepted, the class is created and appears in the class pane of the browser (see Figure 3.4). The editing pane now shows the class definition. Below you get the Quality Assistant's feedback: It runs automatically quality rules on your code and reports them.

About comments

Pharoers put a very high value on the readability of their code, but also good quality comments.

Method comments. People have the tendency to believe that it is not necessary to comment well written methods: it is plain wrong and encourages sloppiness. Of course, bad code should renamed and refactored. Obviously commenting trivial methods makes no sense. A comment should not be the code written in english but an explanation of what the method is doing, its context, or the rationale behind its implementation. When reading a comment, the reader should be comforted that his hypotheses are correct.

Class comments. For the class comment, the Pharo class comment template gives a good idea of a strong class comment. Read it! It is based on CRC for Class Responsibility Collaborators. So in a nutshell the comments state the responsibility of the class in a couple of sentences and how it collaborates with other classes to achieve this responsibilities. In addition we can state the API (main messages an object understands), give an example (usually in Pharo we define examples as class methods), and some details about internal representation or implementation rationale.

Select the comment button and define a class comment following this template

On categories vs. packages

Historically, Pharo packages were implemented as "categories" (a group of classes). With the newer versions of Pharo, the term **category** is being deprecated, and replaced exclusively by **package**.

If you use an older version of Pharo or an old tutorial, the class template will be as follow:

```
SimpleSwitchMorph subclass: #LOCell
    instanceVariableNames: 'mouseAction'
    classVariableNames: ''
    category: 'PBE-LightsOut'
```

It is equivalent to the one we mentioned earlier. In this book we only use the term **package**. The Pharo package is also what you will be using to version your source code using the Monticello versioning tool.

3.4 Adding methods to a class

Now let's add some methods to our class. Select the protocol 'no messages' in the protocol pane. You will see a template for method creation in the editing pane. Select the template text, and replace it by the following (Do not forget to compile it):

```
initialize
    super initialize.
    self label: ''.
    self borderWidth: 2.
    bounds := 0 @ 0 corner: 16 @ 16.
    offColor := Color paleYellow.
    onColor := Color paleBlue darker.
    self useSquareCorners.
```

A first application

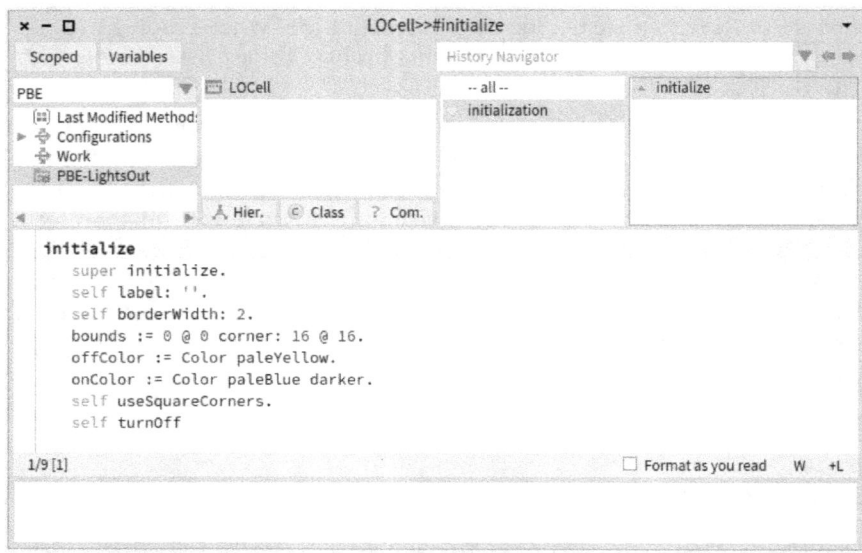

Figure 3.5: The newly-created method `initialize`

```
self turnOff
```

Note that the characters ' ' on line 3 are two separate single quotes with nothing between them, not a double quote! ' ' denotes the empty string. Another way to create an empty string is `String new`. Do not forget to **accept** this method definition.

Initialize methods. Notice that the method is called `initialize`. The name is very significant! By convention, if a class defines a method named `initialize`, it is called right after the object is created. So, when we execute `LOCell new`, the message `initialize` is sent automatically to this newly created object. `initialize` methods are used to set up the state of objects, typically to set their instance variables; this is exactly what we are doing here.

Invoking superclass initialization. The first thing that this method does (line 2) is to execute the `initialize` method of its superclass, `SimpleSwitchMorph`. The idea here is that any inherited state will be properly initialized by the `initialize` method of the superclass. It is always a good idea to initialize inherited state by sending `super initialize` before doing anything else. We don't know exactly what `SimpleSwitchMorph`'s `initialize` method will do (and we don't care), but it's a fair bet that it will set up some instance variables to hold reasonable default values. So we had better call it, or we risk starting in an unclean state.

The rest of the method sets up the state of this object. Sending `self label: ' '`, for example, sets the label of this object to the empty string.

About point and rectangle creation. The expression `0@0 corner: 16@16` probably needs some explanation. `0@0` represents a `Point` object with x and y coordinates both set to 0. In fact, `0@0` sends the message `@` to the number 0 with argument 0. The effect will be that the number 0 will ask the `Point` class to create a new instance with coordinates `(0,0)`. Now we send this newly created point the message `corner: 16@16`, which causes it to create a `Rectangle` with corners `0@0` and `16@16`. This newly created rectangle will be assigned to the bounds variable, inherited from the superclass.

Note that the origin of the Pharo screen is the top left, and the y coordinate increases downwards.

About the rest. The rest of the method should be self-explanatory. Part of the art of writing good Pharo code is to pick good method names so that the code can be read like a kind of pidgin English. You should be able to imagine the object talking to itself and saying "Self, use square corners!", "Self, turn off!".

Notice that there is a little green arrow next to your method (see Figure 3.5). This means the method exists in the superclass and is overridden in your class.

3.5 Inspecting an object

You can immediately test the effect of the code you have written by creating a new LOCell object and inspecting it: Open a `Playground`, type the expression `LOCell new`, and **Inspect** it (using the menu item with the same name).

The left-hand column of the inspector shows a list of instance variables and the value of the instance variable is shown in the right column (see Figure 3.6).

If you click on an instance variable the inspector will open a new pane with the detail of the instance variable (see Figure 3.7).

Executing expressions. The bottom pane of the inspector is a mini-playground. It's useful because in this playground the pseudo-variable `self` is bound to the object selected.

Go to that Playground at the bottom of the pane and type the text `self bounds: (200@200 corner: 250@250)` **Do it**. To refresh the values, click on the update button (the blue little circle) at the top right of the pane. The bounds variable should change in the inspector. Now type the text `self openInWorld` in the mini-playground and **Do it**.

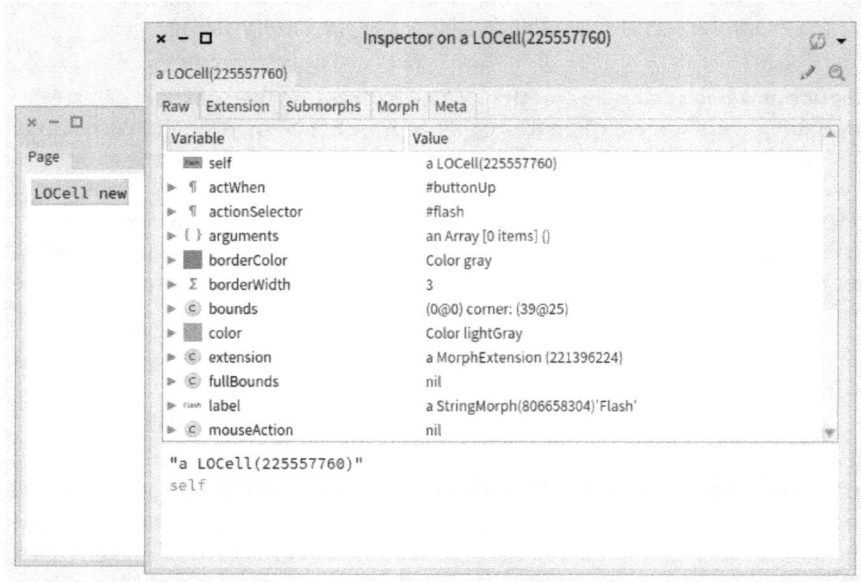

Figure 3.6: The inspector used to examine a LOCell object

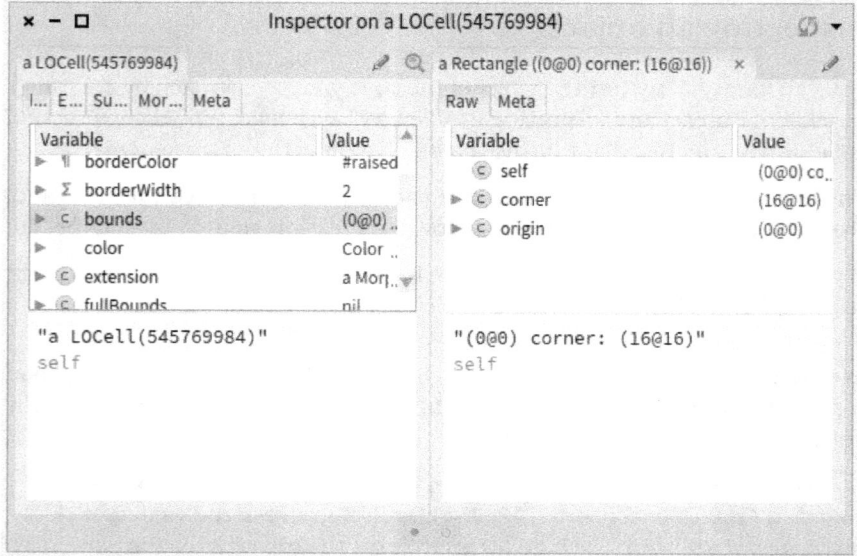

Figure 3.7: When we click on an instance variable, we inspect its value (another object)

3.6 Defining the class LOGame

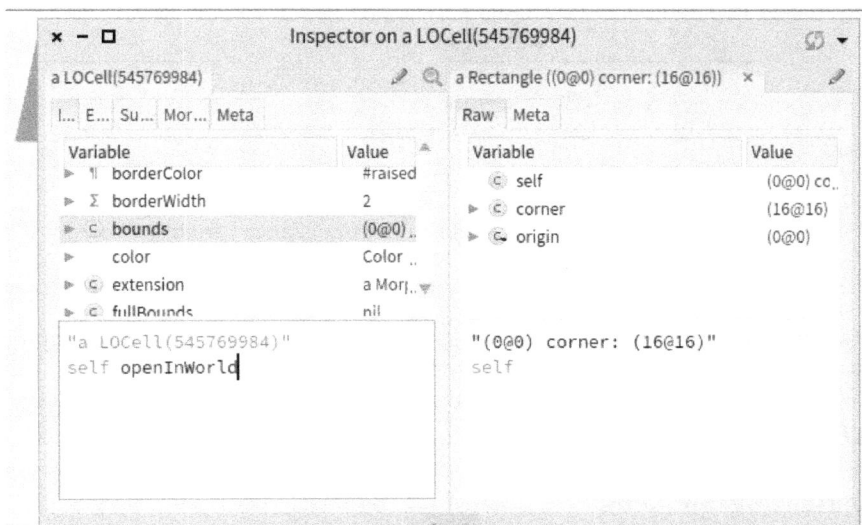

Figure 3.8: An LOCell open in world

The cell should appear near the top left-hand corner of the screen (as shown in Figure 3.8) and exactly where its bounds say that it should appear. Meta-click on the cell to bring up the Morphic halo. Move the cell with the brown (next to top-right) handle and resize it with the yellow (bottom-right) handle. Notice how the bounds reported by the inspector also change. (You may have to click refresh to see the new bounds value.) Delete the cell by clicking on the x in the pink handle.

3.6 Defining the class LOGame

Now let's create the other class that we need for the game, which we will name LOGame.

Class creation

Make the class definition template visible in the browser main window. Do this by clicking on the package name (or right-clicking on the Class pane and selecting Add Class). Edit the code so that it reads as follows, and **Accept** it.

```
BorderedMorph subclass: #LOGame
    instanceVariableNames: ''
    classVariableNames: ''
    package: 'PBE-LightsOut'
```

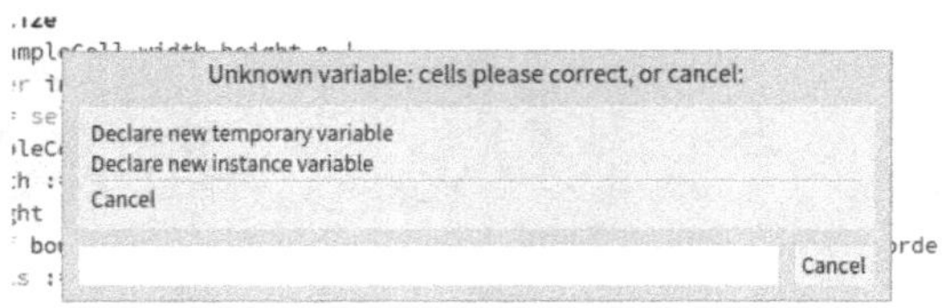

A first application

Figure 3.9: Declaring cells as a new instance variable

Here we subclass BorderedMorph. Morph is the superclass of all of the graphical shapes in Pharo, and (unsurprisingly) a BorderedMorph is a Morph with a border. We could also insert the names of the instance variables between the quotes on the second line, but for now, let's just leave that list empty.

Initializing our game

Now let's define an initialize method for LOGame. Type the following into the browser as a method for LOGame and try to **Accept** it.

```
initialize
    | sampleCell width height n |
    super initialize.
    n := self cellsPerSide.
    sampleCell := LOCell new.
    width := sampleCell width.
    height := sampleCell height.
    self bounds: (5 @ 5 extent: (width * n) @ (height * n) + (2 * self
        borderWidth)).
    cells := Matrix new: n tabulate: [ :i :j | self newCellAt: i at: j ]
```

Pharo will complain that it doesn't know the meaning of cells (see Figure 3.9). It will offer you a number of ways to fix this.

Choose **Declare new instance variable**, because we want cells to be an instance variable.

Taking advantage of the debugger

At this stage if you open a Playground, type LOGame new, and **Do it**, Pharo will complain that it doesn't know the meaning of some of the terms (see Figure 3.10). It will tell you that it doesn't know of a message cellsPerSide, and will open a debugger. But cellsPerSide is not a mistake; it is just a method that we haven't yet defined. We will do so, shortly.

Now let us do it: type LOGame new and **Do it**. Do not close the debugger. Click on the button Create of the debugger, when prompted, select **LOGame**, the class which will contain the method, click on ok, then when prompted for

3.6 Defining the class LOGame

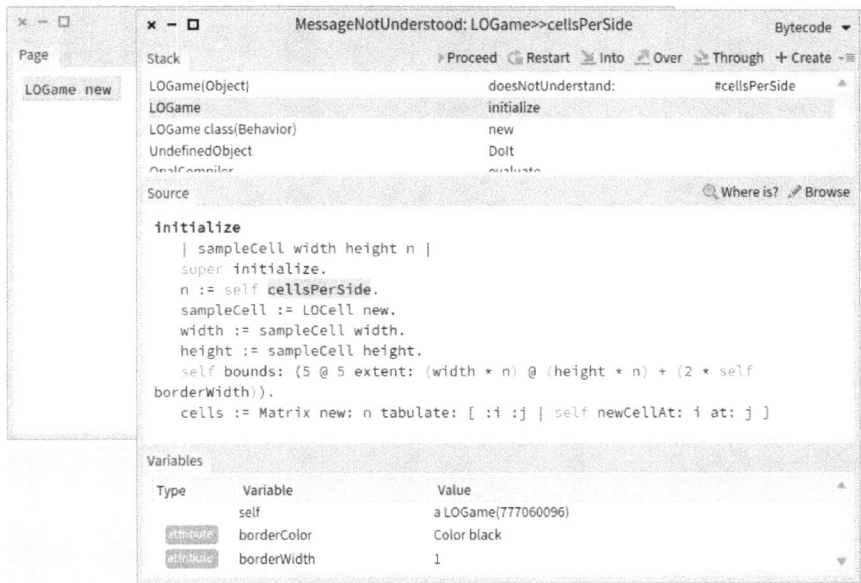

Figure 3.10: Pharo detecting an unknown selector

a method protocol enter accessing. The debugger will create the method cellsPerSide on the fly and invoke it immediately. As there is no magic, the created method will simply raise an exception and the debugger will stop again (as shown in Figure 3.11) giving you the opportunity to define the behavior of the method.

Here you can write your method. This method could hardly be simpler: it answers the constant 10. One advantage of representing constants as methods is that if the program evolves so that the constant then depends on some other features, the method can be changed to calculate this value.

```
cellsPerSide
    "The number of cells along each side of the game"
    ^ 10
```

Define the method cellsPerSide in the debugger. Do not forget to compile the method definition by using **Accept**. You should obtain a situation as shown by Figure 3.12. If you press the button **Proceed** the program will continue its execution - here it will stop since we did not define the method newCellAt:. We could use the same process but for now we stop to explain a bit what we did so far. Close the debugger, and look at the class definition once again (which you can do by clicking on **LOGame** on the second pane of the **System Browser**), you will see that the browser has modified it to include the instance variable cells.

43

A first application

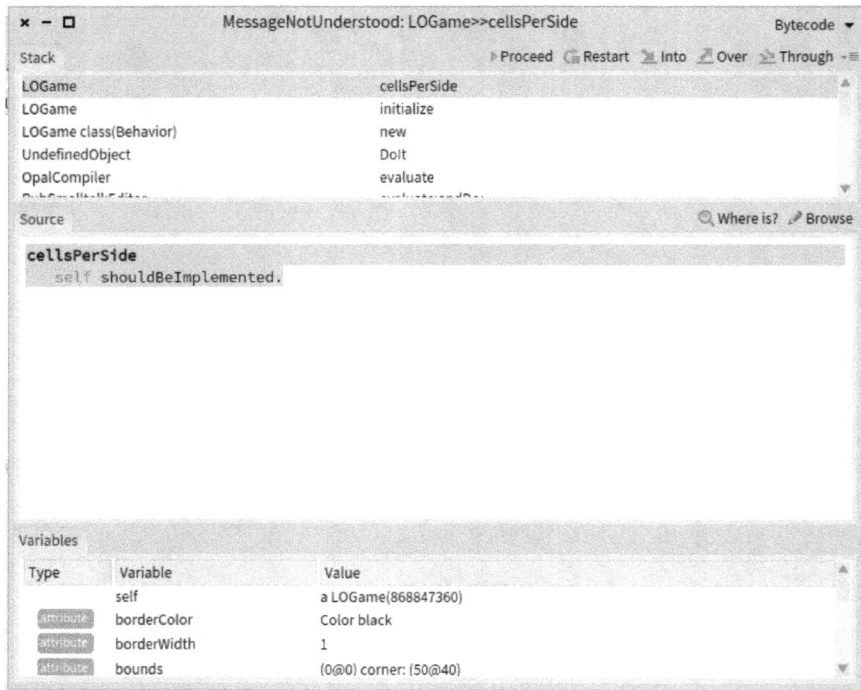

Figure 3.11: The system created a new method with a body to be defined.

Studying the initialize method

Let us now study the method `initialize`.

```
1 initialize
2   | sampleCell width height n |
3   super initialize.
4   n := self cellsPerSide.
5   sampleCell := LOCell new.
6   width := sampleCell width.
7   height := sampleCell height.
8   self bounds: (5 @ 5 extent: (width * n) @ (height * n) + (2 * self
      borderWidth)).
9   cells := Matrix new: n tabulate: [ :i :j | self newCellAt: i at: j ]
```

- At line 2, the expression | sampleCell width height n | declares 4 temporary variables. They are called temporary variables because their scope and lifetime are limited to this method. Temporary variables with explanatory names are helpful in making code more readable. Lines 4-7 set the value of these variables.

- How big should our game board be? Big enough to hold some integral

3.6 Defining the class LOGame

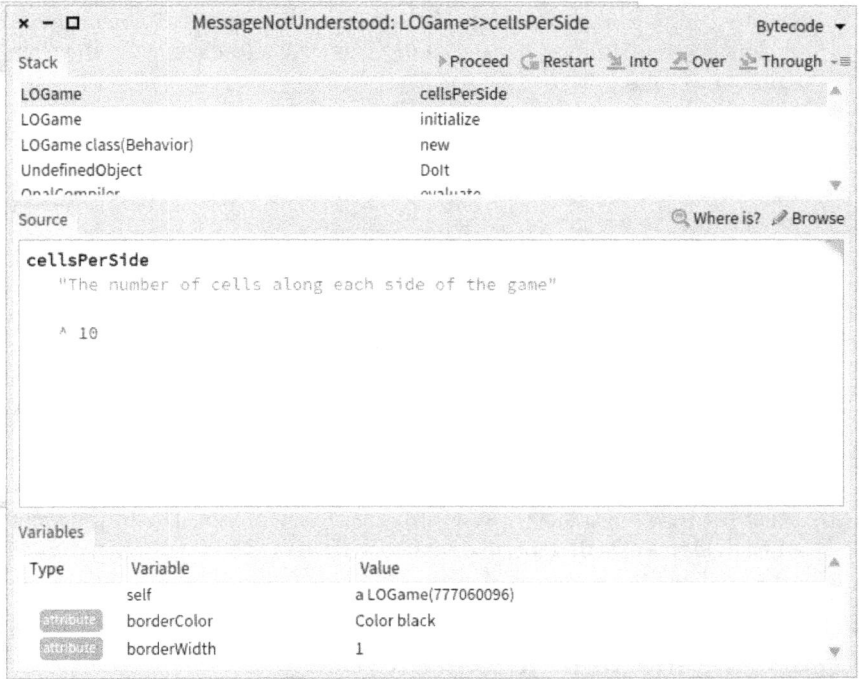

Figure 3.12: Defining cellsPerSide in the debugger

number of cells, and big enough to draw a border around them. How many cells is the right number? 5? 10? 100? We don't know yet, and if we did, we would probably change our minds later. So we delegate the responsibility for knowing that number to another method, which we name cellsPerSide, and which we will write in a minute or two. Don't be put off by this: it is actually good practice to code by referring to other methods that we haven't yet defined. Why? Well, it wasn't until we started writing the initialize method that we realized that we needed it. And at that point, we can give it a meaningful name, and move on, without interrupting our flow.

- The fourth line uses this method, n := self cellsPerSide. sends the message cellsPerSide to self, i.e., to this very object. The response, which will be the number of cells per side of the game board, is assigned to n.
- The next three lines create a new LOCell object, and assign its width and height to the appropriate temporary variables.
- Line 8 sets the bounds of the new object. Without worrying too much about the details just yet, believe us that the expression in parentheses

45

creates a square with its origin (i.e., its top-left corner) at the point (5,5) and its bottom-right corner far enough away to allow space for the right number of cells.

- The last line sets the `LOGame` object's instance variable `cells` to a newly created `Matrix` with the right number of rows and columns. We do this by sending the message `new: tabulate:` to the `Matrix` class (classes are objects too, so we can send them messages). We know that `new: tabulate:` takes two arguments because it has two colons (:) in its name. The arguments go right after the colons. If you are used to languages that put all of the arguments together inside parentheses, this may seem weird at first. Don't panic, it's only syntax! It turns out to be a very good syntax because the name of the method can be used to explain the roles of the arguments. For example, it is pretty clear that `Matrix rows: 5 columns: 2` has 5 rows and 2 columns, and not 2 rows and 5 columns.

- `Matrix new: n tabulate: [ :i :j | self newCellAt: i at: j ]` creates a new n X n matrix and initializes its elements. The initial value of each element will depend on its coordinates. The (i,j)th element will be initialized to the result of evaluating `self newCellAt: i at: j`.

3.7 Organizing methods into protocols

Before we define any more methods, let's take a quick look at the third pane at the top of the browser. In the same way that the first pane of the browser lets us categorize classes into packages, the protocol pane lets us categorize methods so that we are not overwhelmed by a very long list of method names in the method pane. These groups of methods are called "protocols".

The browser also offers us the --all-- virtual protocol, which, you will not be surprised to learn, contains all of the methods in the class.

If you have followed along with this example, the protocol pane may well contain the protocol **as yet unclassified**. Right-click in the protocol pane and select **categorize all uncategorized** to fix this, and move the `initialize` method to a new protocol called **initialization**.

How does the **System Browser** know that this is the right protocol? Well, in general Pharo can't know exactly, but in this case there is also an `initialize` method in the superclass, and it assumes that our `initialize` method should go in the same protocol as the one that it overrides.

A typographic convention. Pharoers frequently use the notation `Class >> method` to identify the class to which a method belongs. For example, the `cellsPerSide` method in class `LOGame` would be referred to as `LOGame >> cellsPerSide`. Just keep in mind that this is not Pharo syntax exactly, but merely a convenient notation to indicate "the instance method `cellsPerSide` which belongs to the class LOGame". (Incidentally, the corresponding notation for a class-side method would be LOGame class >> someClassSideMethod.)

From now on, when we show a method in this book, we will write the name of the method in this form. Of course, when you actually type the code into the browser, you don't have to type the class name or the >>; instead, you just make sure that the appropriate class is selected in the class pane.

3.8 Finishing the game

Now let's define the other method that are used by LOGame >> initialize. Let's define LOGame >> newCellAt: at: in the initialization protocol.

```
LOGame >> newCellAt: i at: j
  "Create a cell for position (i,j) and add it to my on-screen
      representation at the appropriate screen position. Answer the
      new cell"

  | c origin |
  c := LOCell new.
  origin := self innerBounds origin.
  self addMorph: c.
  c position: ((i - 1) * c width) @ ((j - 1) * c height) + origin.
  c mouseAction: [ self toggleNeighboursOfCellAt: i at: j ]
```

Formatting. As you can see there are some tabulation and empty lines. In order to keep the same convention you can right-click on the method edit area and click on Format (or use CMD-Shift-f shortcut). This will format your method.

The method defined above created a new LOCell, initialized to position (i, j) in the Matrix of cells. The last line defines the new cell's mouseAction to be the block [self toggleNeighboursOfCellAt: i at: j]. In effect, this defines the callback behaviour to perform when the mouse is clicked. The corresponding method also needs to be defined.

```
LOGame >> toggleNeighboursOfCellAt: i at: j
  i > 1
    ifTrue: [ (cells at: i - 1 at: j) toggleState ].
  i < self cellsPerSide
    ifTrue: [ (cells at: i + 1 at: j) toggleState ].
  j > 1
    ifTrue: [ (cells at: i at: j - 1) toggleState ].
  j < self cellsPerSide
    ifTrue: [ (cells at: i at: j + 1) toggleState ]
```

The method toggleNeighboursOfCellAt:at: toggles the state of the four cells to the north, south, west and east of cell (i, j). The only complication is

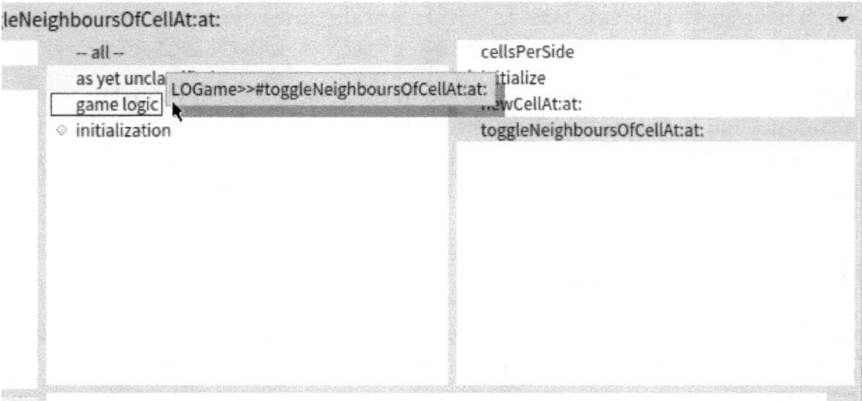

Figure 3.13: Drag a method to a protocol

that the board is finite, so we have to make sure that a neighboring cell exists before we toggle its state.

Place this method in a new protocol called game logic. (Right-click in the protocol pane to add a new protocol.) To move (re-classify) the method, you can simply click on its name and drag it to the newly-created protocol (see Figure 3.13).

To complete the Lights Out game, we need to define two more methods in class LOCell this time to handle mouse events.

```
LOCell >> mouseAction: aBlock
    ^ mouseAction := aBlock
```

The method above does nothing more than set the cell's mouseAction variable to the argument, and then answers the new value. Any method that changes the value of an instance variable in this way is called a *setter method*; a method that answers the current value of an instance variable is called a *getter method*.

Setter/Getter convention. If you are used to getters and setters in other programming languages, you might expect these methods to be called setMouseAction and getMouseAction. The Pharo convention is different. A getter always has the same name as the variable it gets, and a setter is named similarly, but with a trailing ":", hence mouseAction and mouseAction:. Collectively, setters and getters are called *accessor methods*, and by convention they should be placed in the accessing protocol. In Pharo, all instance variables are private to the object that owns them, so the only way for another object to read or write those variables is through accessor methods like this one. In fact, the instance variables can be accessed in subclasses too.

3.9 Let's try our code

Go to the class LOCell, define LOCell >> mouseAction: and put it in the accessing protocol.

Finally, we need to define a method mouseUp:. This will be called automatically by the GUI framework if the mouse button is released while the cursor is over this cell on the screen. Add the method LOCell >> mouseUp: and then **Categorize automatically** the methods.

```
LOCell >> mouseUp: anEvent
    mouseAction value
```

What this method does is to send the message value to the object stored in the instance variable mouseAction. In LOGame >> newCellAt: i at: j we created the *block* [self toggleNeighboursOfCellAt: i at: j] which is toggling all the neighbours of a cell and we assigned this block to the mouseAction of the cell. Therefore sending the value message causes this block to be evaluated, and consequently the state of the cells will toggle.

3.9 Let's try our code

That's it: the Lights Out game is complete! If you have followed all of the steps, you should be able to play the game, consisting of just 2 classes and 7 methods. In a Playground, type LOGame new openInWorld and **Do it** .

The game will open, and you should be able to click on the cells and see how it works. Well, so much for theory... When you click on a cell, a debugger will appear. In the upper part of the debugger window you can see the execution stack, showing all the active methods. Selecting any one of them will show, in the middle pane, the Smalltalk code being executed in that method, with the part that triggered the error highlighted.

Click on the line labeled LOGame >> toggleNeighboursOfCellAt: at: (near the top). The debugger will show you the execution context within this method where the error occurred (see Figure 3.14).

At the bottom of the debugger is a variable zone. You can inspect the object that is the receiver of the message that caused the selected method to execute, so you can look here to see the values of the instance variables. You can also see the values of the method arguments.

Using the debugger, you can execute code step by step, inspect objects in parameters and local variables, evaluate code just as you can in a playground, and, most surprisingly to those used to other debuggers, change the code while it is being debugged! Some Pharoers program in the debugger almost all the time, rather than in the browser. The advantage of this is that you see the method that you are writing as it will be executed, with real parameters in the actual execution context.

In this case we can see in the first line of the top panel that the toggleState message has been sent to an instance of LOGame, while it should clearly have

A first application

Figure 3.14: The debugger, with the method `toggleNeighboursOfCell:at:` selected

been an instance of `LOCell`. The problem is most likely with the initialization of the cells matrix. Browsing the code of `LOGame >> initialize` shows that `cells` is filled with the return values of `newCellAt: at:`, but when we look at that method, we see that there is no return statement there! By default, a method returns `self`, which in the case of `newCellAt: at:` is indeed an instance of `LOGame`. The syntax to return a value from a method in Pharo is `^`.

Close the debugger window. Add the expression `^ c` to the end of the method `LOGame >> newCellAt:at:` so that it returns c.

```
LOGame >> newCellAt: i at: j
    "Create a cell for position (i,j) and add it to my on-screen
        representation at the appropriate screen position. Answer the
        new cell"

    | c origin |
    c := LOCell new.
    origin := self innerBounds origin.
    self addMorph: c.
    c position: ((i - 1) * c width) @ ((j - 1) * c height) + origin.
    c mouseAction: [ self toggleNeighboursOfCellAt: i at: j ].
    ^ c
```

Often, you can fix the code directly in the debugger window and click Proceed to continue running the application. In our case, because the bug was in the initialization of an object, rather than in the method that failed, the easiest thing to do is to close the debugger window, destroy the running instance of the game (with the halo CMD-Alt-Shift and click), and create a new one.

Execute `LOGame new openInWorld` again because if you use the old game instance it will still contain the block with the old logic.

Now the game should work properly... or nearly so. If we happen to move the mouse between clicking and releasing, then the cell the mouse is over will also be toggled. This turns out to be behavior that we inherit from `SimpleSwitchMorph`. We can fix this simply by overriding mouseMove: to do nothing:

```
LOCell >> mouseMove: anEvent
```

Finally we are done!

About the debugger. By default when an error occurs in Pharo, the system displays a debugger. However, we can fully control this behavior. For example we can write the error in a file. We can even serialize the execution stack in a file, zip and reopen it in another image. Now when we are in development mode the debugger is available to let us go as fast as possible. In production system, developers often control the debugger to hide their mistakes from their clients.

3.10 Saving and sharing Pharo code

Now that you have **Lights Out** working, you probably want to save it somewhere so that you can archive it and share it with your friends. Of course, you can save your whole Pharo image, and show off your first program by running it, but your friends probably have their own code in their images, and don't want to give that up to use your image. What you need is a way of getting source code out of your Pharo image so that other programmers can bring it into theirs.

> **Note** We'll be discussing the various ways to save and share code in a future chapter, Chapter : Sharing Code and Source Control. For now, here is an overview of some of the available methods.

Saving plain code

The simplest way of doing this is by "filing out" the code. The right-click menu in the Package pane will give you the option to `File Out` the whole of package PBE-LightsOut. The resulting file is more or less human readable, but is really intended for computers, not humans. You can email this file to your friends, and they can file it into their own Pharo images using the file list browser.

A first application

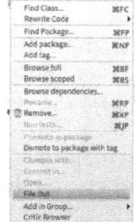

Figure 3.15: File Out our PBE-LightsOut

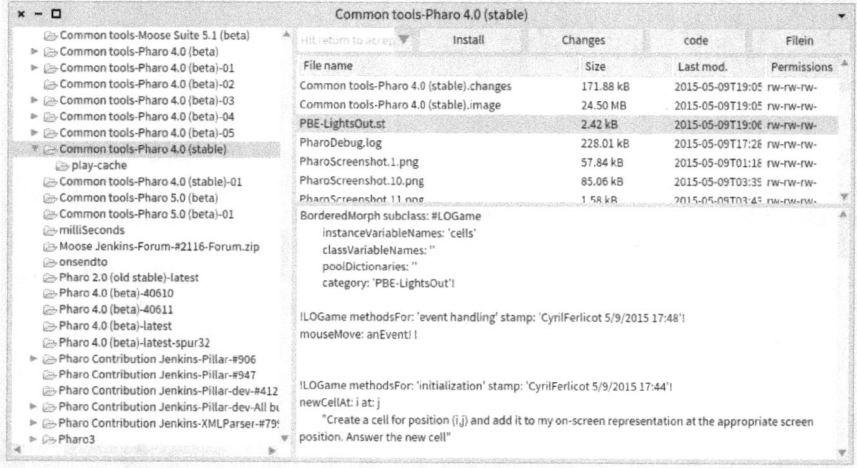

Figure 3.16: Import your code with the file browser

Right-click on the PBE-LightsOut package and file out the contents (see Figure 3.15). You should now find a file named PBE-LightsOut.st in the same folder on disk where your image is saved. Have a look at this file with a text editor.

Open a fresh Pharo image and use the File Browser tool (Tools --> File Browser) to file in the PBE-LightsOut.st fileout (see Figure 3.16) and fileIn. Verify that the game now works in the new image.

Monticello packages

Although fileouts are a convenient way of making a snapshot of the code you have written, they are definitevely "old school". Just as most open-source projects find it much more convenient to maintain their code in a repository using SVN or Git, so Pharo programmers find it more convenient to manage their code using Monticello packages. These packages are represented as files

3.10 Saving and sharing Pharo code

Figure 3.17: Monticello browser. The package PBE-LightsOut is not save yet

with names ending in .mcz. They are actually zip-compressed bundles that contain the complete code of your package.

Using the Monticello package browser, you can save packages to repositories on various types of server, including FTP and HTTP servers. You can also just write the packages to a repository in a local file system directory. A copy of your package is also always cached on your local disk in the package-cache folder. Monticello lets you save multiple versions of your program, merge versions, go back to an old version, and browse the differences between versions. In fact, Monticello is a distributed revision control system. This means it allows developers to save their work on different places, not on a single repository as it is the case with CVS or Subversion.

You can also send a .mcz file by email. The recipient will have to place it in her package-cache folder; she will then be able to use Monticello to browse and load it.

Monticello Browser

Open the Monticello browser from the World menu (see Figure 3.17).

In the right-hand pane of the browser is a list of Monticello repositories, which will include all of the repositories from which code has been loaded into the image that you are using. The top list item is a local directory called the package-cache. It caches copies of the packages that you have loaded or published over the network. This local cache is really handy because it lets you keep your own local history. It also allows you to work in places where you do not have internet access, or where access is slow enough that you do not want to save to a remote repository very frequently.

Saving and loading code with Monticello

On the left-hand side of the Monticello browser is a list of packages that have a version loaded into the image. Packages that have been modified since they were loaded are marked with an asterisk. (These are sometimes referred to as dirty packages.) If you select a package, the list of repositories is restricted to just those repositories that contain a copy of the selected package.

Add the PBE-LightsOut package to your Monticello browser using the + **Package** button and type PBE-LightsOut.

SmalltalkHub: a Github for Pharo

We think that the best way to save your code and share it is to create an account for your project in SmalltalkHub. SmalltalkHub is like GitHub: it is a web front-end to a HTTP Monticello server that lets you manage your projects. There is a public server at http://www.smalltalkhub.com/.

To be able to use SmalltalkHub you will need an account. Open the site in your browser. Then, click on the **Join** link and follow the instructions to create a new account. Finally, **login** to your account. Click on the + **New project** to create a new project. Fill in the information requested and click **Register project** button. You will be sent to your profile page, on the right side you will see the list of your projects and projects you watch by other coders. Click on the project you just created.

Under **Monticello registration** title label you will see a box containing a smalltalk message similar to

```
MCHttpRepository
    location: 'http://www.smalltalkhub.com/mc/UserName/ProjectName/main'
    user: 'YourName'
    password: 'Optional_Password'
```

Copy the contents and go back to Pharo. Once your project has been created on SmalltalkHub, you have to tell your Pharo system to use it. With the PBE-LightsOut package selected, click the **+Repository** button in the Monticello browser. You will see a list of the different Repository types that are available. To add a SmalltalkHub repository select smalltalkhub.com. You will be presented with a dialog in which you can provide the necessary information about the server. You should paste the code snippet you have copied from SmalltalkHub (see Figure 3.18). This message tells Monticello where to find your project online. You can also provide your user name and password. If you do not, then Pharo will ask for them each time you try to save into your online repository at SmalltalkHub.

Once you have accepted, your new repository should be listed on the right-hand side of the Monticello browser. Click on the **Save** button to save a first version of your Lights Out game on SmalltalkHub. Don't forget to put a com-

3.10 Saving and sharing Pharo code

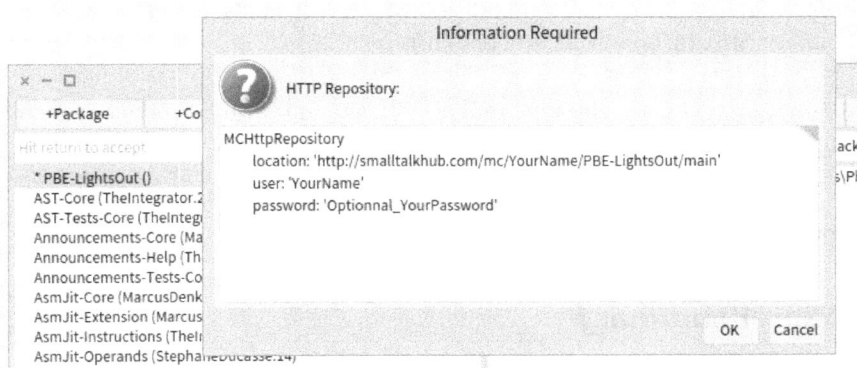

Figure 3.18: Create your first repository on SmalltalkHub

Figure 3.19: Do your first commit

ment so that you, or others, will have an idea of what your commit contains (see Figure 3.19).

To load a package into your image, open Monticello , select the repository where the package is located and click open button. It will open a new window with two columns, left one is the Package to be loaded, the right one is the version of the package to be loaded. Select the Package and the version you want to load and click the load button.

Open the PBE-LightsOut repository you have just saved. You should see the package you just saved.

Monticello has many more capabilities, which will be discussed in depth in Chapter : Sharing Code and Source Control.

About Git. If you are already familiar with Git and Github there are several solutions to manage your projects with Git. This blog posts provides a summary: http://blog.yuriy.tymch.uk/2015/07/pharo-and-github-versioning-revision-2.html#! There is a chapter in preparation on about how to use Git with Pharo. Request it on the Pharo mailing-list.

3.11 Chapter summary

In this chapter you have seen how to create packages, classes and methods. In addition, you have learned how to use the System browser, the inspector, the debugger and the Monticello browser.

- Packages are groups of related classes.
- A new class is created by sending a message to its superclass.
- Protocols are groups of related methods inside a class.
- A new method is created or modified by editing its definition in the browser and then accepting the changes.
- The inspector offers a simple, general-purpose GUI for inspecting and interacting with arbitrary objects.
- The browser detects usage of undeclared variables, and offers possible corrections.
- The `initialize` method is automatically executed after an object is created in Pharo. You can put any initialization code there.
- The debugger provides a high-level GUI to inspect and modify the state of a running program.
- You can share source code by filing out a package, class or method.
- A better way to share code is to use Monticello to manage an external repository, for example defined as a SmalltalkHub project.

CHAPTER 4

Syntax in a nutshell

Pharo adopts a syntax very close to that of its ancestor, Smalltalk. The syntax is designed so that program text can be read aloud as though it were a kind of pidgin English. The following method of the class Week shows an example of the syntax. It checks whether DayNames already contains the argument, i.e. if this argument represents a correct day name. If this is the case, it will assign it to the variable StartDay.

```
startDay: aSymbol

    (DayNames includes: aSymbol)
        ifTrue: [ StartDay := aSymbol ]
        ifFalse: [ self error: aSymbol, ' is not a recognised day name' ]
```

Pharo's syntax is minimal. Essentially there is syntax only for sending messages (i.e. expressions). Expressions are built up from a very small number of primitive elements (message sends, assignments, closures, returns...). There are only 6 keywords, and there is no syntax for control structures or declaring new classes. Instead, nearly everything is achieved by sending messages to objects. For instance, instead of an if-then-else control structure, conditionals are expressed as messages (such as ifTrue:) sent to Boolean objects. New (sub-)classes are created by sending a message to their superclass.

4.1 Syntactic elements

Expressions are composed of the following building blocks:

1. The six reserved keywords, or *pseudo-variables*: self, super, nil, true, false, and thisContext

2. Constant expressions for *literal* objects including numbers, characters, strings, symbols and arrays
3. Variable declarations
4. Assignments
5. Block closures
6. Messages

We can see examples of the various syntactic elements in the Table below.

Syntax	What it represents
startPoint	a variable name
Transcript	a global variable name
self	pseudo-variable
1	decimal integer
2r101	binary integer
1.5	floating point number
2.4e7	exponential notation
$a	the character 'a'
'Hello'	the string 'Hello'
#Hello	the symbol #Hello
#(1 2 3)	a literal array
{ 1 . 2 . 1 + 2 }	a dynamic array
"a comment"	a comment
| x y |	declaration of variables x and y
x := 1	assign 1 to x
[:x | x + 2]	a block that evaluates to x + 2
<primitive: 1>	virtual machine primitive or annotation
3 factorial	unary message factorial
3 + 4	binary message +
2 raisedTo: 6 modulo: 10	keyword message raisedTo:modulo:
^ true	return the value true
x := 2 . x := x + x	expression separator (.)
Transcript show: 'hello'; cr	message cascade (;)

Local variables. startPoint is a variable name, or identifier. By convention, identifiers are composed of words in "camelCase" (i.e., each word except the first starting with an upper case letter). The first letter of an instance variable, method or block argument, or temporary variable must be lower case. This indicates to the reader that the variable has a private scope.

Shared variables. Identifiers that start with upper case letters are global variables, class variables, pool dictionaries or class names. Transcript is a global variable, an instance of the class ThreadSafeTranscript.

The receiver. self is a keyword that refers to the object inside which the current method is executing. We call it "the receiver" because this object

4.1 Syntactic elements

has received the message that caused the method to execute. `self` is called a "pseudo-variable" since we cannot assign to it.

Integers. In addition to ordinary decimal integers like 42, Pharo also provides a radix notation. `2r101` is 101 in radix 2 (i.e., binary), which is equal to decimal 5.

Floating point numbers. can be specified with their base-ten exponent: `2.4e7` is 2.4×10^7.

Characters. A dollar sign introduces a literal character: `$a` is the literal for the character `'a'`. Instances of non-printing characters can be obtained by sending appropriately named messages to the `Character` class, such as `Character space` and `Character tab`.

Strings. Single quotes `' '` are used to define a literal string. If you want a string with a single quote inside, just double the quote, as in `'G''day'`.

Symbols. Symbols are like Strings, in that they contain a sequence of characters. However, unlike a string, a literal symbol is guaranteed to be globally unique. There is only one Symbol object `#Hello` but there may be multiple String objects with the value `'Hello'`.

Compile-time arrays. are defined by `#( )`, surrounding space-separated literals. Everything within the parentheses must be a compile-time constant. For example, `#(27 (true false) abc)` is a literal array of three elements: the integer 27, the compile-time array containing the two booleans, and the symbol #abc. (Note that this is the same as `#(27 #(true false) #abc)`.)

Run-time arrays. Curly braces `{ }` define a (dynamic) array at run-time. Elements are expressions separated by periods. So `{ 1. 2. 1 + 2 }` defines an array with elements 1, 2, and the result of evaluating 1+2.

Comments. are enclosed in double quotes `" "`. "hello" is a comment, not a string, and is ignored by the Pharo compiler. Comments may span multiple lines.

Local variable definitions. Vertical bars `| |` enclose the declaration of one or more local variables in a method (and also in a block).

Assignment. `:=` assigns an object to a variable.

Blocks. Square brackets `[ ]` define a block, also known as a block closure or a lexical closure, which is a first-class object representing a function. As we shall see, blocks may take arguments (`[:i | ...]`) and can have local variables.

Primitives. `< primitive: ... >` denotes an invocation of a virtual machine primitive. For example, `< primitive: 1 >` is the VM primitive for SmallInteger. Any code following the primitive is executed only if the primitive fails. The same syntax is also used for method annotations (pragmas).

59

Unary messages. These consist of a single word (like `factorial`) sent to a receiver (like 3). In `3 factorial`, 3 is the receiver, and `factorial` is the message selector.

Binary messages. These are message with an argument and whose selector looks like mathematical expressions (for example: +) sent to a receiver, and taking a single argument. In `3 + 4`, the receiver is 3, the message selector is +, and the argument is 4.

Keyword messages. They consist of multiple keywords (like `raisedTo: modulo:`), each ending with a colon and taking a single argument. In the expression `2 raisedTo: 6 modulo: 10`, the message selector `raisedTo:modulo:` takes the two arguments 6 and 10, one following each colon. We send the message to the receiver 2.

Method return. ^ is used to *return* a value from a method.

Sequences of statements. A period or full-stop (.) is the statement separator. Putting a period between two expressions turns them into independent statements.

Cascades. Semicolons (;) can be used to send a cascade of messages to a single receiver. In `Transcript show: 'hello'; cr` we first send the keyword message `show: 'hello'` to the receiver `Transcript`, and then we send the unary message `cr` to the same receiver.

The classes `Number`, `Character`, `String` and `Boolean` are described in more detail in Chapter : Basic Classes.

4.2 Pseudo-variables

In Pharo, there are 6 reserved keywords, or pseudo-variables: `nil`, `true`, `false`, `self`, `super`, and `thisContext`. They are called pseudo-variables because they are predefined and cannot be assigned to. `true`, `false`, and `nil` are constants, while the values of `self`, `super`, and `thisContext` vary dynamically as code is executed.

- `true` and `false` are the unique instances of the Boolean classes `True` and `False`. See Chapter : Basic Classes for more details.
- `self` always refers to the receiver of the currently executing method.
- `super` also refers to the receiver of the current method, but when you send a message to `super`, the method-lookup changes so that it starts from the superclass of the class containing the method that uses `super`. For further details see Chapter : The Pharo Object Model.
- `nil` is the undefined object. It is the unique instance of the class `UndefinedObject`. Instance variables, class variables and local variables are initialized to `nil`.

- `thisContext` is a pseudo-variable that represents the top frame of the execution stack. `thisContext` is normally not of interest to most programmers, but it is essential for implementing development tools like the debugger, and it is also used to implement exception handling and continuations.

4.3 Message sends

There are three kinds of messages in Pharo. This distinction has been made to reduce the number of mandatory parentheses.

1. *Unary* messages take no argument. `1 factorial` sends the message `factorial` to the object `1`.
2. *Binary* messages take exactly one argument. `1 + 2` sends the message `+` with argument `2` to the object `1`.
3. *Keyword* messages take an arbitrary number of arguments. `2 raisedTo: 6 modulo: 10` sends the message consisting of the message selector `raisedTo:modulo:` and the arguments 6 and 10 to the object 2.

Unary messages. Unary message selectors consist of alphanumeric characters, and start with a lower case letter.

Binary messages. Binary message selectors consist of one or more characters from the following set:

```
+ - / \ * ~ < > = @ % | & ? ,
```

Keyword message selectors. Keyword message selectors consist of a series of alphanumeric keywords, where each keyword starts with a lower-case letter and ends with a colon.

Message precedence. Unary messages have the highest precedence, then binary messages, and finally keyword messages, so:

```
2 raisedTo: 1 + 3 factorial
>>> 128
```

First we send `factorial` to 3, then we send `+ 6` to 1, and finally we send `raisedTo: 7` to 2. Recall that we use the notation expression `>>>` to show the result of evaluating an expression.

Precedence aside, execution is strictly from left to right, so:

```
1 + 2 * 3
>>> 9
```

return 9 and not 7. Parentheses must be used to alter the order of evaluation:

```
1 + (2 * 3)
>>> 7
```

Periods and semi-colons.   Message sends may be composed with periods and semi-colons. A period separated sequence of expressions causes each expression in the series to be evaluated as a *statement*, one after the other.

```
Transcript cr.
Transcript show: 'hello world'.
Transcript cr
```

This will send cr to the Transcript object, then send it show: 'hello world', and finally send it another cr.

When a series of messages is being sent to the *same* receiver, then this can be expressed more succinctly as a *cascade*. The receiver is specified just once, and the sequence of messages is separated by semi-colons:

```
Transcript
  cr;
  show: 'hello world';
  cr
```

This has precisely the same effect as the previous example.

4.4 Method syntax

Whereas expressions may be evaluated anywhere in Pharo (for example, in a playground, in a debugger, or in a browser), methods are normally defined in a browser window, or in the debugger. Methods can also be filed in from an external medium, but this is not the usual way to program in Pharo.

Programs are developed one method at a time, in the context of a given class. A class is defined by sending a message to an existing class, asking it to create a subclass, so there is no special syntax required for defining classes.

Here is the method lineCount in the class String. The usual *convention* is to refer to methods as ClassName»methodName. Here the method is then String»lineCount. Note that ClassName»methodName is not part of the Pharo syntax just a convention used in books to clearly define a method.

```
String >> lineCount
    "Answer the number of lines represented by the receiver, where every
        cr adds one line."

    | cr count |
    cr := Character cr.
    count := 1 min: self size.
    self do: [:c | c == cr ifTrue: [count := count + 1]].
    ^ count
```

Syntactically, a method consists of:

1. the method pattern, containing the name (i.e., lineCount) and any arguments (none in this example)
2. comments (these may occur anywhere, but the convention is to put one at the top that explains what the method does)
3. declarations of local variables (i.e., cr and count); and
4. any number of expressions separated by dots (here there are four)

The execution of any expression preceded by a ^ (a caret or upper arrow, which is Shift-6 for most keyboards) will cause the method to exit at that point, returning the value of that expression. A method that terminates without explicitly returning some expression will implicitly return self.

Arguments and local variables should always start with lower case letters. Names starting with upper-case letters are assumed to be global variables. Class names, like Character, for example, are simply global variables referring to the object representing that class.

4.5 Block syntax

Blocks (lexical closures) provide a mechanism to defer the execution of expressions. A block is essentially an anonymous function with a definition context. A block is executed by sending it the message value. The block answers the value of the last expression in its body, unless there is an explicit return (with ^) in which case it returns the value of the returned expression.

```
[ 1 + 2 ] value
>>> 3
[ 3 = 3 ifTrue: [ ^ 33 ]. 44 ] value
>>> 33
```

Blocks may take parameters, each of which is declared with a leading colon. A vertical bar separates the parameter declaration(s) from the body of the block. To evaluate a block with one parameter, you must send it the message value: with one argument. A two-parameter block must be sent value:value:, and so on, up to 4 arguments.

```
[ :x | 1 + x ] value: 2
>>> 3
[ :x :y | x + y ] value: 1 value: 2
>>> 3
```

If you have a block with more than four parameters, you must use valueWithArguments: and pass the arguments in an array. (A block with a large number of parameters is often a sign of a design problem.)

Blocks may also declare local variables, which are surrounded by vertical bars, just like local variable declarations in a method. Locals are declared after any arguments:

```
[ :x :y |
   | z |
   z := x + y.
   z ] value: 1 value: 2
>>> 3
```

Blocks are actually lexical closures, since they can refer to variables of the surrounding environment. The following block refers to the variable x of its enclosing environment:

```
| x |
x := 1.
[ :y | x + y ] value: 2
>>> 3
```

Blocks are instances of the class BlockClosure. This means that they are objects, so they can be assigned to variables and passed as arguments just like any other object.

4.6 Conditionals and loops in a nutshell

Pharo offers no special syntax for control constructs. Instead, these are typically expressed by sending messages to booleans, numbers and collections, with blocks as arguments.

Some conditionals

Conditionals are expressed by sending one of the messages ifTrue:, ifFalse: or ifTrue:ifFalse: to the result of a boolean expression. See Chapter : Basic Classes, for more about booleans.

```
(17 * 13 > 220)
   ifTrue: [ 'bigger' ]
   ifFalse: [ 'smaller' ]
>>> 'bigger'
```

Some loops

Loops are typically expressed by sending messages to blocks, integers or collections. Since the exit condition for a loop may be repeatedly evaluated, it should be a block rather than a boolean value. Here is an example of a very procedural loop:

```
n := 1.
[ n < 1000 ] whileTrue: [ n := n*2 ].
```

4.6 Conditionals and loops in a nutshell

```
n
>>> 1024
```

`whileFalse:` reverses the exit condition.
```
n := 1.
[ n > 1000 ] whileFalse: [ n := n*2 ].
n
>>> 1024
```

`timesRepeat:` offers a simple way to implement a fixed iteration:
```
n := 1.
10 timesRepeat: [ n := n*2 ].
n
>>> 1024
```

We can also send the message `to:do:` to a number which then acts as the initial value of a loop counter. The two arguments are the upper bound, and a block that takes the current value of the loop counter as its argument:
```
result := String new.
1 to: 10 do: [:n | result := result, n printString, ' '].
result
>>> '1 2 3 4 5 6 7 8 9 10 '
```

High-order iterators

Collections comprise a large number of different classes, many of which support the same protocol. The most important messages for iterating over collections include `do:`, `collect:`, `select:`, `reject:`, `detect:` and `inject:into:`. These messages define high-level iterators that allow one to write very compact code.

An **Interval** is a collection that lets one iterate over a sequence of numbers from the starting point to the end. `1 to: 10` represents the interval from 1 to 10. Since it is a collection, we can send the message `do:` to it. The argument is a block that is evaluated for each element of the collection.
```
result := String new.
(1 to: 10) do: [:n | result := result, n printString, ' '].
result
>>> '1 2 3 4 5 6 7 8 9 10 '
```

`collect:` builds a new collection of the same size, transforming each element. (You can think of `collect:` as the Map in the MapReduce programming model).
```
(1 to:10) collect: [ :each | each * each ]
>>> #(1 4 9 16 25 36 49 64 81 100)
```

`select:` and `reject:` build new collections, each containing a subset of the elements satisfying (or not) the boolean block condition.

detect: returns the first element satisfying the condition. Don't forget that strings are also collections (of characters), so you can iterate over all the characters.

```
'hello there' select: [ :char | char isVowel ]
>>> 'eoee'
'hello there' reject: [ :char | char isVowel ]
>>> 'hll thr'
'hello there' detect: [ :char | char isVowel ]
>>> $e
```

Finally, you should be aware that collections also support a functional-style fold operator in the inject:into: method. You can also think of it as the Reduce in the MapReduce programming model. This lets you generate a cumulative result using an expression that starts with a seed value and injects each element of the collection. Sums and products are typical examples.

```
(1 to: 10) inject: 0 into: [ :sum :each | sum + each]
>>> 55
```

This is equivalent to 0+1+2+3+4+5+6+7+8+9+10.

More about collections can be found in Chapter : Collections.

4.7 Primitives and pragmas

In Pharo everything is an object, and everything happens by sending messages. Nevertheless, at certain points we hit rock bottom. Certain objects can only get work done by invoking virtual machine primitives.

For example, the following are all implemented as primitives: memory allocation (new, new:), bit manipulation (bitAnd:, bitOr:, bitShift:), pointer and integer arithmetic (+, -, <, >, *, /, =, ==...), and array access (at:, at:put:).

Primitives are invoked with the syntax <primitive: aNumber>. A method that invokes such a primitive may also include Pharo code, which will be executed only if the primitive fails.

Here we see the code for SmallInteger>>+. If the primitive fails, the expression super + aNumber will be executed and returned.

```
+ aNumber
    "Primitive. Add the receiver to the argument and answer with the
        result
    if it is a SmallInteger. Fail if the argument or the result is not a
    SmallInteger Essential No Lookup. See Object documentation
        whatIsAPrimitive."

    <primitive: 1>
    ^ super + aNumber
```

In Pharo, the angle bracket syntax is also used for method annotations called pragmas.

4.8 Chapter summary

- Pharo has only six reserved identifiers (also called pseudo-variables): `true`, `false`, `nil`, `self`, `super`, and `thisContext`.
- There are five kinds of literal objects: numbers (`5`, `2.5`, `1.9e15`, `2r111`), characters (`$a`), strings (`'hello'`), symbols (`#hello`), and arrays (`#('hello' #hi)` or `{ 1 . 2 . 1 + 2 }`)
- Strings are delimited by single quotes, comments by double quotes. To get a quote inside a string, double it.
- Unlike strings, symbols are guaranteed to be globally unique.
- Use `#( ... )` to define a literal array. Use `{ ... }` to define a dynamic array. Note that `#(1+2) size >>> 3`, but `{1+2} size >>> 1`
- There are three kinds of messages: unary (e.g., `1 asString`, `Array new`), binary (e.g., `3 + 4`, `'hi'`, `' there'`), and keyword (e.g., `'hi' at: 2 put: $o`)
- A cascaded message send is a sequence of messages sent to the same target, separated by semi-colons: `OrderedCollection new add: #calvin; add: #hobbes; size >>> 2`
- Local variables are declared with vertical bars. Use `:=` for assignment. `|x| x := 1`
- Expressions consist of message sends, cascades and assignments, evaluated left to right (and optionally grouped with parentheses). Statements are expressions separated by periods.
- Block closures are expressions enclosed in square brackets. Blocks may take arguments and can contain temporary variables. The expressions in the block are not evaluated until you send the block a value message with the correct number of arguments. `[ :x | x + 2 ] value: 4`
- There is no dedicated syntax for control constructs, just messages that conditionally evaluate blocks.

CHAPTER 5

Understanding message syntax

Although Pharo's message syntax is simple, it is unconventional and can take some time getting used to. This chapter offers some guidance to help you get acclimatized to this special syntax for sending messages. If you already feel comfortable with the syntax, you may choose to skip this chapter, or come back to it later.

5.1 Identifying messages

In Pharo, except for the syntactic elements listed in Chapter : Syntax in a Nutshell (:= ^ . ; # () {} [: |] < >), everything is a message send. There is no operators, just messages sent to objects. Therefore you can define a message named + in your class but there is also no precedence because Pharo always takes the simplest form of definition.

The order in which messages are sent is determined by the type of message. There are just three types of messages: **unary**, **binary**, and **keyword messages**. Pharo distinguishes such three types of messages to minimize the number of parentheses. Unary messages are always sent first, then binary messages and finally keyword ones. As in most languages, parentheses can be used to change the order of execution. These rules make Pharo code as easy to read as possible. And most of the time you do not have to think about the rules.

Message structure

As most computation in Pharo is done by message passing, correctly identifying messages is key to avoiding future mistakes. The following terminology

Understanding message syntax

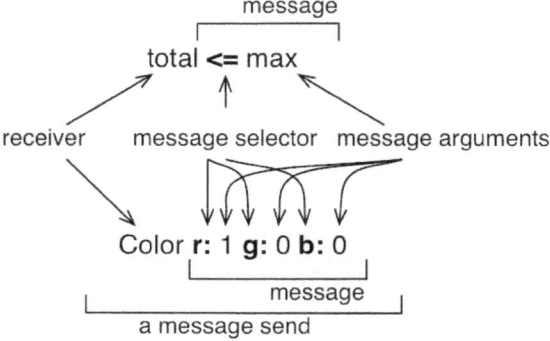

Figure 5.1: Two message sends composed of a receiver, a method selector, and a set of arguments.

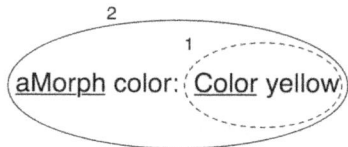

Figure 5.2: aMorph color: Color yellow is composed of two message sends: Color yelow and aMorph color: Color yellow.

will help us:

- A message is composed of the message **selector** and the optional message arguments.
- A message is sent to a **receiver**.
- The combination of a message and its receiver is called a *message send* as shown in Figure 5.1.

A message is always sent to a receiver, which can be a single literal, a block or a variable or the result of evaluating another message.

To help you identify the receiver of a message, we will underline it for you. We will also surround each message send with an ellipse, and number the message sends starting from the first one to help you see the send order in Figure 5.2.

Figure 5.2 represents two message sends, Color yellow and aMorph color: Color yellow, hence there are two ellipses. The message send Color yellow is executed first, so its ellipse is numbered 1. There are two receivers: 1) aMorph which receives the message color: ... and 2) Color which receives the message yellow. Both receivers are underlined.

70

5.2 Three types of messages

A receiver can be the first element of a message, such as 100 in the message send 100 + 200 or `Color` in the message send `Color yellow`. However, a receiver can also be the result of other messages. For example in the message `Pen new go: 100`, the receiver of the message `go: 100` is the object returned by the message send `Pen new`. In all the cases, a message is sent to an object called the *receiver* which may be the result of another message send.

Message send	Message type	Action
`Color yellow`	unary	Creates a color
`aPen go: 100`	keyword	Forwards pen 100 pixels
`100 + 20`	binary	100 receives the message +
`Browser open`	unary	Opens a new browser
`Pen new go: 100`	un. and keyw.	Creates and moves pen 100 px
`aPen go: 100 + 20`	keyw. and bin.	Pen moves forward 120 px

The table shows several characteristics of message sends.

- You should note that not all message sends have arguments. Unary messages like `open` do not have arguments. Single keyword and binary messages like `go: 100` and `+ 20` each have one argument.

- There are also simple messages and composed ones. `Color yellow` and `100 + 20` are simple: a message is sent to an object, while the message send `aPen go: 100 + 20` is composed of two messages: `+ 20` is sent to 100 and `go:` is sent to `aPen` with the argument being the result of the first message.

- A receiver can be an expression (such as an assignment, a message send or a literal) which returns an object. In `Pen new go: 100`, the message `go: 100` is sent to the object that results from the execution of the message send `Pen new`.

5.2 Three types of messages

Pharo distinguishes between three kinds of messages to reduce mandatory parentheses. A few simple rules based on the such different message determine the order in which the messages are sent.

There are three different types of messages:

- *Unary messages* are messages that are sent to an object without any other information. For example, in `3 factorial`, `factorial` is a unary message.

- *Binary messages* are messages consisting of operators (often arithmetic). They are binary because they always involve only two objects: the receiver and the argument object. For example in `10 + 20`, `+` is a binary message sent to the receiver 10 with argument 20.

- *Keyword messages* are messages consisting of one or more keywords, each ending with a colon (:) and taking an argument. For example in `anArray at: 1 put: 10`, the keyword `at:` takes the argument 1 and the keyword `put:` takes the argument 10.

Unary messages

Unary messages are messages that do not require any argument. They follow the syntactic template: `receiver messageName`. The selector is simply made up of a succession of characters not containing : (e.g., `factorial`, `open`, `class`).

```
89 sin
>>> 0.860069405812453
```

```
3 sqrt
>>> 1.732050807568877
```

```
Float pi
>>> 3.141592653589793
```

```
'blop' size
>>> 4
```

```
true not
>>> false
```

```
Object class
>>> Object class "The class of Object is Object class (BANG)"
```

> **Important** Unary messages are messages that do not require any argument. They follow the syntactic template: `receiver selector`.

Binary messages

Binary messages are messages that require exactly one argument *and* whose selector consists of a sequence of one or more characters from the set: +, -, *, /, &, =, >, |, <, ~, and @. Note that -- (double minus) is not allowed for parsing reasons.

```
100@100
>>> 100@100 "creates a Point object"
```

```
3 + 4
>>> 7
```

```
10 - 1
>>> 9
```

```
4 <= 3
>>> false
```

5.2 Three types of messages

```
(4/3) * 3 == 4
>>> true "equality is just a binary message, and Fractions are exact"
```

```
(3/4) == (3/4)
>>> false "two equal Fractions are not the same object"
```

> **Important** Binary messages are messages that require exactly one argument *and* whose selector is composed of a sequence of characters from: +, -, *, /, &, =, >, |, <, ~, and @. -- is not possible. They follow the syntactic template: `receiver selector argument`.

Keyword messages

Keyword messages are messages that require one or more arguments and whose selector consists of one or more keywords each ending in :. Keyword messages follow the syntactic template: `receiver selectorWordOne: argumentOne wordTwo: argumentTwo`.

Each keyword takes an argument. Hence `r:g:b:` is a method with three arguments, `playFileNamed:` and `at:` are methods with one argument, and `at:put:` is a method with two arguments. To create an instance of the class `Color` one can use the method `r:g:b:` (as in `Color r: 1 g: 0 b: 0`), which creates the color red. Note that the colons are part of the selector.

> **Note** In Java or C++, the method invocation `Color r: 1 g: 0 b: 0` would be written `Color.rgb(1, 0, 0)`.

```
1 to: 10
>>> (1 to: 10) "creates an interval"
```

```
Color r: 1 g: 0 b: 0
>>> Color red "creates a new color"
```

```
12 between: 8 and: 15
>>> true
```

```
nums := Array newFrom: (1 to: 5).
nums at: 1 put: 6.
nums
>>> #(6 2 3 4 5)
```

> **Important** Keyword messages are messages that require one or more arguments. Their selector consists of one or more keywords each ending in a colon (:). They follow the syntactic template: `receiver selectorWordOne: argumentOne wordTwo: argumentTwo`.

73

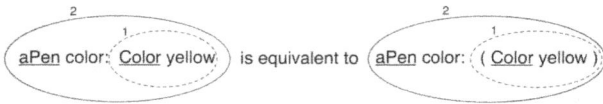

Figure 5.3: Unary messages are sent first so `Color yellow` is sent. This returns a color

5.3 Message composition

The three types of messages each have different precedence, which allows them to be composed in an elegant way and with few parentheses.

- Unary messages are always sent first, then binary messages and finally, keyword messages.
- Messages in parentheses are sent prior to any other messages.
- Messages of the same kind are evaluated from left to right.

These rules lead to a very natural reading order. If you want to be sure that your messages are sent in the order that you want, you can always add more parentheses, as shown in Figure 5.3. In this figure, the message `yellow` is an unary message and the message `color:` a keyword message, therefore the message send `Color yellow` is sent first. However as message sends in parentheses are sent first, putting (unnecessary) parentheses around `Color yellow` just emphasizes that it will be sent first. The rest of the section illustrates each of these points.

Unary > Binary > Keywords

Unary messages are sent first, then binary messages, and finally keyword messages. We also say that unary messages have a higher priority over the other types of messages.

> **Important** *Rule one.* Unary messages are sent first, then binary messages, and finally keyword based messages. Unary > Binary > Keyword

As these examples show, Pharo's syntax rules generally ensure that message sends can be read in a natural way:

```
1000 factorial / 999 factorial
>>> 1000
```

```
2 raisedTo: 1 + 3 factorial
>>> 128
```

Unfortunately the rules are a bit too simplistic for arithmetic message sends, so you need to introduce parentheses whenever you want to impose a priority over binary operators:

5.3 Message composition

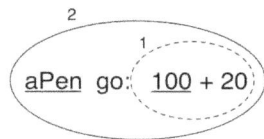

Figure 5.4: Binary messages are sent before keyword

```
1 + 2 * 3
>>> 9
```
```
1 + (2 * 3)
>>> 7
```

Example 1. In the message aPen color: Color yellow, there is one *unary* message yellow sent to the class Color and a *keyword* message color: sent to aPen. Unary messages are sent first so the message send Color yellow is sent (1). This returns a color object which is passed as argument of the message aPen color: aColor (2) as shown in the following script. Figure 5.3 shows graphically how messages are sent.

```
aPen color: Color yellow
"unary message is sent first"
(1) Color yellow
>>> aColor
"keyword message is sent next"
(2) aPen color: aColor
```

Example 2. In the message aPen go: 100 + 20, there is a *binary* message + 20 and a *keyword* message go:. Binary messages are sent prior to keyword messages so 100 + 20 is sent first (1): the message + 20 is sent to the object 100 and returns the number 120. Then the message aPen go: 120 is sent with 120 as argument (2). The following example shows how the message send is executed:

```
aPen go: 100 + 20
"binary message first"
(1) 100 + 20
>>> 120
"then keyword message"
(2) aPen go: 120
```

Example 3. As an exercise we let you decompose the evaluation of the message Pen new go: 100 + 20 which is composed of one unary, one keyword and one binary message (see Figure 5.5).

Understanding message syntax

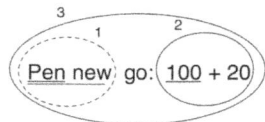

Figure 5.5: Decomposing Pen new go: 100 +

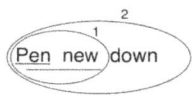

Figure 5.6: Decomposing Pen new

Parentheses first

Parenthesised messages are sent prior to other messages.

```
3 + 4 factorial
>>> 27 "(not 5040)"
(3 + 4) factorial
>>> 5040
```

Here we need the parentheses to force sending `lowMajorScaleOn:` before `play`.

```
(FMSound lowMajorScaleOn: FMSound clarinet) play
"(1) send the message clarinet to the FMSound class to create a
    clarinet sound.
 (2) send this sound to FMSound as argument to the lowMajorScaleOn:
    keyword message.
 (3) play the resulting sound."
```

> **Important** *Rule two.* Parenthesised messages are sent prior to other messages. (Msg) > Unary > Binary > Keyword

Example 4. The message (65@325 extent: 134@100) center returns the center of a rectangle whose top left point is (65, 325) and whose size is 134x100. The following script shows how the message is decomposed and sent. First the message between parentheses is sent. It contains two binary messages, 65@325 and 134@100, that are sent first and return points, and a keyword message extent: which is then sent and returns a rectangle. Finally the unary message center is sent to the rectangle and a point is returned. Evaluating the message without parentheses would lead to an error because the object 100 does not understand the message center.

```
(65@325 extent: 134@100) center
"Expression within parentheses then binary"
```

5.3 Message composition

```
(1) 65@325
>>> aPoint
"binary"
(2)134@100
>>> anotherPoint
"keyword"
(3) aPoint extent: anotherPoint
>>> aRectangle
"unary"
(4) aRectangle center
>>> 132@375
```

From left to right

Now we know how messages of different kinds or priorities are handled. The final question to be addressed is how messages with the same priority are sent. They are sent from the left to the right. Note that you already saw this behaviour in the previous script where the two point creation messages (@) were sent first.

The following script shows that execution from left to right for messages of the same type reduces the need for parentheses.

```
1.5 tan rounded asString = (((1.5 tan) rounded) asString)
>>> true
```

> **Important** *Rule three.* When the messages are of the same kind, the order of evaluation is from left to right.

Example 5. In the message sends Pen new down all messages are unary messages, so the leftmost one, Pen new, is sent first. This returns a newly created pen to which the second message down is sent, as shown in Figure 5.6.

Arithmetic inconsistencies

The message composition rules are simple but they result in inconsistency for the execution of arithmetic message sends expressed in terms of binary messages. Here we see the common situations where extra parentheses are needed.

```
3 + 4 * 5
>>> 35 "(not 23) Binary messages sent from left to right"
```

```
3 + (4 * 5)
>>> 23
```

```
1 + 1/3
>>> (2/3) "and not 4/3"
```

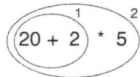

Figure 5.7: The two messages + and * are of the same kind so their execution is from left to right.

```
1 + (1/3)
>>> (4/3)
```

```
1/3 + 2/3
>>> (7/9) "and not 1"
```

```
(1/3) + (2/3)
>>> 1
```

Example 6. In the message sends 20 + 2 * 5, there are only binary messages + and *. However in Pharo there is no special priority for the operations + and *. They are just binary messages, hence * does not have priority over +. Here the leftmost message + is sent first, and then the * is sent to the result as shown in the following script and Figure 5.7.

```
"As there is no priority among binary messages, the leftmost message +
    is evaluated first
even if by the rules of arithmetic the * should be sent first."

20 + 2 * 5
(1) 20 + 2
>>> 22
(2) 22 * 5
>>> 110
```

As shown in the previous example the result of this message send is not 30 but 110. This result is perhaps unexpected but follows directly from the rules used to send messages. This is the price to pay for the simplicity of the Pharo model. To get the correct result, we should use parentheses. When messages are enclosed in parentheses, they are evaluated first. Hence the message send 20 + (2 * 5) returns the result as shown by the following script and Figure 5.8.

```
"The messages surrounded by parentheses are evaluated first therefore *
    is sent prior to + which produces the correct behaviour."

20 + (2 * 5)
(1) (2 * 5)
>>> 10
(2) 20 + 10
>>> 30
```

5.4 Hints for identifying keyword messages

Figure 5.8: Parenthesed expressions are executed first.

Figure 5.9: Equivalent messages using parentheses.

Figure 5.10: Equivalent messages using parentheses.

> **Note** Arithmetic operators such as + and * do not have different priority. + and * are just binary messages, therefore * does not have priority over +. Use parentheses to obtain the desired result.

Table : Message sends and their fully parenthesized equivalents

Implicit precedence	Explicitly parenthesized equivalent
aPen color: Color yellow	aPen color: (Color yellow)
aPen go: 100 + 20	Pen go: (100 + 20)
aPen penSize: aPen penSize + 2	aPen penSize: ((aPen penSize) + 2)
2 factorial + 4	(2 factorial) + 4

Note that the first rule stating that unary messages are sent prior to binary and keyword messages avoids the need to put explicit parentheses around them. Table above shows message sends written following the rules and equivalent message sends if the rules would not exist. Both message sends result in the same effect or return the same value.

5.4 Hints for identifying keyword messages

Often beginners have problems understanding when they need to add parentheses. Let's see how keywords messages are recognized by the compiler.

Parentheses or not?

The characters [,], (and) delimit distinct areas. Within such an area, a keyword message is the longest sequence of words terminated by : that is not cut by the characters ., or ;. When the characters [,], (and { surround some words with colons, these words participate in the keyword message *local* to the area defined.

In this example, there are two distinct keyword messages: rotateBy:magnify:smoothing: and at:put:.

```
aDict
   at: (rotatingForm
         rotateBy: angle
         magnify: 2
         smoothing: 1)
   put: 3
```

> **Note** The characters [,], (and) delimit distinct areas. Within such an area, a keyword message is the longest sequence of words terminated by : that is not cut by the characters ., or ;.When the characters [,], (and) surround some words with colons, these words participate in the keyword message local to the area defined.

Precedence hints

If you have problems with these precedence rules, you may start simply by putting parentheses whenever you want to distinguish two messages having the same precedence.

The following piece of code does not require parentheses because the message send x isNil is unary, and is sent prior to the keyword message ifTrue:.

```
(x isNil)
   ifTrue: [...]
```

The following code requires parentheses because the messages includes: and ifTrue: are both keyword messages.

```
ord := OrderedCollection new.
(ord includes: $a)
   ifTrue: [...]
```

Without parentheses the unknown message includes:ifTrue: would be sent to the collection!

When to use [ ] or ( )

You may also have problems understanding when to use square brackets (blocks) rather than parentheses. The basic principle is that you should use

[ ] when you do not know how many times, potentially zero, an expression should be executed. [expression] will create a block closure (an object, as always) from expression, which may be executed zero or more times, depending on the context. (Recall from Chapter : Syntax in a Nutshell that an expression can either be a message send, a variable, a literal, an assignment or a block.)

Following this principle, the conditional branches of ifTrue: or ifTrue:if-False: require blocks. Similarly, both the receiver and the argument of the whileTrue: message require the use of square brackets since we do not know how many times either the receiver (the loop conditional) or the argument (the "loop body") will be executed.

Parentheses, on the other hand, only affect the order of sending messages. So in (expression), the expression will *always* be executed exactly once.

```
"both the receiver and the argument must be blocks"
[ x isReady ] whileTrue: [ y doSomething ]
```

```
"the argument is evaluated more than once, so must be a block"
4 timesRepeat: [ Beeper beep ]
```

```
"receiver is evaluated once, so is not a block"
(x isReady) ifTrue: [ y doSomething ]
```

5.5 Expression sequences

Expressions (i.e., message sends, assignments and so on) separated by periods are evaluated in sequence. Note that there is no period between a variable definition (the | box | section) and the following expressions. The value of a sequence is the value of the last expression. The values returned by all the expressions except the last one are ignored. Note that the period is a separator between expressions, and not a terminator. Therefore a final period is optional.

```
| box |
box := 20@30 corner: 60@90.
box containsPoint: 40@50
>>> true
```

5.6 Cascaded messages

Pharo offers a way to send multiple messages to the same receiver using a semicolon (;). This is called the cascade in Pharo jargon. It follows the pattern: expression msg1; msg2

```
Transcript show: 'Pharo is '.
Transcript show: 'fun '.
Transcript cr.
```

is equivalent to:

```
Transcript
    show: 'Pharo is';
    show: 'fun ';
    cr
```

Note that the object receiving the cascaded messages can itself be the result of a message send. In fact, the receiver of all the cascaded messages is the receiver of the first message involved in a cascade. In the following example, the first cascaded message is setX:setY since it is followed by a cascade. The receiver of the cascaded message setX:setY: is the newly created point resulting from the evaluation of Point new, and *not* Point. The subsequent message isZero is sent to that same receiver.

```
Point new setX: 25 setY: 35; isZero
>>> false
```

> **Important** expression msg1. expression msg2 is equivalent to expression msg1; msg2

5.7 Chapter summary

- A message is always sent to an object named the *receiver*, which itself may be the result of other message sends.
- There are three types of messages: *unary*, *binary*, and *keyword*.
- Unary messages are messages that do not require any argument. They are of the form of receiver selector.
- Binary messages are messages that involve two objects, the receiver and another object, whose selector is composed of one or more characters from the following list: +, -, *, /, |, &, =, >, <, ~, and @. They are of the form: receiver selector argument.
- Keyword messages are messages that involve more than one object and that contain at least one colon character (:). They are of the form: receiver selectorWordOne: argumentOne wordTwo: argumentTwo.
- **Rule One.** Unary messages are sent first, then binary messages, and finally keyword messages.
- **Rule Two.** Messages in parentheses are sent before any others.
- **Rule Three.** When the messages are of the same type, the order of evaluation is from left to right.
- In Pharo, traditional arithmetic operators such as + and * have the same priority. + and * are just binary messages, therefore * does not

have priority over +. You must use parentheses to obtain the desired arithmetical order of operations.

CHAPTER 6

The Pharo object model

The Pharo programming model is heavily inspired by the one of Smalltalk. It is simple and uniform: everything is an object, and objects communicate only by sending each other messages. Instance variables are private to the object. Methods are all public and dynamically looked up (late-bound). In this chapter we present the core concepts of the Pharo object model. We revisit concepts such as self and super and define precisely their semantics. Then we discuss the consequences of representing classes as objects. This will be extended in Chapter: Classes and Metaclasses.

6.1 The rules of the model

The object model is based on a set of simple rules that are applied *uniformly*. The rules are as follows:

Rule 1. Everything is an object.

Rule 2. Every object is an instance of a class.

Rule 3. Every class has a superclass.

Rule 4. Everything happens by sending messages.

Rule 5. Method lookup dynamically follows the inheritance chain.

Let us look at each of these rules in some detail.

6.2 Everything is an Object

The mantra *everything is an object* is highly contagious. After only a short while working with Pharo, you will start to be surprised at how this rule simplifes everything you do. Integers, for example, are truly objects, so you can send messages to them, just as you do to any other object. At the end of this chapter, we added an implementation note on the object implementation for the curious reader.

```
"send '+ 4' to 3, yielding 7"
3 + 4
>>> 7
```

```
"send factorial, yielding a big number"
20 factorial
>>> 2432902008176640000
```

The object 7 is different than the object returned by `20 factorial`, but because they are both polymorphic objects, none of the code, not even the implementation of `factorial`, needs to know about this.

Coming back to *everything is an object* rule, perhaps the most fundamental consequence of this rule is that classes are objects too. Classes are not second-class objects: they are really first-class objects that you can send messages to, inspect, and change. This means that Pharo is a truly reflective system, which gives a great deal of expressive power to developers.

> **Important**   Classes are objects too.

6.3 Every object is an instance of a class

Every object has a class; you can find out which one by sending it the message `class`.

```
1 class
>>> SmallInteger
```

```
20 factorial class
>>> LargePositiveInteger
```

```
'hello' class
>>> ByteString
```

```
(4@5) class
>>> Point
```

```
Object new class
>>> Object
```

A class defines the *structure* of its instances via instance variables, and the *behavior* of its instances via methods. Each method has a name, called its *selector*, which is unique within the class.

Since *classes are objects*, and *every object is an instance of a class*, it follows that classes must also be instances of classes. A class whose instances are classes is called a *metaclass*. Whenever you create a class, the system automatically creates a metaclass for you. The metaclass defines the structure and behavior of the class that is its instance. 99% of the time you will not need to think about metaclasses, and may happily ignore them. (We will have a closer look at metaclasses in Chapter : Classes and Metaclasses.)

6.4 Instance structure and behavior

Now we will briefly present how we specify the structure and behavior of instances.

Instance variables

Instance variables in Pharo are private to the *instance* itself. This is in contrast to Java and C++, which allow instance variables (also known as *fields* or *member variables*) to be accessed by any other instance that happens to be of the same class. We say that the *encapsulation boundary* of objects in Java and C++ is the class, whereas in Pharo it is the instance.

In Pharo, two instances of the same class cannot access each other's instance variables unless the class defines *accessor methods*. There is no language syntax that provides direct access to the instance variables of any other object. (Actually, a mechanism called reflection does provide a way to ask another object for the values of its instance variables; meta-programming is intended for writing tools like the object inspector, whose sole purpose is to look inside other objects.)

Instance variables can be accessed by name in any of the instance methods of the class that defines them, and also in the methods defined in its subclasses. This means that Pharo instance variables are similar to *protected* variables in C++ and Java. However, we prefer to say that they are private, because it is considered bad style in Pharo to access an instance variable directly from a subclass.

Instance encapsulation example

The method `Point>>dist:` computes the distance between the receiver and another point. The instance variables x and y of the receiver are accessed directly by the method body. However, the instance variables of the other point must be accessed by sending it the messages x and y.

```
Point >> dist: aPoint
    "Answer the distance between aPoint and the receiver."

    | dx dy |
    dx := aPoint x - x.
    dy := aPoint y - y.
```

```
    ^ ((dx * dx) + (dy * dy)) sqrt
1@1 dist: 4@5
>>> 5.0
```

The key reason to prefer instance-based encapsulation to class-based encapsulation is that it enables different implementations of the same abstraction to coexist. For example, the method dist: need not know or care whether the argument aPoint is an instance of the same class as the receiver. The argument object might be represented in polar coordinates, or as a record in a database, or on another computer in a distributed system. As long as it can respond to the messages x and y, the code of method dist (shown above) will still work.

Methods

All methods are *public* and virtual (i.e., dynamically looked up). Methods are grouped into *protocols* that indicate their intent. Some common protocol names have been established by convention, for example, accessing for all accessor methods, and initialization for establishing a consistent initial state for the object. The protocol private is sometimes used to group methods that should not be seen from outside. Nothing, however, prevents you from sending a message that is implemented by such a "private" method.

Methods can access all instance variables of the object. Some developers prefer to access instance variables only through accessors. This practice has some value, but it also clutters the interface of your classes, and worse, exposes its private state to the world.

6.5 The instance side and the class side

Since classes are objects, they can have their own instance variables and their own methods. We call these *class instance variables* and *class methods*, but they are really no different from ordinary instance variables and methods: They simply operate on different objects (classes in this case). An instance variable describes instance state and a method describes instance behavior. Similarly, class instance variables are just instance variables defined by a metaclass (and describe the state of classes - instances of metaclasses), and class methods are just methods defined by a metaclass (and that will be executed on classes).

A class and its metaclass are two separate classes, even though the former is an instance of the latter. However, this is largely irrelevant to you as a programmer: you are concerned with defining the behavior of your objects and the classes that create them.

For this reason, the browser helps you to browse both class and metaclass as if they were a single thing with two "sides": the *instance side* and the *class side*, as shown in Figure 6.1. By default, when you select a class in the browser, you're

6.5 The instance side and the class side

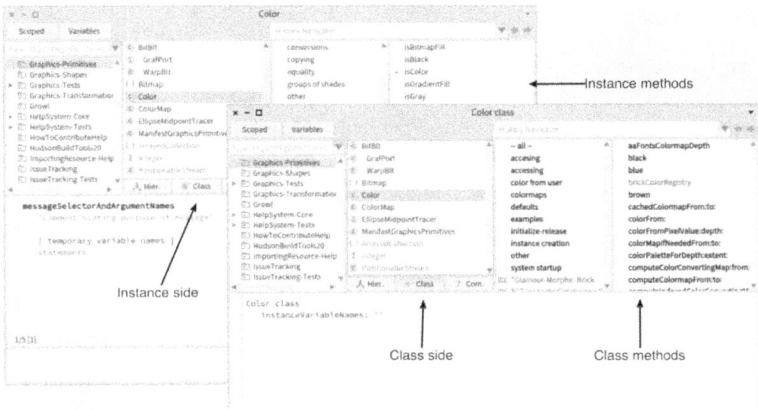

Figure 6.1: Browsing a class and its metaclass

browsing the *instance* side (i.e., the methods that are executed when messages are sent to an *instance* of Color). Clicking on the **Class side** button switches you over to the *class side* (the methods that will be executed when messages are sent to the *class* Color itself).

For example, Color blue sends the message blue to the class Color. You will therefore find the method blue defined on the class side of Color, not on the instance side.

```
"Class-side method blue (convenient instance creation method)"
aColor := Color blue.
>>> Color blue
"Color instances are self-evaluating"
```

```
"Instance-side accessor method red (returns the red RGB value)"
Color blue red
>>> 0.0
```

```
"Instance-side accessor method blue (returns the blue RGB value)"
Color blue blue
>>> 1.0
```

You define a class by filling in the template proposed on the instance side. When you accept this template, the system creates not just the class that you defined, but also the corresponding metaclass (which you can then edit by clicking on the **Class side** button). The only part of the metaclass creation template that makes sense for you to edit directly is the list of the metaclass's instance variable names.

Once a class has been created, browsing its instance side (**Class side** unchecked) lets you edit and browse the methods that will be possessed by instances of that class (and of its subclasses).

Class methods

Class methods can be quite useful; browse Color class for some good examples. You will see that there are two kinds of methods defined on a class: *instance creation methods*, like Color class>>blue, and those that perform a utility function, like Color class>>wheel:. This is typical, although you will occasionally find class methods used in other ways.

It is convenient to place utility methods on the class side because they can be executed without having to create any additional objects first. Indeed, many of them will contain a comment designed to make it easy to execute them.

Browse method Color class>>wheel:, double-click just at the beginning of the comment "(Color wheel: 12) inspect" and press CMD-d. You will see the effect of executing this method.

For those familiar with Java and C++, class methods may seem similar to static methods. However, the uniformity of the Pharo object model (where classes are just regular objects) means that they are somewhat different: whereas Java static methods are really just statically-resolved procedures, Pharo class methods are dynamically-dispatched methods. This means that inheritance, overriding and super-sends work for class methods in Pharo, whereas they don't work for static methods in Java.

Class instance variables

With ordinary instance variables, all the instances of a class have the same set of variable names (though each instance has its own private set of values), and the instances of its subclasses inherit those names. The story is exactly the same with class instance variables: each class has its own private class instance variables. A subclass will inherit those class instance variables, *but the subclass will have its own private copies of those variables*. Just as objects don't share instance variables, neither do classes and their subclasses share class instance variables.

For example, you could use a class instance variable called count to keep track of how many instances you create of a given class. However, any subclass would have its own count variable, so subclass instances would be counted separately.

Example: Class instance variables and subclasses

Suppose we define the class Dog, and its subclass Hyena. Suppose that we add a count class instance variable to the class Dog (i.e. we define it on the metaclass Dog class). Hyena will naturally inherit the class instance variable count from Dog.

```
Object subclass: #Dog
    instanceVariableNames: ''
```

6.5 The instance side and the class side

```
    classVariableNames: ''
    package: 'PBE-CIV'
Dog class
    instanceVariableNames: 'count'
Dog subclass: #Hyena
    instanceVariableNames: ''
    classVariableNames: ''
    package: 'PBE-CIV'
```

Now suppose we define class methods for Dog to initialize its count to 0, and to increment it when new instances are created:

```
Dog class >> initialize
    count := 0.
Dog class >> new
    count := count +1.
    ^ super new
Dog class >> count
    ^ count
```

Now when we create a new Dog, the count value of the class Dog is incremented, and so is that of the class Hyena (but the hyenas are counted separately).

Side note: Notice the use of initialize on the classes, in the following code. In Pharo, when you instantiate an object such as Dog new, initialize is called automatically as part of the new message send (you can see for yourself by browsing Behavior>>new). But with classes, simply defining them does not automatically call initialize, and so we have to call it explicitly here. By default class initialize methods are automatically executed only when classes are loaded. See also the discussion about lazy initialization, below.

```
Dog initialize.
Hyena initialize.
Dog count
>>> 0
Hyena count
>>> 0
```

```
| aDog |
aDog := Dog new.
Dog count
>>> 1 "Incremented"
Hyena count
>>> 0 "Still the same"
```

Class instance variables are private to a class in exactly the same way that instance variables are private to an instance. Since classes and their instances are different objects, this has the following consequences:

1. A class does not have access to the instance variables of its own instances. So, the class Color does not have access to the variables of an object instantiated from it, aColorRed. In other words, just because a class was used to create an instance (using new or a helper instance creation method like Color red), it doesn't give *the class* any special direct access to that instance's variables. The class instead has to go through the accessor methods (a public interface) just like any other object.

2. The reverse is also true: an *instance* of a class does not have access to the class instance variables of its class. In our example above, aDog (an individual instance) does not have direct access to the count variable of the Dog class (except, again, through an accessor method).

> **Important** A class does not have access to the instance variables of its own instances. An instance of a class does not have access to the class instance variables of its class.

For this reason, instance initialization methods must always be defined on the instance side, the class side has no access to instance variables, and so cannot initialize them! All that the class can do is to send initialization messages, using accessors, to newly created instances.

Java has nothing equivalent to class instance variables. Java and C++ static variables are more like Pharo class variables (discussed in Section 6.9), since in those languages all of the subclasses and all of their instances share the same static variable.

Example: Defining a Singleton

The Singleton pattern provides a typical example of the use of class instance variables and class methods. Imagine that we would like to implement a class WebServer, and to use the Singleton pattern to ensure that it has only one instance.

We define the class WebServer as follow.

```
Object subclass: #WebServer
    instanceVariableNames: 'sessions'
    classVariableNames: ''
    package: 'Web'
```

Then, clicking on the **Class side** button, we add the (class) instance variable uniqueInstance.

```
WebServer class
    instanceVariableNames: 'uniqueInstance'
```

As a result, the class WebServer class will have a new instance variable (in addition to the variables that it inherits from Behavior, such as superclass

6.5 The instance side and the class side

and methodDict). It means that the value of this extra instance variable will describe the instance of the class WebServer class i.e. the class WebServer.

```
Object class allInstVarNames
>>> "#('superclass' 'methodDict' 'format' 'layout' 'instanceVariables'
    'organization' 'subclasses' 'name' 'classPool' 'sharedPools'
    'environment' 'category' 'traitComposition' 'localSelectors')"

WebServer class allInstVarNames
>>>"#('superclass' 'methodDict' 'format' 'layout' 'instanceVariables'
    'organization' 'subclasses' 'name' 'classPool' 'sharedPools'
    'environment' 'category' 'traitComposition' 'localSelectors'
    #uniqueInstance)"
```

We can now define a class method named uniqueInstance, as shown below. This method first checks whether uniqueInstance has been initialized. If it has not, the method creates an instance and assigns it to the class instance variable uniqueInstance. Finally the value of uniqueInstance is returned. Since uniqueInstance is a class instance variable, this method can directly access it.

```
WebServer class >> uniqueInstance
    uniqueInstance ifNil: [ uniqueInstance := self new ].
    ^ uniqueInstance
```

The first time that WebServer uniqueInstance is executed, an instance of the class WebServer will be created and assigned to the uniqueInstance variable. The next time, the previously created instance will be returned instead of creating a new one. (This pattern, checking if a variable is nil in an accessor method, and initializing its value if it is nil, is called *lazy initialization*).

Note that the instance creation code in the code above.

is written as self new and not as WebServer new. What is the difference? Since the uniqueInstance method is defined in WebServer class, you might think that there is no difference. And indeed, until someone creates a subclass of WebServer, they are the same. But suppose that ReliableWebServer is a subclass of WebServer, and inherits the uniqueInstance method. We would clearly expect ReliableWebServer uniqueInstance to answer a ReliableWebServer. Using self ensures that this will happen, since self will be bound to the respective receiver, here the classes WebServer and ReliableWebServer. Note also that WebServer and ReliableWebServer will each have a different value for their uniqueInstance instance variable.

A note on lazy initialization. *Do not over-use the lazy initialization pattern.* The setting of initial values for instances of objects generally belongs in the initialize method. Putting initialization calls only in initialize helps from a readability perspective – you don't have to hunt through all the accessor methods to see what the initial values are. Although it may be tempting to instead initialize instance variables in their respective accessor methods (using ifNil: checks), avoid this unless you have a good reason.

For example, in our uniqueInstance method above, we used lazy initialization because users won't typically expect to call WebServer initialize. Instead, they expect the class to be "ready" to return new unique instances. Because of this, lazy initialization makes sense. Similarly, if a variable is expensive to initialize (opening a database connection or a network socket, for example), you will sometimes choose to delay that initialization until you actually need it.

6.6 Every class has a superclass

Each class in Pharo inherits its behaviour and the description of its structure from a single *superclass*. This means that Smalltalk has single inheritance.

```
SmallInteger superclass
>>> Integer
```

```
Integer superclass
>>> Number
```

```
Number superclass
>>> Magnitude
```

```
Magnitude superclass
>>> Object
```

```
Object superclass
>>> ProtoObject
```

```
ProtoObject superclass
>>> nil
```

Traditionally the root of an inheritance hierarchy is the class Object (since everything is an object). In Pharo, the root is actually a class called ProtoObject, but you will normally not pay any attention to this class. ProtoObject encapsulates the minimal set of messages that all objects *must* have and ProtoObject is designed to raise as many as possible errors (to support proxy definition). However, most classes inherit from Object, which defines many additional messages that almost all objects understand and respond to. Unless you have a very good reason to do otherwise, when creating application classes you should normally subclass Object, or one of its subclasses.

A new class is normally created by sending the message subclass: instanceVariableNames: ... to an existing class. There are a few other methods to create classes. To see what they are, have a look at Class and its subclass creation protocol.

Although Pharo does not provide multiple inheritance, it supports a mechanism called Traits for sharing behaviour across unrelated classes. Traits are

6.6 Every class has a superclass

collections of methods that can be reused by multiple classes that are not related by inheritance. Using traits allows one to share code between different classes without duplicating code.

Abstract methods and abstract classes

An abstract class is a class that exists to be subclassed, rather than to be instantiated. An abstract class is usually incomplete, in the sense that it does not define all of the methods that it uses. The "placeholder" methods, those that the other methods assume to be (re)defined are called abstract methods.

Pharo has no dedicated syntax to specify that a method or a class is abstract. Instead, by convention, the body of an abstract method consists of the expression self subclassResponsibility. This indicates that subclasses have the responsibility to define a concrete version of the method. self subclassResponsibility methods should always be overridden, and thus should never be executed. If you forget to override one, and it is executed, an exception will be raised.

Similarly, a class is considered abstract if one of its methods is abstract. Nothing actually prevents you from creating an instance of an abstract class; everything will work until an abstract method is invoked.

Example: the abstract class Magnitude

Magnitude is an abstract class that helps us to define objects that can be compared to each other. Subclasses of Magnitude should implement the methods <, = and hash. Using such messages, Magnitude defines other methods such as >, >=, <=, max:, min:, between:and: and others for comparing objects. Such methods are inherited by subclasses. The method Magnitude>>< is abstract, and defined as shown in the following script.

```
< aMagnitude
    "Answer whether the receiver is less than the argument."

    ^self subclassResponsibility
```

By contrast, the method >= is concrete, and is defined in terms of <.

```
>= aMagnitude
    "Answer whether the receiver is greater than or equal to the
        argument."

    ^(self < aMagnitude) not
```

The same is true of the other comparison methods (they are all defined in terms of the abstract method <).

Character is a subclass of Magnitude; it overrides the < method (which, if you recall, is marked as abstract in Magnitude by the use of self subclassResponsibility) with its own version (see the method definition below).

Character also explicitly defines methods = and hash; it inherits from Magnitude the methods >=, <=, ~= and others.

```
< aCharacter
    "Answer true if the receiver's value < aCharacter's value."

    ^self asciiValue < aCharacter asciiValue
```

Traits

A *trait* is a collection of methods that can be included in the behaviour of a class without the need for inheritance. This makes it easy for classes to have a unique superclass, yet still share useful methods with otherwise unrelated classes.

To define a new trait, simply right-click in the class pane and select Add Trait, or replace the subclass creation template by the trait creation template, below.

```
Trait named: #TAuthor
    uses: { }
    package: 'PBE-LightsOut'
```

Here we define the trait TAuthor in the package PBE-LightsOut. This trait does not *use* any other existing traits. In general we can specify a *trait composition expression* of other traits to use as part of the uses: keyword argument. Here we simply provide an empty array.

Traits may contain methods, but no instance variables. Suppose we would like to be able to add an author method to various classes, independent of where they occur in the hierarchy.

We might do this as follows:

```
TAuthor >> author
    "Returns author initials"

    ^ 'on' "oscar nierstrasz"
```

Now we can use this trait in a class that already has its own superclass, for instance the LOGame class that we defined in Chapter : A First Application. We simply modify the class creation template for LOGame to include a uses: keyword argument that specifies that TAuthor should be used.

```
BorderedMorph subclass: #LOGame
    uses: TAuthor
    instanceVariableNames: 'cells'
    classVariableNames: ''
```

```
    package: 'PBE-LightsOut'
```

If we now instantiate LOGame, it will respond to the author message as expected.

```
LOGame new author
>>> 'on'
```

Trait composition expressions may combine multiple traits using the + operator. In case of conflicts (i.e., if multiple traits define methods with the same name), these conflicts can be resolved by explicitly removing these methods (with -), or by redefining these methods in the class or trait that you are defining. It is also possible to *alias* methods (with @), providing a new name for them.

Traits are used in the system kernel. One good example is the class Behavior.

```
Object subclass: #Behavior
    uses: TPureBehavior @
        {#basicAddTraitSelector:withMethod:->#addTraitSelector:withMethod:}
    instanceVariableNames: 'superclass methodDict format'
    classVariableNames: 'ObsoleteSubclasses'
    package: 'Kernel-Classes'
```

Here we see that the method addTraitSelector:withMethod: defined in the trait TPureBehavior has been aliased to basicAddTraitSelector:withMethod:.

6.7 Everything happens by sending messages

This rule captures the essence of programming in Pharo.

In procedural programming (and in some static features of some object-oriented languages such as Java), the choice of which piece of code to execute when a procedure is called is made by the caller. The caller chooses the procedure to execute *statically*, by name.

In Pharo, we do *not* "invoke methods". Instead, we *send messages*. This is just a terminology point but it is significant. It implies that this is not the responsibility of the client to select the method to be executed, it is the one of the receiver of the message.

When sending a message, we do not decide which method will be executed. Instead, we *tell* an object to do something for us by sending it a message. A message is nothing but a name and a list of arguments. The receiver then decides how to respond by selecting its own *method* for doing what was asked. Since different objects may have different methods for responding to the same message, the method must be chosen *dynamically*, when the message is received.

```
 3 + 4
 >>> 7 "send message + with argument 4 to integer 3"
```

```
 (1@2) + 4
 >>> 5@6 "send message + with argument 4 to point (1@2)"
```

As a consequence, we can send the *same message* to different objects, each of which may have *its own method* for responding to the message. We do not tell the `SmallInteger` 3 or the `Point` (1@2) how to respond to the message + 4. Each has its own method for +, and responds to + 4 accordingly.

One of the consequences of Pharo's model of message sending is that it encourages a style in which objects tend to have very small methods and delegate tasks to other objects, rather than implementing huge, procedural methods that assume too much responsibility. Joseph Pelrine expresses this principle succinctly as follows:

"Don't do anything that you can push off onto someone else."

Many object-oriented languages provide both static and dynamic operations for objects. In Pharo there are only dynamic message sends. For example, instead of providing static class operations, we simply send messages to classes (which are simply objects).

Ok, so *nearly* everything in Pharo happens by sending messages. At some point action must take place:

Variable declarations are not message sends. In fact, variable declarations are not even executable. Declaring a variable just causes space to be allocated for an object reference.

Assignments are not message sends. An assignment to a variable causes that variable name to be freshly bound in the scope of its definition.

Returns are not message sends. A return simply causes the computed result to be returned to the sender.

Primitives (and Pragmas/annotations) are not message sends. They are implemented in the virtual machine.

Other than these few exceptions, pretty much everything else does truly happen by sending messages. In particular, since there are no *public fields* in Pharo, the only way to update an instance variable of another object is to send it a message asking that it update its own field. Of course, providing setter and getter methods for all the instance variables of an object is not good object-oriented style. Joseph Pelrine also states this very nicely:

"Don't let anyone else play with your data."

6.8 Method lookup follows the inheritance chain

What exactly happens when an object receives a message? This is a two step process: method lookup and method execution.

Lookup. First, the method having the same name as the message is looked up.

Method Execution. Second, the found method is applied to the receiver with the message arguments: When the method is found, the arguments are bound to the parameters of the method, and the virtual machine executes it.

The lookup process is quite simple:

1. The class of the receiver looks up the method to use to handle the message.

2. If this class does not have that method method defined, it asks its superclass, and so on, up the inheritance chain.

It is essentially as simple as that. Nevertheless there are a few questions that need some care to answer:

- What happens when a method does not explicitly return a value?
- What happens when a class reimplements a superclass method?
- What is the difference between `self` and `super` sends?
- What happens when no method is found?

The rules for method lookup that we present here are conceptual; virtual machine implementors use all kinds of tricks and optimizations to speed up method lookup. That's their job, but you should never be able to detect that they are doing something different from our rules.

First let us look at the basic lookup strategy, and then consider these further questions.

Method lookup

Suppose we create an instance of `EllipseMorph`.

```
anEllipse := EllipseMorph new.
```

If we now send this object the message `defaultColor`, we get the result `Color yellow`.

```
anEllipse defaultColor
>>> Color yellow
```

The class `EllipseMorph` implements `defaultColor`, so the appropriate method is found immediately.

```
EllipseMorph >> defaultColor
    "Answer the default color/fill style for the receiver"
    ^ Color yellow
```

The Pharo object model

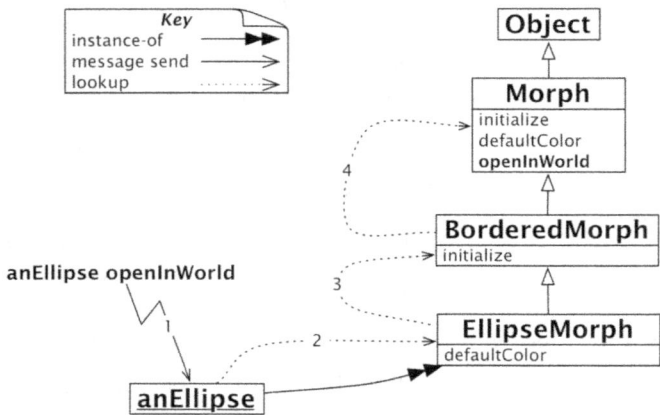

Figure 6.2: Method lookup follows the inheritance hierarchy

In contrast, if we send the message openInWorld to anEllipse, the method is not immediately found, since the class EllipseMorph does not implement openInWorld. The search therefore continues in the superclass, BorderedMorph, and so on, until an openInWorld method is found in the class Morph (see Figure 6.2).

```
Morph >> openInWorld
    "Add this morph to the world."
    self openInWorld: self currentWorld
```

Returning self

Notice that EllipseMorph>>defaultColor explicitly returns Color yellow, whereas Morph>>openInWorld does not appear to return anything.

Actually a method *always* answers a message with a value (which is, of course, an object). The answer may be defined by the ^ construct in the method, but if execution reaches the end of the method without executing a ^, the method still answers a value – it answers the object that received the message. We usually say that the method *answers self*, because in Pharo the pseudo-variable self represents the receiver of the message, much like the keyword this in Java. Other languages, such as Ruby, by default return the value of the last statement in the method. Again, this is not the case in Pharo, instead you can imagine that a method without an explicit return ends with ^ self.

| **Important** self represents the receiver of the message.

This suggests that openInWorld is equivalent to openInWorldReturnSelf, defined below.

6.8 Method lookup follows the inheritance chain

```
Morph >> openInWorld
    "Add this morph to the world."
    self openInWorld: self currentWorld
    ^ self
```

Why is explicitly writing ^ self not a so good thing to do? When you return something explicitly, you are communicating that you are returning something of interest to the sender. When you explicitly return self, you are saying that you expect the sender to use the returned value. This is not the case here, so it is best not to explicitly return self. We only return self on special case to stress that the receiver is returned.

This is a common idiom in Pharo, which Kent Beck refers to as *Interesting return value*:

"Return a value only when you intend for the sender to use the value."

> **Important** By default (if not specified differently) a method returns the message receiver.

Overriding and extension

If we look again at the EllipseMorph class hierarchy in Figure 6.2, we see that the classes Morph and EllipseMorph both implement defaultColor. In fact, if we open a new morph (Morph new openInWorld) we see that we get a blue morph, whereas an ellipse will be yellow by default.

We say that EllipseMorph *overrides* the defaultColor method that it inherits from Morph. The inherited method no longer exists from the point of view of anEllipse.

Sometimes we do not want to override inherited methods, but rather *extend* them with some new functionality, that is, we would like to be able to invoke the overridden method *in addition to* the new functionality we are defining in the subclass. In Pharo, as in many object-oriented languages that support single inheritance, this can be done with the help of super sends.

A frequent application of this mechanism is in the initialize method. Whenever a new instance of a class is initialized, it is critical to also initialize any inherited instance variables. However, the knowledge of how to do this is already captured in the initialize methods of each of the superclass in the inheritance chain. The subclass has no business even trying to initialize inherited instance variables!

It is therefore good practice whenever implementing an initialize method to send super initialize before performing any further initialization:

```
BorderedMorph >> initialize
    "initialize the state of the receiver"

    super initialize.
```

```
self borderInitialize
```

We need super sends to compose inherited behaviour that would otherwise be overridden.

> **Important** It is a good practice that an `initialize` method start by sending `super initialize`.

Self sends and super sends

`self` represents the receiver of the message and the lookup of the method starts in the class of the receiver. Now what is super? super is *not* the superclass! It is a common and natural mistake to think this. It is also a mistake to think that lookup starts in the superclass of the class of the receiver.

> **Important** `self` represents the receiver of the message and the method lookup starts in the class of the receiver.

How do `self` sends differ from super sends?

Like `self`, super represents the receiver of the message. Yes you read it well! The only thing that changes is the method lookup. Instead of lookup starting in the class of the receiver, it starts in the *superclass of the class of the method where the* super *send occurs*.

> **Important** super represents the receiver of the message and the method lookup starts in the superclass of the class of the method where the super send occurs.

We shall see with the following example precisely how this works. Imagine that we define the following three methods:

First we define the method `fullPrintOn:` on class `Morph` that just adds to the stream the name of the class followed by the string ' new' - the idea is that we could execute the resulting string and gets back an instance similar to the receiver.

```
Morph >> fullPrintOn: aStream
    aStream nextPutAll: self class name, ' new'
```

Second we define the method `constructorString` that send the message `fullPrintOn:`.

```
Morph >> constructorString
    ^ String streamContents: [ :s | self fullPrintOn: s ].
```

Finally, we define the method `fullPrintOn:` on the class `BorderedMorph` superclass of `EllipseMorph`. This new method extends the superclass behavior: it invokes it and adds extra behavior.

6.8 Method lookup follows the inheritance chain

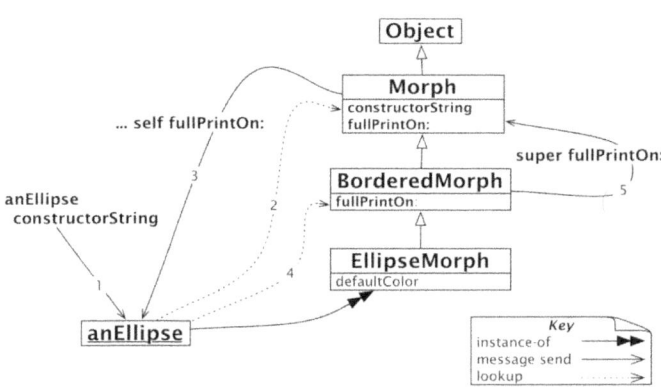

Figure 6.3: self and super sends

```
BorderedMorph >> fullPrintOn: aStream
    aStream nextPutAll: '('.
    super fullPrintOn: aStream.
    aStream
        nextPutAll: ') setBorderWidth: ';
        print: borderWidth;
        nextPutAll: ' borderColor: ', (self colorString: borderColor)
```

Consider the message constructorString sent to an instance of EllipseMorph:

```
EllipseMorph new constructorString
>>> '(EllipseMorph new) setBorderWidth: 1 borderColor: Color black'
```

How exactly is this result obtained through a combination of self and super sends? First, anEllipse constructorString will cause the method constructorString to be found in the class Morph, as shown in Figure 6.3.

The method Morph>>constructorString performs a self send of fullPrintOn:. The message fullPrintOn: is looked up starting in the class EllipseMorph, and the method BorderedMorph>>fullPrintOn: is found in BorderedMorph (see Figure 6.3). What is critical to notice is that the self send causes the method lookup to start again in the class of the receiver, namely the class of anEllipse.

At this point, BorderedMorph>>fullPrintOn: does a super send to extend the fullPrintOn: behaviour it inherits from its superclass. Because this is a super send, the lookup now starts in the superclass of the class where the super send occurs, namely in Morph. We then immediately find and evaluate Morph>>fullPrintOn:.

103

Stepping back

A self send is dynamic in the sense that by looking at the method containing it, we cannot predict which method will be executed. Indeed an instance of a subclass may receive the message containing the self expression and redefine the method in that subclass. Here EllipseMorph could redefine the method fullPrintOn: and this method would be executed by method constructorString. Note that by only looking at the method constructorString, we cannot predict which fullPrintOn: method (either the one of EllipseMorph, BorderedMorph, or Morph) will be executed when executing the method constructorString, since it depends on the receiver the constructorString message.

> **Important** A self send triggers a *method lookup starting in the class of the receiver*. A self send is dynamic in the sense that by looking at the method containing it, we cannot predict which method will be executed.

Note that the super lookup did not start in the superclass of the receiver. This would have caused lookup to start from BorderedMorph, resulting in an infinite loop!

If you think carefully about super send and Figure 6.3, you will realize that super bindings are static: all that matters is the class in which the text of the super send is found. By contrast, the meaning of self is dynamic: it always represents the receiver of the currently executing message. This means that *all* messages sent to self are looked up by starting in the receiver's class.

> **Important** A super send triggers a method lookup starting in the *superclass of the class of the method performing the* super *send*. We say that super sends are *static* because just looking at the method we know the class where the lookup should start (the class above the class containing the method).

Message not understood

What happens if the method we are looking for is not found?

Suppose we send the message foo to our ellipse. First the normal method lookup would go through the inheritance chain all the way up to Object (or rather ProtoObject) looking for this method. When this method is not found, the virtual machine will cause the object to send self doesNotUnderstand: #foo. (See Figure 6.4.)

Now, this is a perfectly ordinary, dynamic message send, so the lookup starts again from the class EllipseMorph, but this time searching for the method doesNotUnderstand:. As it turns out, Object implements doesNotUnderstand:. This method will create a new MessageNotUnderstood object which is capable of starting a Debugger in the current execution context.

6.9 Shared variables

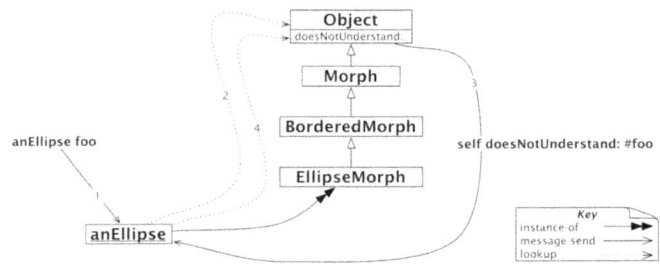

Figure 6.4: Message foo is not understood

Why do we take this convoluted path to handle such an obvious error? Well, this offers developers an easy way to intercept such errors and take alternative action. One could easily override the method Object>>doesNotUnderstand: in any subclass of Object and provide a different way of handling the error.

In fact, this can be an easy way to implement automatic delegation of messages from one object to another. A Delegator object could simply delegate all messages it does not understand to another object whose responsibility it is to handle them, or raise an error itself!

6.9 Shared variables

Now we will look at an aspect of Pharo that is not so easily covered by our five rules: shared variables.

Pharo provides three kinds of shared variables:

1. *Globally* shared variables.

2. *Class variables*: variables shared between instances and classes. (Not to be confused with class instance variables, discussed earlier).

3. *Pool variables*: variables shared amongst a group of classes,

The names of all of these shared variables start with a capital letter, to warn us that they are indeed shared between multiple objects.

Global variables

In Pharo, all global variables are stored in a namespace called Smalltalk, which is implemented as an instance of the class SystemDictionary. Global variables are accessible everywhere. Every class is named by a global variable. In addition, a few globals are used to name special or commonly useful objects.

The variable `Processor` names an instance of `ProcessScheduler`, the main process schedler of Pharo

```
Processor class
>>> ProcessorScheduler
```

Other useful global variables

`Smalltalk` is the instance of `SmalltalkImage`. It contains many functionality to manage the system. In particular it holds a reference to the main namespace `Smalltalk globals`. This namespace includes `Smalltalk` itself since it is a global variable. The keys to this namespace are the symbols that name the global objects in Pharo code. So, for example:

```
Smalltalk globals at: #Boolean
>>> Boolean
```

Since `Smalltalk` is itself a global variable:

```
Smalltalk globals at: #Smalltalk
>>> Smalltalk

(Smalltalk globals at: #Smalltalk) == Smalltalk
>>> true
```

`World` is an instance of `PasteUpMorph` that represents the screen. `World bounds` answers a rectangle that defines the whole screen space; all Morphs on the screen are submorphs of `World`.

`ActiveHand` is the current instance of `HandMorph`, the graphical representation of the cursor. `ActiveHand`'s submorphs hold anything being dragged by the mouse.

`Undeclared` is another dictionary, which contains all the undeclared variables. If you write a method that references an undeclared variable, the browser will normally prompt you to declare it, for example as a global or as an instance variable of the class. However, if you later delete the declaration, the code will then reference an undeclared variable. Inspecting `Undeclared` can sometimes help explain strange behaviour!

Using globals in your code

The recommended practice is to strictly limit the use of global variables. It is usually better to use class instance variables or class variables, and to provide class methods to access them. Indeed, if Pharo were to be implemented from scratch today, most of the global variables that are not classes would be replaced by singletons.

The usual way to define a global is just to perform `Do it` on an assignment to a capitalized but undeclared identifier. The parser will then offer to declare the

6.9 Shared variables

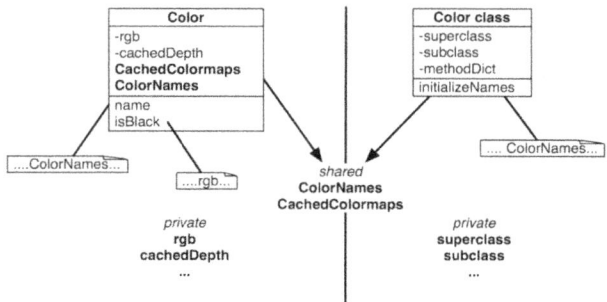

Figure 6.5: Instance and class methods accessing different variables

global for you. If you want to define a global programmatically, just execute `Smalltalk globals at: #AGlobalName put: nil`. To remove it, execute `Smalltalk globals removeKey: #AGlobalName`.

Class variables

Sometimes we need to share some data amongst all the instances of a class and the class itself. This is possible using *class variables*. The term *class variable* indicates that the lifetime of the variable is the same as that of the class. However, what the term does not convey is that these variables are shared amongst all the instances of a class as well as the class itself, as shown in Figure 6.5. Indeed, a better name would have been *shared variables* since this expresses more clearly their role, and also warns of the danger of using them, particularly if they are modified.

In Figure 6.5 we see that `rgb` and `cachedDepth` are instance variables of `Color`, hence only accessible to instances of `Color`. We also see that `superclass`, `subclass`, `methodDict` and so on are *class instance variables*, i.e., instance variables only accessible to the `Color` class.

But we can also see something new: `ColorRegistry` and `CachedColormaps` are *class variables* defined for `Color`. The capitalization of these variables gives us a hint that they are shared. In fact, not only may all instances of `Color` access these shared variables, but also the `Color` class itself, *and any of its subclasses*. Both instance methods and class methods can access these shared variables.

A class variable is declared in the class definition template. For example, the class `Color` defines a large number of class variables to speed up color creation; its definition is shown below.

```
Object subclass: #Color
    instanceVariableNames: 'rgb cachedDepth cachedBitPattern alpha'
    classVariableNames: 'BlueShift CachedColormaps ColorRegistry
        ComponentMask GrayToIndexMap GreenShift HalfComponentMask
```

```
    IndexedColors
 MaskingMap RandomStream RedShift'
 package: 'Graphics-Primitives'
```

The class variable `ColorRegistry` is an instance of `IdentityDictionary` containing the frequently-used colors, referenced by name. This dictionary is shared by all the instances of `Color`, as well as the class itself. It is accessible from all the instance and class methods.

Class initialization

The presence of class variables raises the question: how do we initialize them?

One solution is lazy initialization (discussed earlier in this chapter). This can be done by introducing an accessor method which, when executed, initializes the variable if it has not yet been initialized. This implies that we must use the accessor all the time and never use the class variable directly. This furthermore imposes the cost of the accessor send and the initialization test. It also arguably defeats the point of using a class variable, since in fact it is no longer shared.

Another solution is to override the class method `initialize` (we've seen this before in the Dog example).

```
Color class >> initialize
    ...
    self initializeColorRegistry.
    ...
```

If you adopt this solution, you will need to remember to invoke the `initialize` method after you define it (by evaluating `Color initialize`). Although class side `initialize` methods are executed automatically when code is loaded into memory (from a Monticello repository, for example), they are *not* executed automatically when they are first typed into the browser and compiled, or when they are edited and re-compiled.

Pool variables

Pool variables are variables that are shared between several classes that may not be related by inheritance. Pool variables were originally stored in pool dictionaries; now they should be defined as class variables of dedicated classes (subclasses of `SharedPool`). Our advice is to avoid them; you will need them only in rare and specific circumstances. Our goal here is therefore to explain pool variables just enough so that you can understand them when you are reading code.

A class that accesses a pool variable must mention the pool in its class definition. For example, the class `Text` indicates that it is using the pool dictionary `TextConstants`, which contains all the text constants such as CR and LF. This dictionary has a key #CR that is bound to the value `Character cr`, i.e., the carriage return character.

```
ArrayedCollection subclass: #Text
    instanceVariableNames: 'string runs'
    classVariableNames: ''
    poolDictionaries: 'TextConstants'
    package: 'Collections-Text'
```

This allows methods of the class Text to access the *keys* of the dictionary in the method body *directly*, i.e., by using variable syntax rather than an explicit dictionary lookup. For example, we can write the following method.

```
Text >> testCR
    ^ CR == Character cr
```

Once again, we recommend that you avoid the use of pool variables and pool dictionaries.

6.10 Internal object implementation note

Here is an implementation note for people that really want to go deep inside the way Pharo represents internally objects. The implementation distinguished between two different kinds of objects:

1. Objects with zero or more fields that are passed by reference and exist on the Pharo heap.

2. Immediate objects that are passed by value. Depending on version, these are a range of the integers called SmallInteger, all `Character` objects and possibly a sub-range of 64-bit floating-point numbers called `SmallFloat64`. In the implementation, such immediate objects occupy an object pointer, most of whose bits encode the immediate's value and some of the bits encode the object's class.

The first kind of object, an ordinary object, comes in a number of varieties:

1. Normal objects that have zero or more named instance variables, such as `Point` which has an x and a y instance variable. Each instance variable holds an object pointer, which can be a reference to another ordinary object or an immediate.

2. Indexable objects like arrays that have zero or more indexed instance variables numbered from 1 to N. Each indexed instance variable holds an object pointer, which can be a reference to another ordinary object or an immediate. Indexable objects are accessed using the messages `at:` and `at:put:`. For example `((Array new: 1) at: 1 put: 2; at: 1)` answers 2.

3. Objects like Closure or Context that have both named instance variables and indexed instance variables. In the object, the indexed instance variables follow the named instance variables.

4. Objects like ByteString or Bitmap that have indexed instance variables numbered from 1 to N that contain raw data. Each datum may occupy 8, 16 or 32-bits, depending on its class definition. The data can be accessed as either integers, characters or floating-point numbers, depending on how methods at: and at:put: are implemented. The at: and at:put: methods convert between Pharo objects and raw data, hiding the internal representation, but allowing the system to represent efficiently data such as strings, and bitmaps.

A beauty of Pharo is that you normally don't need to care about the differences between these three kinds of object.

6.11 Chapter summary

The object model of Pharo is both simple and uniform. Everything is an object, and pretty much everything happens by sending messages.

- Everything is an object. Primitive entities like integers are objects, but also classes are first-class objects.

- Every object is an instance of a class. Classes define the structure of their instances via *private* instance variables and the behaviour of their instances via *public* methods. Each class is the unique instance of its metaclass. Class variables are private variables shared by the class and all the instances of the class. Classes cannot directly access instance variables of their instances, and instances cannot access instance variables of their class. Accessors must be defined if this is needed.

- Every class has a superclass. The root of the single inheritance hierarchy is ProtoObject. Classes you define, however, should normally inherit from Object or its subclasses. There is no syntax for defining abstract classes. An abstract class is simply a class with an abstract method (one whose implementation consists of the expression self subclassResponsibility). Although Pharo supports only single inheritance, it is easy to share implementations of methods by packaging them as *traits*.

- Everything happens by sending messages. We do not *call methods*, we *send messages*. The receiver then chooses its own method for responding to the message.

- Method lookup follows the inheritance chain; self sends are dynamic and start the method lookup in the class of the receiver, whereas super sends start the method lookup in the superclass of class in which the super send is written. From this perspective super sends are more static than self sends.

6.11 Chapter summary

- There are three kinds of shared variables. Global variables are accessible everywhere in the system. Class variables are shared between a class, its subclasses and its instances. Pool variables are shared between a selected set of classes. You should avoid shared variables as much as possible.

CHAPTER 7

Some of the key tools of the Pharo environment

The goal of this chapter is to present the main tools of the Pharo programming environment. You have already seen how to define methods and classes using the browser; this chapter will show you more of its features, and introduce you to some of the other browsers.

Of course, very occasionally you may find that your program does not work as you expect. Pharo has an excellent debugger, but like most powerful tools, it can be confusing on first use. We will walk you through a debugging session and demonstrate some of the features of the debugger.

One of the unique features of Pharo (and its ancestors) is that while you are programming, you are living in a world of live objects, not in a world of static program text. This makes it possible to get very rapid feedback while programming, which makes you more productive. There is a tool that let you look at, and indeed change, live objects: the *inspector*.

7.1 Pharo environment overview

The System Browser is the central development tool. You will use it to create, define, and organize your classes and methods. Using it you can also navigate through all the library classes. Unlike other environments where the source code is stored in separate files, in Pharo all classes and methods are contained in the image.

The Finder tool will let you find methods, classes, pragmas, and more. You can look for a method's name, a class name, some source code, a pragma's name or even look for methods by providing an example!

The `Monticello Browser` is the starting point for loading code from, and saving code in, Monticello packages. It is discussed in more detail in Chapter : Sharing Code and Source Control.

The `Process Browser` provides a view of all of the processes (threads) executing in Smalltalk.

The `Test Runner` lets you run and debug SUnit tests, and is described in more detail in Chapter : SUnit.

The `Transcript` is a window on the `Transcript` output stream, which is useful for writing log messages.

The `Playground` is a window into which you can type input. It can be used for any purpose, but is most often used for typing Pharo expressions and executing them via `Do it`. We have already briefly encountered the Playground (and the Transcript) in Chapter : A Quick Tour of Pharo.

The `Debugger` has an obvious role, but you will discover that it has a more central place compared to debuggers for other programming languages, because in Pharo you can *program* in the debugger. The debugger is not launched from a menu; it is normally entered by running a failing test, by typing `CMD-.` to interrupt a running process, or by inserting a `Halt now` expression in code.

Window groups

Managing multiple windows within a Pharo image can become a tedious process. Window Groups are windows that offer tab support similar to the one you are used to on your web browser. To create a window group, click on the down arrow which appears on the top right corner of every window within Pharo, and select `Create window group`. This will turn that window into a window group with a tab bar, containing as its first tab the original contents of the window. You can add other windows to the group (within the Pharo image only, of course), by dragging and dropping their title bars onto the tab bar, next to existing tabs. Each new window that you drag onto the tab bar will be added as a new tab.

Themes and icon sets

If, like some of us, you are not a fan of the default bright theme, there is also a dark theme that can be used with Pharo. It can be found in the Settings browser in the World Menu (`World > System > Settings`), in the Appearance section. The `User interface` theme pulldown allows you to switch between the default `Pharo3` theme and the `Pharo3 Dark` theme. You can also experiment with available icon sets in the next pulldown in that section.

Please note that you may have to close and reopen existing windows to redraw them correctly with the new dark theme.

7.2 The main code browser

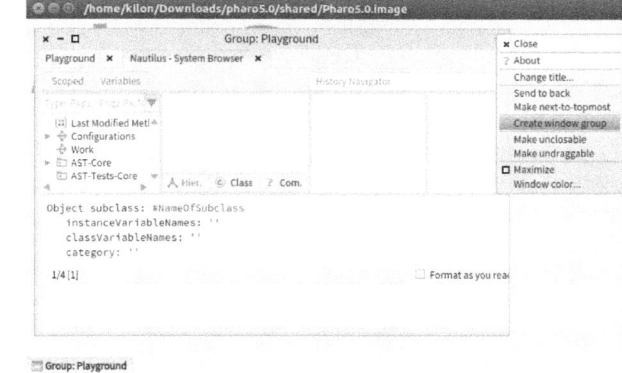

Figure 7.1: Window Group with two tabs, one with Playground and one with System Browser

You can use the `Catalog Browser` to install additional themes. Open `World > Tools > Catalog Browser` and search for theme in the search box. For example, if you want something more colorful, you can download the Nireas theme, which is a blue theme inspired by classic home computers like Amiga 500 and Amstrad CPC 6128. Nireas comes with a GUI tool that allows you to customize the theme's colors to your liking, if blue is not your thing.

Of course, if you are feeling especially adventurous, you can even make your own themes using existing ones as templates.

7.2 The main code browser

Many different class browsers have been developed over the years for Pharo. Pharo simplifies this story by offering a single browser that integrates various views. Figure 7.2 shows the browser as it appears when you first open it.

The four small panes at the top of the browser represent a hierarchic view of the methods in the system, much in the same way as the Mac OS X Finder in column mode provide a view of the files on the disk. The leftmost pane lists *packages* of classes; select one (say `Kernel`) and the pane immediately to the right will then show all of the classes in that package.

Similarly, if you select one of the classes in the second pane, say, `Boolean` (see Figure 7.3), the third pane will show all of the *protocols* defined for that class, as well as a virtual protocol `--all--`. Protocols are a way of categorizing methods; they make it easier to find and think about the behaviour of a class by breaking it up into smaller, conceptually coherent pieces. The fourth pane shows the names of all of the methods defined in the selected protocol. If you then select a method name, the source code of the corresponding method

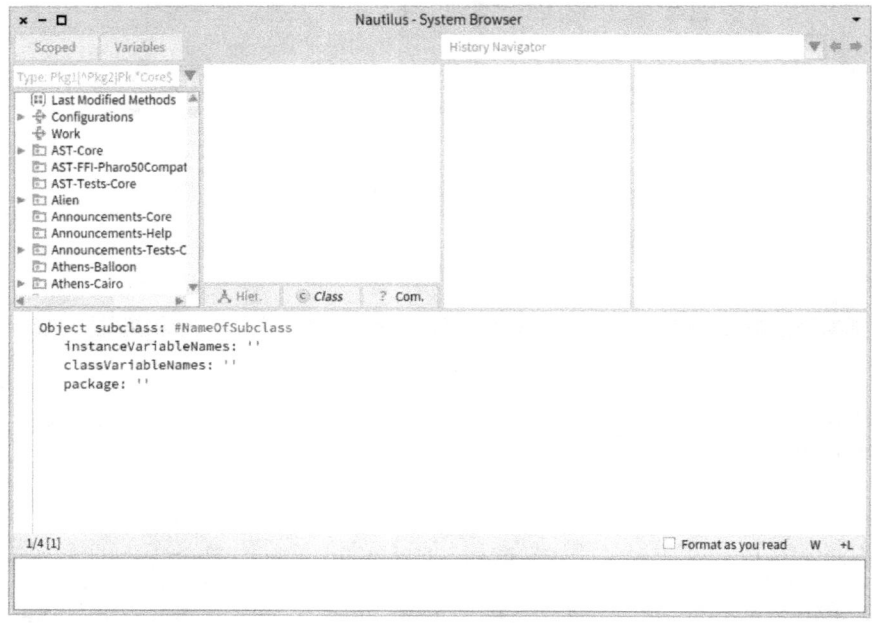

Figure 7.2: The main code browser.

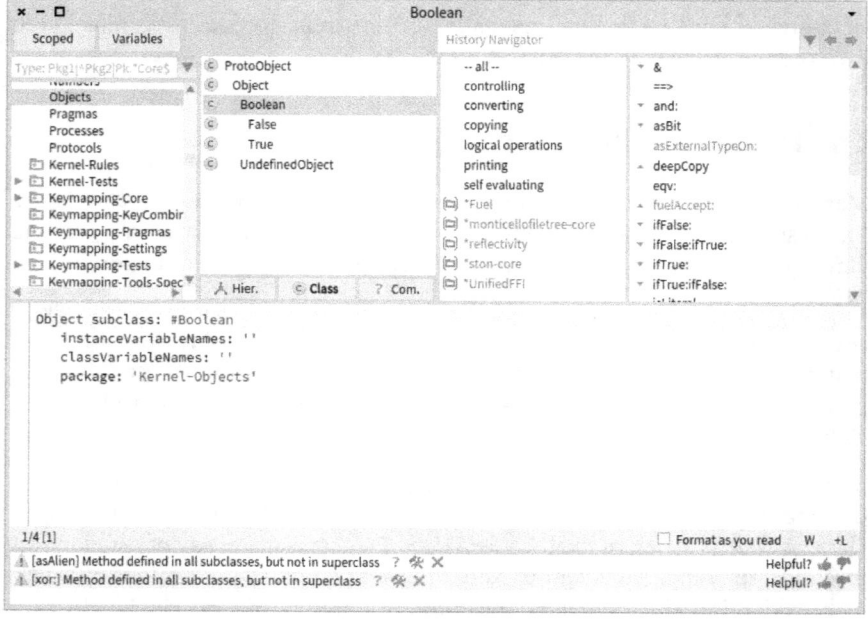

Figure 7.3: The browser with the class `Boolean` selected.

7.2 The main code browser

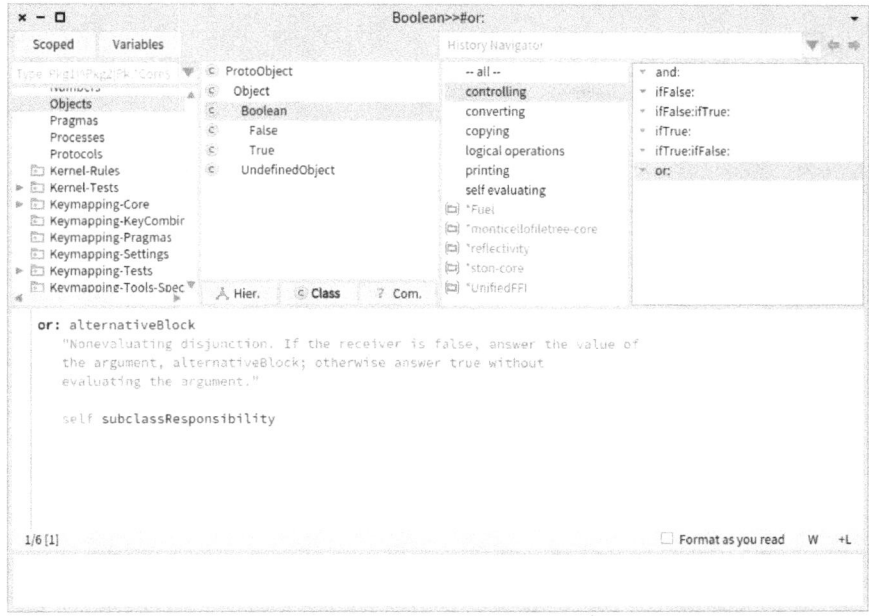

Figure 7.4: Browsing the or: method in class Boolean.

appears in the large pane at the bottom of the browser, where you can view it, edit it, and save the edited version. If you select class Boolean, protocol controlling and the method or:, the browser should look like Figure 7.4.

Unlike directories in a file browser, the four top panes of the browser are not quite equal. Whereas classes and methods are part of the Smalltalk language, packages and protocols are not: they are a convenience introduced by the browser to limit the amount of information that needs to be shown in each pane. For example, if there were no protocols, the browser would have to show a list of all of the methods in the selected class; for many classes this list would be too large to navigate conveniently.

Because of this, the way that you create a new package or a new protocol is different from the way that you create a new class or a new method. To create a new package, right-click in the package pane and select Add package.... To create a new protocol, right-click in the protocol pane and select Add protocol.... Enter the name of the new thing in the dialog, and you are done: there is nothing more to a package or a protocol than its name and its contents.

In contrast, to create a new class or a new method, you will actually have to write some Smalltalk code. If you click the currently selected package (in the left-most pane), the bottom browser pane will display a class creation

117

Some of the key tools of the Pharo environment

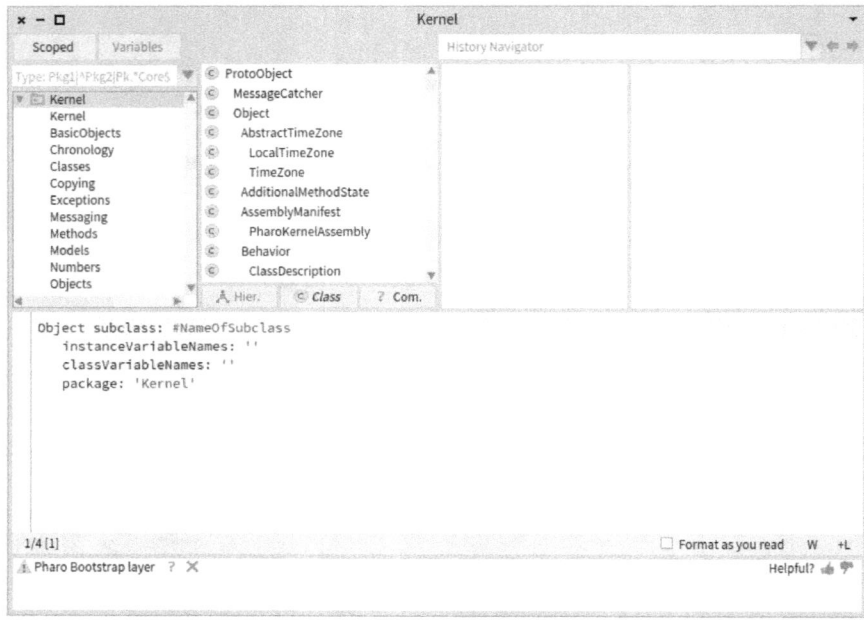

Figure 7.5: Browser showing the class-creation template

template (Figure 7.5). You create a new class by editing this template: replace Object by the name of the existing class of which you wish to create a subclass, replace NameOfSubclass by the name that you would like to give to your new subclass, and fill in the instance variable names if you know them. The package for the new class is by default the currently selected package, but you can change this too if you like. If you already have the browser focused on the class that you wish to subclass, you can get the same template with slightly different initialization by right-clicking in the class pane, and selecting Add Class. You can also just edit the definition of an existing class, changing the class name to something new. In all cases, when you accept the new definition, the new class (the one whose name follows the #) is created (as is the corresponding metaclass). Creating a class also creates a global variable that references the class, which is why you can refer to all of the existing classes by using their names.

Can you see why the name of the new class has to appear as a Symbol (i.e., prefixed with #) in the class creation template, but after the class is created, code can refer to the class by using the name as an identifier (without the #)?

The process of creating a new method is similar. First select the class in which you want the method to live, and then select a protocol. The browser will display a method-creation template, as shown in Figure 7.6, which you can fill-in or edit.

7.2 The main code browser

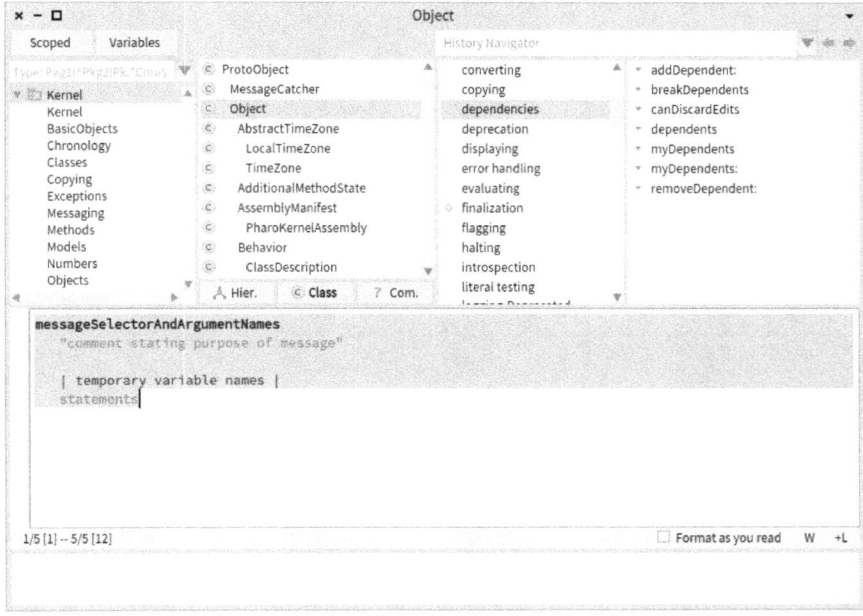

Figure 7.6: Showing the method-creation template.

Navigating the code space

The browser provides several tools for exploring and analyzing code. These tools can be accessed by right-clicking in the various contextual menus, or, in the case of the most frequently used tools, by means of keyboard shortcuts.

Opening a new browser window

Sometimes you want to open multiple browser windows. When you are writing code you will almost certainly need at least two: one for the method that you are typing, and another to browse around the system to see how things work. You can open a browser on a class named by any selected text using the CMD-b keyboard shortcut.

> **To do** Try this: In a playground window, type the name of a class (for instance Morph), select it, and then press CMD-b. This trick is often useful; it works in any text window.

Message senders

While writing new code, refactoring existing code, or while trying to learn how to use unfamiliar libraries, you will frequently want to know the senders

Some of the key tools of the Pharo environment

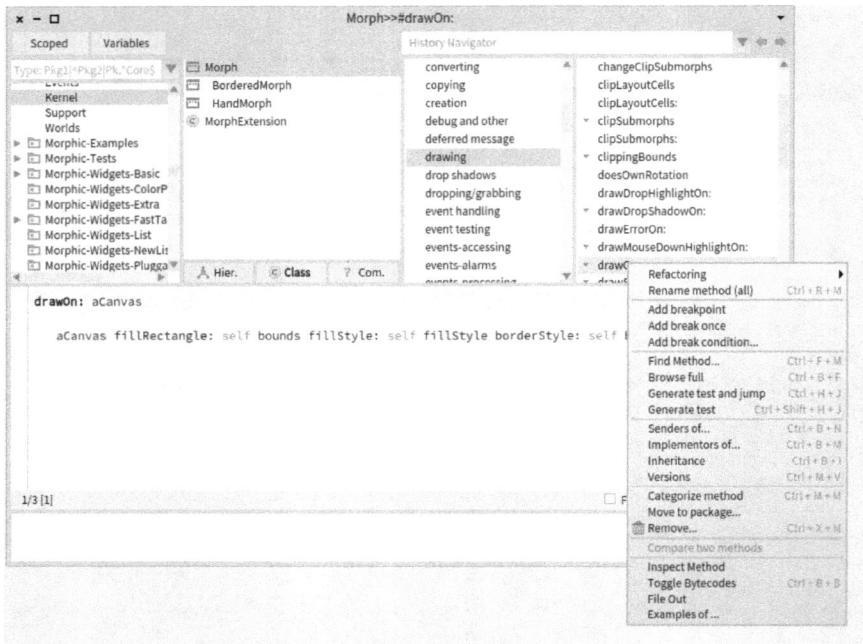

Figure 7.7: The `Senders Of...(b,n)` menu item.

and implementors of various messages.

There are several ways of discovering where in the codebase a message is used, by listing its senders:

1. *From the method pane.* Select a method in the method pane of the browser. You can then right-click on it and select `Senders of...(b,n)` in the context menu. Alternatively, you can also use the shortcut `CMD-b CMD-n` to do the same thing (that's what the b,n in the menu item stands for). To help remember this shortcut, think: browse senders.

2. *From the code pane.* Highlight a particular message in the source code. This can be done in a code pane of a browser, in a Playground window, or in any text window. If you want to find the senders of a keyword message, you highlight all of the keywords in the message, including arguments. Then, you can right-click on the highlighted selector and choose `Code search... > senders of it (n)`. Alternatively, you can use the shortcut `CMD-n` instead of right-clicking.

3. *Using Spotter.* Bring up a particular method in Spotter (press `SHIFT-Enter` to bring up the Spotter search box, type in the message selector, arrow down to a particular Implementor of that message, and press `CMD-right arrow` to focus the search on it.) A list of Senders now appears in the search results.

7.2 The main code browser

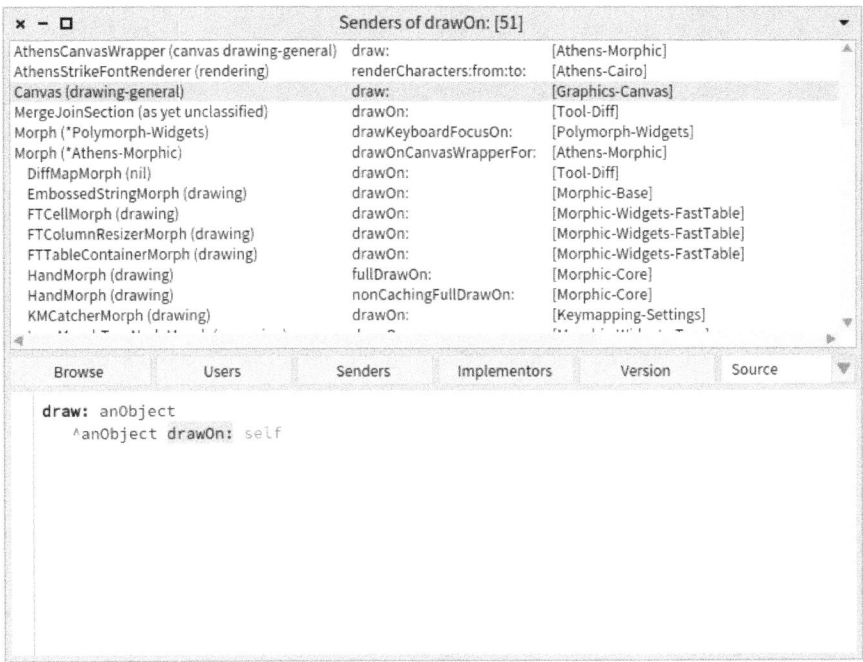

Figure 7.8: The Senders Browser showing that the Canvas>>draw method sends the drawOn: message to its argument.

Only a handful of senders are shown by default, but you can view the full list by clicking on the arrow next to the Senders category (or arrow down to the Senders list and expand it by pressing CMD-SHIFT-right arrow).

Let's try some of these in action.

Open a browser on the Morph class, select the Morph>>drawOn: method in the method pane. If you now press CMD-b CMD-n (or right-click in the method pane and select Senders of... (Figure 7.7)), a browser will open with the list of all methods in the image that send the selected message (Figure 7.8).

Now look at the third sender on the list, Canvas>>draw:. You can see that this method sends drawOn: to whatever object is passed to it as an argument, which could potentially be an instance of any class at all. Dataflow analysis can help figure out the class of the receiver of some messages, but in general, there is no simple way for the browser to know which message-sends might cause which methods to be executed. For this reason, the Senders browser shows exactly what its name suggests: all of the senders of the message with the chosen selector. The senders browser is nevertheless extremely useful when you need to understand how you can *use* a method: it lets you navigate quickly through example uses. Since all of the methods with the same selector

Some of the key tools of the Pharo environment

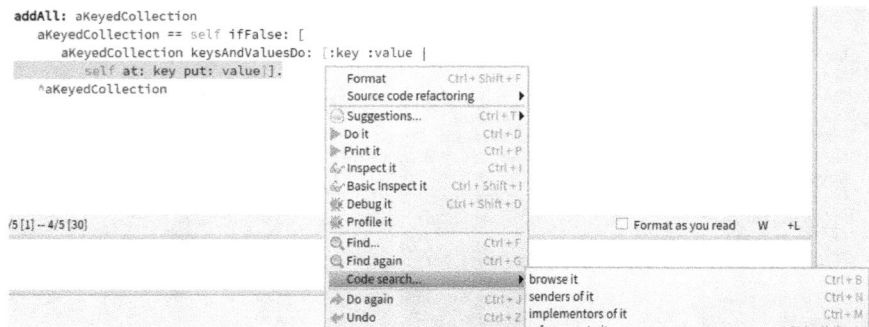

Figure 7.9: Finding senders of a keyword message in the code pane.

should be used in the same way, all of the uses of a given message ought to be similar.

> **To do** Switch to the `Dictionary` class in the browser (remember, you can right-click in the package or class pane and select `Find class...`, or just use the `CMD-f CMD-c` shortcut), and select the `addAll:` method in the method pane.

Looking at the source code, suppose you wanted to see all of the senders of the `at: key put: value` message. You can simply highlight the whole message send, and press `CMD-n` (or right-click and select `Code Search > senders of it (n)`), to bring up the list of senders (see Figure 7.9).

Message implementors

Similarly, you may come across a message, and want to see how it's implemented. This is what the `Implementors` browser is for. It works in the same way as the Senders browser, but instead lists all of the classes that implement a method with the same selector.

1. *From the method pane.* Select a method in the method pane. You can then bring up the Implementors browser by right-clicking on the method and selecting `Implementors of...(b,m)` in the context menu (or use the shortcut `CMD-b CMD-m`). To help remember this shortcut, think: browse implementors.

2. *From the code pane.* Highlight a particular message in the source code (or any text window). If you want to find the implementors of a keyword message, you highlight all of the keywords in the message. Then, you can right-click on the highlited selector and choose `Code search... > implementors of it (m)` from the menu (or just use the shortcut `CMD-n`).

3. *Using Spotter.* Bring up a method in Spotter (press `SHIFT-Enter` to bring up the Spotter search box, and start typing the message selector). The Implementors category will show up in the search results, showing the first handful of implementors. To see the full list, click on the arrow to the right of Implementors category (or arrow down to Implementors and press SHIFT-CMD-right arrow).

Try this out: Press SHIFT-Enter and type drawOn: in the Spotter search box. You should see a list showing 5 out of 100 implementors of that method. It shouldn't be all that surprising that so many classes implement this method: drawOn: is the message that is understood by every object that is capable of drawing itself on the screen.

Notice that if you only typed drawOn and left out the colon (:), the number of implementors in the search results is larger. This is because Spotter is doing a partial search, and including any methods that have 'drawOn' in the name, such as drawOn:offset:, drawOnAthensCanvas:, and so on. This is useful for when you want to find a method but can only remember a part of its name.

Method inheritance and overriding

The inheritance browser displays all the methods overridden by the displayed method. To see how it works, select the ImageMorph>>drawOn: method in the browser. Note the arrow icons next to the method name (Figure 7.10). The upward-pointing arrow tells you that ImageMorph>>drawOn: overrides an inherited method (i.e., Morph>>drawOn:), and the downward-pointing arrow tells you that it is overridden by subclasses. (You can also click on the icons to navigate to these methods.) Now right-click on it in the method pane, and select Inheritance. The inheritance browser shows you the hierarchy of overridden methods (see Figure 7.10).

Hierarchy view

By default, the browser presents a list of packages in the leftmost pane. However it is possible to switch to a class hierarchy view. Simply select a particular class of interest, such as ImageMorph and then click on the Hierarchy button (Hier.). You will then see in the second pane a class hierarchy displaying all superclasses and subclasses of the selected class.

Notice that the package pane is disabled, and the packages are greyed out. When you are in Hierarchy view, you cannot change packages. To be able to change them again, toggle out of the Hierarchy view by clicking on the Hierarchy button again.

In Figure 7.11, the hierarchy view reveals that the direct superclass of ImageMorph is Morph.

Some of the key tools of the Pharo environment

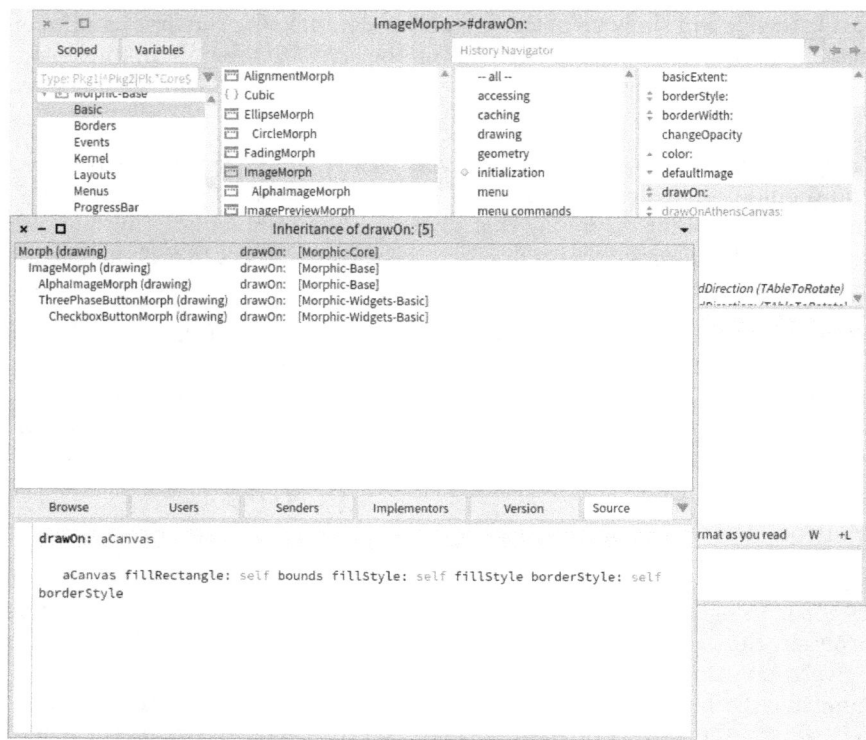

Figure 7.10: `ImageMorph>>drawOn:` and the hierarchy of classes overriding it.

Finding variable references

By right-clicking on a class in the class pane, and selecting `Analyze > Inst var references...` or `Analyze > Class var refs...`, you can find out where an instance variable or a class variable is used. You can also have access to those views by clicking on the `Variables` button, above the package list. Once you click on the button or select the menu item, you will be presented with a dialog that invites you to choose a variable from all of the variables defined in the current class, and all of the variables that it inherits. The list is in inheritance order; it can often be useful to bring up this list just to remind yourself of the name of an instance variable. If you click outside the list, it will go away and no variable browser will be created. If you click on a variable, bounds for example, a *Message Browser* will be created (Figure 7.12).

You can use a similar method to look at direct variable assignments (that is, places that modify the variable without using accessor methods). Right-click on the class and select `Analyze > Inst var assignments`.

7.2 The main code browser

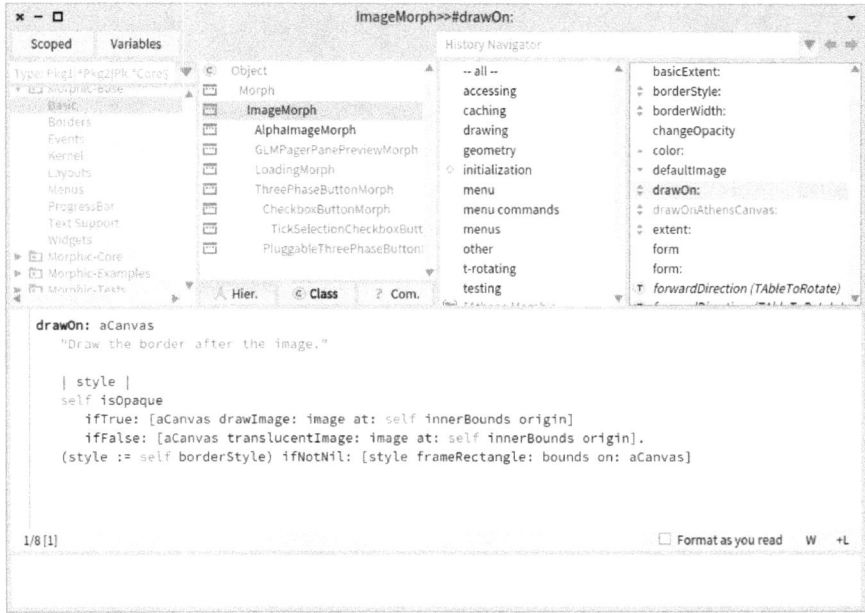

Figure 7.11: A hierarchy view of ImageMorph.

Bytecode source

You have the possibility of browsing the bytecode of a method. To do that, right-click on your method and select `Toggle Bytecodes`, or use the shortcut CMD-b CMD-b (see Figure 7.13). Reselect the method again to get back to the normal view.

Refactorings

The contextual menus offer a large number of standard refactorings. Simply right-click in any of the four panes to see the currently available refactoring operations. See Figure 7.14.

Refactoring was formerly available only in a special browser called the refactoring browser, but it can now be accessed from any browser.

Browser menus

Many additional functions are available by right-clicking in the browser panes. Even if the labels on the menu items are the same, their *meaning* may be context dependent. For example, the package pane, the class pane, the protocol pane and the method pane all have a `File out` menu item. However, they do different things: the package pane's `File out` menu item files out the

Some of the key tools of the Pharo environment

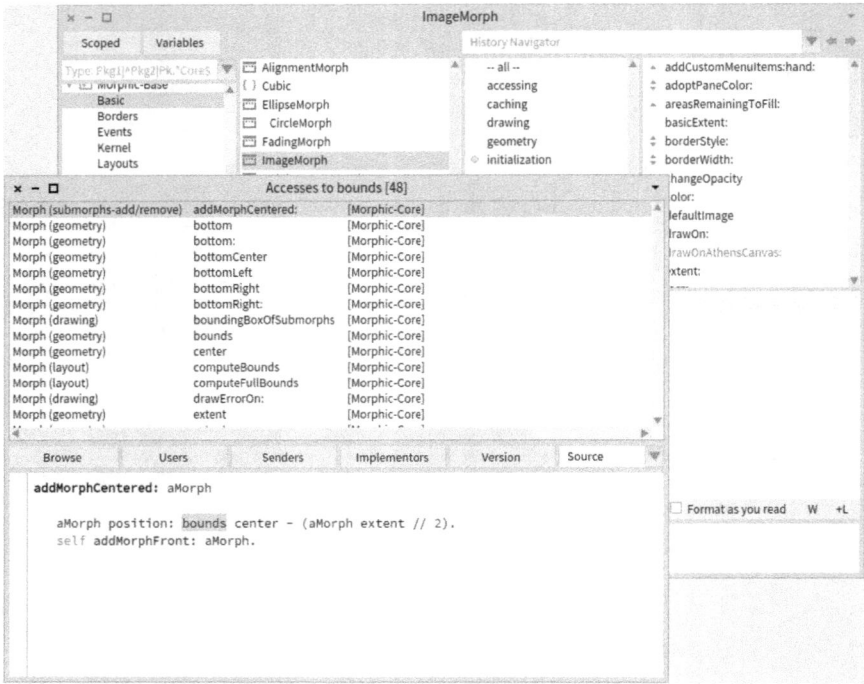

Figure 7.12: A Message Browser for accesses to bounds variable of Morph.

whole package, the class pane's item files out the whole class, the protocol pane's item files out the whole protocol, and the method pane's item files out just the displayed method.

Although this may seem obvious, it can be a source of confusion for beginners.

Possibly the most useful menu item is Find class... (f,c) in the package or class panes. Most of us do not know the package contents of the whole system, and it is much faster to type CMD-f CMD-c followed by the first few characters of the name of a class than to guess which package it might be in.

The History Navigator pulldown, found above the protocol and method panes, can also help you quickly go back to a class or method that you have browsed recently, even if you have forgotten its name.

Another useful method in the class pane is Find method (CMD-f CMD-m), which brings up a menu of all the methods in the class and gives you a search box.

Alternatively, if you are searching for a particular method of the selected class, it is often quicker to browse the --all-- protocol, place the mouse in the method pane, and type the first letter of the name of the method that you are looking for. This will usually scroll the pane so that the sought-for method

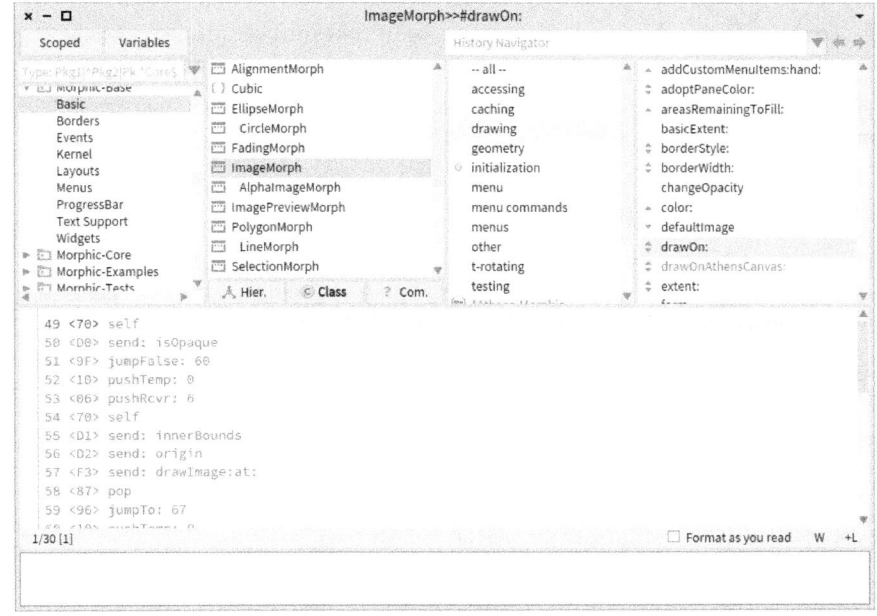

Figure 7.13: Bytecode of the ImageMorph»#DrawOn: compiled method.

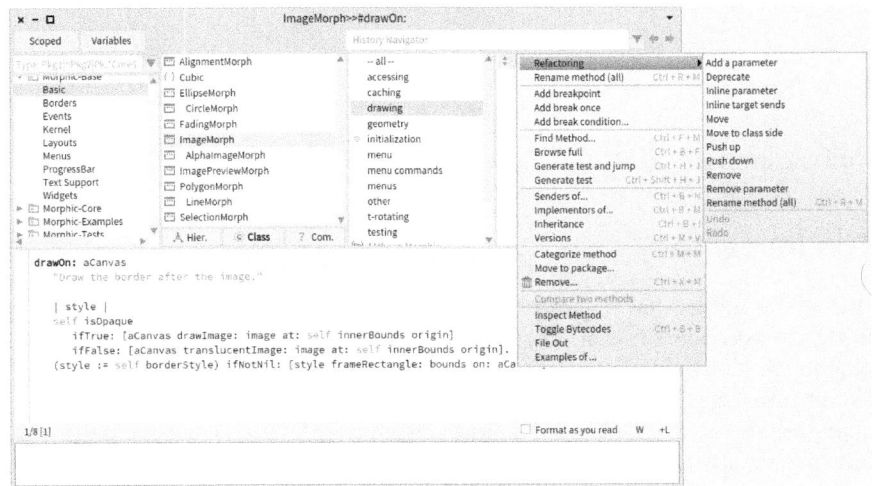

Figure 7.14: Refactoring operations.

name is visible.

> **To do** Try both ways of navigating to `OrderedCollection>>removeAt:`.

There are many other options available in the menus. It pays to spend a few minutes working with the browser and seeing what is there.

Browsing programmatically

The class `SystemNavigation` provides a number of utility methods that are useful for navigating around the system. Many of the functions offered by the system browser are implemented by `SystemNavigation`.

Open a playground and evaluate the following code to browse the senders of `drawOn:`:

```
SystemNavigation default browseAllSendersOf: #drawOn:
```

To restrict the search for senders to the methods of a specific class:

```
SystemNavigation default browseAllSendersOf: #drawOn: localTo:
    ImageMorph
```

Because the development tools are objects, they are completely accessible from programs and you can develop your own tools or adapt the existing tools to your needs.

The programmatic equivalent to the `Implementors of...` menu item is:

```
SystemNavigation default browseAllImplementorsOf: #drawOn:
```

> **To do** To learn more about what is available, explore the class `System-Navigation`

with the browser.

7.3 The inspector

One of the things that makes Pharo so different from many other programming environments is that it provides you with a window onto a world of live objects, not a world of static code. Any of those objects can be examined by the programmer, and even modified (although some care is necessary when changing the basic objects that support the system). By all means experiment, but save your image first!

As an illustration of what you can do with an inspector, type `DateAndTime now` in a playground, and then right-click and choose `Inspect it` (CMD-i) or `Do it and go` (CMD-g) (the latter opens an inspector *inside* the playground window).

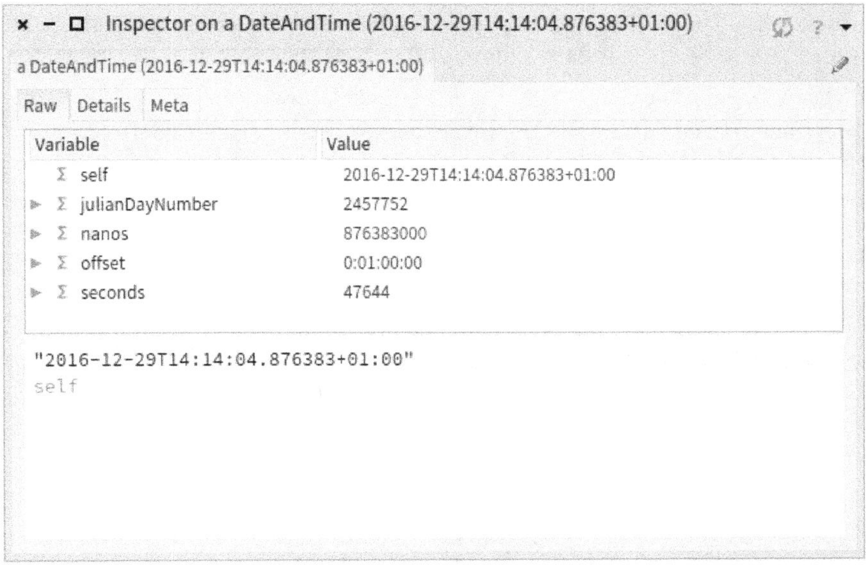

7.3 The inspector

Figure 7.15: Inspecting `DateAndTime now`.

Note that it's often not necessary to select the text before using the menu; if no text is selected, the menu operations work on the whole of the current line.

A window like that shown in Figure 7.15 will appear. This is an inspector, and can be thought of as a window onto the internals of a particular object – in this case, the particular instance of DateAndTime that was created when you evaluated the expression DateAndTime now. The title bar of the window shows the printable representation of the object that is being inspected.

In the default view (the Raw tab), instance variables can be explored by selecting them in the variable list in the Variable column. As you select a variable, its printable representation is shown in the Value column. More importantly, a separate Inspector view for the selected variable opens in the right hand pane.

For variables that are simple types (booleans, integers, etc), the nested inspector view is not much different from the printable representation in the Value column (although it is a full-fledged Inspector). But for most instance variables, the nested Inspector view on the right has its *own* Raw tab, with its own list of instance variables. (You can also see that list in the left pane, by expanding the triangle next to a variable's name.)

You can keep drilling down into the hierarchy of instance variables, with more nested Inspector panes opening to the right of the parent. However, to prevent the multiple panes from being impractical, the panes "scroll" to the right, within the overall inspector window. You can keep track of which "page" you're on, and also back-track to the original instance that you were inspecting, by using the pagination dots at the bottom of the inspector window.

There are special variants of the inspector for Dictionaries, OrderedCollections, CompiledMethods and a few other classes. These variants have other tabs, in addition to the Raw view, that make it easier to examine the contents of these special objects. For example, an inspector on a Dictionary instance, has an additional Items tab that shows that dictionary's keys and values in an intuitive fashion.

The horizontal pane at the bottom of the inspector is a small playground window. It is useful because in this window, the pseudo-variable self is bound to the object that you have selected in the left pane. That means you can write and evaluate arbitrary code expressions that use the selected variable's self, in that bottom pane.

For example, take the inspector on DateAndTime now that you opened earlier in this section. You can select its bottom playground pane, and evaluate the expression self - DateAndTime today. The result will be a Duration object that represents the time interval between midnight today and the instant at which you evaluated DateAndTime now and created the DateAndTime instance that you are inspecting. You can also try evaluating DateAndTime now - self; this will tell you how long you have spent reading this section of this book!

The bottom pane is especially useful if you wanted to change the instance variables of the object being inspected. Provided that you have accessor methods defined for those variables, you can send messages to the root self and change its variables via those accessor methods.

7.4 The debugger

The debugger is arguably the most powerful tool in the Pharo tool suite. It is used not just for debugging, but also for writing new code. To demonstrate the debugger, let's start by creating a bug!

Using the browser, add the following method to the class String:

```
suffix
    "assumes that I'm a file name, and answers my suffix, the part after
        the last dot"

    | dot dotPosition |
    dot := '.'.
    dotPosition := (self size to: 1 by: -1) detect: [ :i | (self at: i)
        = dot ].
    ^ self copyFrom: dotPosition to: self size
```

7.4 The debugger

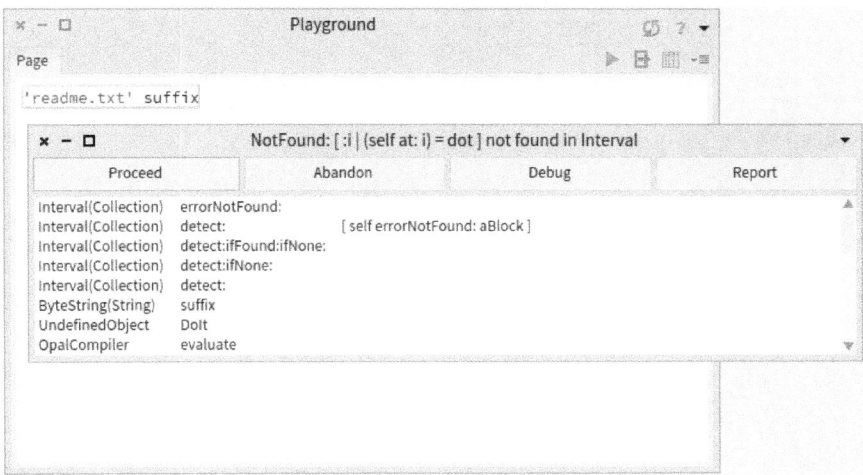

Figure 7.16: A PreDebugWindow notifies us of a bug.

Of course, we are sure that such a trivial method will work, so instead of writing an SUnit test, we just type 'readme.txt' suffix in a playground and Print it (p). What a surprise! Instead of getting the expected answer 'txt', a PreDebugWindow pops up, as shown in Figure 7.16.

The PreDebugWindow has a title bar that tells us what error occurred, and shows us a *stack trace* of the messages that led up to the error. Starting from the bottom of the trace, UndefinedObject>>DoIt represents the code that was compiled and run when we selected 'readme.txt' suffix in the playground and asked Pharo to Print it. This code, of course, sent the message suffix to a ByteString object ('readme.txt'). This caused the inherited suffix method in class String to execute; all this information is encoded in the next line of the stack trace, ByteString(String)>>suffix. Working up the stack, we can see that suffix sent detect:… and eventually detect:ifNone sent errorNotFound:.

To find out *why* the dot was not found, we need the debugger itself, so click on Debug. You can also open the debugger by clicking on any of the lines on the stack trace. If you do this, the debugger will open already focused on the corresponding method.

The debugger is shown in Figure 7.17; it looks intimidating at first, but it is quite easy to use. The title bar and the top pane are very similar to those that we saw in the PreDebugWindow. However, the debugger combines the stack trace with a method browser, so when you select a line in the stack trace, the corresponding method is shown in the pane below. It's important to realize that the execution that caused the error is still in your image, but in a suspended state. Each line of the stack trace represents a frame on the

Some of the key tools of the Pharo environment

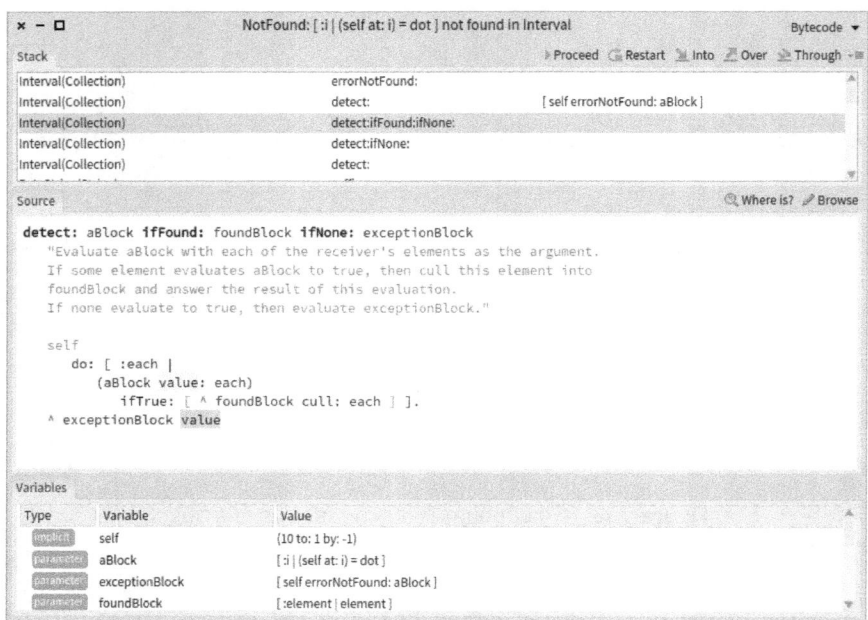

Figure 7.17: The debugger showing the execution stack and the state of various objects.

execution stack that contains all of the information necessary to continue the execution. This includes all of the objects involved in the computation, with their instance variables, and all of the temporary variables of the executing methods.

In Figure 7.17 we have selected the detect:ifFound:IfNone: method in the top pane. The method body is displayed in the center pane; the blue highlight around the message value shows that the current method has sent the message value and is waiting for an answer.

The Variables pane at the bottom of the debugger is actually like a inspector (without playground pane). You can select one variable and open another inspector pane with the well-known inspector panes (Raw, ...), and an Evaluator acting as a Playground for evaluating code within the context of the selected variable. The variables list has up to four types variables it shows.

- **parameter** any parameter passed to this method.
- **temp** any temporaries used in this method.
- **attribute** any instance variable accessible from the context of the current receiver.
- **implicit** pseudo variables (self, thisContext, stackTop) used in the

7.4 The debugger

current context.

As you select different stack frames, the identity of self may change, and so will the contents of the Variables list. If you click on self in the bottom-left pane, you will see that self is the interval (10 to: 1 by -1), which is what we expect. You can always select self and select the Evaluator pane to evaluate some code in the content of the current receiver. But because all of the variables are also in scope in the method pane; you should feel free to type or select expressions directly in the method pane and evaluate them. You can always Cancel (l) your changes using the menu or CMD-l.

Selecting thisContext from the list of (**implicit**) variables, shows the current context object.

As we can see one method lower in the stack trace, the exceptionBlock is [self errorNotFound: ...], so, it is not surprising that we see the corresponding error message.

Incidentally, if you want to open a full inspector on one of the variables shown in the mini-inspectors, just double-click on the name of the variable, or select the name of the variable and right-click to choose Inspect (i). This can be useful if you want to watch how a variable changes while you execute other code.

Looking back at the method window, we see that we expected the penultimate line of the method to find '.' in the string 'readme.txt', and that execution should never have reached the final line. Pharo does not let us run an execution backwards, but it does let us start a method again, which works very well in code that does not mutate objects, but instead creates new ones.

Click Restart, and you will see that the focus of execution returns to the first statement of the current method. The blue highlight shows that the next message to be sent will be do: (see Figure 7.18).

The Into and Over buttons give us two different ways to step through the execution. If you click Over, Pharo executes the current message-send (in this case the do:) in one step, unless there is an error. So Over will take us to the next message-send in the current method, which is value – this is exactly where we started, and not much help. What we need to do is to find out why the do: is not finding the character that we are looking for.

After clicking Over, click Restart to get back to the situation shown in Figure 7.18.

Click Into two times; Pharo will go into the method corresponding to the highlighted message-send, in this case, Interval>>do:.

However, it turns out that this is not much help either; we can be fairly confident that Interval>>do: is not broken. The bug is much more likely to be in *what* we asked Pharo to do. Through is the appropriate button to use in this

Some of the key tools of the Pharo environment

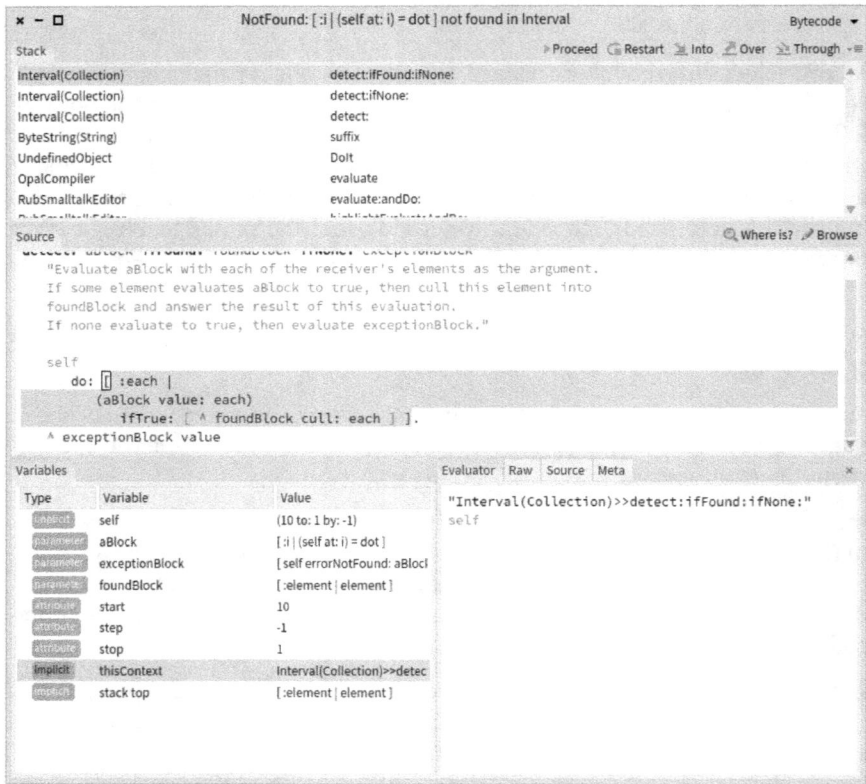

Figure 7.18: The debugger after restarting the detect:ifFound:IfNone: method.

case: we want to ignore the details of the do: itself and focus on the execution of the argument block.

Select the detect:ifFound:IfNone: method again and Restart to get back to the state shown in Figure 7.18. Now click on Through a few times. Select each in the context window as you do so. You should see each count down from 10 as the do: method executes.

When each is 7 we expect the ifTrue: block to be executed, but it isn't. To see what is going wrong, go Into the execution of value: as illustrated in Figure 7.19.

After clicking Into, we find ourselves in the position shown in Figure 7.20. It looks at first that we have gone *back* to the suffix method, but this is because we are now executing the block that suffix provided as argument to detect:.

If you select dot in the context inspector, you will see that its value is '.'. And now you see why they are not equal: the seventh character of 'readme.txt'

7.4 The debugger

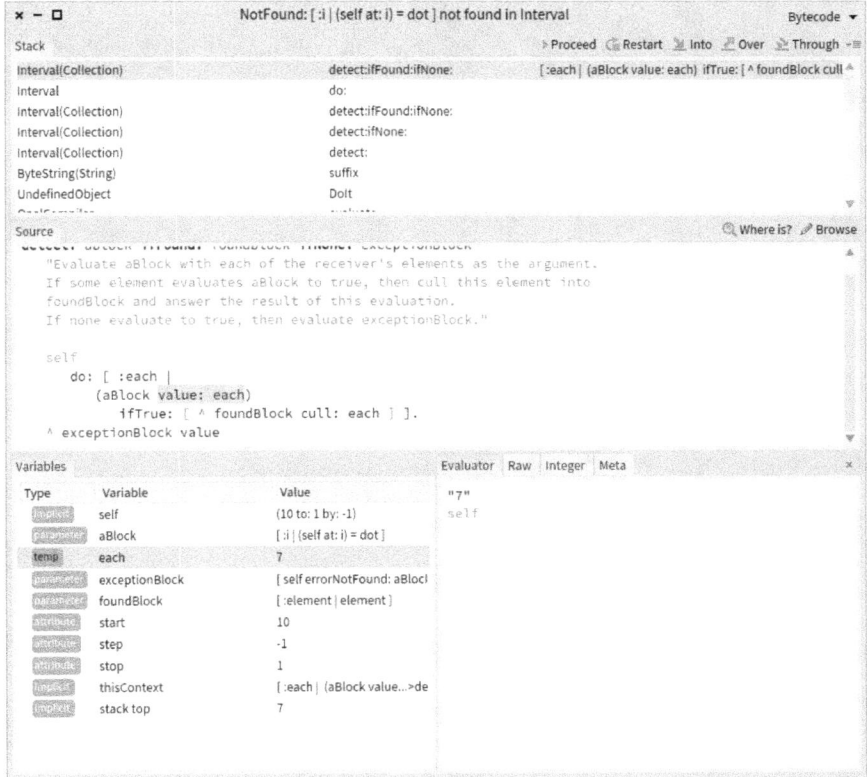

Figure 7.19: The debugger after stepping Through the do: method several times.

is of course a Character, while dot is a String.

Now that we see the bug, the fix is obvious: we have to convert dot to a character before starting to search for it.

Change the code right in the debugger so that the assignment reads dot := $. and accept the change.

Because we are executing code inside a block that is inside a detect:, several stack frames will have to be abandoned in order to make this change. Pharo asks us if this is what we want (see Figure 7.21), and, assuming that we click yes, will save (and compile) the new method.

The evaluation of the expression 'readme.txt' suffix will complete, and print the answer '.txt'.

Is the answer correct? Unfortunately, we can't say for sure. Should the suffix be .txt or txt? The method comment in suffix is not very precise. The way to avoid this sort of problem is to write an SUnit test that defines the answer.

Some of the key tools of the Pharo environment

Figure 7.20: The debugger showing why `'readme.txt' at: 7` is not equal to dot.

```
testSuffixFound
    self assert: 'readme.txt' suffix = 'txt'
```

The effort required to do that was little more than to run the same test in the playground, but using SUnit saves the test as executable documentation, and makes it easy for others to run. Moreover, if you add testSuffix to the class StringTest and run that test suite with SUnit, you can very quickly get back to debugging the error. SUnit opens the debugger on the failing assertion, but you need only go back down the stack one frame, Restart the test and go Into the suffix method, and you can correct the error, as we are doing in Figure 7.22. It is then only a second of work to click on the Run Failures button in the SUnit Test Runner, and confirm that the test now passes.

Here is a better test:

```
testSuffixFound
    self assert: 'readme.txt' suffix = 'txt'.
    self assert: 'read.me.txt' suffix = 'txt'
```

7.4 The debugger

Figure 7.21: Changing the suffix method in the debugger: asking for confirmation of the exit from an inner block.

Why is this test better? Because it tells the reader what the method should do if there is more than one dot in the target String.

There are a few other ways to get into the debugger in addition to catching errors and assertion failures. If you execute code that goes into an infinite loop, you can interrupt it and open a debugger on the computation by typing CMD-. (that's a full stop or a period, depending on where you learned English). (It is also useful to know that you can bring up an emergency debugger at any time by typing CMD-SHIFT-.) You can also just edit the suspect code to insert Halt now.. So, for example, we might edit the suffix method to read as follows:

```
suffix
    "assumes that I'm a file name, and answers my suffix, the part after
        the last dot"

    | dot dotPosition |
    dot := FileDirectory dot first.
    dotPosition := (self size to: 1 by: -1) detect: [ :i | (self at: i)
        = dot ].
    Halt now.
    ^ self copyFrom: dotPosition to: self size
```

Some of the key tools of the Pharo environment

Figure 7.22: Changing the `suffix` method in the debugger: fixing the off-by-one error after an SUnit assertion failure.

When we run this method, the execution of the `Halt` now will bring up the pre-debugger, from where we can either proceed, or go into the debugger (and from there look at variables, step through the computation, and edit the code).

That's all there is to the debugger, but it's not all there is to the `suffix` method. The initial bug should have made you realize that if there is no dot in the target string, the `suffix` method will raise an error. This isn't the behaviour that we want, so let's add a second test to specify what should happen in this case.

```
testSuffixNotFound
    self assert: 'readme' suffix = ''
```

Lastly, add `testNoSuffix` to the test suite in class `StringTest`, and watch the test raise an error. Enter the debugger by selecting the erroneous test in SUnit, and edit the code so that the test passes. The easiest and clearest way to do this is to replace the `detect:` message by `detect:ifNone:`, where the second argument is a block that simply returns the string size.

We will learn more about SUnit in Chapter : SUnit.

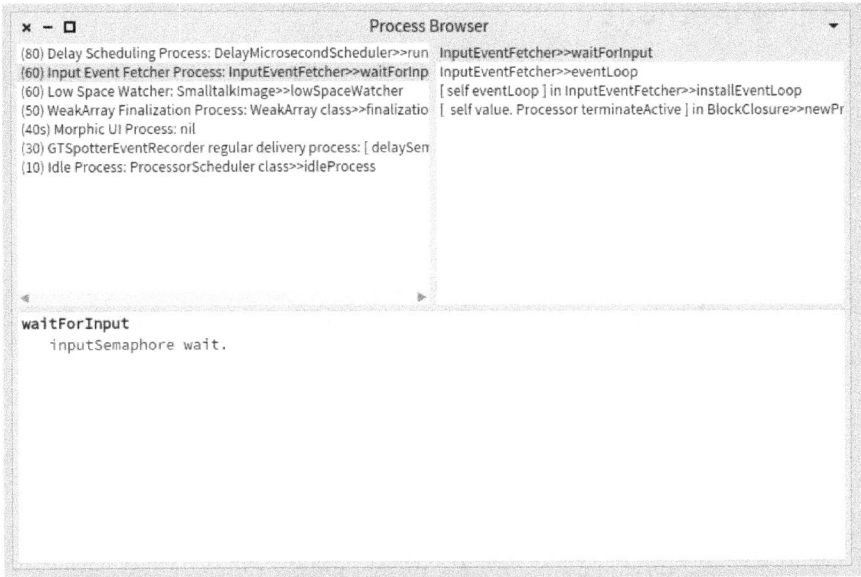

Figure 7.23: The Process Browser showing all the active thread by priority.

7.5 The process browser

Pharo is a multi-threaded system, and there are many lightweight processes (also known as threads) running concurrently in your image. In the future the Pharo virtual machine may take advantage of multiple processors when they are available, but at present, concurrency is implemented by time-slicing.

The Process Browser is a cousin of the debugger that lets you look at the various processes running inside Pharo. You can open it using the World Menu, by selecting Tools > Process Browser (figure 7.23 shows a screenshot). The top-left pane lists all of the processes in Pharo, in priority order, from the timer interrupt watcher at priority 80 to the idle process at priority 10. Of course, on a uniprocessor, the only process that can be running when you look is the UI process; all others will be waiting for some kind of event.

By default, the display of processes is static; it can be updated by right-clicking and selecting Turn on auto-update (a).

If you select a process in the top-left pane, its stack trace is displayed in the top-right pane, just as with the debugger. If you select a stack frame, the corresponding method is displayed in the bottom pane. The process browser is not equipped with mini-inspectors for self and thisContext, but right-clicking on the stack frames provide equivalent functionality.

7.6 Finding methods

The *Finder* is one of several code search tools in Pharo to help you find methods by name (or even functionality). We've discussed it in some length in Chapter : A Quick Tour of Pharo.

7.7 Chapter summary

In order to develop effectively with Pharo, it is important to invest some effort into learning the tools available in the environment.

- The standard *browser* is your main interface for browsing existing packages, classes, method protocols and methods, and for defining new ones.
- The browser offers several useful shortcuts to directly jump to senders or implementors of a message, versions of a method, and so on.
- From any of the tools, you can highlight the name of a class or a method and immediately jump to a browser by using the keyboard shortcut CMD-b.
- You can also browse the Pharo system programmatically by sending messages to `SystemNavigation default`.
- The *Inspector* is a tool that is useful for exploring and interacting with live objects in your image.
- You can even inspect tools by meta-clicking to bring up their morphic halo and selecting the debug handle.
- The *Debugger* is a tool that not only lets you inspect the run-time stack of your program when an error is raised, but it also enables you to interact with all of the objects of your application, including the source code. In many cases you can modify your source code from the debugger and continue executing. The debugger is especially effective as a tool to support test-first development in tandem with SUnit (Chapter : SUnit).
- The *Process Browser* lets you monitor, query and interact with the processes current running in your image.
- The *Finder* is a tool for locating methods.

CHAPTER 8

Sharing code and source control

The consequence of programming in a world of live objects rather than with files and a text editor is that you have to do something explicit to export your program from your Pharo image. The old way of doing this is by creating a *fileout* or a *change set*, which are essentially encoded text files that can be imported into another system. The preferred way of sharing code in Pharo is to save packages and share them using a versioned repository on a server. Up to Pharo 50, this is done using a tool called Monticello, and is a much more powerful and effective way to work, especially when working in a team. In the future Pharo will officially offer support for Git and hosting on servers such as GitHub, BitBucket and more.

We gave you a quick overview of Monticello, Pharo's packaging tool, in Chapter : A First Application. However, Monticello has many more features than were discussed there. Because Monticello manages *packages*, before telling you more about Monticello, it's important that we first explain exactly what a package is.

8.1 Packages: groups of classes and methods

We have pointed out earlier (in Chapter : A First Application) packages are more or less a group of classes and methods. Now we will see exactly what the relationship is. The package system is a simple, lightweight way of organizing Pharo source code that exploits a simple naming convention.

Let's explain this using an example. Suppose that you are developing a framework to facilitate the use of relational databases from Pharo. You have decided to call your framework PharoLink, and have created a couple of classes such as OracleConnection, MySQLConnection, PostgresConnection but also

DBTable, DBRow, DBQuery, and so on. These classes are placed inside a package called PharoLink. However, not all of your code will reside in these classes. For example, you may also have a series of methods to convert objects into an SQL-friendly format: Object>>#asSQL, String>>#asSQL, or Date>>#asSQL.

These methods belong in the same package as the classes. But clearly the whole of class Object does not belong in your package! So you need a way of putting certain *methods* in a package, even though the rest of the class is in another package.

The way that you do this is by placing those methods in a protocol (of Object, String, Date, and so on) named *PharoLink (note the initial asterisk). The *PharoLink protocols added to the package named PharoLink. To be precise, the rules for what goes in a package are as follows.

A package named Foo contains: 1. All *class definitions* of classes in the package Foo.

2. All *methods* in *any class* in protocols named *Foo or *foo (When performing this comparison, the case of the letters in the names is ignored.), or whose name starts with *Foo- or *foo-.

3. All *methods* in classes in the package Foo *except* for those methods in protocols whose names start with *: Because classes of package Foo can be also extended by other packages.

A consequence of these rules is that each class definition and each method belongs to exactly one package.

Accessing packages

The class RPackage represents packages. The class RPackageOrganizer implements a singleton that holds all the Pharo packages. The following expressions are examples of the queries that you can perform.

```
(RPackageOrganizer default packageNamed: 'AST-Core') definedClassNames

(RPackageOrganizer default packageNamed: 'AST-Core') extendedClasses
```

Basic Monticello

When you open the Monticello browser, you will see two list panes and a row of buttons, as shown in Figure 8.1. The left-hand pane lists all of the packages that have been loaded into the image that you are running; the particular version of the package is shown in parentheses after the name.

The right-hand pane lists all of the source code repositories that Monticello knows about, usually because it has loaded code from them. If you select a

8.1 Packages: groups of classes and methods

Figure 8.1: The Monticello browser.

package in the left pane, the right pane is filtered to show only those repositories that contain versions of the selected package.

The package-cache

One of the repositories is a directory named *package-cache*, which is a subdirectory of the directory in which your image is running. When you load code from or write code to a remote repository, a copy is also saved in the package cache. This can be useful if the network is not available and you need to access a package. Also, if you are given a Monticello (.mcz) file directly, for example as an email attachment, the most convenient way to access it is to place it in the package-cache directory.

Adding repositories

To add a new repository to the list, click the +Repository, and choose the kind of repository from the pop-up menu. Let's add an HTTP repository.

> **To do**   Open Monticello, click on +Repository, and select HTTP. Edit the dialog to read:

```
MCHttpRepository
    location: 'http://squeaksource.com/PharoByExample'
    user: ''
    password: ''
```

Click on Open to open a repository browser on this repository. You should see something like Figure 8.2. On the left is a list of all of the packages in the repository; if you select one, then the pane on the right will show all of the versions of the selected package in this repository.

143

Sharing code and source control

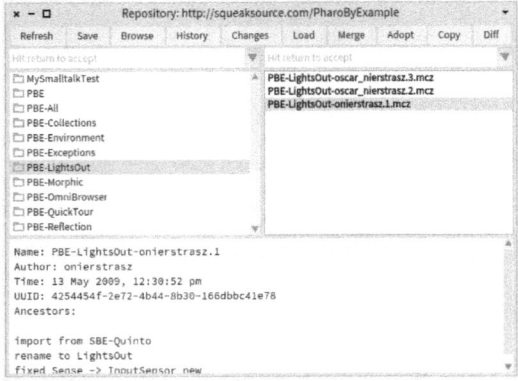

Figure 8.2: A Repository browser.

Browsing versions

If you select one of the versions, you can Browse it (without loading it into your image), Load it, or look at the Changes that will be made to your image by loading the selected version. You can also make a Copy of a version of a package, which you can then write to another repository.

As you can see, the names of versions contain the name of the package, the name of the author of the version, and a version number. The version name is also the name of the file in the repository. Never change these names; correct operation of Monticello depends on them! Monticello version files are just zip archives, and if you are curious you can unpack them with a zip tool, but the best way to look at their contents is using Monticello itself.

Creating a package

To create a package with Monticello, you have to do two things: write some code, and tell Monticello about it.

> **To do**   Create a package called PBE, and put a couple of classes in it, as shown in Figure 8.3. Also, create a method in an existing class, such as Object, and put it in the same package as your classes – see Figure 8.4.

Committing a package

When you add a package via the class browser, Monticello automatically add the package to its list. PBE is now in list of packages; the package entry will be marked with an asterisk to show that the version in the image has not yet been written to any repository (It is said to be *dirty*).

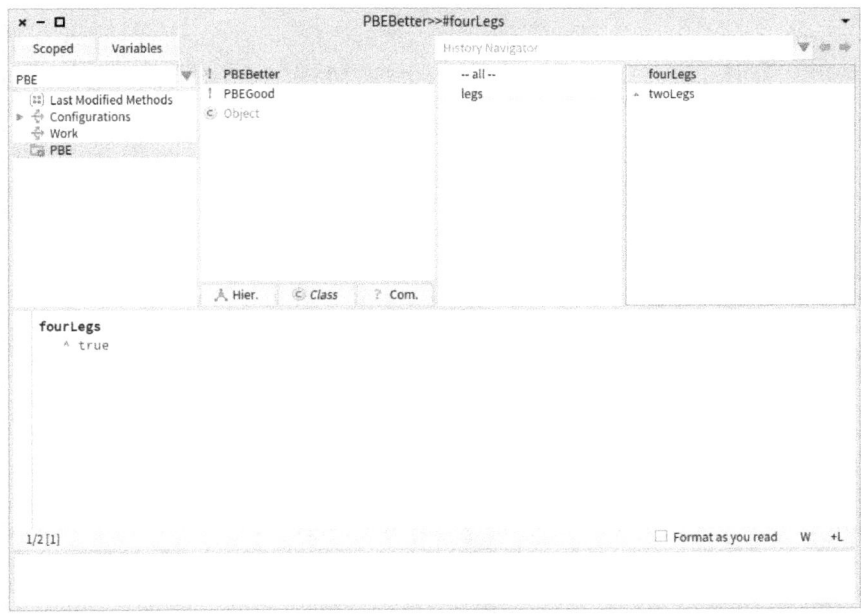

Figure 8.3: Two classes and one extension in the PBE package.

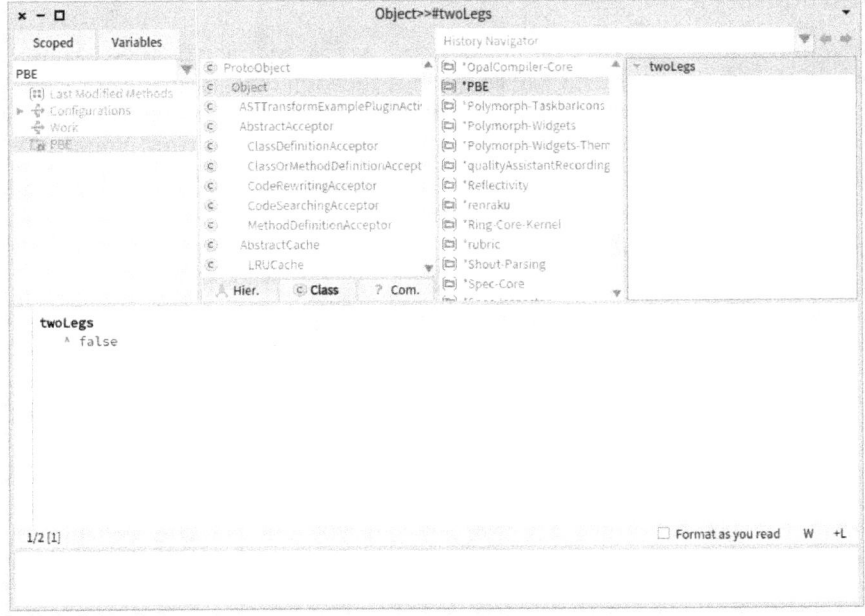

Figure 8.4: An extension method that is also be in the PBE package.

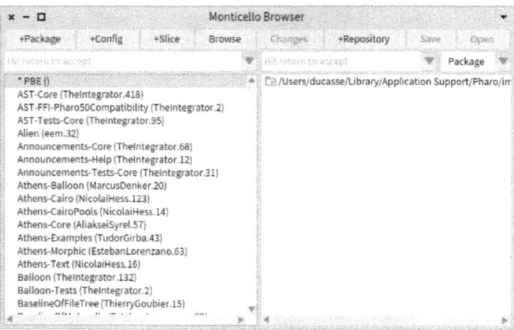

Figure 8.5: The as-yet-unsaved PBE package in Monticello.

Initially, the only repository associated with this package will be your package cache, as shown in Figure 8.5. That's OK: you can still save the code, which will cause it to be written to the package cache. Just click Save and you will be invited to provide a log message for the version of the package that you are about to save, as shown in Figure 8.6; when you accept the message, Monticello will save your package. To indicate this, the asterisk decorating the name in Monticello's package pane will be removed, and the version number added.

Introducing a change

If you then make a change to the package – say by adding a method to one of the classes – the asterisk will re-appear, showing that you have unsaved changes. If you open a repository browser on the package cache, you can select the saved version, and use Changes and the other buttons. You can of course save the new version to the repository too; once you Refresh the repository view, it should look like Figure 8.7.

To save the new package to a repository other than the package cache, you need to first make sure that Monticello knows about the repository, adding it if necessary. Then you can use the Copy in the package-cache repository browser, and select the repository to which the package should be copied. You can also associate the desired repository with the package by right-clicking on the repository and selecting add to package... and select the corresponding package. Once the package knows about a repository, you can save a new version by selecting the repository and the package in the Monticello Browser, and clicking Save. Of course, you must have permission to write to a repository. The PharoByExample repository on SqueakSource is world readable but not world writable, so if you try and save there, you will see an error message.

However, you can create your own repository and save your code there. Nowadays the favorite code repositories are http://www.smalltalkhub.org and http://ss3.gemstone.com. This is especially useful as a mechanism to share

Figure 8.6: Providing a log message for a new version of a package.

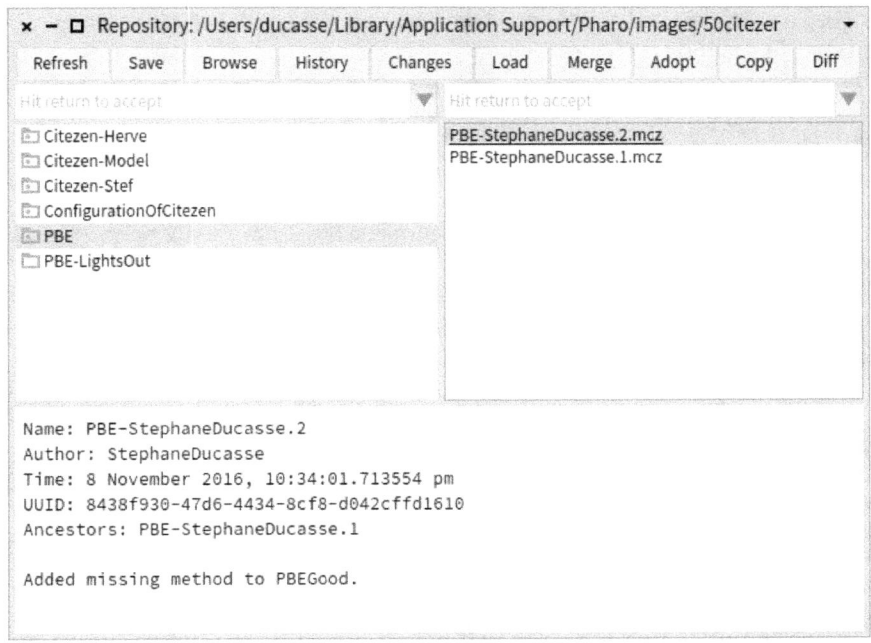

Figure 8.7: Two versions of our package are now in the package cache.

Sharing code and source control

Figure 8.8: The versions browser showing two versions of the `ObjTest>>testIVOffset` method.

your code with others and to make sure that you can use automated build systems such as Jenkins or Travis.

If you do try and save to a repository where you don't have write permission, a version will nevertheless be written to the package-cache. So you can recover by editing the repository information (right-click in the Monticello Browser) or choosing a different repository, and then using Copy from the package-cache browser.

8.2 Source control

Versions of a method

When you save a new version of a method, the old one is not lost. Pharo keeps all of the old versions (assuming that you are using the same image and that you saved it), and allows you to compare different versions and to go back (revert) to an old version.

The `browse > versions (v)` menu item gives access to the successive modifications made to the selected method. In Figure 8.8 we can see two versions of a method.

8.2 Source control

The top pane displays one line for each version of the method, listing the name of the programmer who wrote it, the date and time at which it was saved, the names of the class and the method, and the protocol in which it was defined. The current (active) version is at the top of the list.

The existence of the versions browser means that you never have to worry about preserving code that you think might no longer be needed. If you find that you *do* need it, you can always revert to the old version, or copy the needed code fragment out of the old version and paste it into a another method. Get into the habit of using versions; commenting out code that is no longer needed is a bad practice because it makes the current code harder to read. Pharoers rate code readability extremely highly.

Hint: What if you delete a method entirely, and then decide that you want it back? You can find the deletion in a change set, where you can ask to see versions by right-clicking. The change set browser is described in section 8.2.

Change sets and the changesorter

Whenever you are working in Pharo, any changes that you make to methods and classes are recorded in a *change set*. This includes creating new classes, renaming classes, changing categories, adding methods to existing classes – just about everything of significance. However, arbitrary *Do it*s are not included.

At any time, many change sets exist, but only one of them – ChangeSet current – is collecting the changes that are being made to the image. You can see which change set is current and can examine all of the change sets using the change sorter, available by selecting World > Tools... > Change Sorter.

Figure 8.9 shows the dual change sorter browser. The title bar shows which change set is current, and this change set is selected when the change sorter opens.

Other change sets can be selected in the top-left pane; the right-click menu allows you to make a different change set current, or to create a new change set. The next pane lists all of the classes affected by the selected change set (with their categories). Selecting one of the classes displays the names of its methods that are also in the change set (*not* all of the methods in the class) in the left central pane, and selecting a method name displays the method definition in the bottom pane.

The change sorter also lets you delete classes and methods from the change set using the right-click menu on the corresponding items.

The change sorter allows you to simultaneously view two change sets, one on the left hand side and the other on the right. This layout supports the change sorter's main feature, which is the ability to move or copy changes from one change set to another, as shown by the right-click menu in Figure 8.9. It is also possible to copy individual methods from one side to the other.

Sharing code and source control

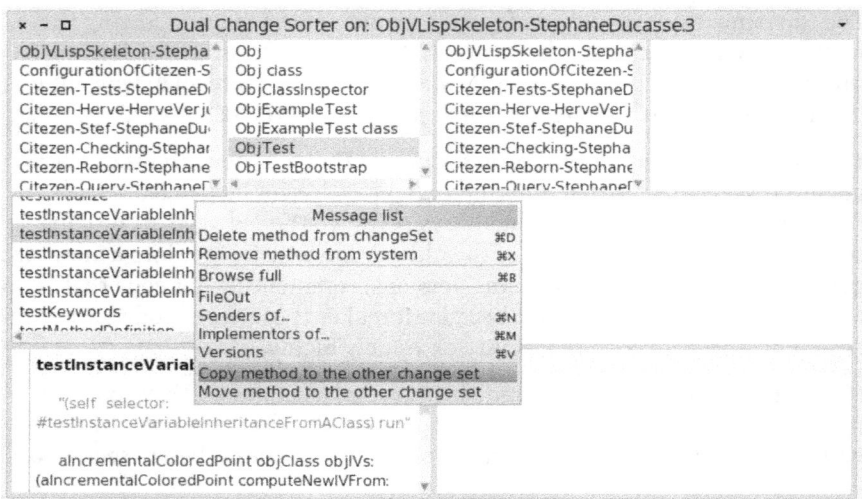

Figure 8.9: The Change Sorter showing all the changes of one changeset and offering actions to move changes to other changesets.

You may be wondering why you should care about the composition of a change set. the answer is that change sets provide a simple mechanism for exporting code from Pharo to the file system, from where it can be imported into another Pharo image. Change set export is known as `Filing-out`, and can be accomplished using the right-click menu on any change set, class or method in either browser. Repeated file outs create new versions of the file, but change sets are not a versioning tool like Monticello: they do not keep track of dependencies.

Before the advent of Monticello, change sets were the main means for exchanging code between Pharoers. They have the advantage of simplicity (the file out is just a text file, although we *don't* recommend that you try to edit them with a text editor), and a degree of portability.

The main drawback of change sets, compared to Monticello packages, is that they do not support the notion of dependencies. In spite of these shortcomings, change sets still have their uses. In particular, you may find change sets on the Internet that you want to look at and perhaps use. So, having filed out a change set using the change sorter, we will now tell you how to file one in. This requires the use of another tool, the file list browser. Note that dropping a changeset on Pharo itself works brings a pop up to ask you whether you want to load or browse the code contained in a changeset.

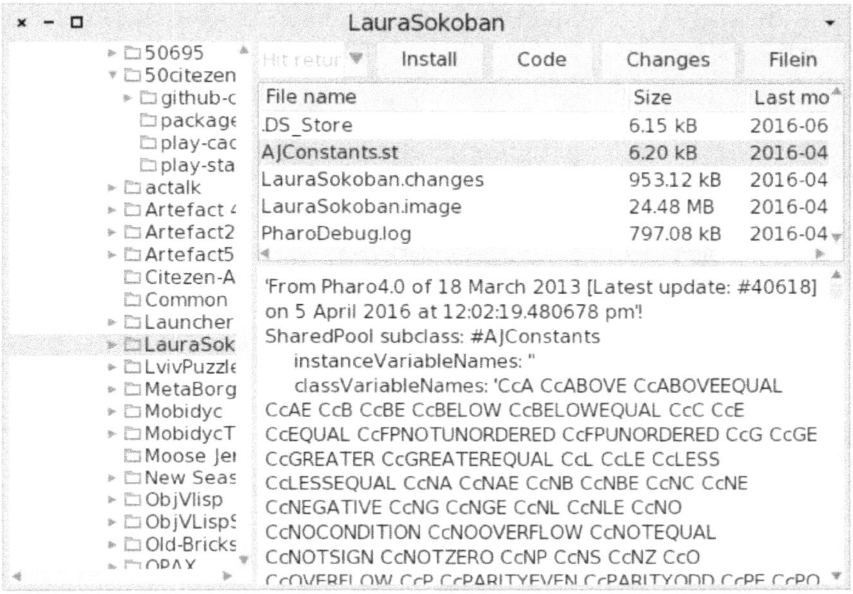

Figure 8.10: A file list browser.

8.3 The File List Browser

The file list browser is in fact a general-purpose tool for browsing the file system (as well as FTP servers) from Pharo. You can open it from the World > Tools... > File Browser menu. What you see of course depends on the contents of your local file system, but a typical view is shown in Figure 8.10.

When you first open a file list browser it will be focused on the current directory, that is, the one from which you started Pharo. The title bar shows the directory name. The larger pane on the left-hand side can be used to navigate the file system in the conventional way. When a directory is selected, the files that it contains (but not the directories) are displayed on the right. This list of files can be filtered by entering a Unix-style pattern in the small box at the top-left of the window. Initially, this pattern is *, which matches all file names, but you can type a different string there and accept it, changing the pattern. (Note that a * is implicitly prepended and appended to the pattern that you type.) The sort order of the files can be changed using the name, date and size buttons. The rest of the buttons depend on the name of the file selected in the browser. In Figure 8.10, the file name has the suffix .st, so the browser assumes that it is pharo code, and provides the possible actions as buttons.

Because the choice of buttons to display depends on the file's *name*, and not on its contents, sometimes the button that you want won't be on the screen.

Sharing code and source control

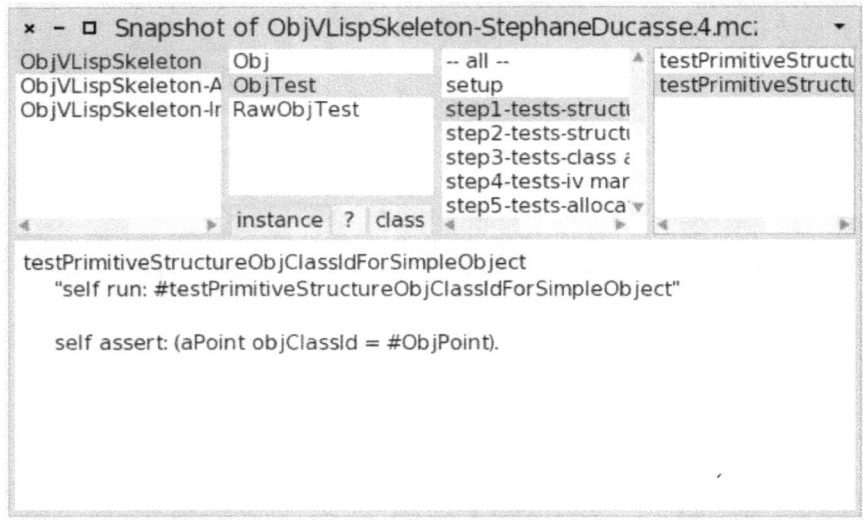

Figure 8.11: A File Contents Browser opened on a package .

However, the full set of options is always available from the right-click more... menu, so you can easily work around this problem.

The code button is perhaps the most useful for working with change sets; it opens a browser on the contents of the change set file or even an MC package; an example is shown in Figure 8.11. The file contents browser is similar to the browser except that the code is not loaded in memory.

8.4 In Pharo, you can't lose code

It is quite possible to crash Pharo: as an experimental system, Pharo lets you change anything, including things that are vital to make Pharo work!

The good news is that you will never lose any work, even if you crash and go back to the last saved version of your image, which might be hours old. This is because all of the code that you executed is saved in the *.changes* file. This excludes Playground snippets , those are stored inside */pharo-local/play-chace*and they can be searched using Spotter (the results are displayed under Playground-cached pages section).

So here are the instructions on how to get your code back. There is no need to read this until you need it. However, when you do need it, you'll find it here waiting for you.

In the worst case, you can use a text editor on the *.changes* file, but since it is many megabytes in size, this can be slow and is not recommended. Pharo offers you better ways.

How to get your code back

Restart Pharo from the most recent snapshot, and select `World > Tools... > Recover lost changes`.

```
Smalltalk recover: 10000.
ChangeList browseRecentLog.
ChangeList browseRecent: 2000.
```

This will give you the opportunity to decide how far back in history you wish to browse. Normally, it's sufficient to browse changes as far back as the last snapshot. (You can get much the same effect by editing `ChangeList browseRecent: 2000` so that the number 2000 becomes something else, using trial and error.)

Once you have a *recent changes* browser, showing, say, changes back as far as your last snapshot, you will have a list of everything that you have done to Pharo during that time. You can delete items from this list using the right-click menu. When you are satisfied, you can file-in what is left, thus incorporating the changes into your new image. It's a good idea to start a new change set, using the ordinary change set browser, before you do the file in, so that all of your recovered code will be in a new change set. You can then file out this change set.

One useful thing to do in the *recent changes* browser is to `remove doIts`. Usually, you won't want to file in (and thus re-execute) doIts. However, there is an exception. Creating a class shows up as a doIt.

Before you can file in the methods for a class, the class must exist. So, if you have created any new classes, *first* file-in the class creation doIts, then `remove doIts` and file in the methods.

When I am finished with the recovery, I like to file out my new change set, quit Pharo without saving the image, restart, and make sure that the new change set files back in cleanly.

8.5 Chapter summary

- *Monticello* is a tool for exporting, importing, versioning and sharing packages of classes and methods.
- A Monticello package consists of classes, and related methods in other packages.
- *Change sets* are automatically generated logs of all changes to the source code of your image. They have largely been superseded by Monticello as a means to store and exchange versions of your source code, but are

still useful, especially for recovering from catastrophic failures, however rare these may be.

- The *file list browser* is a tool for browsing the file system. It also allows you to `File in` source code from the file system.
- In case your image crashes before you could save it or backup your source code with Monticello, you can always recover your most recent changes using a *change list browser*. You can then select the changes you want to replay and file them into the most recent copy of your image.

CHAPTER 9

SUnit

SUnit is a minimal yet powerful framework that supports the creation and deployment of tests. As might be guessed from its name, the design of SUnit focussed on *Unit Tests*, but in fact it can be used for integration tests and functional tests as well. SUnit was originally developed by Kent Beck and subsequently extended by Joseph Pelrine and others to incorporate the notion of a resource (discussed below).

In this chapter we start by discussing why we test, and what makes a good test. We then present a series of small examples showing how to use SUnit. Finally, we look at the implementation of SUnit, so that you can understand how Pharo uses the power of reflection in supporting its tools. Note that the version documented in this chapter and used in Pharo is a modified version of SUnit3.3.

9.1 Introduction

The interest in testing and Test Driven Development is not limited to Pharo. Automated testing has become a hallmark of the *Agile software development* movement, and any software developer concerned with improving software quality would do well to adopt it. Indeed, developers in many languages have come to appreciate the power of unit testing, and versions of *xUnit* now exist for every programming language.

Neither testing, nor the building of test suites, is new. By now, everybody knows that tests are a good way to catch errors. eXtreme Programming, by making testing a core practice and by emphasizing *automated* tests, has helped to make testing productive and fun, rather than a chore that programmers dislike. The Pharo community has a long tradition of testing because of the incremental style of development supported by its programming environment. In traditional Pharo development, the programmer would write tests in a playground as soon as a method was finished. Sometimes a test would be incorporated as a comment at the head of the method that it exercised, or tests that needed some set up would be included as example methods in the class. The problem with these practices is that tests in a playground are not available to other programmers who modify the code. Comments and example methods are better in this respect, but there is still no easy way to keep track of them and to run them automatically. Tests that are not run do not help you to find bugs! Moreover, an example method does not inform the reader of the expected result: you can run the example and see the (perhaps surprising) result, but you will not know if the observed behaviour is correct.

SUnit is valuable because it allows us to write tests that are self-checking: the test itself defines what the correct result should be. It also helps us to organize tests into groups, to describe the context in which the tests must run, and to run a group of tests automatically. In less than two minutes you can write tests using SUnit, so instead of writing small code snippets in a playground, we encourage you to use SUnit and get all the advantages of stored and automatically executable tests.

9.2 Why testing is important

Unfortunately, many developers believe that tests are a waste of their time. After all, *they* do not write bugs, only *other* programmers do that. Most of us have said, at some time or other: *I would write tests if I had more time.* If you never write a bug, and if your code will never be changed in the future, then indeed tests are a waste of your time. However, this most likely also means that your application is trivial, or that it is not used by you or anyone else. Think of tests as an investment for the future: having a suite of tests is quite useful now, but it will be *extremely* useful when your application, or the environment in which it runs, changes in the future.

Tests play several roles. First, they provide documentation of the functionality that they cover. This documentation is active: watching the tests pass tells you that the documentation is up to date. Second, tests help developers to confirm that some changes that they have just made to a package have not broken anything else in the system, and to find the parts that break when that confidence turns out to be misplaced. Finally, writing tests during, or even before, programming forces you to think about the functionality that you want to design, *and how it should appear to the client code*, rather than about how to implement it.

By writing the tests first, i.e., before the code, you are compelled to state the context in which your functionality will run, the way it will interact with the client code, and the expected results. Your code will improve. Try it.

We cannot test all aspects of any realistic application. Covering a complete application is simply impossible and should not be the goal of testing. Even with a good test suite some bugs will still creep into the application, where they can lay dormant waiting for an opportunity to damage your system. If you find that this has happened, take advantage of it! As soon as you uncover the bug, write a test that exposes it, run the test, and watch it fail. Now you can start to fix the bug: the test will tell you when you are done.

9.3 What makes a good test?

Writing good tests is a skill that can be learned by practicing. Let us look at the properties that tests should have to get the maximum benefit.

Tests should be repeatable. You should be able to run a test as often as you want, and always get the same answer.

Tests should run without human intervention. You should be able to run them unattended.

Tests should tell a story. Each test should cover one aspect of a piece of code. A test should act as a scenario that you or someone else can read to understand a piece of functionality.

Tests should have a change frequency lower than that of the functionality they cover. You do not want to have to change all your tests every time you modify your application. One way to achieve this is to write tests based on the public interfaces of the class that you are testing. It is OK to write a test for a private *helper* method if you feel that the method is complicated enough to need the test, but you should be aware that such a test may have to be changed, or thrown away entirely, when you think of a better implementation.

One consequence of such properties is that the number of tests should be somewhat proportional to the number of functions to be tested: changing one aspect of the system should not break all the tests but only a limited number. This is important because having 100 tests fail should send a much stronger message than having 10 tests fail. However, it is not always possible to achieve this ideal: in particular, if a change breaks the initialization of an object, or the set-up of a test, it is likely to cause all of the tests to fail.

Several software development methodologies such as *eXtreme Programming* and Test-Driven Development (TDD) advocate writing tests before writing code. This may seem to go against our deep instincts as software developers. All we can say is: go ahead and try it. We have found that writing the tests before the code helps us to know what we want to code, helps us know when we are done, and helps us conceptualize the functionality of a class and to design its interface. Moreover, test-first development gives us the courage to go fast, because we are not afraid that we will forget something important.

Writing tests is not difficult in itself. Choosing *what* to test is much more difficult. The pragmatic programmers offer the "right-BICEP" principle. It stands for:

- Right: Are the results right?
- B: Are all the boundary conditions correct?
- I: Can you check inverse relationships?
- C: Can you cross-check results using other means?
- E: Can you force error conditions to happen?
- P: Are performance characteristics within bounds?

Now let's write our first test, and show you the benefits of using SUnit.

9.4 SUnit by example

Before going into the details of SUnit, we will show a step by step example. We use an example that tests the class Set. Try entering the code as we go along.

Step 1: Create the test class

First you should create a new subclass of TestCase called MyExampleSetTest. Add two instance variables so that your new class looks like this:

```
TestCase subclass: #MyExampleSetTest
    instanceVariableNames: 'full empty'
    classVariableNames: ''
    package: 'MySetTest'
```

We will use the class MyExampleSetTest to group all the tests related to the class Set. It defines the context in which the tests will run. Here the context is described by the two instance variables full and empty that we will use to represent a full and an empty set.

The name of the class is not critical, but by convention it should end in Test. If you define a class called Pattern and call the corresponding test class PatternTest, the two classes will be alphabetized together in the browser (assuming that they are in the same package). It *is* critical that your class is a subclass of TestCase.

Step 2: Initialize the test context

The message TestCase >> setUp defines the context in which the tests will run, a bit like an initialize method. setUp is invoked before the execution of each test method defined in the test class.

9.4 SUnit by example

Define the `setUp` method as follows, to initialize the `empty` variable to refer to an empty set and the `full` variable to refer to a set containing two elements.

```
MyExampleSetTest >> setUp
    empty := Set new.
    full := Set with: 5 with: 6
```

In testing jargon the context is called the *fixture* for the test.

Step 3: write some test methods

Let's create some tests by defining some methods in the class `MyExampleSetTest`. Each method represents one test. The names of the methods should start with the string `'test'` so that SUnit will collect them into test suites. Test methods take no arguments.

Define the following test methods. The first test, named `testIncludes`, tests the `includes:` method of `Set`. The test says that sending the message `includes: 5` to a set containing 5 should return `true`. Clearly, this test relies on the fact that the `setUp` method has already run.

```
MyExampleSetTest >> testIncludes
    self assert: (full includes: 5).
    self assert: (full includes: 6)
```

The second test, named `testOccurrences`, verifies that the number of occurrences of 5 in `full` set is equal to one, even if we add another element 5 to the set.

```
MyExampleSetTest >> testOccurrences
    self assert: (empty occurrencesOf: 0) = 0.
    self assert: (full occurrencesOf: 5) = 1.
    full add: 5.
    self assert: (full occurrencesOf: 5) = 1
```

Finally, we test that the set no longer contains the element 5 after we have removed it.

```
MyExampleSetTest >> testRemove
    full remove: 5.
    self assert: (full includes: 6).
    self deny: (full includes: 5)
```

Note the use of the method `TestCase >> deny:` to assert something that should not be true. `aTest deny: anExpression` is equivalent to `aTest assert: anExpression not`, but is much more readable.

Step 4: Run the tests

The easiest way to run the tests is directly from the browser. Simply click on the icon of the class name, or on an individual test method, and select *Run tests*

SUnit

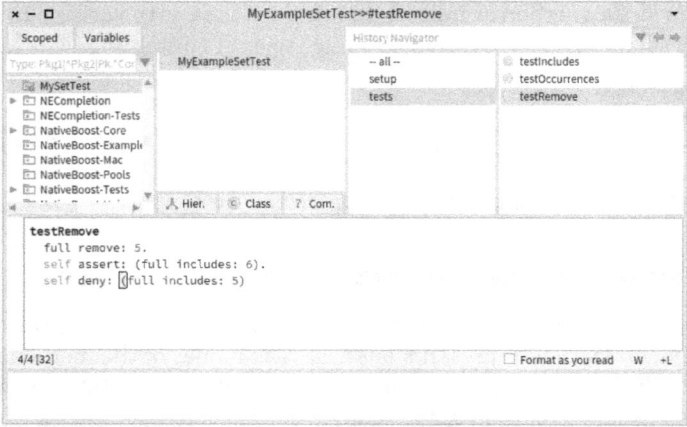

Figure 9.1: Running SUnit tests from the System Browser.

(t) or press the icon. The test methods will be flagged green or red, depending on whether they pass or not (as shown in 9.1).

You can also select sets of test suites to run, and obtain a more detailed log of the results using the SUnit Test Runner, which you can open by selecting World > Test Runner.

The *Test Runner*, shown in Figure 9.2, is designed to make it easy to execute groups of tests.

The left-most pane lists all of the packages that contain test classes (i.e., subclasses of TestCase). When some of these packages are selected, the test classes that they contain appear in the pane to the right. Abstract classes are italicized, and the test class hierarchy is shown by indentation, so subclasses of ClassTestCase are indented more than subclasses of TestCase. ClassTestCase is a class offering utilities methods to compute test coverage.

Open a Test Runner, select the package *MySetTest*, and click the Run Selected button.

You can also run a single test (and print the usual pass/fail result summary) by executing a *Print it* on the following code: MyExampleSetTest run: #testRemove.

Some people include an executable comment in their test methods that allows running a test method with a *Do it* from the browser, as shown below.

```
MyExampleSetTest >> testRemove
    "self run: #testRemove"
    full remove: 5.
    self assert: (full includes: 6).
    self deny: (full includes: 5)
```

9.4 SUnit by example

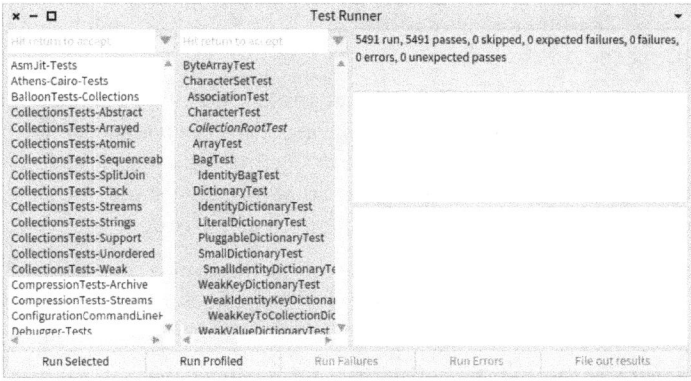

Figure 9.2: Running SUnit tests using the *TestRunner*.

Introduce a bug in `MyExampleSetTest >> testRemove` and run the tests again. For example, change 6 to 7, as in:

```
MyExampleSetTest >> testRemove
    full remove: 5.
    self assert: (full includes: 7).
    self deny: (full includes: 5)
```

The tests that did not pass (if any) are listed in the right-hand panes of the *Test Runner*. If you want to debug one, to see why it failed, just click on the name. Alternatively, you can execute one of the following expressions:

```
(MyExampleSetTest selector: #testRemove) debug

MyExampleSetTest debug: #testRemove
```

Step 5: Interpret the results

The method `assert:` is defined in the class `TestAsserter`. This is a superclass of `TestCase` and therefore all other `TestCase` subclasses and is responsible for all kind of test result assertions. The `assert:` method expects a boolean argument, usually the value of a tested expression. When the argument is true, the test passes; when the argument is false, the test fails.

There are actually three possible outcomes of a test: *passing*, *failing*, and *raising an error*.

- **Passing.** The outcome that we hope for is that all of the assertions in the test are true, in which case the test passes. In the test runner, when all of the tests pass, the bar at the top turns green. However, there are two other ways that running a test can go wrong.

161

- **Failing.** The obvious way is that one of the assertions can be false, causing the test to *fail*.
- **Error.** The other possibility is that some kind of error occurs during the execution of the test, such as a *message not understood* error or an *index out of bounds* error. If an error occurs, the assertions in the test method may not have been executed at all, so we can't say that the test has failed; nevertheless, something is clearly wrong!

In the *test runner*, failing tests cause the bar at the top to turn yellow, and are listed in the middle pane on the right, whereas tests with errors cause the bar to turn red, and are listed in the bottom pane on the right.

Modify your tests to provoke both errors and failures.

9.5 The SUnit cookbook

This section will give you more details on how to use SUnit. If you have used another testing framework such as JUnit, much of this will be familiar, since all these frameworks have their roots in SUnit. Normally you will use SUnit's GUI to run tests, but there are situations where you may not want to use it.

Other assertions

In addition to `assert:` and `deny:`, there are several other methods that can be used to make assertions.

First, `TestAsserter >> assert:description:` and `TestAsserter >> deny:description:` take a second argument which is a message string that describes the reason for the failure, if it is not obvious from the test itself. These methods are described in Section 9.7.

Next, SUnit provides two additional methods, `TestAsserter >> should:raise:` and `TestAsserter >> shouldnt:raise:` for testing exception propagation.

For example, you would use `self should: aBlock raise: anException` to test that a particular exception is raised during the execution of `aBlock`. The method below illustrates the use of `should:raise:`.

```
MyExampleSetTest >> testIllegal
    self should: [ empty at: 5 ] raise: Error.
    self should: [ empty at: 5 put: #zork ] raise: Error
```

Try running this test. Note that the first argument of the `should:` and `shouldnt:` methods is a block that contains the expression to be executed.

Running a single test

Normally, you will run your tests using the Test Runner or using your code browser. If you don't want to launch the Test Runner from the World menu,

9.6 The SUnit framework

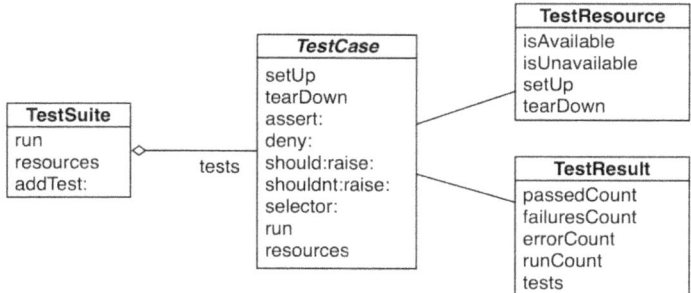

Figure 9.3: The four classes representing the core of SUnit.

you can execute `TestRunner open`. You can also run a single test as follows:

```
MyExampleSetTest run: #testRemove
>>> 1 run, 1 passed, 0 failed, 0 errors
```

Running all the tests in a test class

Any subclass of `TestCase` responds to the message `suite`, which will build a test suite that contains all the methods in the class whose names start with the string *test*.

To run the tests in the suite, send it the message `run`. For example:

```
MyExampleSetTest suite run
>>> 5 run, 5 passed, 0 failed, 0 errors
```

Must I subclass TestCase?

In JUnit you can build a TestSuite from an arbitrary class containing `test*` methods. In SUnit you can do the same but you will then have to create a suite by hand and your class will have to implement all the essential `TestCase` methods like `assert:`. We recommend, however, that you not try to do this. The framework is there: use it.

9.6 The SUnit framework

SUnit consists of four main classes: `TestCase`, `TestSuite`, `TestResult`, and `TestResource`, as shown in Figure 9.3. The notion of a *test resource* represents a resource that is expensive to set-up but which can be used by a whole series of tests. A `TestResource` specifies a `setUp` method that is executed just once before a suite of tests; this is in distinction to the `TestCase >> setUp` method, which is executed before each test.

TestCase

TestCase is an abstract class that is designed to be subclassed. Each of its subclasses represents a group of tests that share a common context (that is, a test suite). Each test is run by creating a new instance of a subclass of TestCase, running setUp, running the test method itself, and then sending the tearDown.

The context is specified by instance variables of the subclass and by the specialization of the method setUp, which initializes those instance variables. Subclasses of TestCase can also override method tearDown, which is invoked after the execution of each test, and can be used to release any objects allocated during setUp.

TestSuite

Instances of the class TestSuite contain a collection of test cases. An instance of TestSuite contains tests, and other test suites. That is, a test suite contains sub-instances of TestCase and TestSuite.

Both individual test cases and test suites understand the same protocol, so they can be treated in the same way (for example, both can be run). This is in fact an application of the Composite pattern in which TestSuite is the composite and the test cases are the leaves.

TestResult

The class TestResult represents the results of a TestSuite execution. It records the number of tests passed, the number of tests failed, and the number of errors signalled.

TestResource

One of the important features of a suite of tests is that they should be independent of each other. The failure of one test should not cause an avalanche of failures of other tests that depend upon it, nor should the order in which the tests are run matter. Performing setUp before each test and tearDown afterwards helps to reinforce this independence.

However, there are occasions where setting up the necessary context is just too time-consuming for it to be done before the execution of each test. Moreover, if it is known that the test cases do not disrupt the resources used by the tests, then it is wasteful to set them up afresh for each test. It is sufficient to set them up once for each suite of tests. Suppose, for example, that a suite of tests needs to query a database, or do analysis on some compiled code. In such cases, it may make sense to set up the database and open a connection to it, or to compile some source code, before any of the tests start to run.

9.6 The SUnit framework

Where should we cache these resources, so that they can be shared by a suite of tests? The instance variables of a particular TestCase subclass won't do, because a TestCase instance persists only for the duration of a single test (as mentioned before, the instance is created anew *for each test method*). A global variable would work, but using too many global variables pollutes the name space, and the binding between the global and the tests that depend on it will not be explicit. A better solution is to put the necessary resources in a singleton object of some class. The class TestResource exists to be subclassed by such resource classes. Each subclass of TestResource understands the message current, which will answer a singleton instance of that subclass. Methods setUp and tearDown should be overridden in the subclass to ensure that the resource is initialized and finalized.

One thing remains: somehow, SUnit has to be told which resources are associated with which test suite. A resource is associated with a particular subclass of TestCase by overriding the *class* method resources.

By default, the resources of a TestSuite are the union of the resources of the TestCases that it contains.

Here is an example. We define a subclass of TestResource called MyTestResource. Then we associate it with MyTestCase by overriding the class method MyTestCase class >> resources to return an array of the test resource classes that MyTestCase will use.

```
TestResource subclass: #MyTestResource
    instanceVariableNames: ''
    ...

MyTestCase class >> resources
    "Associate the resource with this class of test cases"

    ^ { MyTestResource }
```

Exercise

The following trace (written to the Transcript) illustrates that a global set up is run before and after each test in a sequence. Let's see if you can obtain this trace yourself.

```
MyTestResource >> setUp has run.
MyTestCase >> setUp has run.
MyTestCase >> testOne has run.
MyTestCase >> tearDown has run.
MyTestCase >> setUp has run.
MyTestCase >> testTwo has run.
MyTestCase >> tearDown has run.
MyTestResource >> tearDown has run.
```

Create new classes `MyTestResource` and `MyTestCase` which are subclasses of `TestResource` and `TestCase` respectively. Add the appropriate methods so that the following messages are written to the `Transcript` when you run your tests.

Solution. You will need to write the following six methods.

```
MyTestCase >> setUp
    Transcript show: 'MyTestCase>>setUp has run.'; cr

MyTestCase >> tearDown
    Transcript show: 'MyTestCase>>tearDown has run.'; cr

MyTestCase >> testOne
    Transcript show: 'MyTestCase>>testOne has run.'; cr

MyTestCase >> testTwo
    Transcript show: 'MyTestCase>>testTwo has run.'; cr

MyTestCase class >> resources
    ^ Array with: MyTestResource

MyTestResource >> setUp
    Transcript show: 'MyTestResource>>setUp has run'; cr

MyTestResource >> tearDown
    Transcript show: 'MyTestResource>>tearDown has run.'; cr
```

9.7 Advanced features of SUnit

In addition to `TestResource`, SUnit contains assertion description strings, logging support, the ability to skip tests, and resumable test failures.

Assertion description strings

The `TestAsserter` assertion protocol includes a number of methods that allow the programmer to supply a description of the assertion. The description is a `String`; if the test case fails, this string will be displayed by the test runner. Of course, this string can be constructed dynamically.

```
...
e := 42.
self assert: e = 23 description: 'expected 23, got ', e printString
...
```

The relevant methods in `TestAsserter` are:
```
assert:description:
deny:description:
```

9.7 Advanced features of SUnit

```
should:description:
shouldnt:description:
```

Using assert:equals:

In addition to `assert:`, there is also `assert:equals:` that offers a better report in case of error (incidentally, `assert:equals:` uses `assert:description:`).

For example, the two following tests are equivalent. However, the second one will report the value that the test is expecting: this makes easier to understand the failure. In this example, we suppose that aDateAndTime is an instance variable of the test class.

```
testAsDate
   self assert: aDateAndTime asDate = ('February 29, 2004' asDate
      translateTo: 2 hours).

testAsDate
   self
      assert: aDateAndTime asDate
      equals: ('February 29, 2004' asDate translateTo: 2 hours).
```

Logging support

The description strings mentioned above may also be logged to a `Stream`, such as the `Transcript` or a file stream. You can choose whether to log by overriding `isLogging` in your test class; you must also choose where to log by overriding `failureLog` to answer an appropriate stream. By default, the `Transcript` is used to log.

Skipping tests

Sometimes in the middle of a development, you may want to skip a test instead of removing it or renaming it to prevent it from running. You can simply invoke the `TestAsserter` message `skip` on your test case instance. For example, the following test uses it to define a conditional test.

```
OCCompiledMethodIntegrityTest >> testPragmas

   | newCompiledMethod originalCompiledMethod |
   (Smalltalk globals hasClassNamed: #Compiler) ifFalse: [ ^ self skip
      ].
   ...
```

9.8 Continuing after a failure

SUnit also allows us to specify whether or not a test should continue after a failure. This is a really powerful feature that uses Pharo's exception mechanisms. To see what this can be used for, let's look at an example. Consider the following test expression:

```
[ aCollection do: [ :each | self assert: each even ]
```

In this case, as soon as the test finds the first element of the collection that isn't even, the test stops. However, we would usually like to continue, and see both how many elements, and which elements, aren't even (and maybe also log this information). You can do this as follows:

```
aCollection do: [ :each |
    self
        assert: each even
        description: each printString, ' is not even'
        resumable: true ]
```

This will print out a message on your logging stream for each element that fails. It doesn't accumulate failures, i.e, if the assertion fails 10 times in your test method, you'll still only see one failure. All the other assertion methods that we have seen are not resumable by default; assert: p description: s is equivalent to assert: p description: s resumable: false.

9.9 SUnit implementation

The implementation of SUnit makes an interesting case study of a Pharo framework. Let's look at some key aspects of the implementation by following the execution of a test.

Running one test

To execute one test, we execute the expression (aTestClass selector: aSymbol) run.

The method TestCase >> run creates an instance of TestResult that will accumulate the results of the test, then it sends itself the message TestCase >> run: (See Figure 9.4).

```
TestCase >> run
    | result |
    result := self classForTestResult new.
    [ self run: result ]
        ensure: [ self classForTestResource resetResources: self resources
            ].
    ^ result
```

9.9 SUnit implementation

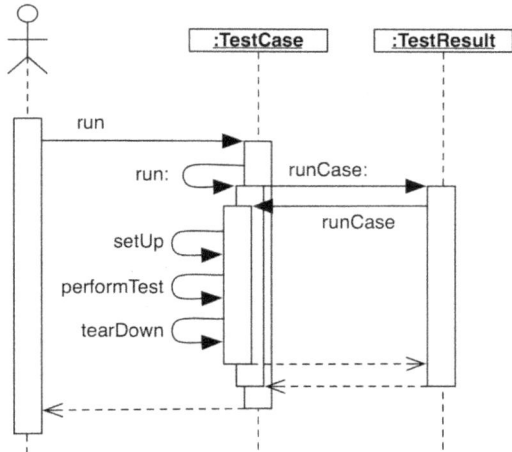

Figure 9.4: Running one test.

The method `TestCase >> run:` sends the message `runCase:` to the test result:

```
TestCase >> run: aResult
    aResult runCase: self
```

The method `TestResult >> runCase:` sends the message `TestCase >> runCase` to an individual test, to execute the test. `TestResult >> runCase` deals with any exceptions that may be raised during the execution of a test, runs a `TestCase` by sending it the `runCase`, and counts the errors, failures, and passes.

```
TestResult >> runCase: aTestCase
    [
    aTestCase announce: TestCaseStarted withResult: self.
    aTestCase runCase.
    aTestCase announce: TestCaseEnded withResult: self.
    self addPass: aTestCase ]
        on: self class failure, self class skip, self class warning, self
            class error
        do: [ :ex | ex sunitAnnounce: aTestCase toResult: self ]
```

The method `TestCase >> runCase` sends the messages `TestCase >> setUp` and `TestCase >> tearDown` as shown below.

```
TestCase >> runCase
    self resources do: [ :each | each availableFor: self ].
    [ self setUp.
    self performTest ] ensure: [
        self tearDown.
        self cleanUpInstanceVariables ]
```

Running a TestSuite

To run more than one test, we send the message run to a TestSuite that contains the relevant tests. TestCase class provides some functionality to build a test suite from its methods. The expression MyTestCase buildSuiteFromSelectors returns a suite containing all the tests defined in the MyTestCase class. The core of this process is:

```
TestCase class >> testSelectors
    ^ (self selectors select: [ :each | (each beginsWith: 'test') and: [
        each numArgs isZero ]])
```

The method TestSuite >> run creates an instance of TestResult, verifies that all the resources are available, and then sends itself the message TestSuite >> run:, which runs all the tests in the suite. All the resources are then released.

```
TestSuite >> run: aResult
    self setUp.
    [ self tests
        do: [ :each |
            each run: aResult.
            self announceTest: each.
            self changed: each ] ]
        ensure: [ self tearDown ]

TestSuite >> setUp
    self resources do: [ :each |
            each isAvailable ifFalse: [ each signalInitializationError ]
        ].

TestSuite >> tearDown
    self resourceClass resetResources: self resources
```

The class TestResource and its subclasses keep track of their currently created singleton instances that can be accessed and created using the class method TestResource class >> current. This instance is cleared when the tests have finished running and the resources are reset.

The resource availability check makes it possible for the resource to be re-created if needed, as shown in the class method TestResource class >> isAvailable. During the TestResource instance creation, it is initialized and the message setUp is sent to a test resource.

```
TestResource class >> isAvailable
    "This is (and must be) a lazy method. If my current has a value, an
        attempt to make me available has already been made: trust its
        result. If not, try to make me available."

    current ifNil: [ self makeAvailable ].
    ^ self isAlreadyAvailable
```

```
TestResource class >> current
    "This is a lazy accessor: the assert of self isAvailable does no
        work unless current isNil. However this method should normally
        be sent only to a resource that should already have been made
        available, e.g. in a test whose test case class has the resource
        class in its #resources, so should never be able to fail the
        assert.
    If the intent is indeed to access a possibly-unprepared or
        reset-in-earlier-test resource lazily, then preface the call of
        'MyResource current' with 'MyResource availableFor: self'."

    self
        assert: self isAvailable
        description:
            'Sent #current to unavailable resource ', self name,
            '. Add it to test case'' class-side #resources (recommended)
                or send #availableFor: beforehand'.
    ^ current
```

9.10 A piece of advices on testing

While the mechanics of testing are easy, writing good tests is not. Here is some advice on how to design tests.

Self-contained tests

You do not want to have to change your tests each time you change your code, so try to write the tests so that they are self-contained. This can be difficult, but pays off in the long term. Writing tests against stable interfaces supports this effort.

Do not over-test

Try to build your tests so that they do not overlap. It is annoying to have many tests covering the same functionality, because one bug in the code will then break many tests at the same time. This is covered by Black's rule, below.

Feathers' Rules for Unit tests

Michael Feathers, an agile process consultant and author, writes:

A test is not a unit test if: it talks to the database, it communicates across the network, it touches the file system, it can't run at the same time as any of your other unit tests, or you have to do special things to your environment (such as editing config files) to run it. Tests that do these things aren't bad. Often they are worth writing, and they can be written in a unit test harness. However, it is important to be able to separate them from true unit tests so that we can keep a set of tests that we can run fast whenever we make our changes. Never get yourself into a situation where you don't want to run your unit test suite because it takes too long.

Unit Tests vs. Acceptance Tests

Unit tests capture one piece of functionality, and as such make it easier to identify bugs in that functionality. As far as possible try to have unit tests for each method that could possibly fail, and group them per class. However, for certain deeply recursive or complex setup situations, it is easier to write tests that represent a scenario in the larger application. These are called acceptance tests (or integration tests, or functional tests). Tests that break Feathers' rules may make good acceptance tests. Group acceptance tests according to the functionality that they test. For example, if you are writing a compiler, you might write acceptance tests that make assertions about the code generated for each possible source language statement. Such tests might exercise many classes, and might take a long time to run because they touch the file system. You can write them using SUnit, but you won't want to run them each time you make a small change, so they should be separated from the true unit tests.

Black's Rule of Testing

For every test in the system, you should be able to identify some property for which the test increases your confidence. It's obvious that there should be no important property that you are not testing. This rule states the less obvious fact that there should be no test that does not add value to the system by increasing your confidence that a useful property holds. For example, several tests of the same property do no good. In fact, they do harm in two ways. First, they make it harder to infer the behaviour of the class by reading the tests. Second, because one bug in the code might then break many tests, they make it harder to estimate how many bugs remain in the code. So, have a property in mind when you write a test.

9.11 Chapter summary

This chapter explained why tests are an important investment in the future of your code. We explained in a step-by-step fashion how to define a few tests for the class Set. Then we gave an overview of the core of the SUnit framework by presenting the classes TestCase, TestResult, TestSuite and TestResources. Finally we looked deep inside SUnit by following the execution of a test and a test suite.

- To maximize their potential, unit tests should be fast, repeatable, independent of any direct human interaction and cover a single unit of functionality.

9.11 Chapter summary

- Tests for a class called `MyClass` belong in a class named `MyClassTest`, which should be introduced as a subclass of `TestCase`.
- Initialize your test data in a `setUp` method.
- Each test method should start with the word *test*.
- Use the `TestCase` methods `assert:`, `deny:` and others to make assertions.
- Run tests!

CHAPTER 10

Basic classes

Pharo is a really simple language but powerful language. Part of its power is not in the language but in its class libraries. To program effectively in it, you will need to learn how the class libraries support the language and environment. The class libraries are entirely written in Pharo, and can easily be extended. (Recall that a package may add new functionality to a class even if it does not define this class.)

Our goal here is not to present in tedious detail the whole of the Pharo class library, but rather to point out the key classes and methods that you will need to use (or subclass/override) to program effectively. In this chapter, we will cover the basic classes that you will need for nearly every application: Object, Number and its subclasses, Character, String, Symbol, and Boolean.

10.1 Object

For all intents and purposes, Object is the root of the inheritance hierarchy. Actually, in Pharo the true root of the hierarchy is ProtoObject, which is used to define minimal entities that masquerade as objects, but we can ignore this point for the time being.

Object defines almost 400 methods (in other words, every class that you define will automatically provide all those methods). *Note:* You can count the number of methods in a class like so:

```
Object selectors size "Count the instance methods in Object"
Object class selectors size "Count the class methods"
```

Class Object provides default behaviour common to all normal objects, such as access, copying, comparison, error handling, message sending, and reflection. Also utility messages that all objects should respond to are defined here. Object has no instance variables, nor should any be added. This is due to several classes of objects that inherit from Object that have special implementations (SmallInteger and UndefinedObject for example) that the VM knows about and depends on the structure and layout of certain standard classes.

If we begin to browse the method protocols on the instance side of Object we will start to see some of the key behaviour it provides.

Printing

Every object can return a printed form of itself. You can select any expression in a textpane and select the Print it menu item: this executes the expression and asks the returned object to print itself. In fact this sends the message printString to the returned object. The method printString, which is a template method, at its core sends the message printOn: to its receiver. The message printOn: is a hook that can be specialized.

Method Object>>printOn: is very likely one of the methods that you will most frequently override. This method takes as its argument a Stream on which a String representation of the object will be written. The default implementation simply writes the class name preceded by a or an. Object>>printString returns the String that is written.

For example, the class OpalCompiler does not redefine the method printOn: and sending the message printString to an instance executes the methods defined in Object.

```
OpalCompiler new printString
>>> 'an OpalCompiler'
```

The class Color shows an example of printOn: specialization. It prints the name of the class followed by the name of the class method used to generate that color.

```
Color >> printOn: aStream
    | name |
    (name := self name).
    name = #unnamed
        ifFalse: [
            ^ aStream
                nextPutAll: 'Color ';
                nextPutAll: name ].
    self storeOn: aStream]]]

[[[
Color red printString
>>> 'Color red'
```

Note that the message printOn: is not the same as storeOn:. The message storeOn: writes to its argument stream an expression that can be used to

10.1 Object

recreate the receiver. This expression is executed when the stream is read using the message `readFrom:`. On the other hand, the message `printOn:` just returns a textual version of the receiver. Of course, it may happen that this textual representation may represent the receiver as a self-evaluating expression.

A word about representation and self-evaluating representation. In functional programming, expressions return values when executed. In Pharo, messages (expressions) return objects (values). Some objects have the nice property that their value is themselves. For example, the value of the object true is itself i.e., the object true. We call such objects *self-evaluating objects*. You can see a *printed* version of an object value when you print the object in a playground. Here are some examples of such self-evaluating expressions.

```
true
>>> true
3@4
>>> (3@4)
$a
>>> $a
#(1 2 3)
>>> #(1 2 3)
Color red
>>> Color red
```

Note that some objects such as arrays are self-evaluating or not depending on the objects they contain. For example, an array of booleans is self-evaluating, whereas an array of persons is not. The following example shows that a dynamic array is self-evaluating only if its elements are:

```
{10@10. 100@100}
>>> {(10@10). (100@100)}
{Nautilus new . 100@100}
>>> an Array(a Nautilus (100@100))
```

Remember that literal arrays can only contain literals. Hence the following array does not contain two points but rather six literal elements.

```
#(10@10 100@100)
>>> #(10 #@ 10 100 #@ 100)
```

Lots of `printOn:` method specializations implement self-evaluating behavior. The implementations of `Point>>printOn:` and `Interval>>printOn:` are self-evaluating.

```
Point >> printOn: aStream
    "The receiver prints on aStream in terms of infix notation."

    aStream nextPut: $(.
    x printOn: aStream.
```

```
    aStream nextPut: $@.
    (y notNil and: [y negative])
       ifTrue: [
          "Avoid ambiguous @- construct"
          aStream space ].
    y printOn: aStream.
    aStream nextPut: $).
```

```
Interval >> printOn: aStream
    aStream nextPut: $(;
       print: start;
       nextPutAll: ' to: ';
       print: stop.
    step ~= 1 ifTrue: [aStream nextPutAll: ' by: '; print: step].
    aStream nextPut: $)
```

```
1 to: 10
>>> (1 to: 10) "intervals are self-evaluating"
```

Identity and equality

In Pharo, the message = tests object *equality* (i.e., whether two objects represent the same value) whereas == tests object *identity* (whether two expressions represent the same object).

The default implementation of object equality is to test for object identity:

```
Object >> = anObject
    "Answer whether the receiver and the argument represent the same
       object.
    If = is redefined in any subclass, consider also redefining the
       message hash."

    ^ self == anObject
```

This is a method that you will frequently want to override. Consider the case of Complex numbers as defined in the SciSmalltalk/PolyMath packages (PolyMath is a set of packages that offer support for numerical methods):

```
(1 + 2 i) = (1 + 2 i)
>>> true "same value"
(1 + 2 i) == (1 + 2 i)
>>> false "but different objects"
```

This works because Complex overrides = as follows:

```
Complex >> = anObject
    ^ anObject isComplex
       ifTrue: [ (real = anObject real) & (imaginary = anObject
          imaginary)]
       ifFalse: [ anObject adaptToComplex: self andSend: #=]
```

10.1 Object

The default implementation of Object>>~= (a test for inequality) simply negates Object>>=, and should not normally need to be changed.

```
(1 + 2 i) ~= (1 + 4 i)
>>> true
```

If you override =, you should consider overriding hash. If instances of your class are ever used as keys in a Dictionary, then you should make sure that instances that are considered to be equal have the same hash value:

```
Complex >> hash
    "Hash is reimplemented because = is implemented."
    ^ real hash bitXor: imaginary hash.
```

Although you should override = and hash together, you should *never* override ==. The semantics of object identity is the same for all classes. Message == is a primitive method of ProtoObject.

Note that Pharo has some strange equality behaviour compared to other Smalltalks. For example a symbol and a string can be equal. (We consider this to be a bug, not a feature.)

```
#'lulu' = 'lulu'
>>> true
'lulu' = #'lulu'
>>> true
```

Class membership

Several methods allow you to query the class of an object.

class. You can ask any object about its class using the message class.

```
1 class
>>> SmallInteger
```

isMemberOf:. Conversely, you can ask if an object is an instance of a specific class:

```
1 isMemberOf: SmallInteger
>>> true   "must be precisely this class"
1 isMemberOf: Integer
>>> false
1 isMemberOf: Number
>>> false
1 isMemberOf: Object
>>> false
```

Since Pharo is written in itself, you can really navigate through its structure using the right combination of superclass and class messages (see Chapter : Classes and Metaclasses).

isKindOf:. Object>>isKindOf: answers whether the receiver's class is either the same as, or a subclass of the argument class.

```
1 isKindOf: SmallInteger
>>> true
1 isKindOf: Integer
>>> true
1 isKindOf: Number
>>> true
1 isKindOf: Object
>>> true
1 isKindOf: String
>>> false

1/3 isKindOf: Number
>>> true
1/3 isKindOf: Integer
>>> false
```

1/3 which is a Fraction is a kind of Number, since the class Number is a superclass of the class Fraction, but 1/3 is not an Integer.

respondsTo:. Object>>respondsTo: answers whether the receiver understands the message selector given as an argument.

```
1 respondsTo: #,
>>> false
```

A note on the usage of respondsTo:. Normally it is a bad idea to query an object for its class, or to ask it which messages it understands. Instead of making decisions based on the class of object, you should simply send a message to the object and let it decide (on the basis of its class) how it should behave. (This concept is sometimes referred to as *duck typing*).

Copying

Copying objects introduces some subtle issues. Since instance variables are accessed by reference, a *shallow copy* of an object would share its references to instance variables with the original object:

```
a1 := { { 'harry' } }.
a1
>>> #(#('harry'))
a2 := a1 shallowCopy.
a2
>>> #(#('harry'))
(a1 at: 1) at: 1 put: 'sally'.
a1
>>> #(#('sally'))
a2
```

10.1 Object

```
>>> #(#('sally')) "the subarray is shared!"
```

Object>>shallowCopy is a primitive method that creates a shallow copy of an object. Since a2 is only a shallow copy of a1, the two arrays share a reference to the nested Array that they contain.

Object>>deepCopy makes an arbitrarily deep copy of an object.

```
a1 := { { { 'harry' } } } .
a2 := a1 deepCopy.
(a1 at: 1) at: 1 put: 'sally'.
a1
>>> #(#('sally'))
a2
>>> #(#(#('harry')))
```

The problem with deepCopy is that it will not terminate when applied to a mutually recursive structure:

```
a1 := { 'harry' }.
a2 := { a1 }.
a1 at: 1 put: a2.
a1 deepCopy
>>> !''... does not terminate!''!
```

An alternate solution is to use message copy. It is implemented on Object as follows:

```
Object >> copy
    "Answer another instance just like the receiver.
    Subclasses typically override postCopy;
    they typically do not override shallowCopy."

    ^ self shallowCopy postCopy
```

```
Object >> postCopy
    ^ self
```

By default postCopy returns self. It means that by default copy is doing the same as shallowCopy but each subclass can decide to customise the postCopy method which acts as a hook. You should override postCopy to copy any instance variables that should not be shared. In addition there is a good chance that postCopy should always do a super postCopy to ensure that state of the superclass is also copied.

Debugging

halt. The most important method here is halt. To set a breakpoint in a method, simply insert the expression send self halt at some point in the body of the method. (Note that since halt is defined on Object you can also write 1 halt). When this message is sent, execution will be interrupted and a debugger will open to this point in your program (See Chapter : The Pharo Environment for more details about the debugger.).

You can also use `Halt once` or `Halt if: aCondition`. Have a look at the class `Halt` which is an special exception.

assert:. The next most important message is `assert:`, which expects a block as its argument. If the block evaluates to `true`, execution continues. Otherwise an `AssertionFailure` exception will be raised. If this exception is not otherwise caught, the debugger will open to this point in the execution. `assert:` is especially useful to support *design by contract*. The most typical usage is to check non-trivial pre-conditions to public methods of objects. `Stack>>pop` could easily have been implemented as follows (Note that this definition is anhypothetical example and not in the Pharo 50 system):

```
Stack >> pop
    "Return the first element and remove it from the stack."

    self assert: [ self isNotEmpty ].
    ^ self linkedList removeFirst element
```

Do not confuse `Object>>assert:` with `TestCase>>assert:`, which occurs in the SUnit testing framework (see Chapter : SUnit). While the former expects a block as its argument (actually, it will take any argument that understands `value`, including a `Boolean`), the latter expects a `Boolean`. Although both are useful for debugging, they each serve a very different purpose.

Error handling

This protocol contains several methods useful for signaling run-time errors.

deprecated:. Sending `self deprecated:` signals that the current method should no longer be used, if deprecation has been turned on. You can turn it on/off in the Debugging section using the Settings browser. The argument should describe an alternative. Look for senders of the message `deprecated:` to get an idea.

doesNotUnderstand:. `doesNotUnderstand:` (commonly abbreviated in discussions as DNU or MNU) is sent whenever message lookup fails. The default implementation, i.e., `Object>>doesNotUnderstand:` will trigger the debugger at this point. It may be useful to override `doesNotUnderstand:` to provide some other behaviour.

error. `Object>>error` and `Object>>error:` are generic methods that can be used to raise exceptions. (Generally it is better to raise your own custom exceptions, so you can distinguish errors arising from your code from those coming from kernel classes.)

subclassResponsibility. Abstract methods are implemented by convention with the body self subclassResponsibility. Should an abstract class be instantiated by accident, then calls to abstract methods will result in Object>>subclassResponsibility being executed.

```
Object >> subclassResponsibility
    "This message sets up a framework for the behavior of the class'
        subclasses.
    Announce that the subclass should have implemented this message."

    self error: 'My subclass should have overridden ', thisContext
        sender selector printString
```

Magnitude, Number, and Boolean are classical examples of abstract classes that we shall see shortly in this chapter.

```
Number new + 1
>>> !''Error: My subclass should have overridden #+''!
```

shouldNotImplement. self shouldNotImplement is sent by convention to signal that an inherited method is not appropriate for this subclass. This is generally a sign that something is not quite right with the design of the class hierarchy. Due to the limitations of single inheritance, however, sometimes it is very hard to avoid such workarounds.

A typical example is Collection>>remove: which is inherited by Dictionary but flagged as not implemented. (A Dictionary provides removeKey: instead.)

Testing

The testing methods have nothing to do with SUnit testing! A testing method is one that lets you ask a question about the state of the receiver and returns a Boolean.

Numerous testing methods are provided by Object. There are isArray, isBoolean, isBlock, isCollection and so on. Generally such methods are to be avoided since querying an object for its class is a form of violation of encapsulation. Instead of testing an object for its class, one should simply send a request and let the object decide how to handle it.

Nevertheless some of these testing methods are undeniably useful. The most useful are probably ProtoObject>>isNil and Object>>notNil (though the Null Object design pattern can obviate the need for even these methods).

Initialize

A final key method that occurs not in Object but in ProtoObject is initialize.

Basic classes

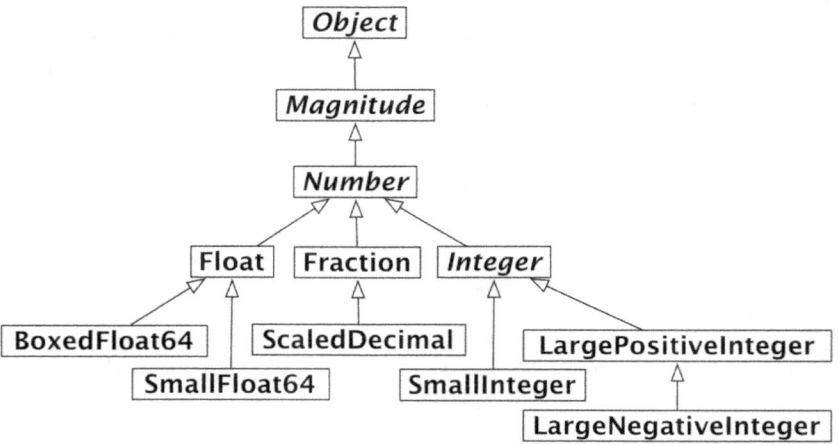

Figure 10.1: The number hierarchy.

```
ProtoObject >> initialize
    "Subclasses should redefine this method to perform initializations
        on instance creation"
```

The reason this is important is that in Pharo, the default new method defined for every class in the system will send initialize to newly created instances.

```
Behavior >> new
    "Answer a new initialized instance of the receiver (which is a
        class) with no indexable
    variables. Fail if the class is indexable."
    ^ self basicNew initialize
```

This means that simply by overriding the initialize hook method, new instances of your class will automatically be initialized. The initialize method should normally perform a super initialize to establish the class invariant for any inherited instance variables.

10.2 Numbers

Numbers in Pharo are not primitive data values but true objects. Of course numbers are implemented efficiently in the virtual machine, but the Number hierarchy is as perfectly accessible and extensible as any other portion of the class hierarchy.

The abstract root of this hierarchy is Magnitude, which represents all kinds of classes supporting comparison operators. Number adds various arithmetic and other operators as mostly abstract methods. Float and Fraction represent,

10.2 Numbers

respectively, floating point numbers and fractional values. Float subclasses (BoxedFloat64 and SmallFloat64) represent Float on certain architectures. For example BoxedFloat64 is only available for 64 bit systems. Integer is also abstract, thus distinguishing between subclasses SmallInteger, LargePositiveInteger and LargeNegativeInteger. For the most part, users do not need to be aware of the difference between the three Integer classes, as values are automatically converted as needed.

Magnitude

Magnitude is the parent not only of the Number classes, but also of other classes supporting comparison operations, such as Character, Duration and Timespan.

Methods < and = are abstract. The remaining operators are generically defined. For example:

```
Magnitude >> < aMagnitude
    "Answer whether the receiver is less than the argument."

    ^ self subclassResponsibility

Magnitude >> > aMagnitude
    "Answer whether the receiver is greater than the argument."

    ^ aMagnitude < self
```

Number

Similarly, Number defines +, -, * and / to be abstract, but all other arithmetic operators are generically defined.

All Number objects support various *converting* operators, such as asFloat and asInteger. There are also numerous *shortcut constructor methods* which generate Durations, such as hour, day and week.

Numbers directly support common *math functions* such as sin, log, raiseTo:, squared, sqrt and so on.

The method Number>>printOn: is implemented in terms of the abstract method Number>>printOn:base:. (The default base is 10.)

Testing methods include even, odd, positive and negative. Unsurprisingly Number overrides isNumber. More interestingly, isInfinite is defined to return false.

Truncation methods include floor, ceiling, integerPart, fractionPart and so on.

```
1 + 2.5
>>> 3.5 "Addition of two numbers"
```

```
3.4 * 5
>>> 17.0 "Multiplication of two numbers"
```
```
8 / 2
>>> 4 "Division of two numbers"
```
```
10 - 8.3
>>> 1.7 "Subtraction of two numbers"
```
```
12 = 11
>>> false "Equality between two numbers"
```
```
12 ~= 11
>>> true "Test if two numbers are different"
```
```
12 > 9
>>> true "Greater than"
```
```
12 >= 10
>>> true "Greater or equal than"
```
```
12 < 10
>>> false "Smaller than"
```
```
100@10
>>> 100@10 "Point creation"
```

The following example works surprisingly well in Pharo:

```
1000 factorial / 999 factorial
>>> 1000
```

Note that `1000 factorial` is really calculated, which in many other languages can be quite difficult to compute. This is an excellent example of automatic coercion and exact handling of a number.

> **To do** Try to display the result of `1000 factorial`. It takes more time to display it than to calculate it!

Float

Float implements the abstract Number methods for floating point numbers.

More interestingly, Float class (i.e., the class-side of Float) provides methods to return the following *constants*: e, infinity, nan and pi.

```
Float pi
>>> 3.141592653589793
```
```
Float infinity
>>> Infinity
```
```
Float infinity isInfinite
>>> true
```

Fraction

Fractions are represented by instance variables for the numerator and denominator, which should be Integers. Fractions are normally created by Integer division (rather than using the constructor method Fraction>>numerator:denominator:):

```
6/8
>>> (3/4)
```

```
(6/8) class
>>> Fraction
```

Multiplying a Fraction by an Integer or another Fraction may yield an Integer:

```
6/8 * 4
>>> 3
```

Integer

Integer is the abstract parent of three concrete integer implementations. In addition to providing concrete implementations of many abstract Number methods, it also adds a few methods specific to integers, such as factorial, atRandom, isPrime, gcd: and many others.

SmallInteger is special in that its instances are represented compactly — instead of being stored as a reference, a SmallInteger is represented directly using the bits that would otherwise be used to hold a reference. The first bit of an object reference indicates whether the object is a SmallInteger or not. Now the virtual machine abstracts that from you, therefore you cannot see this directly when inspecting the object.

The class methods minVal and maxVal tell us the range of a SmallInteger:

```
SmallInteger maxVal = ((2 raisedTo: 30) - 1)
>>> true
```

```
SmallInteger minVal = (2 raisedTo: 30) negated
>>> true
```

When a SmallInteger goes out of this range, it is automatically converted to a LargePositiveInteger or a LargeNegativeInteger, as needed:

```
(SmallInteger maxVal + 1) class
>>> LargePositiveInteger
```

```
(SmallInteger minVal - 1) class
>>> LargeNegativeInteger
```

Large integers are similarly converted back to small integers when appropriate.

As in most programming languages, integers can be useful for specifying iterative behaviour. There is a dedicated method `timesRepeat:` for evaluating a block repeatedly. We have already seen a similar example in Chapter : Syntax in a Nutshell.

```
| n |
n := 2.
3 timesRepeat: [ n := n * n ].
n
>>> 256
```

10.3 Characters

`Character` is defined a subclass of `Magnitude`. Printable characters are represented in Pharo as `$<char>`. For example:

```
$a < $b
>>> true
```

Non-printing characters can be generated by various class methods. `Character class>>value:` takes the Unicode (or ASCII) integer value as argument and returns the corresponding character. The protocol `accessing untypeable characters` contains a number of convenience constructor methods such as `backspace`, `cr`, `escape`, `euro`, `space`, `tab`, and so on.

```
Character space = (Character value: Character space asciiValue)
>>> true
```

The `printOn:` method is clever enough to know which of the three ways to generate characters offers the most appropriate representation:

```
Character value: 1
>>> Character home
```

```
Character value: 2
>>> Character value: 2
```

```
Character value: 32
>>> Character space
```

```
Character value: 97
>>> $a
```

Various convenient *testing* methods are built in: `isAlphaNumeric`, `isCharacter`, `isDigit`, `isLowercase`, `isVowel`, and so on.

To convert a `Character` to the string containing just that character, send `asString`. In this case `asString` and `printString` yield different results:

```
$a asString
>>> 'a'
```

10.4 Strings

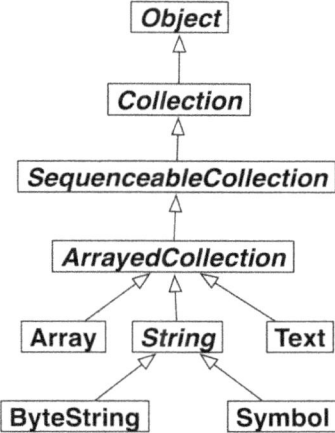

Figure 10.2: The String Hierarchy.

```
$a
>>> $a
```

```
$a printString
>>> '$a'
```

Like SmallInteger, a Character is a immediate value not a object reference. Most of the time you won't see any difference and can use objects of class Character like any other too. But this means, equal value characters are always *identical*:

```
(Character value: 97) == $a
>>> true
```

10.4 Strings

A String is an indexed Collection that holds only Characters.

In fact, String is abstract and Pharo strings are actually instances of the concrete class ByteString.

```
'hello world' class
>>> ByteString
```

The other important subclass of String is Symbol. The key difference is that there is only ever a single instance of Symbol with a given value. (This is sometimes called *the unique instance property*). In contrast, two separately constructed Strings that happen to contain the same sequence of characters will often be different objects.

```
'hel','lo' == 'hello'
>>> false
```

```
('hel','lo') asSymbol == #hello
>>> true
```

Another important difference is that a `String` is mutable, whereas a `Symbol` is immutable.

```
'hello' at: 2 put: $u; yourself
>>> 'hullo'
```

```
#hello at: 2 put: $u
>>> error!
```

It is easy to forget that since strings are collections, they understand the same messages that other collections do:

```
#hello indexOf: $o
>>> 5
```

Although `String` does not inherit from `Magnitude`, it does support the usual comparing methods, <, = and so on. In addition, `String>>match:` is useful for some basic glob-style pattern-matching:

```
'*or*' match: 'zorro'
>>> true
```

Regular expressions will be discussed in more detail in Chapter : Regular Expressions in Pharo.

Strings support a rather large number of conversion methods. Many of these are shortcut constructor methods for other classes, such as `asDate`, `asInteger` and so on. There are also a number of useful methods for converting a string to another string, such as `capitalized` and `translateToLowercase`.

For more on strings and collections, see Chapter : Collections.

10.5 Booleans

The class `Boolean` offers a fascinating insight into how much of the Pharo language has been pushed into the class library. `Boolean` is the abstract superclass of the singleton classes `True` and `False`.

Most of the behaviour of `Booleans` can be understood by considering the method `ifTrue:ifFalse:`, which takes two `Blocks` as arguments.

```
4 factorial > 20
   ifTrue: [ 'bigger' ]
   ifFalse: [ 'smaller' ]
>>> 'bigger'
```

10.5 Booleans

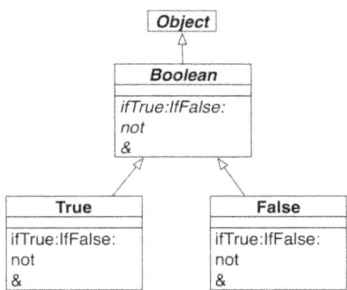

Figure 10.3: The Boolean Hierarchy.

The method ifTrue:ifFalse: is abstract in class Boolean. The implementations in its concrete subclasses are both trivial:

```
True >> ifTrue: trueAlternativeBlock ifFalse: falseAlternativeBlock
    ^ trueAlternativeBlock value

False >> ifTrue: trueAlternativeBlock ifFalse: falseAlternativeBlock
    ^ falseAlternativeBlock value
```

Each of them execute the correct block depending on the receiver of the message. In fact, this is the essence of OOP: when a message is sent to an object, the object itself determines which method will be used to respond. In this case an instance of True simply executes the *true* alternative, while an instance of False executes the *false* alternative. All the abstract Boolean methods are implemented in this way for True and False. For example the implementation of negation (message not) is defined the same way:

```
True >> not
    "Negation--answer false since the receiver is true."
    ^ false

False >> not
    "Negation--answer true since the receiver is false."
    ^ true
```

Booleans offer several useful convenience methods, such as ifTrue:, if-False:, and ifFalse:ifTrue. You also have the choice between eager and lazy conjunctions and disjunctions.

```
( 1 > 2 ) & ( 3 < 4 )
>>> false "Eager, must evaluate both sides"
```

```
( 1 > 2 ) and: [ 3 < 4 ]
>>> false "Lazy, only evaluate receiver"
```

```
( 1 > 2 ) and: [ ( 1 / 0 ) > 0 ]
>>> false "argument block is never executed, so no exception"
```

In the first example, both `Boolean` subexpressions are executed, since & takes a `Boolean` argument. In the second and third examples, only the first is executed, since `and:` expects a `Block` as its argument. The `Block` is executed only if the first argument is `true`.

> **To do** Try to imagine how `and:` and `or:` are implemented. Check the implementations in `Boolean`, `True` and `False`.

10.6 Chapter summary

- If you override = then you should override `hash` as well.
- Override `postCopy` to correctly implement copying for your objects.
- Use `self halt.` to set a breakpoint.
- Return `self subclassResponsibility` to make a method abstract.
- To give an object a `String` representation you should override `printOn:`.
- Override the hook method `initialize` to properly initialize instances.
- Number methods automatically convert between `Floats`, `Fractions` and `Integers`.
- `Fractions` truly represent rational numbers rather than floats.
- All `Characters` are like unique instances.
- `Strings` are mutable; `Symbols` are not. Take care not to mutate string literals, however!
- `Symbols` are unique; `Strings` are not.
- `Strings` and `Symbols` are `Collections` and therefore support the usual `Collection` methods.

CHAPTER **11**

Collections

11.1 Introduction

The collection classes form a loosely-defined group of general-purpose subclasses of Collection and Stream. Many of these (like Bitmap, FileStream and CompiledMethod) are special-purpose classes crafted for use in other parts of the system or in applications, and hence not categorized as *Collections* by the system organization. For the purposes of this chapter, we use the term *Collection Hierarchy* to mean Collection and its subclasses that are *also* in the packages labelled Collections-*. We use the term *Stream Hierarchy* to mean Stream and its subclasses that are *also* in the Collections-Streams packages.

In this chapter we focus mainly on the subset of collection classes shown in Figure 11.1. Streams will be discussed separately in Chapter : Streams.

11.2 The varieties of collections

To make good use of the collection classes, the reader needs at least a superficial knowledge of the wide variety of collections that they implement, and their commonalities and differences.

Programming with collections using high-order functions rather than individual elements is an important way to raise the level of abstraction of a program. The Lisp function map, which applies an argument function to every element of a list and returns a new list containing the results is an early example of this style. Following its Smalltalk root, Pharo adopts this collection-based high-order programming as a central tenet. Modern functional programming languages such as ML and Haskell have followed Smalltalk's lead.

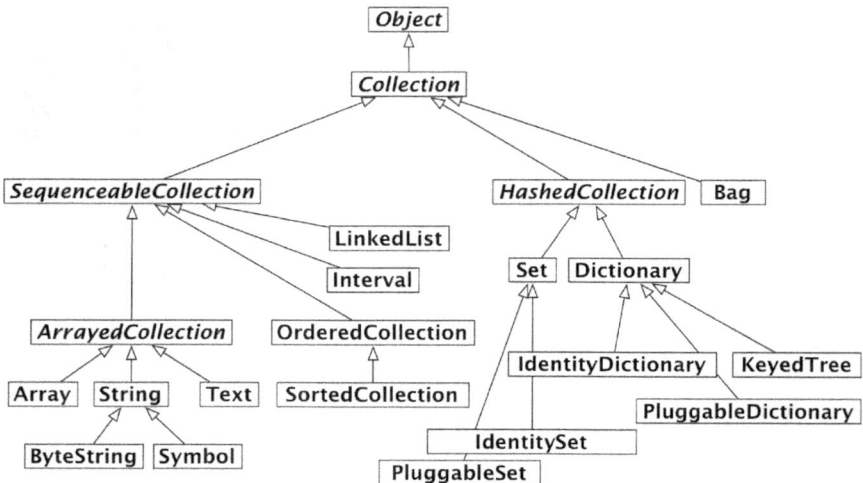

Figure 11.1: Some of the key collection classes in Pharo.

Why is this a good idea? Suppose you have a data structure containing a collection of student records, and wish to perform some action on all of the students that meet some criterion. Programmers raised to use an imperative language will immediately reach for a loop. But the Pharo programmer will write:

```
students
    select: [ :each | each gpa < threshold ]
```

This expression returns a new collection containing precisely those elements of students for which the block (the bracketed function) returns true. The block can be thought of as a lambda-expression defining an anonymous function x. x gpa < threshold. This code has the simplicity and elegance of a domain-specific query language.

The message select: is understood by *all* collections in Pharo. There is no need to find out if the student data structure is an array or a linked list: the select: message is understood by both. Note that this is quite different from using a loop, where one must know whether students is an array or a linked list before the loop can be set up.

In Pharo, when one speaks of a collection without being more specific about the kind of collection, one means an object that supports well-defined protocols for testing membership and enumerating the elements. *All* collections understand the testing messages includes:, isEmpty and occurrencesOf:. *All* collections understand the enumeration messages do:, select:, reject: (which is the opposite of select:), collect: (which is like Lisp's map), detect:ifNone:, inject:into: (which performs a left fold) and many more. It

11.2 The varieties of collections

is the ubiquity of this protocol, as well as its variety, that makes it so powerful.

The table below summarizes the standard protocols supported by most of the classes in the collection hierarchy. These methods are defined, redefined, optimized or occasionally even forbidden by subclasses of Collection.

Protocol	Methods
accessing	size, capacity, at:, at:put:
testing	isEmpty, includes:, contains:, occurrencesOf:
adding	add:, addAll:
removing	remove:, remove:ifAbsent:, removeAll:
enumerating	do:, collect:, select:, reject:
	detect:, detect:ifNone:, inject:into:
converting	asBag, asSet, asOrderedCollection, asSortedCollection, asArray, asSortedCollection:
creation	with:, with:with:, with:with:with:, with:with:with:with:, withAll:

Beyond this basic uniformity, there are many different kinds of collection either supporting different protocols, or providing different behaviour for the same requests. Let us briefly survey some of the key differences:

Sequenceable: Instances of all subclasses of SequenceableCollection start from a first element and proceed in a well-defined order to a last element. Instances of Set, Bag and Dictionary, on the other hand, are not sequenceable.

Sortable: A SortedCollection maintains its elements in sort order.

Indexable: Most sequenceable collections are also indexable, that is, elements can be retrieved with message at: anIndex. Array is the familiar indexable data structure with a fixed size; anArray at: n retrieves the nth element of anArray, and anArray at: n put: v changes the nth element to v. LinkedLists and SkipLists are sequenceable but not indexable, that is, they understand first and last, but not the message at:.

Keyed: Instances of Dictionary and its subclasses are accessed by keys instead of indices.

Mutable: Most collections are mutable, but Intervals and Symbols are not. An Interval is an immutable collection representing a range of Integers. For example, 5 to: 16 by: 2 is an interval that contains the elements 5, 7, 9, 11, 13 and 15. It is indexable with message at: anIndex, but cannot be changed with message at: anIndex put: aValue.

Growable: Instances of Interval and Array are always of a fixed size. Other kinds of collections (sorted collections, ordered collections, and linked lists) can grow after creation. The class OrderedCollection is more

Arrayed Implementation	Ordered Implementation	Hashed Implementation	Linked Implementation	Interval Implementation
Array String Symbol	OrderedCollection SortedCollection Text Heap	Set IdentitySet PluggableSet Bag IdentityBag Dictionary IdentityDictionary PluggableDictionary	LinkedList SkipList	Interval

Figure 11.2: Some collection classes categorized by implementation technique.

general than Array; the size of an OrderedCollection grows on demand, and it defines messages addFirst: anElement and addLast: anElement as well as messages at: anIndex and at: anIndex put: aValue.

Accepts duplicates: A Set filters out duplicates, but a Bag does not. Classes Dictionary, Set and Bag use the = method provided by the elements; the Identity variants of these classes use the == method, which tests whether the arguments are the same object, and the Pluggable variants use an arbitrary equivalence relation supplied by the creator of the collection.

Heterogeneous: Most collections will hold any kind of element. A String, CharacterArray or Symbol, however, only holds Characters. An Array will hold any mix of objects, but a ByteArray only holds Bytes. A LinkedList is constrained to hold elements that conform to the Link accessing protocol.

11.3 Collection implementations

These categorizations by functionality are not our only concern; we must also consider how the collection classes are implemented. As shown in Figure 11.2, five main implementation techniques are employed.

- Arrays store their elements in the (indexable) instance variables of the collection object itself; as a consequence, arrays must be of a fixed size, but can be created with a single memory allocation.

- OrderedCollections and SortedCollections store their elements in an array that is referenced by one of the instance variables of the collection. Consequently, the internal array can be replaced with a larger one if the collection grows beyond its storage capacity.

- The various kinds of set and dictionary also reference a subsidiary array for storage, but use the array as a hash table. Bags use a subsidiary

Dictionary, with the elements of the bag as keys and the number of occurrences as values.
- LinkedLists use a standard singly-linked representation.
- Intervals are represented by three integers that record the two endpoints and the step size.

In addition to these classes, there are also *weak* variants of Array, Set and of the various kinds of dictionary. These collections hold onto their elements weakly, i.e., in a way that does not prevent the elements from being garbage collected. The Pharo virtual machine is aware of these classes and handles them specially.

11.4 Examples of key classes

We present now the most common or important collection classes using simple code examples. The main protocols of collections are:

- messages at:, at:put: — to access an element,
- messages add:, remove: — to add or remove an element,
- messages size, isEmpty, include: — to get some information about the collection,
- messages do:, collect:, select: — to iterate over the collection.

Each collection may implement (or not) such protocols, and when they do, they interpret them to fit with their semantics. We suggest you browse the classes themselves to identify specific and more advanced protocols.

We will focus on the most common collection classes: OrderedCollection, Set, SortedCollection, Dictionary, Interval, and Array.

Common creation protocol. There are several ways to create instances of collections. The most generic ones use the message new: aSize and with: anElement.

- new: anInteger creates a collection of size anInteger whose elements will all be nil.
- with: anObject creates a collection and adds anObject to the created collection.

Different collections will realize this behaviour differently.

You can create collections with initial elements using the methods with:, with:with: etc. for up to six elements.

```
Array with: 1
>>> #(1)
```

```
Array with: 1 with: 2
>>> #(1 2)
```

```
Array with: 1 with: 2 with: 3
>>> #(1 2 3)
```

```
Array with: 1 with: 2 with: 3 with: 4
>>> #(1 2 3 4)
```

```
Array with: 1 with: 2 with: 3 with: 4 with: 5
>>> #(1 2 3 4 5)
```

```
Array with: 1 with: 2 with: 3 with: 4 with: 5 with: 6
>>> #(1 2 3 4 5 6)
```

You can also use message addAll: aCollection to add all elements of one kind of collection to another kind:

```
(1 to: 5) asOrderedCollection addAll: '678'; yourself
>>> an OrderedCollection(1 2 3 4 5 6 7 8)
```

Take care that addAll: returns its argument, and not the receiver!

You can also create many collections with withAll: aCollection.

```
Array withAll: #(7 3 1 3)
>>> #(7 3 1 3)
```

```
OrderedCollection withAll: #(7 3 1 3)
>>> an OrderedCollection(7 3 1 3)
```

```
SortedCollection withAll: #(7 3 1 3)
>>> a SortedCollection(1 3 3 7)
```

```
Set withAll: #(7 3 1 3)
>>> a Set(7 1 3)
```

```
Bag withAll: #(7 3 1 3)
>>> a Bag(7 1 3 3)
```

Array

An Array is a fixed-sized collection of elements accessed by integer indices. Contrary to the C convention in Pharo, the first element of an array is at position 1 and not 0. The main protocol to access array elements is the method at: and at:put:. at: anInteger returns the element at index anInteger. at: anInteger put: anObject puts anObject at index anInteger. Arrays are fixed-size collections therefore we cannot add or remove elements at the end of an array. The following code creates an array of size 5, puts values in the first 3 locations and returns the first element.

```
| anArray |
anArray := Array new: 5.
anArray at: 1 put: 4.
```

11.4 Examples of key classes

```
anArray at: 2 put: 3/2.
anArray at: 3 put: 'ssss'.
anArray at: 1
>>> 4
```

There are several ways to create instances of the class Array. We can use new:, with:, and the constructs #( ) (literal arrays) and { . } (dynamic compact syntax).

Creation with new: The message new: anInteger creates an array of size anInteger. Array new: 5 creates an array of size 5. (Note: the value of each element is initialized to nil).

Creation using with: The with:* messages allow one to specify the value of the elements. The following code creates an array of three elements consisting of the number 4, the fraction 3/2 and the string 'lulu'.

```
Array with: 4 with: 3/2 with: 'lulu'
>>> {4. (3/2). 'lulu'}
```

Literal creation with #() The expression #() creates literal arrays with constants or *literal* elements that have to be known when the expression is compiled, and not when it is executed. The following code creates an array of size 2 where the first element is the (literal) number 1 and the second the (literal) string 'here'.

```
#(1 'here') size
>>> 2
```

Now, if you execute the expression #(1+2), you do not get an array with a single element 3 but instead you get the array #(1 #+ 2) i.e., with three elements: 1, the symbol #+ and the number 2.

```
#(1+2)
>>> #(1 #+ 2)
```

This occurs because the construct #() does not execute the expressions it contains. The elements are only objects that are created when parsing the expression (called literal objects). The expression is scanned and the resulting elements are fed to a new array. Literal arrays contain numbers, nil, true, false, symbols, strings and other literal arrays. During the execution of #() expressions, there are no messages sent.

Dynamic creation with { . } Finally, you can create a dynamic array using the construct { . }. The expression { a . b } is totally equivalent to Array with: a with: b. This means in particular that the expressions enclosed by { and } are executed (contrary to the case of #()).

```
{ 1 + 2 }
>>> #(3)
```

```
{(1/2) asFloat} at: 1
>>> 0.5
```

```
{10 atRandom. 1/3} at: 2
>>> (1/3)
```

Element Access Elements of all sequenceable collections can be accessed with messages at: anIndex and at: anIndex put: anObject.

```
| anArray |
anArray := #(1 2 3 4 5 6) copy.
anArray at: 3 >>> 3
anArray at: 3 put: 33.
anArray at: 3
>>> 33
```

Be careful: as a general principle do not modify literal arrays! Literal arrays are kept in compiled method literal frames (a space where literals appearing in a method are stored), therefore unless you copy the array, the second time you execute the code your *literal* array may not have the value you expect. In the example, without copying the array, the second time around, the literal #(1 2 3 4 5 6) will actually be #(1 2 33 4 5 6)! Dynamic arrays do not have this problem because they are not stored in literal frames.

OrderedCollection

OrderedCollection is one of the collections that can grow, and to which elements can be added sequentially. It offers a variety of messages such as add:, addFirst:, addLast:, and addAll:.

```
| ordCol |
ordCol := OrderedCollection new.
ordCol add: 'Seaside'; add: 'SmalltalkHub'; addFirst: 'Monticello'.
ordCol
>>> an OrderedCollection('Monticello' 'Seaside' 'SmalltalkHub')
```

Removing Elements The message remove: anObject removes the first occurrence of an object from the collection. If the collection does not include such an object, it raises an error.

```
ordCol add: 'Monticello'.
ordCol remove: 'Monticello'.
ordCol
>>> an OrderedCollection('Seaside' 'SmalltalkHub' 'Monticello')
```

11.4 Examples of key classes

There is a variant of `remove:` named `remove:ifAbsent:` that allows one to specify as second argument a block that is executed in case the element to be removed is not in the collection.

```
result := ordCol remove: 'zork' ifAbsent: [33].
result
>>> 33
```

Conversion It is possible to get an `OrderedCollection` from an `Array` (or any other collection) by sending the message `asOrderedCollection`:

```
#(1 2 3) asOrderedCollection
>>> an OrderedCollection(1 2 3)
```

```
'hello' asOrderedCollection
>>> an OrderedCollection($h $e $l $l $o)
```

Interval

The class `Interval` represents ranges of numbers. For example, the interval of numbers from 1 to 100 is defined as follows:

```
Interval from: 1 to: 100
>>> (1 to: 100)
```

The result of `printString` reveals that the class `Number` provides us with a convenience method called `to:` to generate intervals:

```
(Interval from: 1 to: 100) = (1 to: 100)
>>> true
```

We can use `Interval class>>from:to:by:` or `Number>>to:by:` to specify the step between two numbers as follow:

```
(Interval from: 1 to: 100 by: 0.5) size
>>> 199
```

```
(1 to: 100 by: 0.5) at: 198
>>> 99.5
```

```
(1/2 to: 54/7 by: 1/3) last
>>> (15/2)
```

Dictionary

Dictionaries are important collections whose elements are accessed using keys. Among the most commonly used messages of dictionary you will find at: aKey, at: aKey put: aValue, at: aKey ifAbsent: aBlock, keys, and values.

```
| colors |
colors := Dictionary new.
```

```
colors at: #yellow put: Color yellow.
colors at: #blue put: Color blue.
colors at: #red put: Color red.
colors at: #yellow
>>> Color yellow
colors keys
>>> #(#red #blue #yellow)
colors values
>>> {Color blue . Color yellow . Color red}
```

Dictionaries compare keys by equality. Two keys are considered to be the same if they return true when compared using =. A common and difficult to spot bug is to use as key an object whose = method has been redefined but not its hash method. Both methods are used in the implementation of dictionary and when comparing objects.

In its implementation, a Dictionary can be seen as consisting of a set of (key value) associations created using the message ->. We can create a Dictionary from a collection of associations, or we may convert a dictionary to an array of associations.

```
| colors |
colors := Dictionary newFrom: { #blue->Color blue . #red->Color red .
    #yellow->Color yellow }.
colors removeKey: #blue.
colors associations
>>> {#yellow->Color yellow. #red->Color red}
```

IdentityDictionary   While a dictionary uses the result of the messages = and hash to determine if two keys are the same, the class IdentityDictionary uses the identity (message ==) of the key instead of its values, i.e., it considers two keys to be equal *only* if they are the same object.

Often Symbols are used as keys, in which case it is natural to use an IdentityDictionary, since a Symbol is guaranteed to be globally unique. If, on the other hand, your keys are Strings, it is better to use a plain Dictionary, or you may get into trouble:

```
a := 'foobar'.
b := a copy.
trouble := IdentityDictionary new.
trouble at: a put: 'a'; at: b put: 'b'.
trouble at: a
>>> 'a'
trouble at: b
>>> 'b'
trouble at: 'foobar'
>>> 'a'
```

11.4 Examples of key classes

Since a and b are different objects, they are treated as different objects. Interestingly, the literal 'foobar' is allocated just once, so is really the same object as a. You don't want your code to depend on behaviour like this! A plain Dictionary would give the same value for any key equal to 'foobar'.

Use only globally unique objects (like Symbols or SmallIntegers) as keys for an IdentityDictionary, and Strings (or other objects) as keys for a plain Dictionary.

Note that the expression Smalltalk globals returns an instance of SystemDictionary, a subclass of IdentityDictionary, hence all its keys are Symbols (actually, ByteSymbols, which contain only 8-bit characters).

```
Smalltalk globals keys collect: [ :each | each class ] as:Set
>>> a Set(ByteSymbol)
```

Here we are using collect:as: to specify the result collection to be of class Set, that way we collect each kind of class used as a key only once.

Set

The class Set is a collection which behaves as a mathematical set, i.e., as a collection with no duplicate elements and without any order. In a Set, elements are added using the message add: and they cannot be accessed using the message at:. Objects put in a set should implement the methods hash and =.

```
s := Set new.
s add: 4/2; add: 4; add:2.
s size
>>> 2
```

You can also create sets using Set class>>newFrom: or the conversion message Collection>>asSet:

```
(Set newFrom: #( 1 2 3 1 4 )) = #(1 2 3 4 3 2 1) asSet
>>> true
```

asSet offers us a convenient way to eliminate duplicates from a collection:

```
{ Color black. Color white. (Color red + Color blue + Color green) }
    asSet size
>>> 2
```

Note that **red + blue + green = white.**

A Bag is much like a Set except that it does allow duplicates:

```
{ Color black. Color white. (Color red + Color blue + Color green) }
    asBag size
>>> 3
```

The set operations *union, intersection* and *membership test* are implemented by the Collection messages union:, intersection:, and includes:. The receiver is first converted to a Set, so these operations work for all kinds of collections!

```
(1 to: 6) union: (4 to: 10)
>>> a Set(1 2 3 4 5 6 7 8 9 10)
```

```
'hello' intersection: 'there'
>>> 'he'
```

```
#Smalltalk includes: $k
>>> true
```

As we explain below, elements of a set are accessed using iterators (see Section 11.5).

SortedCollection

In contrast to an OrderedCollection, a SortedCollection maintains its elements in sort order. By default, a sorted collection uses the message <= to establish sort order, so it can sort instances of subclasses of the abstract class Magnitude, which defines the protocol of comparable objects (<, =, >, >=, between:and:...). (See Chapter : Basic Classes).

You can create a SortedCollection by creating a new instance and adding elements to it:

```
SortedCollection new add: 5; add: 2; add: 50; add: -10; yourself.
>>> a SortedCollection(-10 2 5 50)
```

More usually, though, one will send the conversion message asSortedCollection to an existing collection:

```
#(5 2 50 -10) asSortedCollection
>>> a SortedCollection(-10 2 5 50)
```

```
'hello' asSortedCollection
>>> a SortedCollection($e $h $l $l $o)
```

How do you get a String back from this result? asString unfortunately returns the printString representation, which is not what we want:

```
'hello' asSortedCollection asString
>>> 'a SortedCollection($e $h $l $l $o)'
```

The correct answer is to either use String class>>newFrom:, String class>>withAll: or Object>>as::

```
'hello' asSortedCollection as: String
>>> 'ehllo'
String newFrom: 'hello' asSortedCollection
>>> 'ehllo'
```

11.4 Examples of key classes

```
String withAll: 'hello' asSortedCollection
>>> 'ehllo'
```

It is possible to have different kinds of elements in a SortedCollection as long as they are all comparable. For example, we can mix different kinds of numbers such as integers, floats and fractions:

```
{ 5 . 2/ -3 . 5.21 } asSortedCollection
>>> a SortedCollection((-2/3) 5 5.21)
```

Imagine that you want to sort objects that do not define the method <= or that you would like to have a different sorting criterion. You can do this by supplying a two argument block, called a sortblock, to the sorted collection. For example, the class Color is not a Magnitude and it does not implement the method <=, but we can specify a block stating that the colors should be sorted according to their luminance (a measure of brightness).

```
col := SortedCollection
        sortBlock: [ :c1 :c2 | c1 luminance <= c2 luminance ].
col addAll: { Color red . Color yellow . Color white . Color black }.
col
>>> a SortedCollection(Color black Color red Color yellow Color white)
```

String

In Pharo, a String is a collection of Characters. It is sequenceable, indexable, mutable and homogeneous, containing only Character instances. Like Arrays, Strings have a dedicated syntax, and are normally created by directly specifying a String literal within single quotes, but the usual collection creation methods will work as well.

```
'Hello'
>>> 'Hello'
```

```
String with: $A
>>> 'A'
```

```
String with: $h with: $i with: $!
>>> 'hi!'
```

```
String newFrom: #($h $e $l $l $o)
>>> 'hello'
```

In actual fact, String is abstract. When we instantiate a String we actually get either an 8-bit ByteString or a 32-bit WideString. To keep things simple, we usually ignore the difference and just talk about instances of String.

While strings are delimited by single quotes, a string can contain a single quote: to define a string with a single quote we should type it twice. Note that the string will contain only one element and not two as shown below:

```
'l''idiot' at: 2
>>> $'
```
```
'l''idiot' at: 3
>>> $i
```

Two instances of String can be concatenated with a comma.

```
s := 'no', ' ', 'worries'.
s
>>> 'no worries'
```

Since a string is a mutable collection we can also change it using the message at:put:.

```
s at: 4 put: $h; at: 5 put: $u.
s
>>> 'no hurries'
```

Note that the comma method is defined by Collection, so it will work for any kind of collection!

```
(1 to: 3), '45'
>>> #(1 2 3 $4 $5)
```

We can also modify an existing string using replaceAll:with: or replaceFrom:to:with: as shown below. Note that the number of characters and the interval should have the same size.

```
s replaceAll: $n with: $N.
s
>>> 'No hurries'
s replaceFrom: 4 to: 5 with: 'wo'.
s
>>> 'No worries'
```

In contrast to the methods described above, the method copyReplaceAll: creates a new string. (Curiously, here the arguments are substrings rather than individual characters, and their sizes do not have to match.)

```
s copyReplaceAll: 'rries' with: 'mbats'
>>> 'No wombats'
```

A quick look at the implementation of these methods reveals that they are defined not only for Strings, but for any kind of SequenceableCollection, so the following also works:

```
(1 to: 6) copyReplaceAll: (3 to: 5) with: { 'three' . 'etc.' }
>>> #(1 2 'three' 'etc.' 6)
```

String matching It is possible to ask whether a pattern matches a string by sending the match: message. The pattern can use * to match an arbitrary

11.4 Examples of key classes

series of characters and # to match a single character. Note that match: is sent to the pattern and not the string to be matched.

```
'Linux *' match: 'Linux mag'
>>> true
'GNU#Linux #ag' match: 'GNU/Linux tag'
>>> true
```

More advanced pattern matching facilities are also available in the Regex package.

Substrings For substring manipulation we can use messages like first, first:, allButFirst:, copyFrom:to: and others, defined in SequenceableCollection.

```
'alphabet' at: 6
>>> $b
```

```
'alphabet' first
>>> $a
```

```
'alphabet' first: 5
>>> 'alpha'
```

```
'alphabet' allButFirst: 3
>>> 'habet'
```

```
'alphabet' copyFrom: 5 to: 7
>>> 'abe'
```

```
'alphabet' copyFrom: 3 to: 3
>>> 'p' (not $p)
```

Be aware that result type can be different, depending on the method used. Most of the substring-related methods return String instances. But the messages that always return one element of the String collection, return a Character instance (for example, 'alphabet' at: 6 returns the character $b). For a complete list of substring-related messages, browse the SequenceableCollection class (especially the accessing protocol).

Some tests on strings The following examples illustrate the use of isEmpty, includes: and anySatisfy: which are also messages defined not only on Strings but more generally on collections.

```
'Hello' isEmpty
>>> false
```

```
'Hello' includes: $a
>>> false
```

```
'JOE' anySatisfy: [ :c | c isLowercase ]
>>> false
```

```
'Joe' anySatisfy: [ :c | c isLowercase ]
>>> true
```

String templating There are three messages that are useful to manage string templating: `format:`, `expandMacros` and `expandMacrosWith:`.

```
'{1} is {2}' format: {'Pharo' . 'cool'}
>>> 'Pharo is cool'
```

The messages of the expandMacros family offer variable substitution, using <n> for carriage return, <t> for tabulation, <1s>, <2s>, <3s> for arguments (<1p>, <2p>, surrounds the string with single quotes), and <1?value1:value2> for conditional.

```
'look-<t>-here' expandMacros
>>> 'look- -here'
```

```
'<1s> is <2s>' expandMacrosWith: 'Pharo' with: 'cool'
>>> 'Pharo is cool'
```

```
'<2s> is <1s>' expandMacrosWith: 'Pharo' with: 'cool'
>>> 'cool is Pharo'
```

```
'<1p> or <1s>' expandMacrosWith: 'Pharo' with: 'cool'
>>> '''Pharo'' or Pharo'
```

```
'<1?Quentin:Thibaut> plays' expandMacrosWith: true
>>> 'Quentin plays'
```

```
'<1?Quentin:Thibaut> plays' expandMacrosWith: false
>>> 'Thibaut plays'
```

Some other utility methods The class String offers numerous other utilities including the messages asLowercase, asUppercase and capitalized.

```
'XYZ' asLowercase
>>> 'xyz'
```

```
'xyz' asUppercase
>>> 'XYZ'
```

```
'hilaire' capitalized
>>> 'Hilaire'
```

```
'Hilaire' uncapitalized
>>> 'hilaire'
```

```
'1.54' asNumber
>>> 1.54
```

```
'this sentence is without a doubt far too long' contractTo: 20
>>> 'this sent...too long'
```

Note that there is generally a difference between asking an object its string representation by sending the message printString and converting it to a string by sending the message asString. Here is an example of the difference.

```
#ASymbol printString
>>> '#ASymbol'
```

```
#ASymbol asString
>>> 'ASymbol'
```

A symbol is similar to a string but is guaranteed to be globally unique. For this reason symbols are preferred to strings as keys for dictionaries, in particular for instances of IdentityDictionary. See also Chapter : Basic Classes for more about String and Symbol.

11.5 Collection iterators

In Pharo loops and conditionals are simply messages sent to collections or other objects such as integers or blocks (see also Chapter : Syntax in a Nutshell). In addition to low-level messages such as to:do: which evaluates a block with an argument ranging from an initial to a final number, the collection hierarchy offers various high-level iterators. Using such iterators will make your code more robust and compact.

Iterating (do:)

The method do: is the basic collection iterator. It applies its argument (a block taking a single argument) to each element of the receiver. The following example prints all the strings contained in the receiver to the transcript.

```
#('bob' 'joe' 'toto') do: [:each | Transcript show: each; cr].
```

Variants. There are a lot of variants of do:, such as do:without:, doWithIndex: and reverseDo:.

For the indexed collections (Array, OrderedCollection, SortedCollection) the message doWithIndex: also gives access to the current index. This message is related to to:do: which is defined in class Number.

```
#('bob' 'joe' 'toto')
    doWithIndex: [ :each :i | (each = 'joe') ifTrue: [ ^ i ] ]
>>> 2
```

For ordered collections, the message reverseDo: walks the collection in the reverse order.

The following code shows an interesting message: do:separatedBy: which executes the second block only in between two elements.

```
| res |
res := ''.
#('bob' 'joe' 'toto')
    do: [ :e | res := res, e ]
    separatedBy: [ res := res, '.' ].
res
>>> 'bob.joe.toto'
```

Note that this code is not especially efficient since it creates intermediate strings and it would be better to use a write stream to buffer the result (see Chapter : Streams):

```
String streamContents: [ :stream |
    #('bob' 'joe' 'toto') asStringOn: stream delimiter: '.' ]
>>> 'bob.joe.toto'
```

Dictionaries

When the message do: is sent to a dictionary, the elements taken into account are the values, not the associations. The proper messages to use are keysDo:, valuesDo:, and associationsDo:, which iterate respectively on keys, values or associations.

```
colors := Dictionary newFrom: { #yellow -> Color yellow. #blue -> Color
        blue. #red -> Color red }.
colors keysDo: [ :key | Transcript show: key; cr ].
colors valuesDo: [ :value | Transcript show: value; cr ].
colors associationsDo: [:value | Transcript show: value; cr].
```

Collecting results (collect:)

If you want to apply a function to the elements of a collection and get a new collection with the results, rather than using do:, you are probably better off using collect:, or one of the other iterator methods. Most of these can be found in the enumerating protocol of Collection and its subclasses.

Imagine that we want a collection containing the doubles of the elements in another collection. Using the method do: we must write the following:

```
| double |
double := OrderedCollection new.
#(1 2 3 4 5 6) do: [ :e | double add: 2 * e ].
double
>>> an OrderedCollection(2 4 6 8 10 12)
```

The message collect: executes its argument block for each element and returns a new collection containing the results. Using collect: instead, the code is much simpler:

11.5 Collection iterators

```
#(1 2 3 4 5 6) collect: [ :e | 2 * e ]
>>> #(2 4 6 8 10 12)
```

The advantages of `collect:` over `do:` are even more important in the following example, where we take a collection of integers and generate as a result a collection of absolute values of these integers:

```
aCol := #( 2 -3 4 -35 4 -11).
result := aCol species new: aCol size.
1 to: aCol size do: [ :each | result at: each put: (aCol at: each) abs
    ].
result
>>> #(2 3 4 35 4 11)
```

Contrast the above with the much simpler following expression:

```
#( 2 -3 4 -35 4 -11) collect: [ :each | each abs ]
>>> #(2 3 4 35 4 11)
```

A further advantage of the second solution is that it will also work for sets and bags. Generally you should avoid using `do:`, unless you want to send messages to each of the elements of a collection.

Note that sending the message `collect:` returns the same kind of collection as the receiver. For this reason the following code fails. (A `String` cannot hold integer values.)

```
'abc' collect: [ :ea | ea asciiValue ]
>>> "error!"
```

Instead we must first convert the string to an `Array` or an `OrderedCollection`:

```
'abc' asArray collect: [ :ea | ea asciiValue ]
>>> #(97 98 99)
```

Actually `collect:` is not guaranteed to return a collection of exactly the same class as the receiver, but only the same *species*. In the case of an `Interval`, the species is an `Array`!

```
(1 to: 5) collect: [ :ea | ea * 2 ]
>>> #(2 4 6 8 10)
```

Selecting and rejecting elements

The message `select:` returns the elements of the receiver that satisfy a particular condition:

```
(2 to: 20) select: [ :each | each isPrime ]
>>> #(2 3 5 7 11 13 17 19)
```

The message `reject:` does the opposite:

```
(2 to: 20) reject: [ :each | each isPrime ]
>>> #(4 6 8 9 10 12 14 15 16 18 20)
```

Identifying an element with detect:

The message detect: returns the first element of the receiver that matches block argument.

```
'through' detect: [ :each | each isVowel ]
>>> $o
```

The message detect:ifNone: is a variant of the method detect:. Its second block is evaluated when there is no element matching the block.

```
Smalltalk globals allClasses
    detect: [:each | '*cobol*' match: each asString]
    ifNone: [ nil ]
>>> nil
```

Accumulating results with inject:into:

Functional programming languages often provide a higher-order function called *fold* or *reduce* to accumulate a result by applying some binary operator iteratively over all elements of a collection. In Pharo this is done by Collection>>inject:into:.

The first argument is an initial value, and the second argument is a two-argument block which is applied to the result this far, and each element in turn.

A trivial application of inject:into: is to produce the sum of a collection of numbers. In Pharo we could write this expression to sum the first 100 integers:

```
(1 to: 100) inject: 0 into: [ :sum :each | sum + each ]
>>> 5050
```

Another example is the following one-argument block which computes factorials:

```
factorial := [ :n | (1 to: n) inject: 1 into: [ :product :each |
    product * each ] ].
factorial value: 10
>>> 3628800
```

Other messages

There are many other iterator messages. Just check the Collection class.

11.6 Some hints for using collections

count: The message `count:` returns the number of elements satisfying a condition. The condition is represented as a boolean block.

```
Smalltalk globals allClasses
    count: [ :each | 'Collection*' match: each asString ]
>>> 6
```

includes: The message `includes:` checks whether the argument is contained in the collection.

```
| colors |
colors := {Color white . Color yellow . Color blue . Color orange}.
colors includes: Color blue.
>>> true
```

anySatisfy: The message `anySatisfy:` answers true if at least one element of the collection satisfies the condition represented by the argument.

```
colors anySatisfy: [ :c | c red > 0.5 ]
>>> true
```

11.6 Some hints for using collections

A common mistake with add: The following error is one of the most frequent Smalltalk mistakes.

```
| collection |
collection := OrderedCollection new add: 1; add: 2.
collection
>>> 2
```

Here the variable `collection` does not hold the newly created collection but rather the last number added. This is because the method `add:` returns the element added and not the receiver.

The following code yields the expected result:

```
| collection |
collection := OrderedCollection new.
collection add: 1; add: 2.
collection
>>> an OrderedCollection(1 2)
```

You can also use the message `yourself` to return the receiver of a cascade of messages:

```
| collection |
collection := OrderedCollection new add: 1; add: 2; yourself
>>> an OrderedCollection(1 2)
```

Removing an element of the collection you are iterating on Another mistake you may make is to remove an element from a collection you are currently iterating over.

```
| range |
range := (2 to: 20) asOrderedCollection.
range do: [ :aNumber | aNumber isPrime
                        ifFalse: [ range remove: aNumber ] ].
range
>>> an OrderedCollection(2 3 5 7 9 11 13 15 17 19)
```

This result is clearly incorrect since 9 and 15 should have been filtered out!

The solution is to copy the collection before going over it.

```
| range |
range := (2 to: 20) asOrderedCollection.
range copy do: [ :aNumber | aNumber isPrime
                        ifFalse: [ range remove: aNumber ] ].
range
>>> an OrderedCollection(2 3 5 7 11 13 17 19)
```

Redefining = but not hash A difficult error to spot is when you redefine = but not hash. The symptoms are that you will lose elements that you put in sets or other strange behaviour. One solution proposed by Kent Beck is to use `bitXor:` to redefine hash. Suppose that we want two books to be considered equal if their titles and authors are the same. Then we would redefine not only = but also hash as follows:

```
Book >> = aBook
    self class = aBook class ifFalse: [ ^ false ].
    ^ title = aBook title and: [ authors = aBook authors ]

Book >> hash
    ^ title hash bitXor: authors hash
```

Another nasty problem arises if you use a mutable object, i.e., an object that can change its hash value over time, as an element of a `Set` or as a key to a `Dictionary`. Don't do this unless you love debugging!

11.7 Chapter summary

The collection hierarchy provides a common vocabulary for uniformly manipulating a variety of different kinds of collections.

- A key distinction is between `SequenceableCollections`, which maintain their elements in a given order, `Dictionary` and its subclasses, which maintain key-to-value associations, and `Sets` and `Bags`, which are unordered.

11.7 Chapter summary

- You can convert most collections to another kind of collection by sending them the messages asArray, asOrderedCollection etc..
- To sort a collection, send it the message asSortedCollection.
- #(...) creates arrays containing only literal objects (i.e., objects created without sending messages). { ... } creates dynamic arrays using a compact form.
- A Dictionary compares keys by equality. It is most useful when keys are instances of String. An IdentityDictionary instead uses object identity to compare keys. It is more suitable when Symbols are used as keys, or when mapping object references to values.
- Strings also understand the usual collection messages. In addition, a String supports a simple form of pattern-matching. For more advanced application, look instead at the RegEx package.
- The basic iteration message is do:. It is useful for imperative code, such as modifying each element of a collection, or sending each element a message.
- Instead of using do:, it is more common to use collect:, select:, reject:, includes:, inject:into: and other higher-level messages to process collections in a uniform way.
- Never remove an element from a collection you are iterating over. If you must modify it, iterate over a copy instead.
- If you override =, remember to override hash as well!

CHAPTER **12**

Streams

Streams are used to iterate over sequences of elements such as sequenced collections, files, and network streams. Streams may be either readable, or writeable, or both. Reading or writing is always relative to the current position in the stream. Streams can easily be converted to collections, and vice versa.

12.1 Two sequences of elements

A good metaphor to understand a stream is the following. A stream can be represented as two sequences of elements: a past element sequence and a future element sequence. The stream is positioned between the two sequences. Understanding this model is important, since all stream operations in Pharo rely on it. For this reason, most of the Stream classes are subclasses of PositionableStream. Figure 12.1 presents a stream which contains five characters. This stream is in its original position, i.e., there is no element in the past. You can go back to this position using the message reset defined in PositionableStream.

Reading an element conceptually means removing the first element of the future element sequence and putting it after the last element in the past

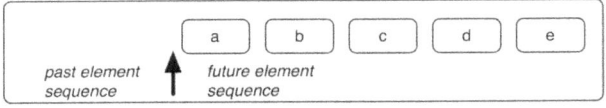

Figure 12.1: A stream positioned at its beginning.

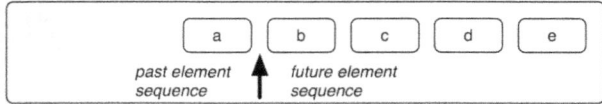

Figure 12.2: The same stream after the execution of the method next: the character a is *in the past* whereas b, c, d and e are *in the future*.

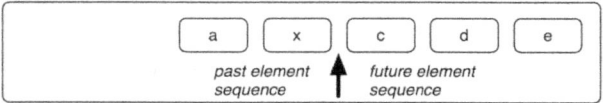

Figure 12.3: The same stream after having written an x.

element sequence. After having read one element using the message next, the state of your stream is that shown in Figure 12.2.

Writing an element means replacing the first element of the future sequence by the new one and moving it to the past. Figure 12.3 shows the state of the same stream after having written an x using the message nextPut: anElement defined in Stream.

12.2 Streams vs. collections

The collection protocol supports the storage, removal and enumeration of the elements of a collection, but does not allow these operations to be intermingled. For example, if the elements of an OrderedCollection are processed by a do: method, it is not possible to add or remove elements from inside the do: block. Nor does the collection protocol offer ways to iterate over two collections at the same time, choosing which collection goes forward and which does not. Procedures like these require that a traversal index or position reference is maintained outside of the collection itself: this is exactly the role of ReadStream, WriteStream and ReadWriteStream.

These three classes are defined to *stream over* some collection. For example, the following snippet creates a stream on an interval, then it reads two elements.

```
| r |
r := ReadStream on: (1 to: 1000).
r next.
>>> 1
r next.
>>> 2
r atEnd.
>>> false
```

12.3 Streaming over collections

WriteStreams can write data to the collection:

```
| w |
w := WriteStream on: (String new: 5).
w nextPut: $a.
w nextPut: $b.
w contents.
>>> 'ab'
```

It is also possible to create `ReadWriteStreams` that support both the reading and writing protocols.

Streams are not only meant for collections, they can be used for files or sockets too. The following example creates a file named test.txt, writes two strings to it, separated by a carriage return, and closes the file.

```
StandardFileStream
    fileNamed: 'test.txt'
    do: [:str | str
                nextPutAll: '123';
                cr;
                nextPutAll: 'abcd' ].
```

The following sections present the protocols in more depth.

12.3 Streaming over collections

Streams are really useful when dealing with collections of elements, and can be used for reading and writing those elements. We will now explore the stream features for collections.

Reading collections

Using a stream to read a collection essentially provides you a pointer into the collection. That pointer will move forward on reading, and you can place it wherever you want. The class `ReadStream` should be used to read elements from collections.

Messages `next` and `next:` defined in `ReadStream` are used to retrieve one or more elements from the collection.

```
| stream |
stream := ReadStream on: #(1 (a b c) false).
stream next.
>>> 1
stream next.
>>> #(#a #b #c)
stream next.
>>> false
```

219

```
| stream |
stream := ReadStream on: 'abcdef'.
stream next: 0.
>>> ''
stream next: 1.
>>> 'a'
stream next: 3.
>>> 'bcd'
stream next: 2.
>>> 'ef'
```

The message peek defined in PositionableStream is used when you want to know what is the next element in the stream without going forward.

```
stream := ReadStream on: '-143'.
"look at the first element without consuming it."
negative := (stream peek = $-).
negative.
>>> true
"ignores the minus character"
negative ifTrue: [ stream next ].
number := stream upToEnd.
number.
>>> '143'
```

This code sets the boolean variable negative according to the sign of the number in the stream, and number to its absolute value. The message upToEnd defined in ReadStream returns everything from the current position to the end of the stream and sets the stream to its end. This code can be simplified using the message peekFor: defined in PositionableStream, which moves forward if the following element equals the parameter and doesn't move otherwise.

```
| stream |
stream := '-143' readStream.
(stream peekFor: $-)
>>> true
stream upToEnd
>>> '143'
```

peekFor: also returns a boolean indicating if the parameter equals the element.

You might have noticed a new way of constructing a stream in the above example: one can simply send the message readStream to a sequenceable collection (such as a String) to get a reading stream on that particular collection.

Positioning

There are messages to position the stream pointer. If you have the index, you can go directly to it using position: defined in PositionableStream. You

12.3 Streaming over collections

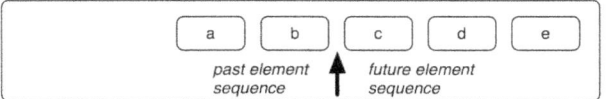

Figure 12.4: A stream at position 2.

can request the current position using position. Please remember that a stream is not positioned on an element, but between two elements. The index corresponding to the beginning of the stream is 0.

You can obtain the state of the stream depicted in 12.4 with the following code:

```
| stream |
stream := 'abcde' readStream.
stream position: 2.
stream peek
>>> $c
```

To position the stream at the beginning or the end, you can use the message reset or setToEnd. The messages skip: and skipTo: are used to go forward to a location relative to the current position: skip: accepts a number as argument and skips that number of elements whereas skipTo: skips all elements in the stream until it finds an element equal to its parameter. Note that it positions the stream after the matched element.

```
| stream |
stream := 'abcdef' readStream.
stream next.
>>> $a "stream is now positioned just after the a"
stream skip: 3. "stream is now after the d"
stream position.
>>> 4
stream skip: -2. "stream is after the b"
stream position.
>>> 2
stream reset.
stream position.
>>> 0
stream skipTo: $e. "stream is just after the e now"
stream next.
>>> $f
stream contents.
>>> 'abcdef'
```

As you can see, the letter e has been skipped.

The message contents always returns a copy of the entire stream.

Testing

Some messages allow you to test the state of the current stream: atEnd returns true if and only if no more elements can be read, whereas isEmpty returns true if and only if there are no elements at all in the collection.

Here is a possible implementation of an algorithm using atEnd that takes two sorted collections as parameters and merges those collections into another sorted collection:

```
| stream1 stream2 result |
stream1 := #(1 4 9 11 12 13) readStream.
stream2 := #(1 2 3 4 5 10 13 14 15) readStream.

"The variable result will contain the sorted collection."
result := OrderedCollection new.
[stream1 atEnd not & stream2 atEnd not ]
  whileTrue: [
    stream1 peek < stream2 peek
      "Remove the smallest element from either stream and add it to
          the result."
      ifTrue: [result add: stream1 next ]
      ifFalse: [result add: stream2 next ] ].

"One of the two streams might not be at its end. Copy whatever remains."
result
  addAll: stream1 upToEnd;
  addAll: stream2 upToEnd.

result.
>>> an OrderedCollection(1 1 2 3 4 4 5 9 10 11 12 13 13 14 15)
```

Writing to collections

We have already seen how to read a collection by iterating over its elements using a ReadStream. We'll now learn how to create collections using WriteStreams.

WriteStreams are useful for appending a lot of data to a collection at various locations. They are often used to construct strings that are based on static and dynamic parts, as in this example:

```
| stream |
stream := String new writeStream.
stream
  nextPutAll: 'This Smalltalk image contains: ';
  print: Smalltalk allClasses size;
  nextPutAll: ' classes.';
  cr;
  nextPutAll: 'This is really a lot.'.
```

12.3 Streaming over collections

```
stream contents.
>>> 'This Smalltalk image contains: 2322 classes.
This is really a lot.'
```

This technique is used in the different implementations of the method printOn:, for example. There is a simpler and more efficient way of creating strings if you are only interested in the content of the stream:

```
| string |
string := String streamContents:
    [ :stream |
      stream
          print: #(1 2 3);
          space;
          nextPutAll: 'size';
          space;
          nextPut: $=;
          space;
          print: 3. ].
string.
>>> '#(1 2 3) size = 3'
```

The message streamContents: defined SequenceableCollection creates a collection and a stream on that collection for you. It then executes the block you gave passing the stream as a parameter. When the block ends, streamContents: returns the contents of the collection.

The following WriteStream methods are especially useful in this context:

nextPut: adds the parameter to the stream;

nextPutAll: adds each element of the collection, passed as a parameter, to the stream;

print: adds the textual representation of the parameter to the stream.

There are also convenient messages for printing useful characters to a stream, such as space, tab and cr (carriage return). Another useful method is ensureASpace which ensures that the last character in the stream is a space; if the last character isn't a space it adds one.

About String Concatenation

Using nextPut: and nextPutAll: on a WriteStream is often the best way to concatenate characters. Using the comma concatenation operator (,) is far less efficient:

```
[| temp |
  temp := String new.
  (1 to: 100000)
    do: [:i | temp := temp, i asString, ' ' ] ] timeToRun
>>> 115176 "(milliseconds)"
```

Figure 12.5: A new history is empty. Nothing is displayed in the web browser.

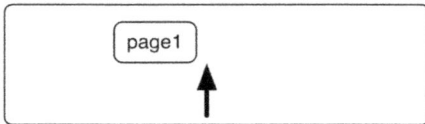

Figure 12.6: The user opens to page 1.

```
[| temp |
  temp := WriteStream on: String new.
  (1 to: 100000)
    do: [:i | temp nextPutAll: i asString; space ].
  temp contents ] timeToRun
>>> 1262 "(milliseconds)"
```

The reason that using a stream can be much more efficient is that using a comma creates a new string containing the concatenation of the receiver and the argument, so it must copy both of them. When you repeatedly concatenate onto the same receiver, it gets longer and longer each time, so that the number of characters that must be copied goes up exponentially. This also creates a lot of garbage, which must be collected. Using a stream instead of string concatenation is a well-known optimization.

In fact, you can use the message streamContents: defined in Sequenceable Collection class (mentioned earlier) to help you do this:

```
String streamContents: [ :tempStream |
  (1 to: 100000)
    do: [:i | tempStream nextPutAll: i asString; space ] ]
```

Reading and writing at the same time

It's possible to use a stream to access a collection for reading and writing at the same time. Imagine you want to create a History class which will manage backward and forward buttons in a web browser. A history would react as in figures 12.5 to 12.11.

This behaviour can be implemented using a ReadWriteStream.

```
Object subclass: #History
  instanceVariableNames: 'stream'
```

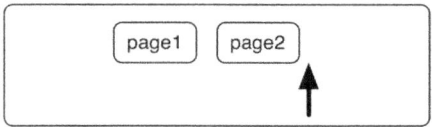

Figure 12.7: The user clicks on a link to page 2.

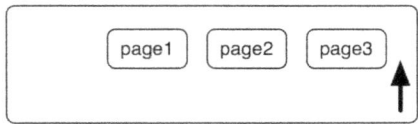

Figure 12.8: The user clicks on a link to page 3.

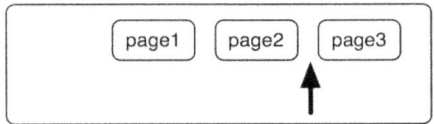

Figure 12.9: The user clicks on the Back button. They are now viewing page 2 again.

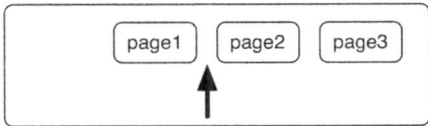

Figure 12.10: The user clicks again the back button. Page 1 is now displayed.

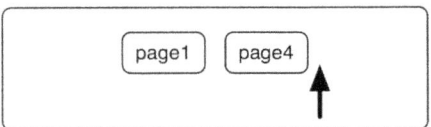

Figure 12.11: From page 1, the user clicks on a link to page 4. The history forgets pages 2 and 3.

```
classVariableNames: ''
package: 'PBE-Streams'

History >> initialize
    super initialize.
    stream := ReadWriteStream on: Array new.
```

Nothing really difficult here, we define a new class which contains a stream. The stream is created during the `initialize` method.

We need methods to go backward and forward:

```
History >> goBackward
  self canGoBackward
    ifFalse: [ self error: 'Already on the first element' ].
  stream skip: -2.
  ^ stream next.

History >> goForward
  self canGoForward
    ifFalse: [ self error: 'Already on the last element' ].
  ^ stream next
```

Up to this point, the code is pretty straightforward. Next, we have to deal with the `goTo:` method which should be activated when the user clicks on a link. A possible implementation is:

```
History >> goTo: aPage
    stream nextPut: aPage.
```

This version is incomplete however. This is because when the user clicks on the link, there should be no more future pages to go to, *i.e.*, the forward button must be deactivated. To do this, the simplest solution is to write `nil` just after, to indicate that history is at the end:

```
History >> goTo: anObject
    stream nextPut: anObject.
    stream nextPut: nil.
    stream back.
```

Now, only methods `canGoBackward` and `canGoForward` remain to be implemented.

A stream is always positioned between two elements. To go backward, there must be two pages before the current position: one page is the current page, and the other one is the page we want to go to.

```
History >> canGoBackward
  ^ stream position > 1

History >> canGoForward
  ^ stream atEnd not and: [stream peek notNil ]
```

12.4 Using streams for file access

Let us add a method to peek at the contents of the stream:

```
History >> contents
   ^ stream contents
```

And the history works as advertised:

```
History new
   goTo: #page1;
   goTo: #page2;
   goTo: #page3;
   goBackward;
   goBackward;
   goTo: #page4;
   contents
>>> #(#page1 #page4 nil nil)
```

12.4 Using streams for file access

You have already seen how to stream over collections of elements. It's also possible to stream over files on your hard disk. Once created, a stream on a file is really like a stream on a collection; you will be able to use the same protocol to read, write or position the stream. The main difference appears in the creation of the stream. There are several different ways to create file streams, as we shall now see.

Creating file streams

To create file streams, you will have to use one of the following instance creation messages offered by the class `FileStream`:

fileNamed: Open a file with the given name for reading and writing. If the file already exists, its prior contents may be modified or replaced, but the file will not be truncated on close. If the name has no directory part, then the file will be created in the default directory.

newFileNamed: Create a new file with the given name, and answer a stream opened for writing on that file. If the file already exists, ask the user what to do.

forceNewFileNamed: Create a new file with the given name, and answer a stream opened for writing on that file. If the file already exists, delete it without asking before creating the new file.

oldFileNamed: Open an existing file with the given name for reading and writing. If the file already exists, its prior contents may be modified or replaced, but the file will not be truncated on close. If the name has no directory part, then the file will be created in the default directory.

readOnlyFileNamed: Open an existing file with the given name for reading.

You have to remember that each time you open a stream on a file, you have to close it too. This is done through the =close message defined in FileStream.

```
| stream |
stream := FileStream forceNewFileNamed: 'test.txt'.
stream
    nextPutAll: 'This text is written in a file named ';
    print: stream localName.
stream close.

stream := FileStream readOnlyFileNamed: 'test.txt'.
stream contents.
>>> 'This text is written in a file named ''test.txt'''
stream close.
```

The message localName defined in class FileStream answers the last component of the name of the file. You can also access the full path name using the message fullName.

You will soon notice that manually closing the file stream is painful and error-prone. That's why FileStream offers a message called forceNewFileNamed:do: to automatically close a new stream after evaluating a block that sets its contents.

```
| string |
FileStream
    forceNewFileNamed: 'test.txt'
    do: [ :stream |
        stream
            nextPutAll: 'This text is written in a file named ';
            print: stream localName ].
string := FileStream
            readOnlyFileNamed: 'test.txt'
            do: [ :stream | stream contents ].
string
>>> 'This text is written in a file named ''test.txt'''
```

The stream creation methods that take a block as an argument first create a stream on a file, then execute the block with the stream as an argument, and finally close the stream. These methods return what is returned by the block, which is to say, the value of the last expression in the block. This is used in the previous example to get the content of the file and put it in the variable string.

Binary streams

By default, created streams are text-based which means you will read and write characters. If your stream must be binary, you have to send the message binary to your stream.

When your stream is in binary mode, you can only write numbers from 0 to 255 (1 Byte). If you want to use nextPutAll: to write more than one number at a time, you have to pass a ByteArray as argument.

```
FileStream
  forceNewFileNamed: 'test.bin'
  do: [ :stream |
        stream
          binary;
          nextPutAll: #(145 250 139 98) asByteArray ].
```

```
FileStream
  readOnlyFileNamed: 'test.bin'
  do: [ :stream |
        stream binary.
        stream size.
      >>> 4
        stream next.
      >>> 145
        stream upToEnd.
      >>> #[250 139 98 ]
      ].
```

Here is another example which creates a picture in a file named test.pgm (portable graymap file format). You can open this file with your favorite drawing program.

```
FileStream
  forceNewFileNamed: 'test.pgm'
  do: [ :stream |
   stream
      nextPutAll: 'P5'; cr;
      nextPutAll: '4 4'; cr;
      nextPutAll: '255'; cr;
      binary;
      nextPutAll: #(255 0 255 0) asByteArray;
      nextPutAll: #(0 255 0 255) asByteArray;
      nextPutAll: #(255 0 255 0) asByteArray;
      nextPutAll: #(0 255 0 255) asByteArray ]
```

This creates a 4x4 checkerboard as shown in 12.12.

12.5 Chapter summary

Streams offer a better way (compared to collections) to incrementally read and write a sequence of elements. There are easy ways to convert back and forth between streams and collections.

- Streams may be either readable, writeable or both readable and writeable.

Figure 12.12: A 4x4 checkerboard you can draw using binary streams.

- To convert a collection to a stream, define a stream *on* a collection, *e.g.*, ReadStream on: (1 to: 1000), or send the messages readStream, etc. to the collection.
- To convert a stream to a collection, send the message contents.
- To concatenate large collections, instead of using the comma operator, it is more efficient to create a stream, append the collections to the stream with nextPutAll:, and extract the result by sending contents.
- File streams are by default character-based. Send binary to explicitly make them binary.

CHAPTER 13

Morphic

Morphic is the name given to Pharo's graphical interface. Morphic is written in Pharo, so it is fully portable between operating systems. As a consequence, Pharo looks exactly the same on Unix, MacOS and Windows. What distinguishes Morphic from most other user interface toolkits is that it does not have separate modes for *composing* and *running* the interface: all the graphical elements can be assembled and disassembled by the user, at any time. (We thank Hilaire Fernandes for permission to base this chapter on his original article in French.)

13.1 The history of Morphic

Morphic was developed by John Maloney and Randy Smith for the Self programming language, starting around 1993. Maloney later wrote a new version of Morphic for Squeak, but the basic ideas behind the Self version are still alive and well in Pharo Morphic: *directness* and *liveness*. Directness means that the shapes on the screen are objects that can be examined or changed directly, that is, by clicking on them using a mouse. Liveness means that the user interface is always able to respond to user actions: information on the screen is continuously updated as the world that it describes changes. A simple example of this is that you can detach a menu item and keep it as a button.

Bring up the World Menu and meta-click once on it to bring up its morphic halo, then meta-click again on a menu item you want to detach, to bring up that item's halo. (Recall that you should set `halosEnabled` in the Preferences browser.) Now drag that item elsewhere on the screen by grabbing the black handle (see Figure 13.1), as shown in Figure 13.2.

Figure 13.1: The grab handle.

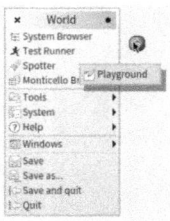

Figure 13.2: Detaching a morph, here the `Playground` menu item, to make it an independent button.

All of the objects that you see on the screen when you run Pharo are *Morphs*, that is, they are instances of subclasses of class Morph. Morph itself is a large class with many methods; this makes it possible for subclasses to implement interesting behaviour with little code. You can create a morph to represent any object, although how good a representation you get depends on the object!

To create a morph to represent a string object, execute the following code in a Playground.

```
'Morph' asMorph openInWorld
```

This creates a Morph to represent the string 'Morph', and then opens it (that is, displays it) in the *world*, which is the name that Pharo gives to the screen. You should obtain a graphical element (a Morph), which you can manipulate by meta-clicking.

Of course, it is possible to define morphs that are more interesting graphical representations than the one that you have just seen. The method asMorph has a default implementation in class Object class that just creates a String-Morph. So, for example, Color tan asMorph returns a StringMorph labeled with the result of Color tan printString. Let's change this so that we get a coloured rectangle instead.

Open a browser on the Color class and add the following method to it:

```
Color >> asMorph
    ^ Morph new color: self
```

Now execute `Color orange asMorph openInWorld` in a Playground. Instead of the string-like morph, you get an orange rectangle (see Figure 13.3)!

13.2 Manipulating morphs

Figure 13.3: `Color orange asMorph openInWorld` with our new method.

13.2 Manipulating morphs

Morphs are objects, so we can manipulate them like any other object in Pharo: by sending messages, we can change their properties, create new subclasses of Morph, and so on.

Every morph, even if it is not currently open on the screen, has a position and a size. For convenience, all morphs are considered to occupy a rectangular region of the screen; if they are irregularly shaped, their position and size are those of the smallest rectangular *box* that surrounds them, which is known as the morph's bounding box, or just its *bounds*. The `position` method returns a `Point` that describes the location of the morph's upper left corner (or the upper left corner of its bounding box). The origin of the coordinate system is the screen's upper left corner, with *y* coordinates increasing *down* the screen and *x* coordinates increasing to the right. The `extent` method also returns a point, but this point specifies the width and height of the morph rather than a location.

Type the following code into a playground and `Do it`:

```
joe := Morph new color: Color blue.
joe openInWorld.
bill := Morph new color: Color red.
bill openInWorld.
```

Then type `joe position` and then `Print it`. To move joe, execute `joe position: (joe position + (10@3))` repeatedly (see Figure 13.4).

It is possible to do a similar thing with size. `joe extent` answers joe's size; to have joe grow, execute `joe extent: (joe extent * 1.1)`. To change the color of a morph, send it the `color:` message with the desired `Color` object as

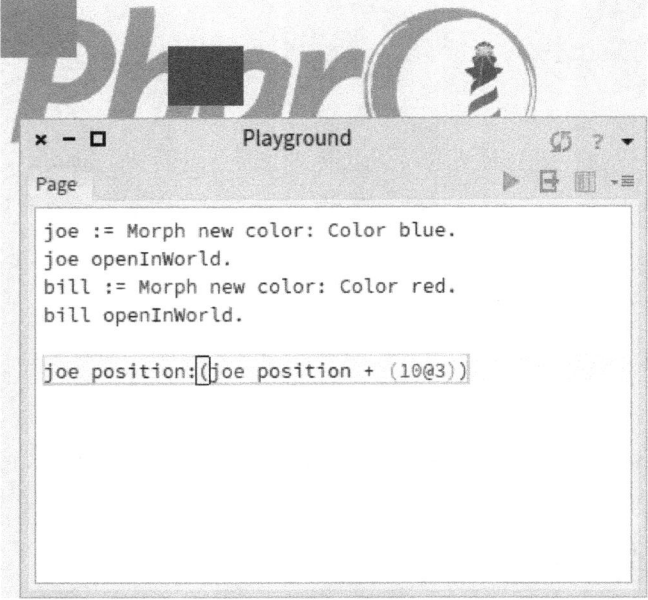

Figure 13.4: Bill and Joe after 10 moves.

argument, for instance, joe color: Color orange. To add transparency, try joe color: (Color orange alpha: 0.5).

To make bill follow joe, you can repeatedly execute this code:

```
bill position: (joe position + (100@0))
```

If you move joe using the mouse and then execute this code, bill will move so that it is 100 pixels to the right of joe.

You can see the result on Figure 13.5

13.3 Composing morphs

One way of creating new graphical representations is by placing one morph inside another. This is called *composition*; morphs can be composed to any depth.

You can place a morph inside another by sending the message addMorph: to the container morph.

Try adding a morph to another one:

```
balloon := BalloonMorph new color: Color yellow.
joe addMorph: balloon.
```

13.3 Composing morphs

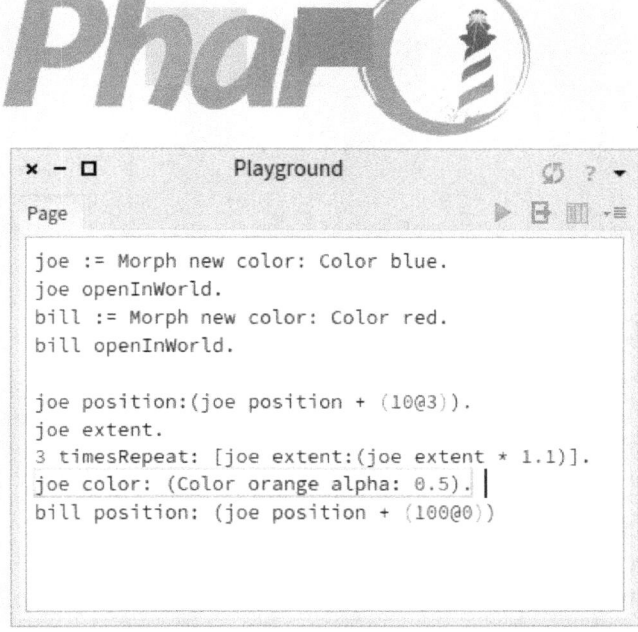

Figure 13.5: Bill follows Joe.

Figure 13.6: The balloon is contained inside joe, the translucent orange morph.

```
balloon position: joe position.
```

The last line positions the balloon at the same coordinates as joe. Notice that the coordinates of the contained morph are still relative to the screen, not to the containing morph. There are many methods available to position a morph; browse the geometry protocol of class Morph to see for yourself. For example, to center the balloon inside joe, execute `balloon center: joe center`.

If you now try to grab the balloon with the mouse, you will find that you actually grab joe, and the two morphs move together: the balloon is *embedded* inside joe. It is possible to embed more morphs inside joe. In addition to doing this programmatically, you can also embed morphs by direct manipulation.

235

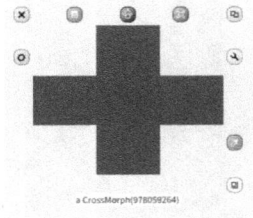

Figure 13.7: A CrossMorph with its halo; you can resize it as you wish.

13.4 Creating and drawing your own morphs

While it is possible to make many interesting and useful graphical representations by composing morphs, sometimes you will need to create something completely different.

To do this you define a subclass of Morph and override the drawOn: method to change its appearance.

The morphic framework sends the message drawOn: to a morph when it needs to redisplay the morph on the screen. The parameter to drawOn: is a kind of Canvas; the expected behaviour is that the morph will draw itself on that canvas, inside its bounds. Let's use this knowledge to create a cross-shaped morph.

Using the browser, define a new class CrossMorph inheriting from Morph:

```
Morph subclass: #CrossMorph
    instanceVariableNames: ''
    classVariableNames: ''
    package: 'PBE-Morphic'
```

We can define the drawOn: method like this:

```
CrossMorph >> drawOn: aCanvas
    | crossHeight crossWidth horizontalBar verticalBar |
    crossHeight := self height / 3.0.
    crossWidth := self width / 3.0.
    horizontalBar := self bounds insetBy: 0 @ crossHeight.
    verticalBar := self bounds insetBy: crossWidth @ 0.
    aCanvas fillRectangle: horizontalBar color: self color.
    aCanvas fillRectangle: verticalBar color: self color
```

Sending the bounds message to a morph answers its bounding box, which is an instance of Rectangle. Rectangles understand many messages that create other rectangles of related geometry. Here, we use the insetBy: message with a point as its argument to create first a rectangle with reduced height, and then another rectangle with reduced width.

To test your new morph, execute CrossMorph new openInWorld.

13.4 Creating and drawing your own morphs

The result should look something like Figure 13.7. However, you will notice that the sensitive zone — where you can click to grab the morph — is still the whole bounding box. Let's fix this.

When the Morphic framework needs to find out which Morphs lie under the cursor, it sends the message containsPoint: to all the morphs whose bounding boxes lie under the mouse pointer. So, to limit the sensitive zone of the morph to the cross shape, we need to override the containsPoint: method.

Define the following method in class CrossMorph:

```
CrossMorph >> containsPoint: aPoint
    | crossHeight crossWidth horizontalBar verticalBar |
    crossHeight := self height / 3.0.
    crossWidth := self width / 3.0.
    horizontalBar := self bounds insetBy: 0 @ crossHeight.
    verticalBar := self bounds insetBy: crossWidth @ 0.
    ^ (horizontalBar containsPoint: aPoint) or: [ verticalBar
        containsPoint: aPoint ]
```

This method uses the same logic as drawOn:, so we can be confident that the points for which containsPoint: answers true are the same ones that will be colored in by drawOn. Notice how we leverage the containsPoint: method in class Rectangle to do the hard work.

There are two problems with the code in the two methods above.

The most obvious is that we have duplicated code. This is a cardinal error: if we find that we need to change the way that horizontalBar or verticalBar are calculated, we are quite likely to forget to change one of the two occurrences. The solution is to factor out these calculations into two new methods, which we put in the private protocol:

```
CrossMorph >> horizontalBar
    | crossHeight |
    crossHeight := self height / 3.0.
    ^ self bounds insetBy: 0 @ crossHeight
```

```
CrossMorph >> verticalBar
    | crossWidth |
    crossWidth := self width / 3.0.
    ^ self bounds insetBy: crossWidth @ 0
```

We can then define both drawOn: and containsPoint: using these methods:

```
CrossMorph >> drawOn: aCanvas
    aCanvas fillRectangle: self horizontalBar color: self color.
    aCanvas fillRectangle: self verticalBar color: self color
```

```
CrossMorph >> containsPoint: aPoint
    ^ (self horizontalBar containsPoint: aPoint) or: [ self verticalBar
        containsPoint: aPoint ]
```

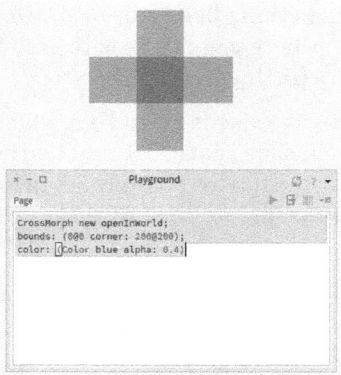

Figure 13.8: The center of the cross is filled twice with the color.

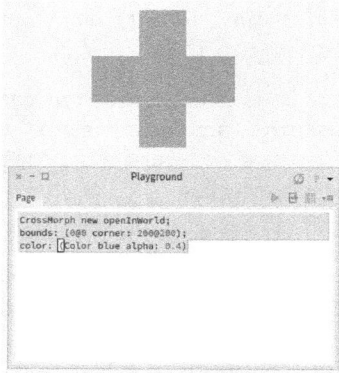

Figure 13.9: The cross-shaped morph, showing a row of unfilled pixels.

This code is much simpler to understand, largely because we have given meaningful names to the private methods. In fact, it is so simple that you may have noticed the second problem: the area in the center of the cross, which is under both the horizontal and the vertical bars, is drawn twice. This doesn't matter when we fill the cross with an opaque colour, but the bug becomes apparent immediately if we draw a semi-transparent cross, as shown in Figure 13.8.

Execute the following code in a playground, line by line:

```
CrossMorph new openInWorld;
    bounds: (0@0 corner: 200@200);
    color: (Color blue alpha: 0.4)
```

The fix is to divide the vertical bar into three pieces, and to fill only the top

13.5 Interaction and animation

and bottom. Once again we find a method in class `Rectangle` that does the hard work for us: `r1 areasOutside: r2` answers an array of rectangles comprising the parts of r1 outside r2. Here is the revised code:

```
CrossMorph >> drawOn: aCanvas
    | topAndBottom |
    aCanvas fillRectangle: self horizontalBar color: self color.
    topAndBottom := self verticalBar areasOutside: self horizontalBar.
    topAndBottom do: [ :each | aCanvas fillRectangle: each color: self
        color ]
```

This code seems to work, but if you try it on some crosses and resize them, you may notice that at some sizes, a one-pixel wide line separates the bottom of the cross from the remainder, as shown in Figure 13.9. This is due to rounding: when the size of the rectangle to be filled is not an integer, `fillRectangle: color:` seems to round inconsistently, leaving one row of pixels unfilled. We can work around this by rounding explicitly when we calculate the sizes of the bars.

```
CrossMorph >> horizontalBar
    | crossHeight |
    crossHeight := (self height / 3.0) rounded.
    ^ self bounds insetBy: 0 @ crossHeight
```

```
CrossMorph >> verticalBar
    | crossWidth |
    crossWidth := (self width / 3.0) rounded.
    ^ self bounds insetBy: crossWidth @ 0
```

13.5 Interaction and animation

To build live user interfaces using morphs, we need to be able to interact with them using the mouse and keyboard. Moreover, the morphs need to be able respond to user input by changing their appearance and position — that is, by animating themselves.

Mouse events

When a mouse button is pressed, Morphic sends each morph under the mouse pointer the message `handlesMouseDown:`. If a morph answers `true`, then Morphic immediately sends it the `mouseDown:` message; it also sends the `mouseUp:` message when the user releases the mouse button. If all morphs answer `false`, then Morphic initiates a drag-and-drop operation. As we will discuss below, the `mouseDown:` and `mouseUp:` messages are sent with an argument — a `MouseEvent` object — that encodes the details of the mouse action.

Let's extend `CrossMorph` to handle mouse events. We start by ensuring that all crossMorphs answer `true` to the `handlesMouseDown:` message.

Figure 13.10: Move Handle button.

Figure 13.11: Grab Handle button.

Add this method to `CrossMorph`:

```
CrossMorph >> handlesMouseDown: anEvent
    ^ true
```

Suppose that when we click on the cross, we want to change the color of the cross to red, and when we action-click on it, we want to change the color to yellow. This can be accomplished by the `mouseDown:` method as follows:

```
CrossMorph >> mouseDown: anEvent
    anEvent redButtonPressed
        ifTrue: [ self color: Color red ].   "click"
    anEvent yellowButtonPressed
        ifTrue: [ self color: Color yellow ].   "action-click"
    self changed
```

Notice that in addition to changing the color of the morph, this method also sends `self changed`. This makes sure that morphic sends `drawOn:` in a timely fashion.

Note also that once the morph handles mouse events, you can no longer grab it with the mouse and move it. Instead you have to use the halo: meta-click on the morph to make the halo appear and grab either the brown move handle (see Figure 13.10) or the black pickup handle (see Figure 13.11) at the top of the morph.

The `anEvent` argument of `mouseDown:` is an instance of `MouseEvent`, which is a subclass of `MorphicEvent`. `MouseEvent` defines the `redButtonPressed` and `yellowButtonPressed` methods. Browse this class to see what other methods it provides to interrogate the mouse event.

Keyboard events

To catch keyboard events, we need to take three steps.

1. Give the *keyboard focus* to a specific morph. For instance, we can give focus to our morph when the mouse is over it.
2. Handle the keyboard event itself with the `handleKeystroke:` method. This message is sent to the morph that has keyboard focus when the user presses a key.

13.5 Interaction and animation

3. Release the keyboard focus when the mouse is no longer over our morph.

Let's extend CrossMorph so that it reacts to keystrokes. First, we need to arrange to be notified when the mouse is over the morph. This will happen if our morph answers true to the handlesMouseOver: message

Declare that CrossMorph will react when it is under the mouse pointer.

```
CrossMorph >> handlesMouseOver: anEvent
    ^true
```

This message is the equivalent of handlesMouseDown: for the mouse position. When the mouse pointer enters or leaves the morph, the mouseEnter: and mouseLeave: messages are sent to it.

Define two methods so that CrossMorph catches and releases the keyboard focus, and a third method to actually handle the keystrokes.

```
CrossMorph >> mouseEnter: anEvent
    anEvent hand newKeyboardFocus: self
```

```
CrossMorph >> mouseLeave: anEvent
    anEvent hand newKeyboardFocus: nil
```

```
CrossMorph >> handleKeystroke: anEvent
    | keyValue |
    keyValue := anEvent keyValue.
    keyValue = 30 "up arrow"
        ifTrue: [self position: self position - (0 @ 1)].
    keyValue = 31 "down arrow"
        ifTrue: [self position: self position + (0 @ 1)].
    keyValue = 29 "right arrow"
        ifTrue: [self position: self position + (1 @ 0)].
    keyValue = 28 "left arrow"
        ifTrue: [self position: self position - (1 @ 0)]
```

We have written this method so that you can move the morph using the arrow keys. Note that when the mouse is no longer over the morph, the handleKeystroke: message is not sent, so the morph stops responding to keyboard commands. To discover the key values, you can open a Transcript window and add Transcript show: anEvent keyValue to the handleKeystroke: method.

The anEvent argument of handleKeystroke: is an instance of KeyboardEvent, another subclass of MorphicEvent. Browse this class to learn more about keyboard events.

Morphic animations

Morphic provides a simple animation system with two main methods: step is sent to a morph at regular intervals of time, while stepTime specifies the time

Figure 13.12: The debug handle button.

in milliseconds between steps. stepTime is actually the *minimum* time between steps. If you ask for a stepTime of 1 ms, don't be surprised if Pharo is too busy to step your morph that often. In addition, startStepping turns on the stepping mechanism, while stopStepping turns it off again. isStepping can be used to find out whether a morph is currently being stepped.

Make CrossMorph blink by defining these methods as follows:

```
CrossMorph >> stepTime
    ^ 100
```

```
CrossMorph >> step
    (self color diff: Color black) < 0.1
        ifTrue: [ self color: Color red ]
        ifFalse: [ self color: self color darker ]
```

To start things off, you can open an inspector on a CrossMorph using the debug handle (see Figure 13.12) in the morphic halo, type self startStepping in the small playground pane at the bottom, and Do it.

Alternatively, you can modify the handleKeystroke: method so that you can use the + and - keys to start and stop stepping. Add the following code to the handleKeystroke: method:

```
keyValue = $+ asciiValue
    ifTrue: [ self startStepping ].
keyValue = $- asciiValue
    ifTrue: [ self stopStepping ].
```

13.6 Interactors

To prompt the user for input, the UIManager class provides a large number of ready to use dialog boxes. For instance, the request:initialAnswer: method returns the string entered by the user (Figure 13.13).

```
UIManager default request: 'What''s your name?' initialAnswer: 'no name'
```

To display a popup menu, use one of the various chooseFrom: methods (Figure 13.14):

```
UIManager default
    chooseFrom: #('circle' 'oval' 'square' 'rectangle' 'triangle')
    lines: #(2 4) message: 'Choose a shape'
```

Browse the UIManager class and try out some of the interaction methods offered.

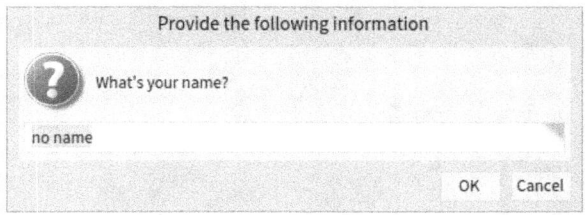

Figure 13.13: An input dialog.

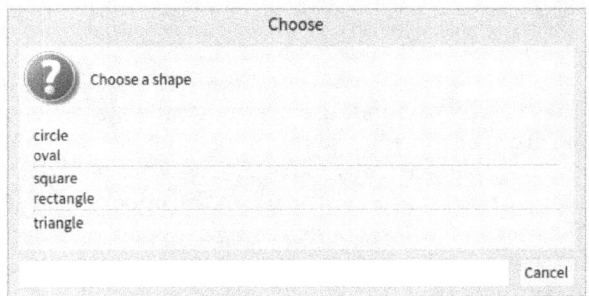

Figure 13.14: Pop-up menu.

13.7 Drag-and-drop

Morphic also supports drag-and-drop. Let's examine a simple example with two morphs, a receiver morph and a dropped morph. The receiver will accept a morph only if the dropped morph matches a given condition: in our example, the morph should be blue. If it is rejected, the dropped morph decides what to do.

Let's first define the receiver morph:

```
Morph subclass: #ReceiverMorph
    instanceVariableNames: ''
    classVariableNames: ''
    package: 'PBE-Morphic'
```

Now define the initialization method in the usual way:

```
ReceiverMorph >> initialize
    super initialize.
    color := Color red.
    bounds := 0 @ 0 extent: 200 @ 200
```

How do we decide if the receiver morph will accept or reject the dropped morph? In general, both of the morphs will have to agree to the interaction.

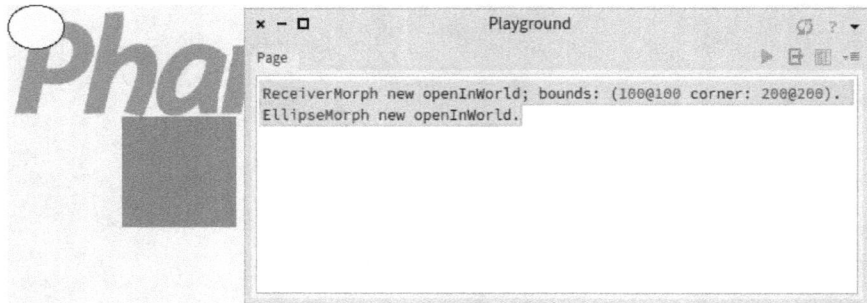

Figure 13.15: A ReceiverMorph and an EllipseMorph.

The receiver does this by responding to wantsDroppedMorph:event:. Its first argument is the dropped morph, and the second the mouse event, so that the receiver can, for example, see if any modifier keys were held down at the time of the drop. The dropped morph is also given the opportunity to check and see if it likes the morph onto which it is being dropped, by responding to the message wantsToBeDroppedInto:. The default implementation of this method (in class Morph) answers true.

```
ReceiverMorph >> wantsDroppedMorph: aMorph event: anEvent
    ^ aMorph color = Color blue
```

What happens to the dropped morph if the receiving morph doesn't want it? The default behaviour is for it to do nothing, that is, to sit on top of the receiving morph, but without interacting with it. A more intuitive behavior is for the dropped morph to go back to its original position. This can be achieved by the receiver answering true to the message repelsMorph:event: when it doesn't want the dropped morph:

```
ReceiverMorph >> repelsMorph: aMorph event: anEvent
    ^ (self wantsDroppedMorph: aMorph event: anEvent) not
```

That's all we need as far as the receiver is concerned.

Create instances of ReceiverMorph and EllipseMorph in a playground:

```
ReceiverMorph new openInWorld;
    bounds: (100@100 corner: 200@200).
EllipseMorph new openInWorld.
```

Try to drag and drop the yellow EllipseMorph onto the receiver. It will be rejected and sent back to its initial position.

To change this behaviour, change the color of the ellipse morph to the color blue (by sending it the message color: Color blue; right after new). Blue morphs should be accepted by the ReceiverMorph.

Let's create a specific subclass of `Morph`, named `DroppedMorph`, so we can experiment a bit more:

```
Morph subclass: #DroppedMorph
    instanceVariableNames: ''
    classVariableNames: ''
    package: 'PBE-Morphic'
```

```
DroppedMorph >> initialize
    super initialize.
    color := Color blue.
    self position: 250 @ 100
```

Now we can specify what the dropped morph should do when it is rejected by the receiver; here it will stay attached to the mouse pointer:

```
DroppedMorph >> rejectDropMorphEvent: anEvent
    | h |
    h := anEvent hand.
    WorldState addDeferredUIMessage: [ h grabMorph: self ].
    anEvent wasHandled: true
```

Sending the `hand` message to an event answers the *hand*, an instance of `HandMorph` that represents the mouse pointer and whatever it holds. Here we tell the `World` that the hand should grab `self`, the rejected morph.

Create two instances of `DroppedMorph`, and then drag and drop them onto the receiver.

```
ReceiverMorph new openInWorld.
morph := (DroppedMorph new color: Color blue) openInWorld.
morph position: (morph position + (70@0)).
(DroppedMorph new color: Color green) openInWorld.
```

The green morph is rejected and therefore stays attached to the mouse pointer.

13.8 A complete example

Let's design a morph to roll a die. Clicking on it will display the values of all sides of the die in a quick loop, and another click will stop the animation.

Define the die as a subclass of `BorderedMorph` instead of `Morph`, because we will make use of the border.

```
BorderedMorph subclass: #DieMorph
    instanceVariableNames: 'faces dieValue isStopped'
    classVariableNames: ''
    package: 'PBE-Morphic'
```

The instance variable `faces` records the number of faces on the die; we allow dice with up to 9 faces! `dieValue` records the value of the face that is

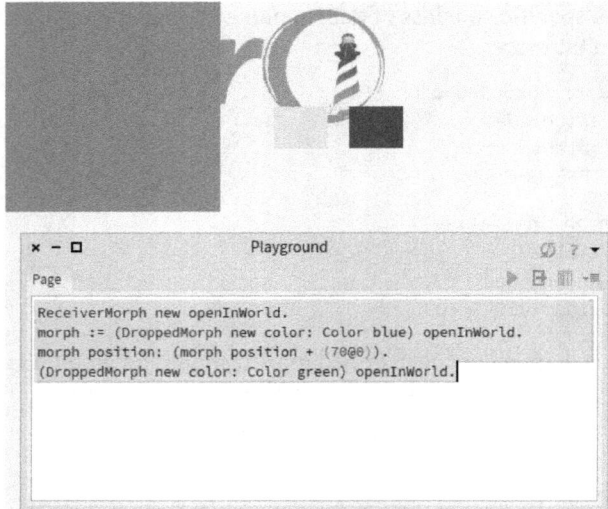

Figure 13.16: Creation of DroppedMorph and ReceiverMorph.

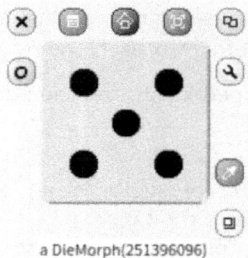

Figure 13.17: The die in Morphic

currently displayed, and isStopped is true if the die animation has stopped running. To create a die instance, we define the faces: n method on the *class* side of DieMorph to create a new die with n faces.

```
DieMorph class >> faces: aNumber
    ^ self new faces: aNumber
```

The initialize method is defined on the instance side in the usual way; remember that new automatically sends initialize to the newly-created instance.

```
DieMorph >> initialize
    super initialize.
    self extent: 50 @ 50.
    self
```

13.8 A complete example

```
        useGradientFill;
        borderWidth: 2;
        useRoundedCorners.
    self setBorderStyle: #complexRaised.
    self fillStyle direction: self extent.
    self color: Color green.
    dieValue := 1.
    faces := 6.
    isStopped := false
```

We use a few methods of BorderedMorph to give a nice appearance to the die: a thick border with a raised effect, rounded corners, and a color gradient on the visible face. We define the instance method faces: to check for a valid parameter as follows:

```
DieMorph >> faces: aNumber
    "Set the number of faces"

    ((aNumber isInteger and: [ aNumber > 0 ]) and: [ aNumber <= 9 ])
        ifTrue: [ faces := aNumber ]
```

It may be good to review the order in which the messages are sent when a die is created. For instance, if we start by evaluating DieMorph faces: 9:

- The class method DieMorph class >> faces: sends new to DieMorph class.
- The method for new (inherited by DieMorph class from Behavior) creates the new instance and sends it the initialize message.
- The initialize method in DieMorph sets faces to an initial value of 6.
- DieMorph class >> new returns to the class method DieMorph class >> faces:, which then sends the message faces: 9 to the new instance.
- The instance method DieMorph >> faces: now executes, setting the faces instance variable to 9.

Before defining drawOn:, we need a few methods to place the dots on the displayed face:

```
DieMorph >> face1
    ^ {(0.5 @ 0.5)}
```

```
DieMorph >> face2
    ^{0.25@0.25 . 0.75@0.75}
```

```
DieMorph >> face3
    ^{0.25@0.25 . 0.75@0.75 . 0.5@0.5}
```

```
DieMorph >> face4
    ^{0.25@0.25 . 0.75@0.25 . 0.75@0.75 . 0.25@0.75}
```

```
DieMorph >> face5
    ^{0.25@0.25 . 0.75@0.25 . 0.75@0.75 . 0.25@0.75 . 0.5@0.5}
```

```
DieMorph >> face6
    ^{0.25@0.25 . 0.75@0.25 . 0.75@0.75 . 0.25@0.75 . 0.25@0.5 .
        0.75@0.5}
```

```
DieMorph >> face7
    ^{0.25@0.25 . 0.75@0.25 . 0.75@0.75 . 0.25@0.75 . 0.25@0.5 .
        0.75@0.5 . 0.5@0.5}
```

```
DieMorph >> face8
    ^{0.25@0.25 . 0.75@0.25 . 0.75@0.75 . 0.25@0.75 . 0.25@0.5 .
        0.75@0.5 . 0.5@0.5 . 0.5@0.25}
```

```
DieMorph >> face9
    ^{0.25@0.25 . 0.75@0.25 . 0.75@0.75 . 0.25@0.75 . 0.25@0.5 .
        0.75@0.5 . 0.5@0.5 . 0.5@0.25 . 0.5@0.75}
```

These methods define collections of the coordinates of dots for each face. The coordinates are in a square of size 1x1; we will simply need to scale them to place the actual dots.

The drawOn: method does two things: it draws the die background with the super-send, and then draws the dots.

```
DieMorph >> drawOn: aCanvas
    super drawOn: aCanvas.
    (self perform: ('face', dieValue asString) asSymbol)
        do: [:aPoint | self drawDotOn: aCanvas at: aPoint]
```

The second part of this method uses the reflective capacities of Pharo. Drawing the dots of a face is a simple matter of iterating over the collection given by the faceX method for that face, sending the drawDotOn:at: message for each coordinate. To call the correct faceX method, we use the perform: method which sends a message built from a string, ('face', dieValue asString) asSymbol. You will encounter this use of perform: quite regularly.

```
DieMorph >> drawDotOn: aCanvas at: aPoint
    aCanvas
        fillOval: (Rectangle
            center: self position + (self extent * aPoint)
            extent: self extent / 6)
        color: Color black
```

Since the coordinates are normalized to the [0:1] interval, we scale them to the dimensions of our die: self extent * aPoint.

We can already create a die instance from a playground (see result on Figure 13.18):

```
(DieMorph faces: 6) openInWorld.
```

13.8 A complete example

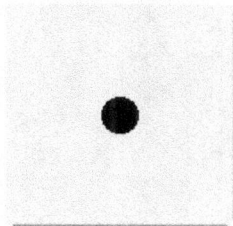

Figure 13.18: A new die 6 with (DieMorph faces: 6) openInWorld

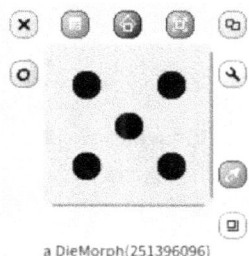

Figure 13.19: Result of (DieMorph faces: 6) openInWorld; dieValue: 5.

To change the displayed face, we create an accessor that we can use as myDie dieValue: 5:

```
DieMorph >> dieValue: aNumber
   ((aNumber isInteger and: [ aNumber > 0 ]) and: [ aNumber <= faces ])
      ifTrue: [
         dieValue := aNumber.
         self changed ]
```

Now we will use the animation system to show quickly all the faces:

```
DieMorph >> stepTime
   ^ 100
```

```
DieMorph >> step
   isStopped ifFalse: [self dieValue: (1 to: faces) atRandom]
```

Now the die is rolling!

To start or stop the animation by clicking, we will use what we learned previously about mouse events. First, activate the reception of mouse events:

```
DieMorph >> handlesMouseDown: anEvent
   ^ true
```

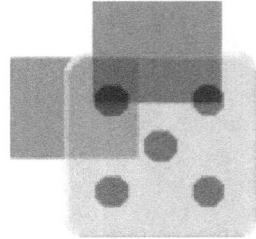

Figure 13.20: The die displayed with alpha-transparency

```
DieMorph >> mouseDown: anEvent
    anEvent redButtonPressed
        ifTrue: [isStopped := isStopped not]
```

Now the die will roll or stop rolling when we click on it.

13.9 More about the canvas

The drawOn: method has an instance of Canvas as its sole argument; the canvas is the area on which the morph draws itself. By using the graphics methods of the canvas you are free to give the appearance you want to a morph. If you browse the inheritance hierarchy of the Canvas class, you will see that it has several variants. The default variant of Canvas is FormCanvas, and you will find the key graphics methods in Canvas and FormCanvas. These methods can draw points, lines, polygons, rectangles, ellipses, text, and images with rotation and scaling.

It is also possible to use other kinds of canvas, for example to obtain transparent morphs, more graphics methods, antialiasing, and so on. To use these features you will need an AlphaBlendingCanvas or a BalloonCanvas. But how can you obtain such a canvas in a drawOn: method, when drawOn: receives an instance of FormCanvas as its argument? Fortunately, you can transform one kind of canvas into another.

To use a canvas with a 0.5 alpha-transparency in DieMorph, redefine drawOn: like this:

```
DieMorph >> drawOn: aCanvas
    | theCanvas |
    theCanvas := aCanvas asAlphaBlendingCanvas: 0.5.
    super drawOn: theCanvas.
    (self perform: ('face', dieValue asString) asSymbol)
        do: [:aPoint | self drawDotOn: theCanvas at: aPoint]
```

That's all you need to do!

13.10 Chapter summary

Morphic is a graphical framework in which graphical interface elements can be dynamically composed.

- You can convert an object into a morph and display that morph on the screen by sending it the messages asMorph openInWorld.

- You can manipulate a morph by meta-clicking on it and using the handles that appear. (Handles have help balloons that explain what they do.)

- You can compose morphs by embedding one onto another, either by drag and drop or by sending the message addMorph:.

- You can subclass an existing morph class and redefine key methods, like initialize and drawOn:.

- You can control how a morph reacts to mouse and keyboard events by redefining the methods handlesMouseDown:, handlesMouseOver:, etc.

- You can animate a morph by defining the methods step (what to do) and stepTime (the number of milliseconds between steps).

CHAPTER **14**

Seaside by example

Seaside is a framework for building web applications in Smalltalk, originally developed by Avi Bryant and Julian Fitzell in 2002. Once mastered, Seaside makes web applications almost as easy to write as desktop applications. Seaside is really interesting for developing fast complex applications. For example http://allstocker.com is a Seaside commercial applications or the Quuve, FinWorks and CableExpertise application from http://www.pharo.org/success have been developed in Seaside.

Seaside is unusual in that it is thoroughly object-oriented: there are no HTML templates, no complicated control flows through web pages, and no encoding of state in URLs. Instead, you just send messages to objects. What a nice idea!

14.1 Why do we need Seaside?

Modern web applications try to interact with the user in the same way as desktop applications: they ask the user questions and the user responds, usually by filling in a form or clicking a button. But the web works the other way around: the user's browser makes a request of the server, and the server responds with a new web page. So web application development frameworks have to cope with a host of problems, chief among them being the management of this *inverted* control flow. Because of this, many web applications try to forbid the use of the browser's *Back* button due to the difficulty of keeping track of the state of a session. Expressing non-trivial control flows across multiple web pages is often cumbersome, and multiple control flows can be difficult or impossible to express.

Seaside is a component-based framework that makes web development easier in several ways. First, control flow can be expressed naturally using message sends. Seaside keeps track of which web page corresponds to which point in the execution of the web application. This means that the browser's *Back* button works correctly.

Second, state is managed for you. As the developer, you have the choice of enabling backtracking of state, so that navigation *Back* in time will undo side-effects. Alternatively, you can use the transaction support built into Seaside to prevent users from undoing permanent side-effects when they use the back button. You do not have to encode state information in the URL — this too is managed automatically for you.

Third, web pages are built up from nested components, each of which can support its own, independent control flow. There are no HTML templates — instead valid HTML is generated programmatically using a simple Smalltalk-based protocol. Seaside supports Cascading Style Sheets (CSS), so content and layout are cleanly separated.

Finally, Seaside provides a convenient web-based development interface, making it easy to develop applications iteratively, debug applications interactively, and recompile and extend applications while the server is running.

14.2 Getting started

The Seaside community

The Seaside.st website (http://www.seaside.st) contains many Seaside-related resources, including downloads, documentation and tutorials. (Keep in mind that Seaside has evolved considerably over the years, and not all available material refers to the latest version.) There are also several active mailing lists, which you can find at http://www.seaside.st/community/mailinglist.

In addition, the Wiki on the Seaside GitHub repository (https://github.com/seasidest/seaside/wiki) provides some crucial documentation, including the Release Notes for each version of Seaside.

Installing Seaside using the one-click experience image

The easiest way to get started is to download the `Seaside One-Click Experience 3.1` from the Pharo Downloads section of the Seaside web site (http://www.seaside.st/download/pharo). This is a prepackaged version of the latest stable version of Seaside for Mac OSX, Linux and Windows, built on Pharo 4. The current latest Seaside version is 3.2. These are full Pharo distributions, which include the Pharo VM as well as a development image with many Seaside-related packages preloaded, and a helpful Seaside control panel that starts when you open the image.

Download and launch the Seaside One-Click image (feel free to refer to the `Getting Started` section of Chapter : A Quick Tour of Pharo for an in-depth

14.2 Getting started

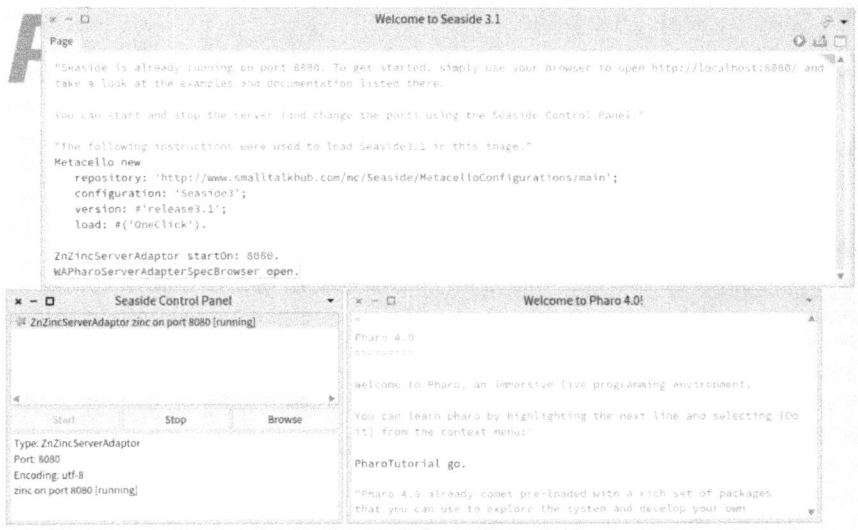

Figure 14.1: Start up the Seaside One-Click Experience image.

discussion of launching Pharo images). Once started, you should see something similar to Figure 14.1 - a familiar Pharo development environment with some windows pre-opened, such as welcome messages as well as a Seaside Control Panel.

Starting the Seaside server

The easiest way to start and stop the Seaside web server is through the Seaside Control Panel. If you're using the Seaside One-Click Experience image, it should already be open (and running a server adapter) when you open the image for the first time. You can manually open it at any time, however, by evaluating WAPharoServerAdapterSpecBrowser open.

Right-clicking on the top pane of the Seaside Control Panel lets you add new server adapters. For example, you can add a ZnZincServerAdaptor, specify a port number, then start it using the Start button on the control panel, which launches a new Seaside server that listens on that port.

```
ZnZincServerAdaptor startOn: 8080. "start on port 8080"
ZnZincServerAdaptor stop.
```

You can also start and stop the Seaside web server from a playground, by sendning the startOn: and stop messages to your server adapter of choice.

The Seaside welcome page

Once the Seaside server is running, navigate to http://localhost:8080/ in your web browser. You should see a web page that looks like Figure 14.2.

The Welcome page contains links to some sample Seaside applications. It also links to various documents and resources, and (in the sidebar) links to the Configuration and Browse applications that allow you to interact with Seaside applications registered in your image.

Let's look at one of the example applications that demonstrates the Counter component: click on the Counter link.

This page is a small Seaside application: it displays a counter component that can be incremented or decremented by clicking on the ++ and -- links (see Figure 14.3).

Play with the counter by clicking on these links. Use your browser's *Back* button to go back to a previous state, and then click on ++ again. Notice how the counter is correctly incremented with respect to the currently displayed state, rather than the state that the counter was in when you started using the *Back* button.

Notice the toolbar at the bottom of the web page in Figure 14.2. Seaside supports a notion of *sessions* to keep track of the state of the application for different users. New Session will start a new session on the counter application. Configure allows you to configure the settings of your application through a web interface. (To close the Configure view, click on the x in the top right corner.) Halos provides a way to explore the state of the application running on the Seaside server. Profile and Memory provide detailed information about the run-time performance of the application. XHTML can be used to validate the generated web page, but works only when the web page is publicly accessible from the Internet, because it uses the W3C validation service.

Single components

Seaside applications are built up from pluggable *components*. In fact, components are ordinary Smalltalk objects. The only thing that is special about them is that they are instances of classes that inherit from the Seaside framework class WAComponent. We can explore components and their classes from the Pharo image, or directly from the web interface using halos.

Click on the Halos link at the bottom of the page to toggle on halo functionality. You'll see a number of nested components each with their own halo icons, including the Counter component (you may have to scroll down a bit to reach it), like the one seen in Figure 14.4.

At the top left of the component, the text WACounter tells us the class of the Seaside component that implements its behavior. Next to this are three clickable icons. The first is the Class Browser (the notepad with pencil icon),

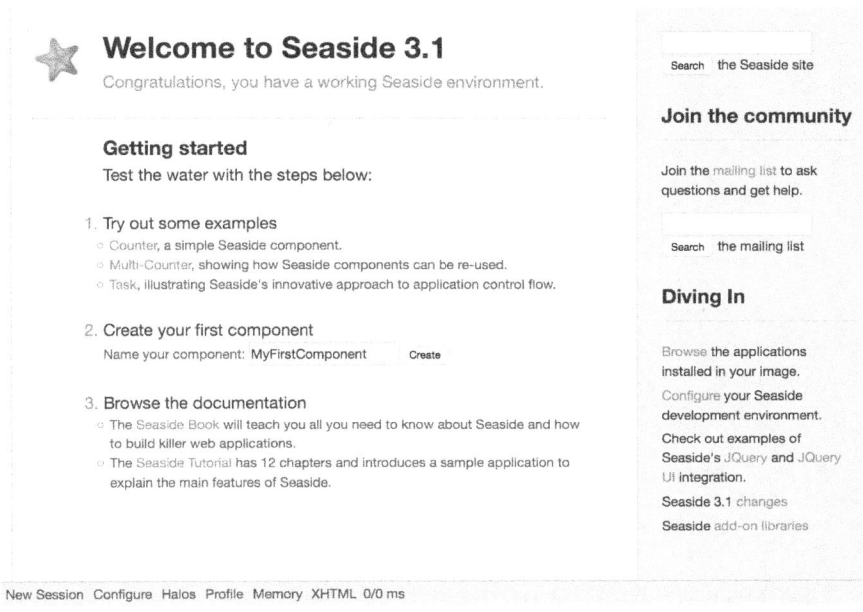

Figure 14.2: The Seaside Welcome application at `http://localhost:8080/`.

Example: Counter

[go back]

The counter is an example of a very simple Seaside component. It increments and decrements a number by clicking on a link. Test the example below by clicking on the "++" and "--" links:

Figure 14.3: The counter.

Figure 14.4: Halos.

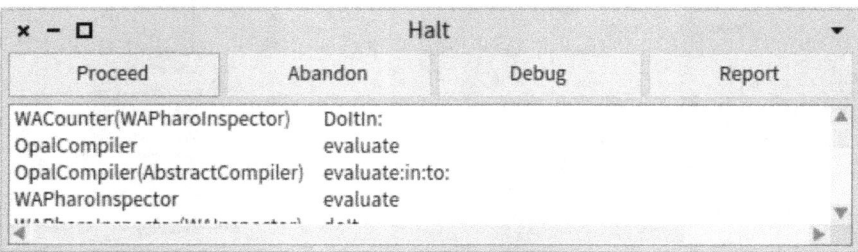

Figure 14.5: Debugging the running Counter application in the Pharo image.

which opens up a (web-based) Seaside class browser on this component's class. The second is the Object Inspector (notepad with magnifying glass icon), which opens a web-based object inspector on the actual WACounter instance. The third is the CSS Style Manager (the coloured circles icon), opens a Seaside view to display the CSS style sheet for this component.

At the top right of the component, the Render / Source links let you toggle between the Rendered and (formatted) Source views of the component's HTML source code. Experiment with all of these links. Note that the ++ and − links are also active in the source view.

The Seaside Class Browser and Object Inspector can be very convenient when the server is running on another computer, especially when the server does not have a display, or if it is in remote place. However, when you are first developing a Seaside application, the server will be running locally, and it is easy to use the ordinary Pharo development tools in the server image.

Using the Object Inspector link in the web browser, open an inspector on the underlying Pharo counter object, type self halt and click the doIt button.

The form submits, and the browser will hang, spinning. Now switch to the Pharo Seaside image. You should see a pre-debugger window (Figure 14.5) showing a WACounter object executing a halt. Examine this execution in the debugger, and then Proceed. Go back to the web browser and notice that the

14.2 Getting started

Figure 14.6: Independent subcomponents.

Counter application is running again.

Multiple components

Seaside components can be instantiated multiple times and in different contexts.

Now, point your web browser to http://localhost:8080/examples/multicounter.

You will see a simple application composed of a number of independent instances of the WACounter component, nested inside a WAMultiCounter. Increment and decrement several of the counters. Verify that they behave correctly even if you use the *Back* button. Toggle the halos to see how the application is built out of nested components. Use the Seaside class browser to view the implementation of WAMultiCounter. You should see two methods on the class side (description, and initialize) and three on the instance side (children, initialize, and renderContentOn:). Note that an application is simply a component that is willing to be at the root of the component containment hierarchy; this willingness is indicated by defining a class-side method canBeRoot to answer true.

You can use the Seaside web interface to configure, copy or remove individual applications (which are root-level components). Try making the following configuration change.

Point your web browser to http://localhost:8080/config.

If you are asked for a login, supply the default login and password (admin and seaside). You can see a list of a registered applications and dispatchers.

Seaside by example

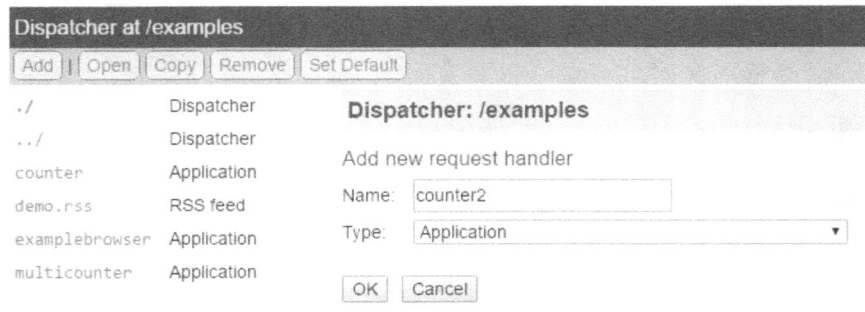

Figure 14.7: Add a new application.

Change into the examples dispatcher list by clicking on the link on the left side. With the buttons at the topbar, we can add new request handlers, open the current, copy, remove or set it as the default page. We want to add a new example application. Select Add, enter the name counter2 and choose the type Application, click OK (see Figure 14.7).

On the next screen, set the Root Component to WACounter, apply the changes (Figure 14.8).

Now we have a new counter installed at http://localhost:8080/examples/counter2. Use the same Remove-button in the configuration interface to remove this entry point.

Seaside operates in two modes: *development* mode, which is what we have seen so far, and *deployment* mode, in which the toolbar is not available.

You can put a Seaside Application into deployment mode by removing the inherited Root Decoration Class (again, see Figure 14.8).

Alternatively, you can disable the development toolbar for all new aplications by evaluating the code:

```
AAdmin applicationDefaults
    removeParent: WADevelopmentConfiguration instance
```

If you want to enable the password protection, you need to add the WAAuth-Configuration in the Inherited Configuration. Choose WAAuthConfiguration from the list of possible parents, after adding this configuration, you can define the Login and Password setting.

14.3 Seaside components

As we mentioned in the previous section, Seaside applications are built out of components. Let's take a closer look at how Seaside works by implementing

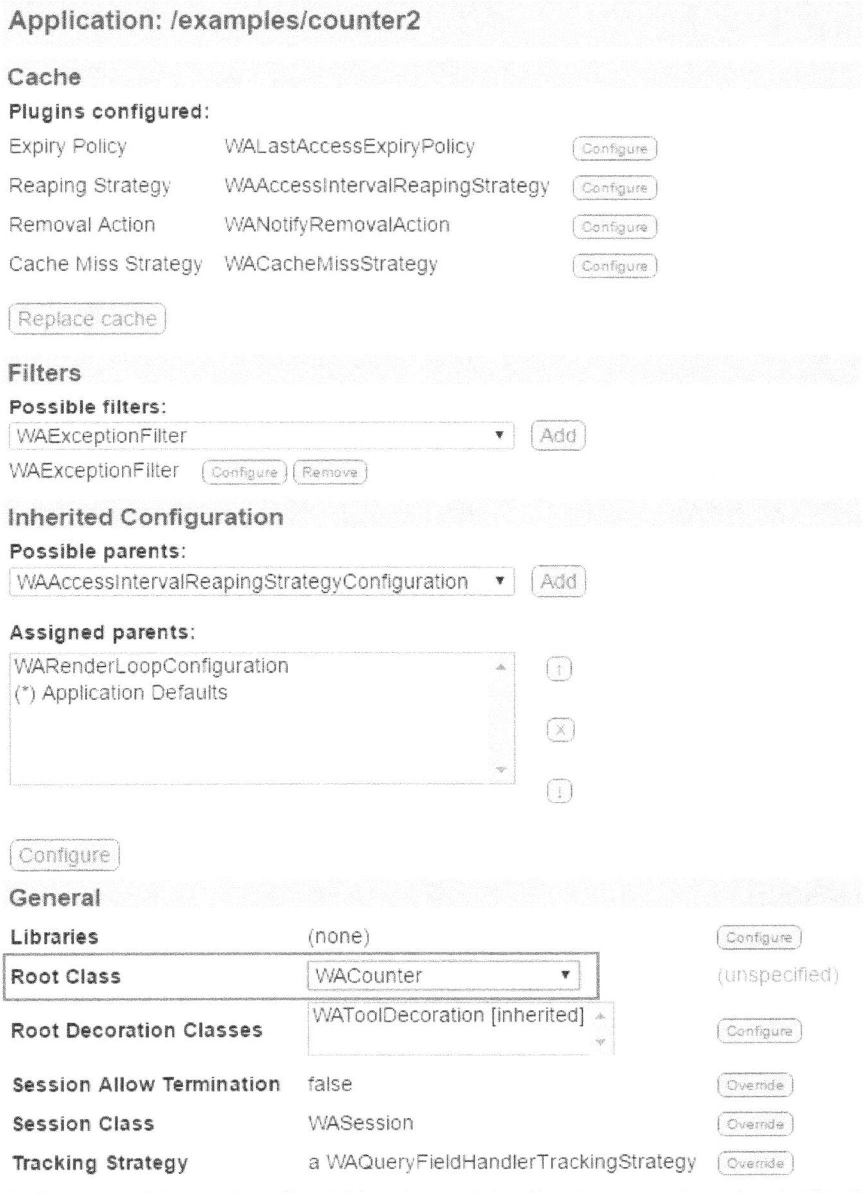

Application: /examples/counter2

Cache
Plugins configured:

Expiry Policy	WALastAccessExpiryPolicy	[Configure]
Reaping Strategy	WAAccessIntervalReapingStrategy	[Configure]
Removal Action	WANotifyRemovalAction	[Configure]
Cache Miss Strategy	WACacheMissStrategy	[Configure]

[Replace cache]

Filters
Possible filters:
[WAExceptionFilter ▼] [Add]
WAExceptionFilter [Configure] [Remove]

Inherited Configuration
Possible parents:
[WAAccessIntervalReapingStrategyConfiguration ▼] [Add]

Assigned parents:
WARenderLoopConfiguration
(*) Application Defaults

[Configure]

General

Libraries	(none)	[Configure]
Root Class	WACounter ▼	(unspecified)
Root Decoration Classes	WAToolDecoration [inherited]	[Configure]
Session Allow Termination	false	[Override]
Session Class	WASession	[Override]
Tracking Strategy	a WAQueryFieldHandlerTrackingStrategy	[Override]

Figure 14.8: Configure the new application.

Figure 14.9: *Hello World* in Seaside.

the *Hello World* component.

Every Seaside component should inherit directly or indirectly from WAComponent, as shown in Figure 14.10. (Incidentally, the 'WA' prefix often used in Seaside code stands for 'Web Application'.)

Define a subclass of WAComponent called WAHelloWorld.

Components must know how to render themselves. Usually this is done by implementing the method renderContentOn:, which gets as its argument an instance of WAHtmlCanvas, which knows how to render HTML.

Implement the following method, and put it in a protocol called rendering:

```
WAHelloWorld >> renderContentOn: html
    html text: 'hello world'
```

Now we must inform Seaside that this component is willing to be a standalone application.

Implement the following method on the class side of WAHelloWorld.

```
WAHelloWorld class >> canBeRoot
    ^ true
```

We are almost done!

Point your web browser at http://localhost:8080/config, add a new entry point called hello, and set its root component to be WAHelloWorld.

Now navigate to http://localhost:8080/hello. That's it! You should see a web page similar to Figure 14.9.

14.3 Seaside components

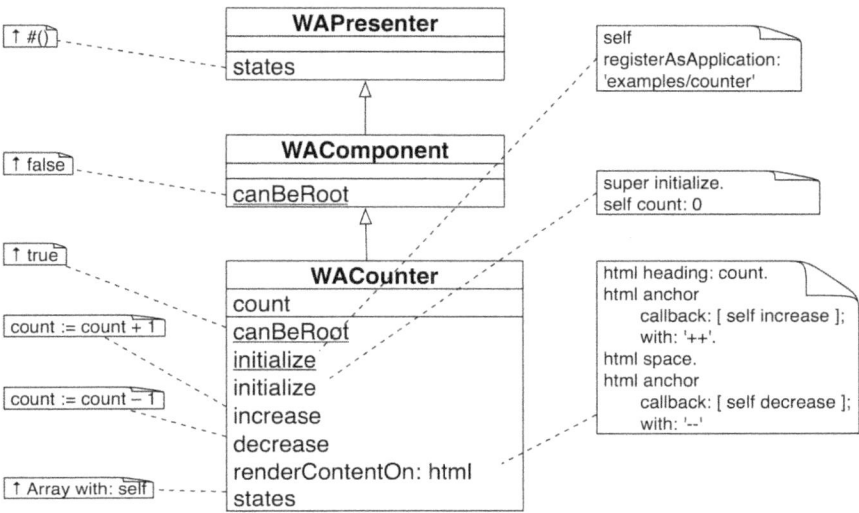

Figure 14.10: The WACounter class, which implements the *counter* application. Methods with underlined names are on the class-side; those with plain-text names are on the instance side.

State backtracking and the Counter application

The *counter* application is only slightly more complex than the *hello world* application.

The class WACounter is a standalone application, so WACounter class must answer true to the canBeRoot message. It must also register itself as an application; this is done in its class-side initialize method, as shown in Figure 14.10.

WACounter defines two methods, increase and decrease, which will be triggered from the ++ and -- links on the web page. It also defines an instance variable count to record the state of the counter. However, we also want Seaside to synchronize the counter with the browser page: when the user clicks on the browser's *Back* button, we want seaside to *backtrack* the state of the WACounter object. Seaside includes a general mechanism for backtracking, but each application has to tell Seaside which parts of its state to track.

A component enables backtracking by implementing the states method on the instance side: states should answer an array containing all the objects to be tracked. In this case, the WACounter object adds itself to Seaside's table of backtrackable objects by returning Array with: self.

Backtracking caveat There is a subtle but important point to watch for when declaring objects for backtracking. Seaside tracks state by making a *copy* of all the objects declared in the states array. It does this using a WASnapshot object; WASnapshot is a subclass of IdentityDictionary that records the objects to be tracked as keys and shallow copies of their state as values. If the state of an application is backtracked to a particular snapshot, the state of each object entered into the snapshot dictionary is overwritten by the copy saved in the snapshot.

Here is the point to watch out for: In the case of WACounter, you might think that the state to be tracked is a number — the value of the count instance variable. However, having the states method answer Array with: count won't work. This is because the object named by count is an integer, and integers are immutable. The increase and decrease methods don't change the state of the object 0 into 1 or the object 3 into 2. Instead, they make count hold a different integer: every time the count is incremented or decremented, the object named by count is *replaced* by another. This is why WACounter>>states must return Array with: self. When the state of a WACounter object is replaced by a previous state, the *value* of each of the instance variable in the object is replaced by a previous value; this correctly replaces the current value of count by a prior value.

14.4 Rendering HTML

The purpose of a web application is to create, or *render*, web pages. As we mentioned in Section 14.3, each Seaside component is responsible for rendering itself. So, let's start our exploration of rendering by seeing how the counter component renders itself.

Rendering the Counter

The rendering of the counter is relatively straightforward; the code is shown in Figure 14.10. The current value of the counter is displayed as an HTML heading, and the increment and decrement operations are implemented as HTML anchors (that is, links) with callbacks to blocks that will send increase and decrease to the counter object.

We will have a closer look at the rendering protocol in a moment. But before we do, let's have a quick look at the multi-counter.

From Counter to MultiCounter

WAMultiCounter, shown in Figure 14.11 is also a standalone application, so it overrides canBeRoot to answer true. In addition, it is a *composite* component, so Seaside requires it to declare its children by implementing a method children that answers an array of all the components it contains. It renders itself by rendering each of its subcomponents, separated by a horizontal rule. Aside

14.4 Rendering HTML

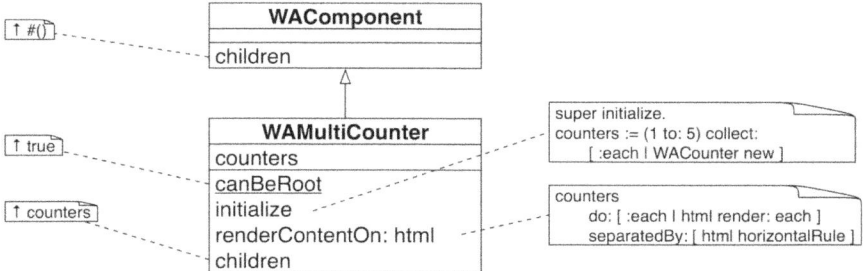

Figure 14.11: WAMultiCounter.

from instance and class-side initialization methods, there is nothing else to the multi-counter!

More about rendering HTML

As you can see from these examples, Seaside does not use templates to generate web pages. Instead it generates HTML programmatically. The basic idea is that every Seaside component should override the method renderContentOn:; this message will be sent by the framework to each component that needs to be rendered. This renderContentOn: message will have an argument that is an *HTML canvas* onto which the component should render itself. By convention, the HTML canvas parameter is called html. An HTML canvas is analogous to the graphics canvas used by Morphic (and most other drawing frameworks) to abstract away from the device-dependent details of drawing.

Here are some of the most basic rendering methods:

```
html text: 'hello world'. "render a plain text string"
html html: '&ndash;'. "render an HTML incantation"
html render: 1. "render any object"
```

The message render: anyObject can be sent to an HTML canvas to render anyObject; it is normally used to render subcomponents. anyObject will itself be sent the message renderContentOn: this is what happens in the multi-counter (see Figure 14.11).

Using brushes

A canvas provides a number of *brushes* that can be used to render (*i.e.*, *paint*) content on the canvas. There are brushes for every kind of HTML element — paragraphs, tables, lists, and so on. To see the full protocol of brushes and convenience methods, you should browse the class WACanvas and its subclasses. The argument to renderContentOn: is actually an instance of the subclass WARender.

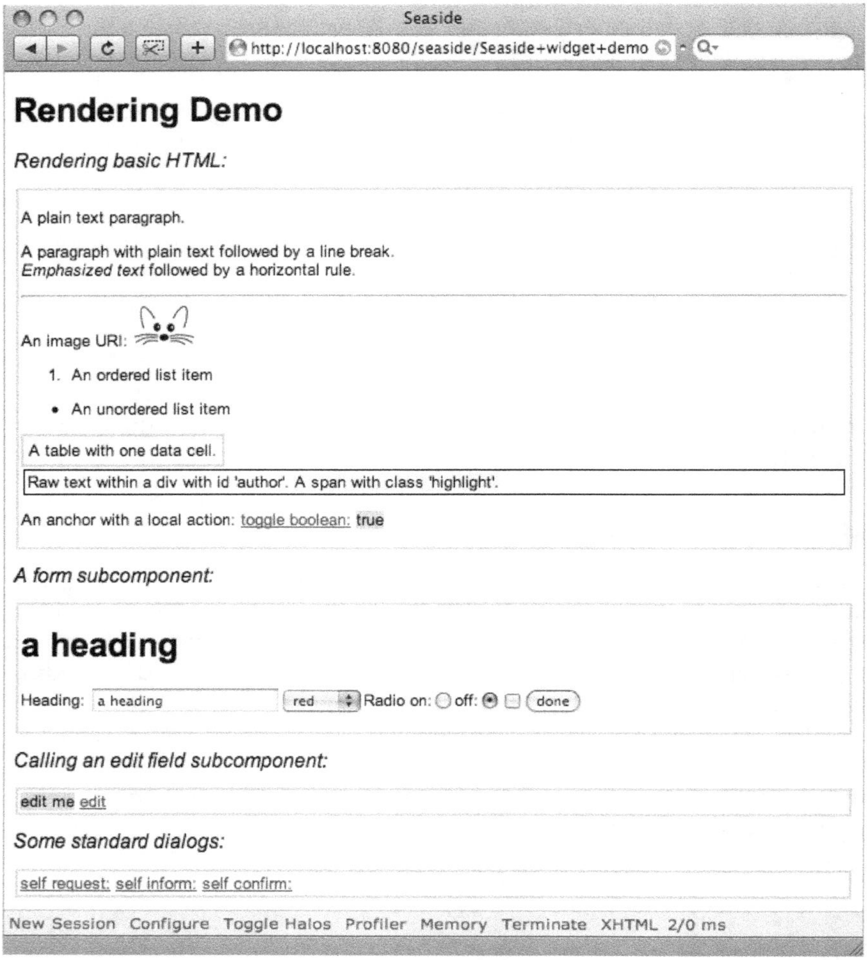

Figure 14.12: RenderingDemo.

We have already seen the following brush used in the counter and multi-counter examples:

```
html horizontalRule.
```

In Figure 14.12 we can see the output of many of the basic brushes offered by Seaside. (The source code for method `SeasideDemo >> renderContentOn:` defined below is in the package `PBE-SeasideDemo` in the project http://www.squeaksource.com/PharoByExample.) The root component `SeasideDemo` simply renders its subcomponents, which are instances of `SeasideHtmlDemo`, `SeasideFormDemo`, `SeasideEditCallDemo` and `SeasideDialogDemo`, as shown below.

14.4 Rendering HTML

```
SeasideDemo >> renderContentOn: html
   html heading: 'Rendering Demo'.
   html heading
      level: 2;
      with: 'Rendering basic HTML: '.
   html div
      class: 'subcomponent';
      with: htmlDemo.
   "render the remaining components ..."
```

Recall that a root component must always declare its children, or Seaside will refuse to render them.

```
SeasideDemo >> children
   ^ { htmlDemo . formDemo . editDemo . dialogDemo }
```

Notice that there are two different ways of instantiating the `heading` brush. The first way is to set the text directly by sending the message `heading:`. The second way is to instantiate the brush by sending `heading`, and then to send a cascade of messages to the brush to set its properties and render it. Many of the available brushes can be used in these two ways.

> **Important** If you send a cascade of messages to a brush including the message `with:`, then `with:` should be the *final* message. `with:` both sets the content and renders the result.

In method `renderContentOn:` above, the first heading is at level 1, since this is the default. We explicitly set the level of the second heading to 2. The subcomponent is rendered as an HTML *div* with the CSS class *subcomponent*. (More on CSS in Section 14.5.) Also note that the argument to the `with:` keyword message need not be a literal string: it can be another component, or even — as in the next example — a block containing further rendering actions.

The `SeasideHtmlDemo` component demonstrates many of the most basic brushes. Most of the code should be self-explanatory.

```
SeasideHtmlDemo >> renderContentOn: html
   self renderParagraphsOn: html.
   self renderListsAndTablesOn: html.
   self renderDivsAndSpansOn: html.
   self renderLinkWithCallbackOn: html
```

It is common practice to break up long rendering methods into many helper methods, as we have done here.

A word of advice: Don't put all your rendering code into a single method.

Instead, split it into helper methods named using the pattern `render*On:`. All rendering methods go in the `rendering` protocol. Don't send `renderContentOn:` from your own code, use `render:` instead.

Look at the following code. The first helper method, SeasideHtmlDemo>>renderParagraphsOn:, shows you how to generate HTML paragraphs, plain and emphasized text, and images. Note that in Seaside simple elements are rendered by specifying the text they contain directly, whereas complex elements are specified using blocks. This is a simple convention to help you structure your rendering code.

```
SeasideHtmlDemo >> renderParagraphsOn: html
   html paragraph: 'A plain text paragraph.'.
   html paragraph: [
      html
         text: 'A paragraph with plain text followed by a line break. ';
         break;
         emphasis: 'Emphasized text ';
         text: 'followed by a horizontal rule.';
         horizontalRule;
         text: 'An image URI: '.
      html image
         url: self squeakImageUrl;
         width: '50']
```

The next helper method, SeasideHtmlDemo>>renderListsAndTablesOn:, shows you how to generate lists and tables. A table uses two levels of blocks to display each of its rows and the cells within the rows.

```
SeasideHtmlDemo >> renderListsAndTablesOn: html
   html orderedList: [
      html listItem: 'An ordered list item'].
   html unorderedList: [
      html listItem: 'An unordered list item'].
   html table: [
      html tableRow: [
         html tableData: 'A table with one data cell.']]
```

The next example shows how we can specify class or id attributes for div and span elements (for use with CSS). Of course, the messages class: and id: can also be sent to the other brushes, not just to div and span. The method SeasideDemoWidget>>style defines how these HTML elements should be displayed (see Section 14.5).

```
SeasideHtmlDemo >> renderDivsAndSpansOn: html
   html div
      id: 'author';
      with: [
         html text: 'Raw text within a div with id ''author''. '.
         html span
            class: 'highlight';
            with: 'A span with class ''highlight''.']
```

Finally we see a simple example of a link, created by binding a simple callback to an *anchor* (*i.e.*, a link). Clicking on the link will cause the subsequent text

14.4 Rendering HTML

to toggle between `true` and `false` by toggling the instance variable `toggleValue`.

```
SeasideHtmlDemo >> renderLinkWithCallbackOn: html
   html paragraph: [
      html text: 'An anchor with a local action: '.
      html span with: [
         html anchor
            callback: [toggleValue := toggleValue not];
            with: 'toggle boolean:'].
      html space.
      html span
         class: 'boolean';
         with: toggleValue ]
```

Note that actions should appear only in callbacks.

The code executed while rendering should not change the state of the application!

Forms

Forms are rendered just like the other examples that we have already seen. Here is the code for the `SeasideFormDemo` component in Figure 14.12.

```
SeasideFormDemo >> renderContentOn: html
   | radioGroup |
   html heading: heading.
   html form: [
      html span: 'Heading: '.
      html textInput on: #heading of: self.
      html select
         list: self colors;
         on: #color of: self.
      radioGroup := html radioGroup.
      html text: 'Radio on:'.
      radioGroup radioButton
         selected: radioOn;
         callback: [radioOn := true].
      html text: 'off:'.
      radioGroup radioButton
         selected: radioOn not;
         callback: [radioOn := false].
      html checkbox on: #checked of: self.
      html submitButton
         text: 'done' ]
```

Since a form is a complex entity, it is rendered using a block. Note that all the state changes happen in the callbacks, not as part of the rendering.

There is one Seaside feature used here that is worth special mention, namely the message on:of:. In the example, this message is used to bind a text input field to the variable heading. Anchors and buttons also support this message. The first argument is the name of an instance variable for which accessors have been defined; the second argument is the object to which this instance variable belongs. Both observer (heading) and mutator (heading:) accessor messages must be understood by the object, with the usual naming convention. In the case of a text input field, this saves us the trouble of having to define a callback that updates the field as well as having to bind the default contents of the HTML input field to the current value of the instance variable. Using on: #heading of: self, the heading variable is updated automatically whenever the user updates the text input field.

The same message is used twice more in this example, to cause the selection of a colour on the HTML form to update the color variable, and to bind the result of the checkbox to the checked variable. Many other examples can be found in the functional tests for Seaside. Have a look at the package Seaside-Tests-Functional, or just point your browser to http://localhost:8080/tests/functional. Select WAInputPostFunctionalTest and click on the Restart button to see most of the features of forms.

Don't forget, if you toggle Halos, you can browse the source code of the examples directly using the Seaside class browser.

14.5 CSS: Cascading style sheets

Cascading Style Sheets (http://www.w3.org/Style/CSS/), or CSS for short, are a standard way for web applications to separate style from content. Seaside relies on CSS to avoid cluttering your rendering code with layout considerations.

You can set the CSS style sheet for your web components by defining the method style, which should return a string containing the CSS rules for that component. The styles of all the components displayed on a web page are joined together, so each component can have its own style. A better approach can be to define an abstract class for your web application that defines a common style for all its subclasses.

Actually, for deployed applications, it is more common to define style sheets as external files. This way the look and feel of the component is completely separate from its functionality. (Have a look at WAFileLibrary, which provides a way to serve static files without the need for a standalone server.)

If you already are familiar with CSS, then that's all you need to know. Otherwise, read on for a very brief introduction to CSS.

Instead of directly encoding display attributes in the paragraph and text elements of your web pages, CSS lets you define different *classes* of elements, and place all display considerations in a separate style sheet.

14.5 CSS: Cascading style sheets

To put it another way, a CSS style sheet consists of a set of rules that specify how to format given HTML elements. Each rule consists of two parts. There is a *selector* that specifies which HTML elements the rule applies to, and there is a *declaration* which sets a number of attributes for that element.

```
SeasideDemoWidget >> style
    ^ '
body {
    font: 10pt Arial, Helvetica, sans-serif, Times New Roman;
}
h2 {
    font-size: 12pt;
    font-weight: normal;
    font-style: italic;
}
table { border-collapse: collapse; }
td {
    border: 2px solid #CCCCCC;
    padding: 4px;
}
#author {
    border: 1px solid black;
    padding: 2px;
    margin: 2px;
}
.subcomponent {
    border: 2px solid lightblue;
    padding: 2px;
    margin: 2px;
}
.highlight { background-color: yellow; }
.boolean { background-color: lightgrey; }
.field { background-color: lightgrey; }
'
```

The previous method illustrates a simple style sheet for the rendering demo shown earlier in Figure 14.12. The first rule specifies a preference for the fonts to use for the body of the web page. The next few rules specify properties of second-level headings (h2), tables (table), and table data (td).

The remaining rules have selectors that will match HTML elements that have the given class or id attributes. CSS selectors for class attributes start with a . and those for id attributes with #. The main difference between class and id attributes is that many elements may have the same class, but only one element may have a given id (i.e., an *identifier*). So, whereas a class attribute, such as highlight, may occur multiple times on any page, an id must identify a *unique* element on the page, such as a particular menu, the modified date, or author. Note that a particular HTML element may have multiple classes, in which case all the applicable display attributes will be applied in sequence.

Selector conditions may be combined, so the selector div.subcomponent will only match an HTML element if it is both a div *and* it has a class attribute equal to subcomponent.

It is also possible to specify nested elements, though this is seldom necessary. For example, the selector p span will match a span within a paragraph but not within a div.

There are numerous books and web sites to help you learn CSS. For a dramatic demonstration of the power of CSS, we recommend you to have a look at the CSS Zen Garden (http://www.csszengarden.com/), which shows how the same content can be rendered in radically different ways simply by changing the CSS style sheet.

14.6 Managing control flow

Seaside makes it particularly easy to design web applications with non-trivial control flow. There are basically two mechanisms that you can use:

1. A component can *call* another component by sending caller call: callee. The caller is temporarily replaced by the callee, until the callee returns control by sending answer:. The caller is usually self, but could also be any other currently visible component.

2. A workflow can be defined as a *task*. This is a special kind of component that subclasses WATask (instead of WAComponent). Instead of defining renderContentOn:, it defines no content of its own, but rather defines a go method that sends a series of call: messages to activate various subcomponents in turn.

Call and answer

Call and answer are used to realize simple dialogues.

There is a trivial example of call: and answer: in the rendering demo of Figure 14.12. The component SeasideEditCallDemo displays a text field and an edit link. The callback for the edit link calls a new instance of SeasideEditAnswerDemo initialized to the value of the text field. The callback also updates this text field to the result which is sent as an answer.

(We underline the call: and answer: sends to draw attention to them.)

```
SeasideEditCallDemo >> renderContentOn: html
    html span
        class: 'field';
        with: self text.
    html space.
    html anchor
        callback: [self text: (self call: (SeasideEditAnswerDemo new text:
            self text))];
        with: 'edit'
```

14.6 Managing control flow

What is particularly elegant is that the code makes absolutely no reference to the new web page that must be created. At run-time, a new page is created in which the SeasideEditCallDemo component is replaced by a SeasideEditAnswerDemo component; the parent component and the other peer components are untouched.

It is important to keep in mind that call: and answer: should never be used while rendering. They may safely be sent from within a callback, or from within the go method of a task.

The SeasideEditAnswerDemo component is also remarkably simple. It just renders a form with a text field. The submit button is bound to a callback that will answer the final value of the text field.

```
SeasideEditAnswerDemo >> renderContentOn: html
   html form: [
      html textInput
         on: #text of: self.
      html submitButton
         callback: [ self answer: self text ];
         text: 'ok'.
      ]
```

That's it.

Seaside takes care of the control flow and the correct rendering of all the components. Interestingly, the *Back* button of the browser will also work just fine (though side effects are not rolled back unless we take additional steps).

Convenience methods

Since certain call–answer dialogues are very common, Seaside provides some convenience methods to save you the trouble of writing components like SeasideEditAnswerDemo. The generated dialogues are shown in Figure 14.13. We can see these convenience methods being used within SeasideDialogDemo>>renderContentOn:

The message request: performs a call to a component that will let you edit a text field. The component answers the edited string. An optional label and default value may also be specified.

```
SeasideDialogDemo >> renderContentOn: html
   html anchor
      callback: [ self request: 'edit this' label: 'done' default: 'some
         text' ];
      with: 'self request:'.
...
```

The message inform: calls a component that simply displays the argument message and waits for the user to click Ok. The called component just returns self.

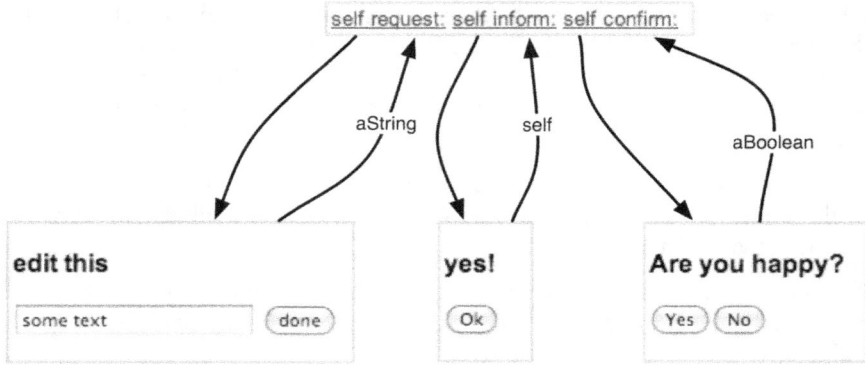

Figure 14.13: Some standard dialogs.

```
...
html space.
html anchor
    callback: [ self inform: 'yes!' ];
    with: 'self inform:'.
...
```

The message confirm: asks a question and waits for the user to select either Yes or No. The component answers a boolean, which can be used to perform further actions.

```
...
html space.
html anchor
    callback: [
        (self confirm: 'Are you happy?')
            ifTrue: [ self inform: ':-)' ]
            ifFalse: [ self inform: ':-(' ]
        ];
    with: 'self confirm:'.
```

A few further convenience methods, such as chooseFrom:caption:, are defined in the convenience protocol of WAComponent.

Tasks

A task is a component that subclasses WATask. It does not render anything itself, but simply calls other components in a control flow defined by implementing the method go.

WAConvenienceTest is a simple example of a task defined in the package Seaside-Tests-Functional. To see its effect, just point your browser to http:

14.6 Managing control flow

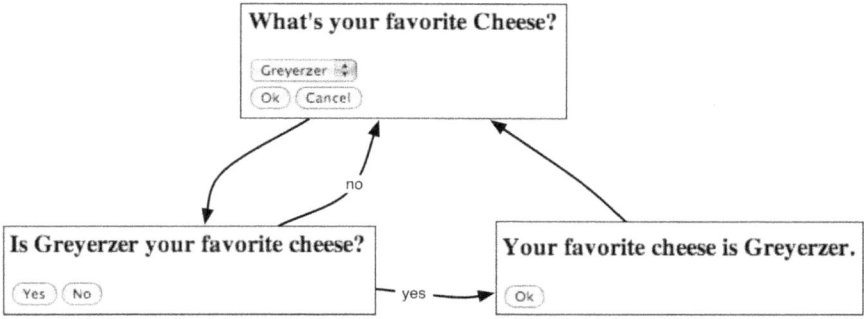

Figure 14.14: A simple task.

//localhost:8080/tests/functional, select WAFlowConvenienceFunctionalTest and click Restart.

```
WAFlowConvenienceFunctionalTest >> go
    [ self chooseCheese.
      self confirmCheese ] whileFalse.
    self informCheese
```

This task calls in turn three components. The first, generated by the convenience method chooseFrom: caption:, is a WAChoiceDialog that asks the user to choose a cheese.

```
WAFlowConvenienceFunctionalTest >> chooseCheese
    cheese := self
        chooseFrom: #('Greyerzer' 'Tilsiter' 'Sbrinz')
        caption: 'What''s your favorite Cheese?'.
    cheese isNil ifTrue: [ self chooseCheese ]
```

The second is a WAYesOrNoDialog to confirm the choice (generated by the convenience method confirm:).

```
WAFlowConvenienceFunctionalTest >> confirmCheese
    ^self confirm: 'Is ', cheese, ' your favorite cheese?'
```

Finally a WAFormDialog is called (via the convenience method inform:).

```
WAFlowConvenienceFunctionalTest >> informCheese
    self inform: 'Your favorite cheese is ', cheese, '.'
```

The generated dialogues are shown in Figure 14.14.

Transactions

We saw in Section 14.3 that Seaside can keep track of the correspondence between the state of components and individual web pages by having components register their state for backtracking: all that a component need do

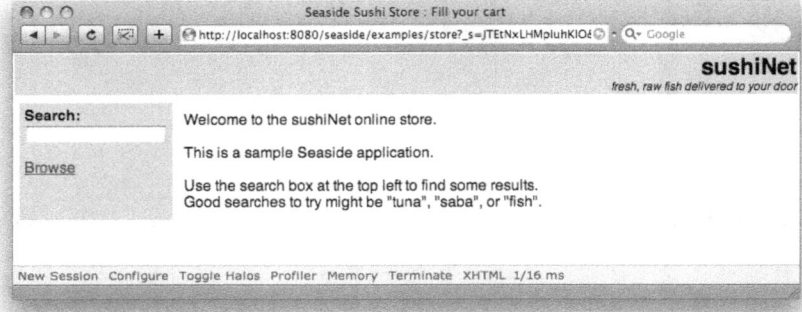

Figure 14.15: The Sushi Store.

is implement the method `states` to answer an array of all the objects whose state must be tracked.

Sometimes, however, we do not want to backtrack state: instead we want to *prevent* the user from accidentally undoing effects that should be permanent. This is often referred to as "the shopping cart problem". Once you have checked out your shopping cart and paid for the items you have purchased, it should not be possible to go *Back* with the browser and add more items to the shopping cart!

Seaside allows you to enforce restriction this by defining a task within which certain actions are grouped together as *transactions*. You can backtrack within a transaction, but once a transaction is complete, you can no longer go back to it. The corresponding pages are *invalidated*, and any attempt to go back to them will cause Seaside to generate a warning and redirect the user to the most recent valid page.

The Seaside *Sushi Store* is sample application that illustrates many of the features of Seaside, including transactions. This application is bundled with your installation of Seaside, so you can try it out by pointing your browser at http://localhost:8080/seaside/examples/store. (If you cannot find it in your image, there is a version of the sushi store available on SqueakSource from http://www.squeaksource.com/SeasideExamples/.)

The sushi store supports the following workflow:

- Visit the store.
- Browse or search for sushi.
- Add sushi to your shopping cart.
- Checkout.
- Verify your order.

14.6 Managing control flow

- Enter shipping address.
- Verify shipping address.
- Enter payment information.
- Your fish is on its way!

If you toggle the halos, you will see that the top-level component of the sushi store is an instance of WAStore. It does nothing but render the title bar, and then it renders task, an instance of WAStoreTask.

```
WAStore >> renderContentOn: html
    "... render the title bar ..."
    html div id: 'body'; with: task
```

WAStoreTask captures this workflow sequence. At a couple of points it is critical that the user not be able to go back and change the submitted information.

Purchase some sushi and then use the *Back* button to try to put more sushi into your cart.

You will get the message *That page has expired.*

Seaside lets the programmer say that a certain part of a workflow acts like a transaction: once the transaction is complete, the user cannot go back and undo it. This is done by sending isolate: to a task with the transactional block as its argument. We can see this in the sushi store workflow as follows:

```
WAStoreTask >> go
    | shipping billing creditCard |
    cart := WAStoreCart new.
    self isolate:
       [[ self fillCart.
        self confirmContentsOfCart ]
           whileFalse ].

    self isolate:
       [ shipping := self getShippingAddress.
        billing := (self useAsBillingAddress: shipping)
                ifFalse: [ self getBillingAddress ]
                ifTrue: [ shipping ].
        creditCard := self getPaymentInfo.
        self shipTo: shipping billTo: billing payWith: creditCard ].

    self displayConfirmation.
```

Here we see quite clearly that there are two transactions. The first fills the cart and closes the shopping phase. (The helper methods such as fillCart take care of instantiating and calling the right subcomponents.) Once you have confirmed the contents of the cart you cannot go back without starting a new session. The second transaction completes the shipping and payment data. You can navigate back and forth within the second transaction until you

277

confirm payment. However, once both transactions are complete, any attempt to navigate back will fail.

Transactions may also be nested. A simple demonstration of this is found in the class WANestedTransaction. The first isolate: takes as argument a block that contains another, nested isolate:

```
WANestedTransaction >> go
    self inform: 'Before parent txn'.
    self isolate:
        [self inform: 'Inside parent txn'.
        self isolate: [self inform: 'Inside child txn'].
        self inform: 'Outside child txn'].
    self inform: 'Outside parent txn'
```

Go to http://localhost:8080/tests/functionals, select WATransactionTest and click on Restart. Try to navigate back and forth within the parent and child transaction by clicking the *Back* button and then clicking Ok. Note that as soon as a transaction is complete, you can no longer go back inside the transaction without generating an error upon clicking Ok.

14.7 A complete tutorial example

Let's see how we can build a complete Seaside application from scratch. (The exercise should take at most a couple of hours. If you prefer to just look at the completed source code, you can grab it from the SqueakSource project http://www.squeaksource.com/PharoByExample. The package to load is PBE-SeasideRPN. The tutorial that follows uses slightly different class names so that you can compare your implementation with ours.) We will build a RPN (Reverse Polish Notation) calculator as a Seaside application that uses a simple stack machine as its underlying model. Furthermore, the Seaside interface will let us toggle between two displays — one which just shows us the current value on top of the stack, and the other which shows us the complete state of the stack. The calculator with the two display options is shown in Figure 14.16.

We begin by implementing the stack machine and its tests.

First, Define a new class called MyStackMachine with an instance variable contents initialized to a new OrderedCollection.

```
MyStackMachine >> initialize
    super initialize.
    contents := OrderedCollection new.
```

The stack machine should provide operations to push: and pop values, view the top of the stack, and perform various arithmetic operations to add, subtract, multiply and divide the top values on the stack.

Write some tests for the stack operations and then implement these operations. Here is a sample test:

14.7 A complete tutorial example

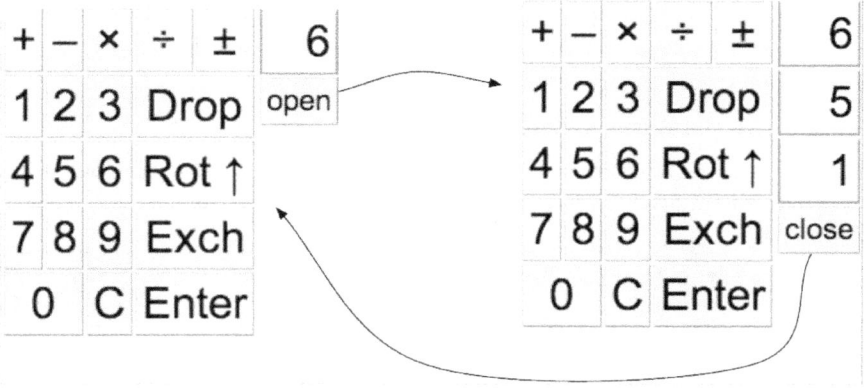

Figure 14.16: RPN calculator and its stack machine.

```
MyStackMachineTest >> testDiv
    stack
        push: 3;
        push: 4;
        div.
    self assert: stack size = 1.
    self assert: stack top = (4/3).
```

You might consider using some helper methods for the arithmetic operations to check that there are two numbers on the stack before doing anything, and raising an error if this precondition is not fulfilled. (It's a good idea to use Object>>assert: to specify the preconditions for an operation. This method will raise an AssertionFailure if the user tries to use the stack machine in an invalid state.) If you do this, most of your methods will just be one or two lines long.

You might also consider implementing MyStackMachine>>printOn: to make it easier to debug your stack machine implementation with the help of an object inspector. (Hint: just delegate printing to the contents variable.)

Complete the MyStackMachine by writing operations dup (push a duplicate of the top value onto the stack), exch (exchange the top two values), and rotUp (rotate the entire stack contents up — the top value will move to the bottom).

Now we have a simple stack machine implementation. We can start to implement the Seaside RPN Calculator.

We will make use of 5 classes:

1. MyRPNWidget — this should be an abstract class that defines the common CSS style sheet for the application, and other common behavior for the components of the RPN calculator. It is a subclass of WAComponent and the direct superclass of the following four classes.

279

2. `MyCalculator` — this is the root component. It should register the application (on the class side), it should instantiate and render its subcomponents, and it should register any state for backtracking.

3. `MyKeypad` - this displays the keys that we use to interact with the calculator.

4. `MyDisplay` — this component displays the top of the stack and provides a button to call another component to display the detailed view.

5. `MyDisplayStack` — this component shows the detailed view of the stack and provides a button to answer back. It is a subclass of `MyDisplay`.

Create a package `MyCalculator`, and define `MyRPNWidget`.

Define the common `style` for the application.

Here is a minimal CSS for the application. You can make it more fancy if you like.

```
MyRPNWidget >> style
   ^ 'table.keypad { float: left; }
td.key {
   border: 1px solid grey;
   background: lightgrey;
   padding: 4px;
   text-align: center;
}
table.stack { float: left; }
td.stackcell {
   border: 2px solid white;
   border-left-color: grey;
   border-right-color: grey;
   border-bottom-color: grey;
   padding: 4px;
   text-align: right;
}
td.small { font-size: 8pt; }'
```

Define `MyCalculator` to be a root component and register itself as an application (*i.e.*, implement `canBeRoot` and `initialize` on the class side).

Implement `MyCalculator>>renderContentOn:` to render something trivial (such as its name), and verify that the application runs in a browser.

`MyCalculator` is responsible for instantiating `MyStackMachine`, `MyKeypad` and `MyDisplay`.

Define `MyKeypad` and `MyDisplay` as subclasses of `MyRPNWidget`.

All three components will need access to a common instance of the stack machine, so define the instance variable `stackMachine` and an initialization method `setMyStackMachine:` in the common parent, `MyRPNWidget`. Add instance variables `keypad` and `display` to `MyCalculator` and initialize them in `MyCalculator>>initialize`. (Don't forget to send `super initialize`!)

14.7 A complete tutorial example

Figure 14.17: Displaying the top of the stack.

Pass the shared instance of the stack machine to the keypad and the display in the same initialize method.

Implement MyCalculator>>renderContentOn: to simply render in turn the keypad and the display. To correctly display the subcomponents, you must implement MyCalculator>>children to return an array with the keypad and the display. Implement placeholder rendering methods for the keypad and the display and verify that the calculator now displays its two subcomponents.

Now we will change the implementation of the display to show the top value of the stack.

Use a table with class keypad containing a row with a single table data cell with class stackcell.

Change the rendering method of the keypad to ensure that the number 0 is pushed on the stack in case it is empty. (Define and use MyKeypad>>ensureStackMachineNotEmpty.) Also make it display an empty table with class keypad. Now the calculator should display a single cell containing the value 0. If you toggle the halos, you should see something like this: Figure 14.17

Now let's implement an interface to interact with the stack.

First, define the following helper methods, which will make it easier to script the interface:

```
MyKeypad >> renderStackButton: text callback: aBlock colSpan: anInteger
    on: html
  html tableData
    class: 'key';
    colSpan: anInteger;
    with:
        [ html anchor
            callback: aBlock;
            with: [ html html: text ]]

MyKeypad >> renderStackButton: text callback: aBlock on: html
  self
    renderStackButton: text
```

```
        callback: aBlock
        colSpan: 1
        on: html
```

We will use these two methods to define the buttons on the keypad with appropriate callbacks. Certain buttons may span multiple columns, but the default is to occupy just one column.

Use the two helper methods to script the keypad as follows.

(Hint: start by getting the digit and Enter keys working, then the arithmetic operators.)

```
MyKeypad >> renderContentOn: html
  self ensureStackMachineNotEmpty.
  html table
    class: 'keypad';
    with: [
      html tableRow: [
        self renderStackButton: '+' callback: [self stackOp: #add] on:
          html.
        self renderStackButton: '&ndash;' callback: [self stackOp:
          #min] on: html.
        self renderStackButton: '&times;' callback: [self stackOp:
          #mul] on: html.
        self renderStackButton: '&divide;' callback: [self stackOp:
          #div] on: html.
        self renderStackButton: '&plusmn;' callback: [self stackOp:
          #neg] on: html ].
      html tableRow: [
        self renderStackButton: '1' callback: [self type: '1'] on:
          html.
        self renderStackButton: '2' callback: [self type: '2'] on:
          html.
        self renderStackButton: '3' callback: [self type: '3'] on:
          html.
        self renderStackButton: 'Drop' callback: [self
          stackPopIfNotEmpty]
          colSpan: 2 on: html ].
" and so on ... "
      html tableRow: [
        self renderStackButton: '0' callback: [self type: '0']
          colSpan: 2 on: html.
        self renderStackButton: 'C' callback: [self stackClearTop] on:
          html.
        self renderStackButton: 'Enter'
          callback: [self stackOp: #dup. self setClearMode]
          colSpan: 2 on: html ]]
```

Check that the keypad displays properly. If you try to click on the keys, however, you will find that the calculator does not work yet.

14.7 A complete tutorial example

Implement MyKeypad>>type: to update the top of the stack by appending the typed digit. You will need to convert the top value to a string, update it, and convert it back to an integer, something like this:

```
MyKeypad >> type: aString
   stackMachine push: (self stackPopTopOrZero asString, aString)
      asNumber.
```

The two methods stackPopTopOrZero and stackPopIfNotEmpty are used to guard against operating on an empty stack.

```
MyKeypad >> stackPopTopOrZero
   ^ stackMachine isEmpty
      ifTrue: [ 0 ]
      ifFalse: [ stackMachine pop ]
```

```
MyKeypad >> stackPopIfNotEmpty
   stackMachine isEmpty
      ifFalse: [ stackMachine pop ]
```

Now when you click on the digit keys the display should be updated. (Be sure that MyStackMachine>>pop returns the value popped, or this will not work!)

Next, we must implement MyKeypad>>stackOp:. Something like this will do the trick:

```
MyKeypad >> stackOp: op
   [ stackMachine perform: op ] on: AssertionFailure do: [ ].
```

The point is that we are not sure that all operations will succeed. For example, addition will fail if we do not have two numbers on the stack. For the moment we can just ignore such errors. If we are feeling more ambitious later on, we can provide some user feedback in the error handler block.

The first version of the calculator should be working now. Try to enter some numbers by pressing the digit keys, hitting Enter to push a copy of the current value, and entering + to sum the top two values.

You will notice that typing digits does not behave the way you might expect. Actually the calculator should be aware of whether you are typing a *new* number, or appending to an existing number.

Adapt MyKeypad>>type: to behave differently depending on the current typing mode.

Introduce an instance variable mode which takes on one of the three values: the symbol #typing (when you are typing), #push (after you have performed a calculator operation and typing should force the top value to be pushed), or #clear (after you have performed Enter and the top value should be cleared before typing). The new type: method might look like this:

```
MyKeypad >> type: aString
   self inPushMode ifTrue: [
```

283

```
        stackMachine push: stackMachine top.
        self stackClearTop ].
    self inClearMode ifTrue: [ self stackClearTop ].
    stackMachine push: (self stackPopTopOrZero asString, aString)
        asNumber.
```

Typing might work better now, but it is still frustrating not to be able to see what is on the stack.

Define `MyDisplayStack` as a subclass of `MyDisplay`.

Add a button to the rendering method of `MyDisplay` which will call a new instance of `MyDisplayStack`. You will need an HTML anchor that looks something like this:

```
html anchor
    callback: [ self call: (MyDisplayStack new setMyStackMachine:
        stackMachine)];
    with: 'open'
```

The callback will cause the current instance of `MyDisplay` to be temporarily replaced by a new instance of `MyDisplayStack` whose job it is to display the complete stack. When this component signals that it is done (*i.e.*, by sending `self answer`), then control will return to the original instance of `MyDisplay`.

Define the rendering method of `MyDisplayStack` to display all of the values on the stack.

(You will either need to define an accessor for the stack machine's contents or you can define `MyStackMachine>>do:` to iterate over the stack values.) The stack display should also have a button labelled `close` whose callback will simply perform `self answer`.

```
html anchor
    callback: [ self answer];
    with: 'close'
```

Now you should be able to *open* and *close* the stack while you are using the calculator.

There is, however, one thing we have forgotten. Try to perform some operations on the stack. Now use the *Back* button of your browser and try to perform some more stack operations. For example, open the stack, type 1, Enter twice and +. The stack should display *2* and *1*. Now hit the *Back* button. The stack now shows three times *1* again. Now if you type +, the stack shows *3*. Backtracking is not yet working.

Implement `MyCalculator>>states` to return an array with the contents of the stack machine.

Check that backtracking now works correctly.

14.8 A quick look at AJAX

AJAX (Asynchronous JavaScript and XML) is a technique to make web applications more interactive by exploiting JavaScript functionality on the client side.

Two well-known JavaScript libraries are Prototype (http://www.prototypejs.org) and script.aculo.us (http://script.aculo.us). Prototype provides a framework to ease writing JavaScript. script.aculo.us provides some additional features to support animations and drag-and-drop on top of Prototype. Both frameworks are supported in Seaside through the package Scriptaculous.

All ready made images have the Scriptaculous package extensions already loaded. The latest version is available from http://www.squeaksource.com/Seaside. An online demo is available at http://scriptaculous.seasidehosting.st. Alternatively, if you have a enabled image running, simply go to http://localhost:8080/javascript/scriptaculous.

The Scriptaculous extensions follow the same approach as Seaside itself — simply configure Pharo objects to model your application, and the needed Javascript code will be generated for you.

Let us look at a simple example of how client-side Javascript support can make our RPN calculator behave more naturally. Currently every keystroke to enter a digit generates a request to refresh the page. We would like instead to handle editing of the display on the client-side by updating the display in the existing page.

To address the display from JavaScript code, we must first give it a unique id.

Update the calculator's rendering method as follows. (If you have not implemented the tutorial example yourself, you can simply load the complete example (PBE-SeasideRPN) from http://www.squeaksource.com/PharoByExample and apply the suggested changes to the classes RPN* instead of My*.

```
MyCalculator >> renderContentOn: html
    html div id: 'keypad'; with: keypad.
    html div id: 'display'; with: display.
```

To be able to re-render the display when a keyboard button is pressed, the keyboard needs to know the display component.

Add a display instance variable to MyKeypad, an initialize method MyKeypad>>setDisplay:, and call this from MyCalculator>>initialize. Now we are able to assign some JavaScript code to the buttons by updating MyKeypad>>renderStackButton:callback:colSpan:on: as follows:

```
MyKeypad >> renderStackButton: text callback: aBlock colSpan: anInteger
      on: html
    html tableData
      class: 'key';
      colSpan: anInteger;
```

```
with: [
    html anchor
        callback: aBlock;
        onClick:    "handle Javascript event"
            (html scriptaculous updater
                id: 'display';
                callback: [ :r |
                    aBlock value.
                    r render: display ];
                return: false);
        with: [ html html: text ] ]
```

`onClick:` specifies a JavaScript event handler. `html updater` returns an instance of `PTUpdater`, a Smalltalk object representing the JavaScript AJAX Updater object (http://www.prototypejs.org/api/ajax/updater). This object performs AJAX requests and updates a container's contents based on the response text. `id:` tells the updater what HTML DOM element to update, in this case the contents of the `div` element with the id 'display'. `callback:` specifies a block that is triggered when the user presses the button. The block argument is a new renderer `r`, which we can use to render the display component. (Note: Even though HTML is still accessible, it is not valid anymore at the time this callback block is evaluated). Before rendering the display component we evaluate aBlock to perform the desired action.

`return: false` tells the JavaScript engine to not trigger the original link callback, which would cause a full refresh. We could instead remove the original anchor `callback:`, but like this the calculator will still work even if JavaScript is disabled.

Try the calculator again, and notice how a full page refresh is triggered every time you press a digit key. (The URL of the web page is updated at each keystroke.)

Although we have implemented the client-side behavior, we have not yet activated it. Now we will enable the Javascript event handling.

Click on the Configure link in the toolbar of the calculator.

Configure the `Libraries` attribute under the `General` section. (You may need to enable the modification of this attribute, by first selecting `Modify`). From the list of available libraries, select `PTDevelopmentLibrary` and apply the changes.

Instead of manually adding the library, you may also do it programmatically when you register the application:

```
MyCalculator class >> initialize
    (WAAdmin register: self asApplicationAt: self applicationName)
        addLibrary: PTDevelopmentLibrary
```

14.8 A quick look at AJAX

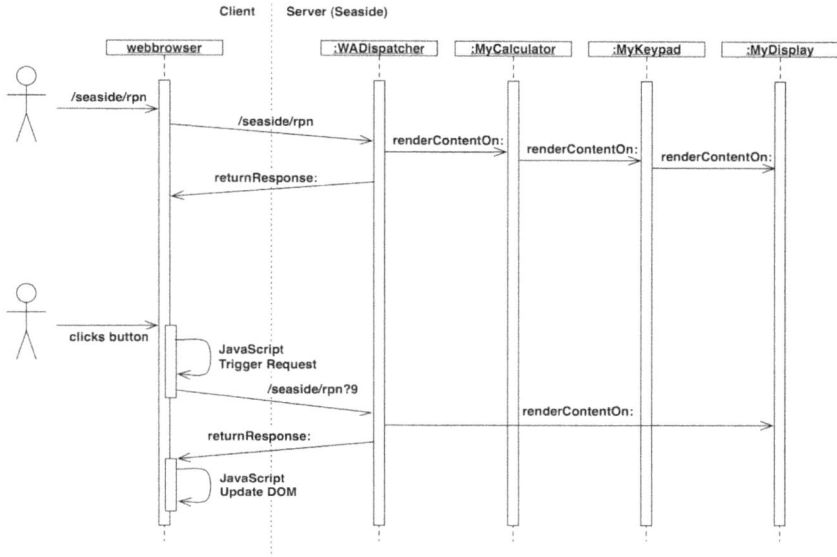

Figure 14.18: Seaside AJAX processing (simplified).

For this example the `PTDevelopmentLibrary` is sufficient, but for the full set of the scriptaculous extensions you need to add the `SUDevelopmentLibrary`, too.

Try the revised application. Note that the feedback is much more natural. In particular, a new URL is not generated with each keystroke.

You may well ask, *yes, but how does this work?* Figure 14.18 shows how the RPN applications would both without and with AJAX. Basically AJAX short-circuits the rendering to *only* update the display component. Javascript is responsible both for triggering the request and updating the corresponding DOM element. Have a look at the generated source-code, especially the JavaScript code:

```
new Ajax.Updater(
  'display',
  'http://localhost/seaside/RPN+Calculator',
  {'evalScripts': true,
    'parameters': ['UNDERSCOREs=zcdqfonqwbeYzkza',
      'UNDERSCOREk=jMORHtqr','9'].join('&')});
```

```
 return false
```

For more advanced examples, have a further look at http://localhost:8080/javascript/scriptaculous.

Hints

In case of server side problems use the Debugger. In case of client side problems use FireFox (http://www.mozilla.com) with the JavaScript debugger FireBug (http://www.getfirebug.com/) plugin enabled.

14.9 Chapter summary

- The easiest way to get started is to download the *Seaside One-Click Experience* from http://seaside.st
- Turn the server on and off by evaluating `ZnZincServerAdaptor startOn: 8080` and `ZnZincServerAdaptor stop`.
- Toggle `Halos` to directly view application source code, run-time objects, CSS and HTML.
- Remove the root decoration class `WAToolDecoration` in the application configuration, to disable the toolbar
- Send `WAAdmin applicationDefaults removeParent: WADevelopmentConfiguration instance`, to disable toolbar for new Components
- Seaside web applications are composed of components, each of which is an instance of a subclass of `WAComponent`.
- Only a root component may be registered as an application. It should implement `canBeRoot` on the class side. Alternatively it may register itself as an application in its class-side `initialize` method by sending `WAAdmin register: self asApplicationAt:` *application path*. If you override `description` it is possible to return a descriptive application name that will be displayed in the configuration editor.
- To backtrack state, a component must implement the `states` method to answer an array of objects whose state will be restored if the user clicks the browser's *Back* button.
- A component renders itself by implementing `renderContentOn:`. The argument to this method is an HTML rendering *canvas* (usually called `html`).
- A component can render a subcomponent by sending `self render:` *subcomponent*.

14.9 Chapter summary

- HTML is generated programmatically by sending messages to *brushes*. A brush is obtained by sending a message, such as paragraph or div, to the HTML canvas.

- If you send a cascade of messages to a brush that includes the message with:, then with: should be the last message sent. The with: message sets the contents *and* renders the result.

- Actions should appear only in callbacks. You should not change the state of the application while you are rendering it.

- You can bind various form widgets and anchors to instance variables with accessors by sending the message on: *instance variable* of: *object* to the brush.

- You can define the CSS for a component hierarchy by defining the method style, which should return a string containing the style sheet. (For deployed applications, it is more usual to refer to a style sheet located at a static URL.)

- Control flows can be programmed by sending x call: y, in which case component x will be replaced by y until y answers by sending answer: with a result in a callback. The receiver of call: is usually self, but may in general be any visible component.

- A control flow can also be specified as a *task* — a instance of a subclass of WATask. It should implement the method go, which should call: a series of components in a workflow.

- Use WAComponents's convenience methods request:, inform:, confirm: and chooseFrom:caption: for basic interactions.

- To prevent the user from using the browser's *Back* button to access a previous execution state of the web application, you can declare portions of the workflow to be a *transaction* by enclosing them in an isolate: block.

CHAPTER 15

Classes and metaclasses

As we saw in preceding chapters, in Pharo, everything is an object, and every object is an instance of a class. Classes are no exception: classes are objects, and class objects are instances of other classes. This object model captures the essence of object-oriented programming, and is lean, simple, elegant and uniform. However, the implications of this uniformity may confuse newcomers.

Note that you do not need to fully understand the implications of this uniformity to program fluently in Pharo. Nevertheless, the goal of this chapter is twofold: (1) go as deep as possible and (2) show that there is nothing complex, *magic* or special here: just simple rules applied uniformly. By following these rules you can always understand why the situation is the way that it is.

15.1 Rules for classes and metaclasses

The Pharo object model is based on a limited number of concepts applied uniformly. To refresh your memory, here are the rules of the object model that we explored in Chapter : The Pharo Object Model.

Rule 1 Everything is an object.

Rule 2 Every object is an instance of a class.

Rule 3 Every class has a superclass.

Rule 4 Everything happens by sending messages.

Rule 5 Method lookup follows the inheritance chain.

As we mentioned in the introduction to this chapter, a consequence of Rule 1 is that *classes are objects too*, so Rule 2 tells us that classes must also be in-

Classes and metaclasses

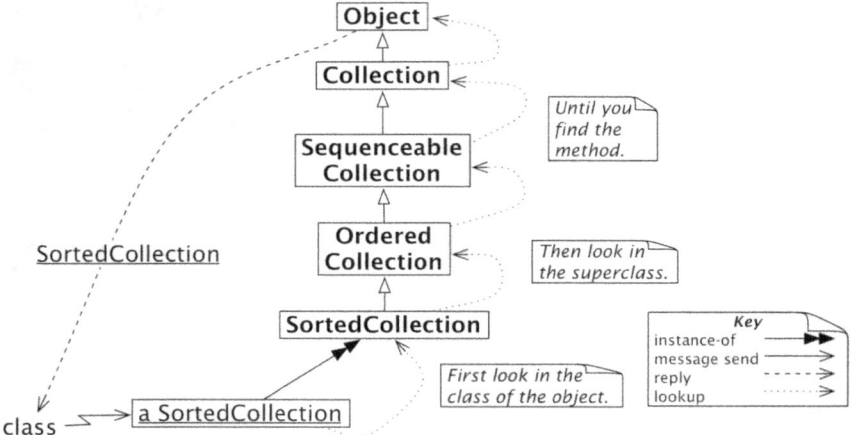

Figure 15.1: Sending the message class to a sorted collection

stances of classes. The class of a class is called a *metaclass*. A metaclass is created automatically for you whenever you create a class. Most of the time you do not need to care or think about metaclasses. However, every time that you use the browser to browse the *class side* of a class, it is helpful to recall that you are actually browsing a different class. A class and its metaclass are two separate classes, even though the former is an instance of the latter.

To properly explain classes and metaclasses, we need to extend the rules from Chapter : The Pharo Object Model with the following additional rules.

Rule 6 Every class is an instance of a metaclass.

Rule 7 The metaclass hierarchy parallels the class hierarchy.

Rule 8 Every metaclass inherits from `Class` and `Behavior`.

Rule 9 Every metaclass is an instance of `Metaclass`.

Rule 10 The metaclass of `Metaclass` is an instance of `Metaclass`.

Together, these 10 rules complete Pharo's object model.

We will first briefly revisit the 5 rules from Chapter : The Pharo Object Model with a small example. Then we will take a closer look at the new rules, using the same example.

15.2 Revisiting the Pharo object model

Rule 1. Since everything is an object, an ordered collection in Pharo is also an object.

15.3 Every class is an instance of a metaclass

```
OrderedCollection withAll: #(4 5 6 1 2 3)
>>> an OrderedCollection(4 5 6 1 2 3)
```

Rule 2. Every object is an instance of a class. The class of an ordered collection is the class `OrderedCollection`:

```
(OrderedCollection withAll: #(4 5 6 1 2 3)) class
>>> OrderedCollection
```

Rule 3. Every class has a superclass. The superclass of `OrderedCollection` is `SequenceableCollection` and the superclass of `SequenceableCollection` is `Collection`:

```
OrderedCollection superclass
>>> SequenceableCollection
```

```
SequenceableCollection superclass
>>> Collection
```

```
Collection superclass
>>> Object
```

Let us take an example. When we send the message asSortedCollection, we convert the ordered collection into a sorted collection. We verify simply as follows:

```
(OrderedCollection withAll: #(4 5 6 1 2 3)) asSortedCollection class
>>> SortedCollection
```

Rule 4. Everything happens by sending messagess, so we can deduce that `withAll:` is a message to `OrderedCollection` and `asSortedCollection` are messages sent to the ordered collection instance, and `superclass` is a message to `OrderedCollection` and `SequenceableCollection`, and `Collection`. The receiver in each case is an object, since everything is an object, but some of these objects are also classes.

Rule 5. Method lookup follows the inheritance chain, so when we send the message class to the result of (`OrderedCollection withAll: #(4 5 6 1 2 3)) asSortedCollection`, the message is handled when the corresponding method is found in the class `Object`, as shown in Figure 15.1.

15.3 Every class is an instance of a metaclass

As we mentioned earlier in Section 15.1, classes whose instances are themselves classes are called metaclasses.

Metaclasses are implicit

Metaclasses are automatically created when you define a class. We say that they are *implicit* since as a programmer you never have to worry about them.

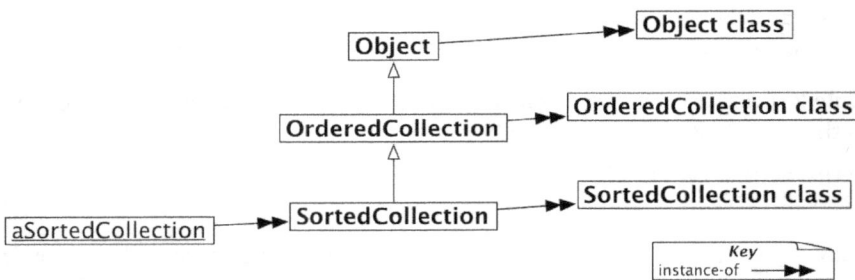

Figure 15.2: The metaclasses of SortedCollection and its superclasses (elided).

An implicit metaclass is created for each class you create, so each metaclass has only a single instance.

Whereas ordinary classes are named, metaclasses are anonymous. However, we can always refer to them through the class that is their instance. The class of SortedCollection, for instance, is SortedCollection class, and the class of Object is Object class:

```
SortedCollection class
>>> SortedCollection class
```

```
Object class
>>> Object class
```

In fact metaclasses are not truly anonymous, their name is deduced from the one of their single instance

```
SortedCollection class name
>>> 'SortedCollection class'
```

Figure 15.2 shows how each class is an instance of its metaclass. Note that we only skip SequenceableCollection and Collection from the figures and explanation due to space constraints. Their absence does not change the overall meaning.

Querying Metaclasses

The fact that classes are also objects makes it easy for us to query them by sending messages. Let's have a look:

```
OrderedCollection subclasses
>>> {SortedCollection . ObjectFinalizerCollection .
    WeakOrderedCollection . OCLiteralList . GLMMultiValue}
```

```
SortedCollection subclasses
>>> #()
```

15.4 The metaclass hierarchy parallels the class hierarchy

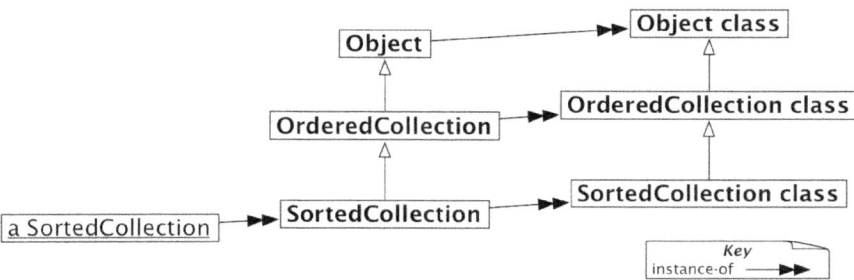

Figure 15.3: The metaclass hierarchy parallels the class hierarchy (elided).

```
SortedCollection allSuperclasses
>>> an OrderedCollection(OrderedCollection SequenceableCollection
    Collection Object ProtoObject)
```

```
SortedCollection instVarNames
>>> #('sortBlock')
```

```
SortedCollection allInstVarNames
>>> #('array' 'firstIndex' 'lastIndex' 'sortBlock')
```

```
SortedCollection selectors
>>> #(#indexForInserting: #sort:to: #addAll: #reSort #sortBlock:
    #copyEmpty #addFirst: #insert:before: #defaultSort:to: #median
    #at:put: #add: #= #collect: #flatCollect: #sort: #join: #sortBlock)
```

15.4 The metaclass hierarchy parallels the class hierarchy

Rule 7 says that the superclass of a metaclass cannot be an arbitrary class: it is constrained to be the metaclass of the superclass of the metaclass's unique instance.

```
SortedCollection class superclass
>>> OrderedCollection class
```

```
SortedCollection superclass class
>>> OrderedCollection class
```

This is what we mean by the metaclass hierarchy being parallel to the class hierarchy. Figure 15.3 shows how this works in the SortedCollection hierarchy.

```
SortedCollection class
>>> SortedCollection class
```

```
SortedCollection class superclass
>>> OrderedCollection class
```

295

Classes and metaclasses

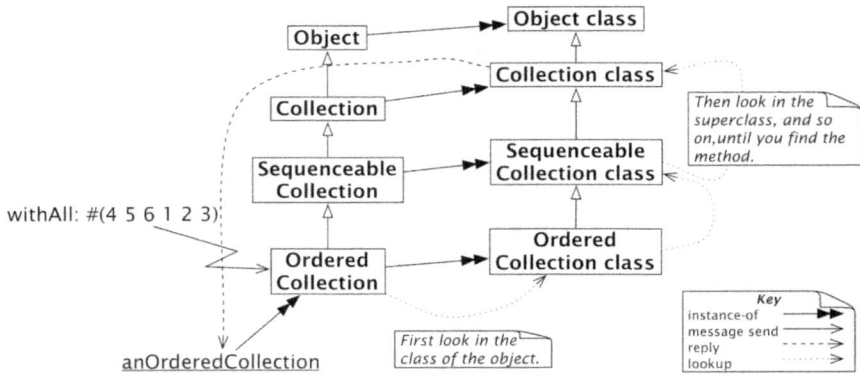

Figure 15.4: Message lookup for classes is the same as for ordinary objects.

```
SortedCollection class superclass superclass
>>> SequenceableCollection class
```

```
SortedCollection class superclass superclass superclass superclass
>>> Object class
```

Uniformity between Classes and Objects

It is interesting to step back a moment and realize that there is no difference between sending a message to an object and to a class. In both cases the search for the corresponding method starts in the *class of the receiver*, and *proceeds up the inheritance chain*.

Thus, messages sent to classes must follow the metaclass inheritance chain. Consider, for example, the method withAll:, which is implemented on the class side of Collection. When we send the message withAll: to the class OrderedCollection, then it is looked up the same way as any other message. The lookup starts in OrderedCollection class (since it starts in the class of the receiver and the receiver is OrderedCollection), and proceeds up the metaclass hierarchy until it is found in Collection class (see Figure 15.4). It returns a new instance of OrderedCollection.

```
OrderedCollection withAll: #(4 5 6 1 2 3)
>>> an OrderedCollection (4 5 6 1 2 3)
```

Only one method lookup

Thus we see that there is one uniform kind of method lookup in Pharo. Classes are just objects, and behave like any other objects. Classes have the power to create new instances only because classes happen to respond to the message new, and because the method for new knows how to create new instances.

296

15.5 Every metaclass inherits from Class and Behavior

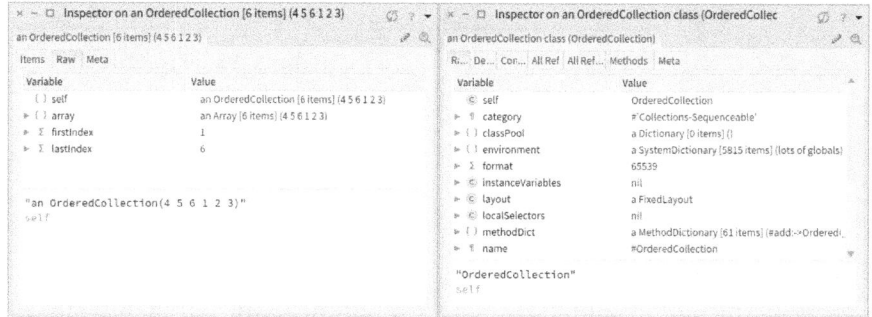

Figure 15.5: Classes are objects too.

Normally, non-class objects do not understand this message, but if you have a good reason to do so, there is nothing stopping you from adding a new method to a non-metaclass.

Inspecting objects and classes

Since classes are objects, we can also inspect them.

Inspect OrderedCollection withAll: #(4 5 6 1 2 3) and OrderedCollection.

Notice that in one case you are inspecting an instance of OrderedCollection and in the other case the OrderedCollection class itself. This can be a bit confusing, because the title bar of the inspector names the *class* of the object being inspected.

The inspector on OrderedCollection allows you to see the superclass, instance variables, method dictionary, and so on, of the OrderedCollection class, as shown in Figure 15.5.

15.5 Every metaclass inherits from Class and Behavior

Every metaclass is a kind of a class (a class with a single instance), hence inherits from Class. Class in turn inherits from its superclasses, ClassDescription and Behavior. Since everything in Pharo is an object, these classes all inherit eventually from Object. We can see the complete picture in Figure 15.6.

Where is new defined?

To understand the importance of the fact that metaclasses inherit from Class and Behavior, it helps to ask where new is defined and how it is found. When

Classes and metaclasses

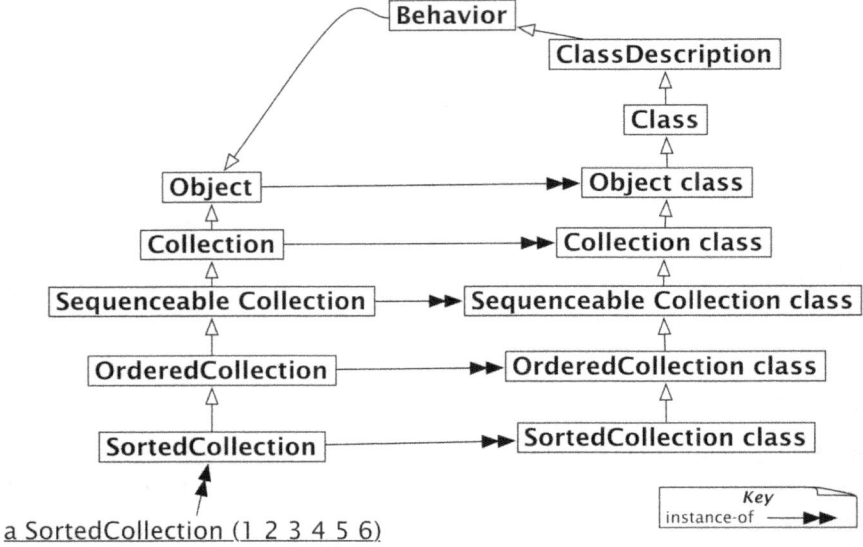

Figure 15.6: Metaclasses inherit from Class and Behavior.

the message new is sent to a class, it is looked up in its metaclass chain and ultimately in its superclasses Class, ClassDescription and Behavior as shown in Figure 15.7.

The question *Where is* new *defined?* is crucial. new is first defined in the class Behavior, and it can be redefined in its subclasses, including any of the metaclass of the classes we define, when this is necessary. Now when a message new is sent to a class it is looked up, as usual, in the metaclass of this class, continuing up the superclass chain right up to the class Behavior, if it has not been redefined along the way.

Note that the result of sending SortedCollection new is an instance of SortedCollection and *not* of Behavior, even though the method is looked up in the class Behavior! new always returns an instance of self, the class that receives the message, even if it is implemented in another class.

```
SortedCollection new class
>>> SortedCollection "not Behavior!"
```

Common mistake. A common mistake is to look for new in the superclass of the receiving class. The same holds for new:, the standard message to create an object of a given size. For example, Array new: 4 creates an array of 4 elements. You will not find this method defined in Array or any of its superclasses. Instead you should look in Array class and its superclasses, since that is where the lookup will start (See Figure 15.7).

298

15.5 Every metaclass inherits from Class and Behavior

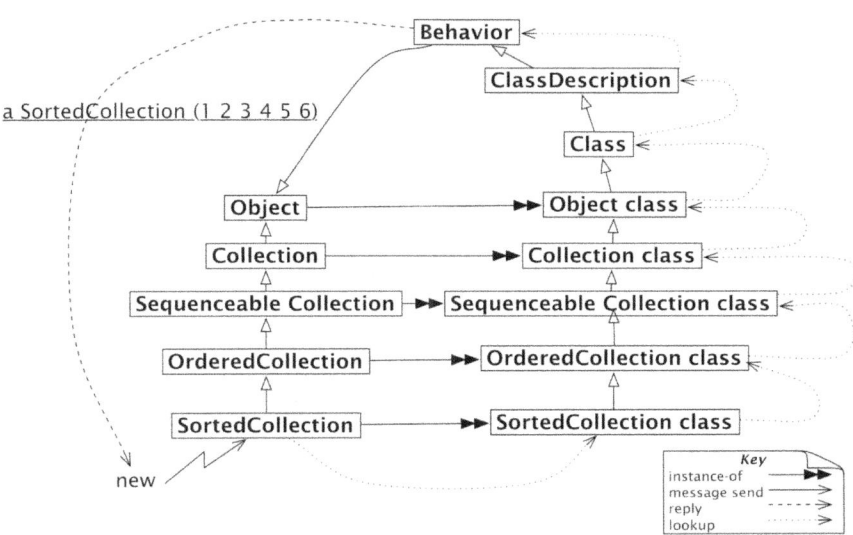

Figure 15.7: new is an ordinary message looked up in the metaclass chain.

Responsibilities of Behavior, ClassDescription, and Class

Behavior provides the minimum state necessary for objects that have instances, which includes a superclass link, a method dictionary and the class format. The class format is an integer that encodes the pointer/non-pointer distinction, compact/non-compact class distinction, and basic size of instances. Behavior inherits from Object, so it, and all of its subclasses, can behave like objects.

Behavior is also the basic interface to the compiler. It provides methods for creating a method dictionary, compiling methods, creating instances (i.e., new, basicNew, new:, and basicNew:), manipulating the class hierarchy (i.e., superclass:, addSubclass:), accessing methods (i.e., selectors, allSelectors, compiledMethodAt:), accessing instances and variables (i.e., allInstances, instVarNames...), accessing the class hierarchy (i.e., superclass, subclasses) and querying (i.e., hasMethods, includesSelector, canUnderstand:, inheritsFrom:, isVariable).

ClassDescription is an abstract class that provides facilities needed by its two direct subclasses, Class and Metaclass. ClassDescription adds a number of facilities to the base provided by Behavior: named instance variables, the categorization of methods into protocols, the maintenance of change sets and the logging of changes, and most of the mechanisms needed for filing out changes.

Class represents the common behaviour of all classes. It provides a class name, compilation methods, method storage, and instance variables. It pro-

299

Classes and metaclasses

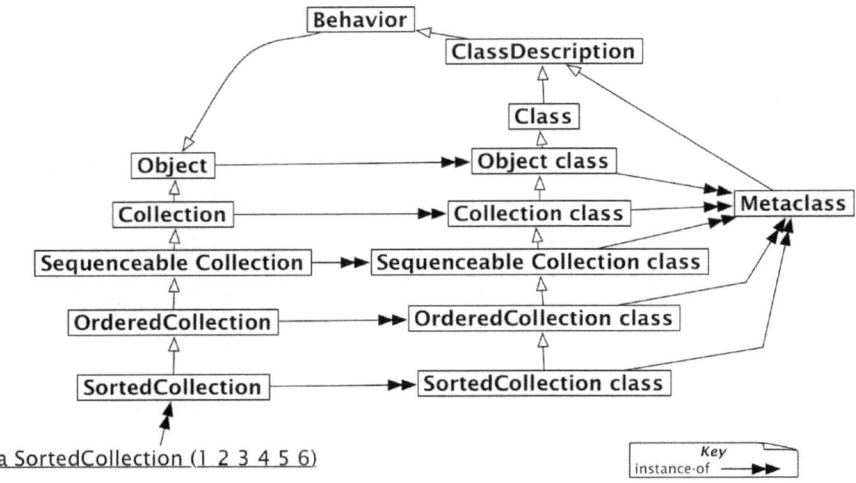

Figure 15.8: Every metaclass is a `Metaclass`.

vides a concrete representation for class variable names and shared pool variables (`addClassVarName:`, `addSharedPool:`, `initialize`). Since a metaclass is a class for its sole instance (*i.e.*, the non-meta class), all metaclasses ultimately inherit from `Class` (as shown by Figure 15.9).

15.6 Every metaclass is an instance of `Metaclass`

One question left is since metaclasses are objects too, they should be instances of another class, but which one? Metaclasses are objects too; they are instances of the class `Metaclass` as shown in Figure 15.8. The instances of class `Metaclass` are the anonymous metaclasses, each of which has exactly one instance, which is a class.

`Metaclass` represents common metaclass behaviour. It provides methods for instance creation (`subclassOf:`), creating initialized instances of the metaclass's sole instance, initialization of class variables, metaclass instance, method compilation, and class information (inheritance links, instance variables, etc.).

15.7 The metaclass of `Metaclass` is an instance of `Metaclass`

The final question to be answered is: what is the class of `Metaclass class`? The answer is simple: it is a metaclass, so it must be an instance of `Metaclass`, just like all the other metaclasses in the system (see Figure 15.9).

300

15.7 The metaclass of Metaclass is an instance of Metaclass

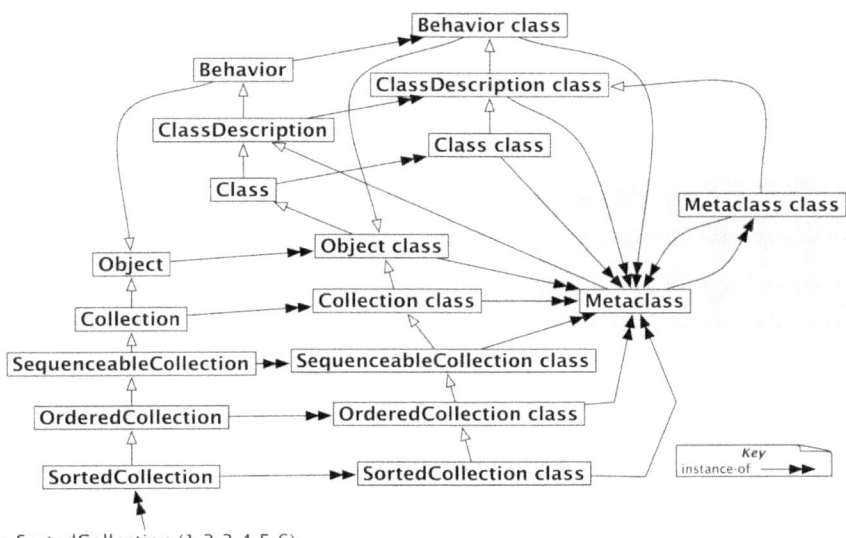

Figure 15.9: All metaclasses are instances of the class Metaclass, even the metaclass of Metaclass.

Figure 15.9 shows how all metaclasses are instances of Metaclass, including the metaclass of Metaclass itself. If you compare Figures 15.8 and 15.9 you will see how the metaclass hierarchy perfectly mirrors the class hierarchy, all the way up to Object class.

The following examples show us how we can query the class hierarchy to demonstrate that Figure 15.9 is correct. (Actually, you will see that we told a white lie — Object class superclass --> ProtoObject class, not Class. In Pharo, we must go one superclass higher to reach Class.)

```
Collection superclass
>>> Object
```

```
Collection class superclass
>>> Object class
Object class superclass superclass
>>> Class "NB: skip ProtoObject class"
Class superclass
>>> ClassDescription
ClassDescription superclass
>>> Behavior
Behavior superclass
>>> Object
```

```
Collection class class
>>> Metaclass
```

```
Object class class
>>> Metaclass
Behavior class class
>>> Metaclass

Metaclass class class
>>> Metaclass
Metaclass superclass
>>> ClassDescription
```

15.8 Chapter summary

This chapter gave an in-depth look into the uniform object model, and a more thorough explanation of how classes are organized. If you get lost or confused, you should always remember that message passing is the key: you look for the method in the class of the receiver. This works on *any* receiver. If the method is not found in the class of the receiver, it is looked up in its superclasses.

- Every class is an instance of a metaclass. Metaclasses are implicit. A metaclass is created automatically when you create the class that is its sole instance. A metaclass is simply a class whose unique instance is a class.

- The metaclass hierarchy parallels the class hierarchy. Method lookup for classes parallels method lookup for ordinary objects, and follows the metaclass's superclass chain.

- Every metaclass inherits from `Class` and `Behavior`. Every class *is a* `Class`. Since metaclasses are classes too, they must also inherit from `Class`. `Behavior` provides behaviour common to all entities that have instances.

- Every metaclass is an instance of `Metaclass`. `ClassDescription` provides everything that is common to `Class` and `Metaclass`.

- The metaclass of `Metaclass` is an instance of `Metaclass`. The *instance-of* relation forms a closed loop, so `Metaclass class class` is `Metaclass`.

CHAPTER 16

Reflection

Pharo is a reflective programming language. In a nutshell, this means that programs are able to *reflect* on their own execution and structure. More technically, this means that the *metaobjects* of the runtime system can be *reified* as ordinary objects, which can be queried and inspected. The metaobjects in Pharo are classes, metaclasses, method dictionaries, compiled methods, but also the run-time stack, processes, and so on. This form of reflection is also called *introspection*, and is supported by many modern programming languages.

Conversely, it is possible in Pharo to modify reified metaobjects and *reflect* these changes back to the runtime system (see Figure 16.1). This is also called

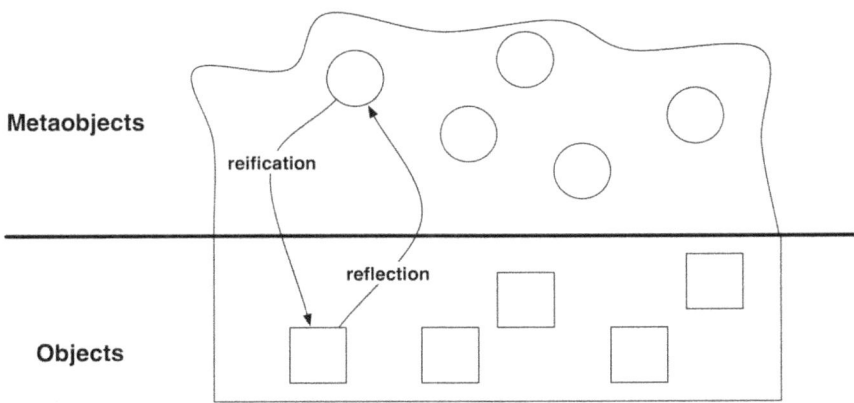

Figure 16.1: Reification and reflection.

intercession, and is supported mainly by dynamic programming languages, and only to a very limited degree by static languages. So pay attention when people say that Java is a reflective language, it is an introspective one not a reflective one.

A program that manipulates other programs (or even itself) is a *metaprogram*. For a programming language to be reflective, it should support both introspection and intercession. Introspection is the ability to *examine* the data structures that define the language, such as objects, classes, methods and the execution stack. Intercession is the ability to *modify* these structures, in other words to change the language semantics and the behavior of a program from within the program itself. *Structural reflection* is about examining and modifying the structures of the run-time system, and *behavioural reflection* is about modifying the interpretation of these structures.

In this chapter we will focus mainly on structural reflection. We will explore many practical examples illustrating how Pharo supports introspection and metaprogramming.

16.1 Introspection

Using the inspector, you can look at an object, change the values of its instance variables, and even send messages to it.

Evaluate the following code in a playground:

```
w := GTPlayground openLabel: 'My Playground'.
w inspect
```

This will open a second playground and an inspector. The inspector shows the internal state of this new playground, listing its instance variables on the left (borderColor, borderWidth, bounds...) and the value of the selected instance variable on the right. The bounds instance variable represents the precise area occupied by the playground.

Now choose the inspector and click the playground area of the inspector which has a comment on top and type self bounds: (Rectangle origin: 10@10 corner: 300@300) in it of select asshown in Figure 16.2 and then *Do It* like you do with a code of a Playground.

Immediately you will see the Playground we created change and resize itself.

Accessing instance variables

How does the inspector work? In Pharo, all instance variables are protected. In theory, it is impossible to access them from another object if the class doesn't define any accessor. In practice, the inspector can access instance variables without needing accessors, because it uses the reflective abilities of Pharo. Classes define instance variables either by name or by numeric

16.1 Introspection

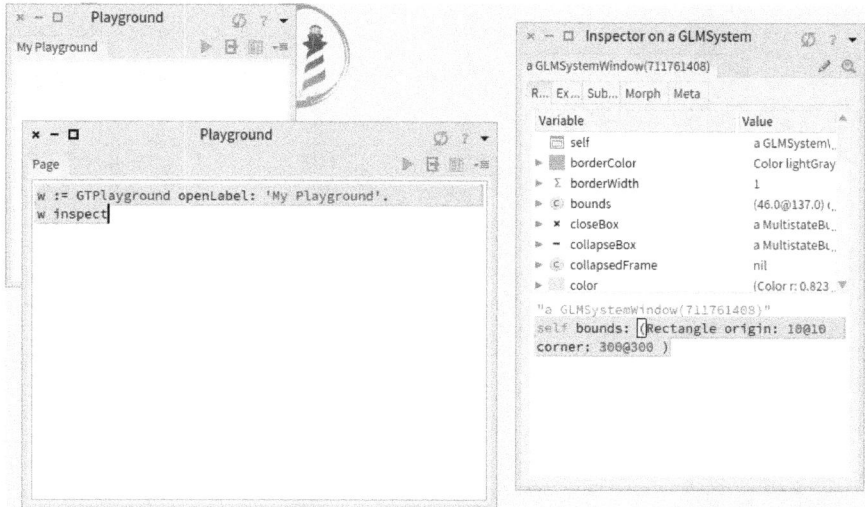

Figure 16.2: Inspecting a Workspace.

indices. The inspector uses methods defined by the Object class to access them: instVarAt: index and instVarNamed: aString can be used to get the value of the instance variable at position index or identified by aString, respectively. Similarly, to assign new values to these instance variables, it uses instVarAt:put: and instVarNamed:put:.

For instance, you can change the value of the w binding of the first workspace by evaluating:

```
w instVarNamed:'bounds' put: (Rectangle origin: 10@10 corner: 500@500).
```

> **Important**   Caveat: Although these methods are useful for building development tools, using them to develop conventional applications is a bad idea: these reflective methods break the encapsulation boundary of your objects and can therefore make your code much harder to understand and maintain.

Both instVarAt: and instVarAt:put: are primitive methods, meaning that they are implemented as primitive operations of the Pharo virtual machine. If you consult the code of these methods, you will see the special pragma syntax <primitive: N> where N is an integer.

```
Object >> instVarAt: index
    "Primitive. Answer a fixed variable in an object. ..."

    <primitive: 173 error: ec>
    self primitiveFailed
```

305

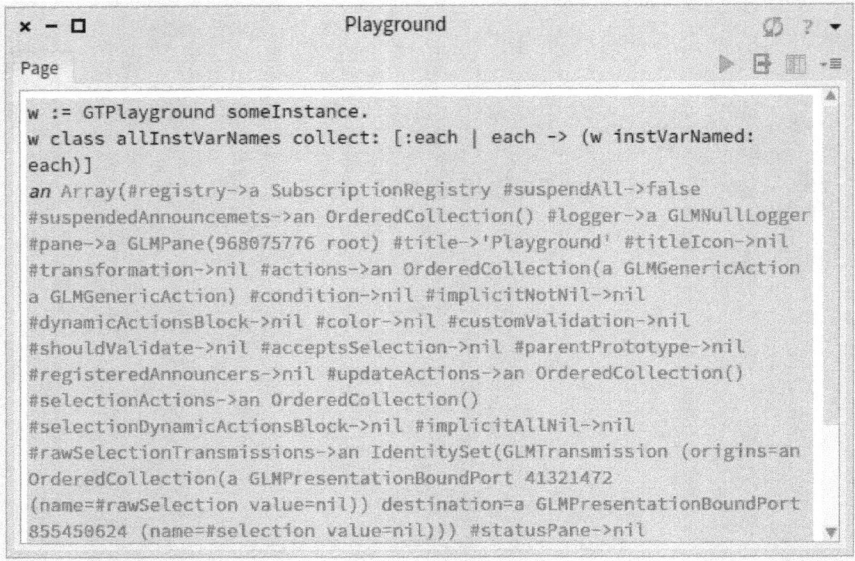

Figure 16.3: Displaying all instance variables of a GTPlayground.

Any Pharo code after the primitive declaration is executed only if the primitive fails. This also allows the debugger to be started on primitive methods. In this specific case, there is no way to implement this method, so the whole method just fails.

Other methods are implemented on the VM for faster execution. For example some arithmetic operations on SmallInteger:

```
* aNumber
    "Primitive. Multiply the receiver by the argument and answer with the
    result if it is a SmallInteger. Fail if the argument or the result
        is not a
    SmallInteger. Essential. No Lookup. See Object documentation
        whatIsAPrimitive."

    <primitive: 9>
    ^ super * aNumber
```

If this primitive fails, for example if the VM does not handle the type of the argument, the Pharo code is executed. Although it is possible to modify the code of primitive methods, beware that this can be risky business for the stability of your Pharo system.

Figure 16.3 shows how to display the values of the instance variables of an arbitrary instance (w) of class GTPlayground. The method allInstVarNames returns all the names of the instance variables of a given class.

16.1 Introspection

```
GTPlayground allInstVarNames
>>>
#(#registry #suspendAll #suspendedAnnouncemets #logger #pane #title
    #titleIcon #transformation #actions #condition #implicitNotNil
    #dynamicActionsBlock #color #customValidation #shouldValidate
    #acceptsSelection #parentPrototype #registeredAnnouncers
    #updateActions #selectionActions #selectionDynamicActionsBlock
    #implicitAllNil #rawSelectionTransmissions #statusPane #sourceLink
    #initializationBlock #cachedDisplayedValue #labelActionBlock
    #portChangeActions #wantsSteps #stepTime #stepCondition
    #presentations #arrangement)
```

```
w := GTPlayground someInstance.
w class allInstVarNames collect: [:each | each -> (w instVarNamed:
    each)]
```

In the same spirit, it is possible to gather instances that have specific properties iterating over instances of a class using an iterator such as select:. For instance, to get all objects who are directly included in the world morph (the main root of the graphical displayed elements), try this expression:

```
Morph allSubInstances
    select: [ :each |
            | own |
            own := (each instVarNamed: 'owner').
            own isNotNil and: [ own isWorldMorph ]]
```

Querying classes and interfaces

The development tools in Pharo (system browser, debugger, inspector...) all use the reflective features we have seen so far.

Here are a few other messages that might be useful to build development tools:

isKindOf: aClass returns true if the receiver is instance of aClass or of one of its superclasses. For instance:

```
1.5 class
>>> BoxedFloat64
```

```
1.5 isKindOf: Float
>>> true
```

```
1.5 isKindOf: Number
>>> true
```

```
1.5 isKindOf: Integer
>>> false
```

respondsTo: aSymbol returns true if the receiver has a method whose selector is aSymbol. For instance:

```
1.5 respondsTo: #floor
>>> true "since Number implements floor"
```

```
1.5 floor
>>> 1
```

```
Exception respondsTo: #,
>>> true "exception classes can be grouped"
```

Important Caveat: Although these features are especially useful for implementing development tools, they are normally not appropriate for typical applications. Asking an object for its class, or querying it to discover which messages it understands, are typical signs of design problems, since they violate the principle of encapsulation. Development tools, however, are not normal applications, since their domain is that of software itself. As such these tools have a right to dig deep into the internal details of code.

Code metrics

Let's see how we can use Pharo's introspection features to quickly extract some code metrics. Code metrics measure such aspects as the depth of the inheritance hierarchy, the number of direct or indirect subclasses, the number of methods or of instance variables in each class, or the number of locally defined methods or instance variables. Here are a few metrics for the class Morph, which is the superclass of all graphical objects in Pharo, revealing that it is a huge class, and that it is at the root of a huge hierarchy. Maybe it needs some refactoring!

```
"inheritance depth"
Morph allSuperclasses size.
>>> 2
```

```
"number of methods"
Morph allSelectors size.
>>> 1304
```

```
"number of instance variables"
Morph allInstVarNames size.
>>> 6
```

```
"number of new methods"
Morph selectors size.
>>> 896
```

```
"number of new variables"
Morph instVarNames size.
>>> 6
```

```
"direct subclasses"
Morph subclasses size.
>>> 63
```

```
"total subclasses"
Morph allSubclasses size.
>>> 376
```

```
"total lines of code!"
Morph linesOfCode.
>>> 4964
```

One of the most interesting metrics in the domain of object-oriented languages is the number of methods that extend methods inherited from the superclass. This informs us about the relation between the class and its superclasses. In the next sections we will see how to exploit our knowledge of the runtime structure to answer such questions.

16.2 Browsing code

In Pharo, everything is an object. In particular, classes are objects that provide useful features for navigating through their instances. Most of the messages we will look at now are implemented in Behavior, so they are understood by all classes.

For example, you can obtain a random instance of a given class by sending it the message someInstance.

```
Point someInstance
>>> 0@0
```

You can also gather all the instances with allInstances, or the number of active instances in memory with instanceCount.

```
ByteString allInstances
>>> #('collection' 'position' ...)
```

```
ByteString instanceCount
>>> 104565
```

```
String allSubInstances size
>>> 101675
```

These features can be very useful when debugging an application, because you can ask a class to enumerate those of its methods exhibiting specific properties. Here are some more interesting and useful methods for code discovery through reflection.

whichSelectorsAccess: returns the list of all selectors of methods that read or write the instance variable named by the argument

whichSelectorsStoreInto: returns the selectors of methods that modify the value of an instance variable

whichSelectorsReferTo: returns the selectors of methods that send a given message

```
Point whichSelectorsAccess: 'x'
>>> #(#degrees #grid: #roundTo: #nearestPointAlongLineFrom:to: ...)
```

```
Point whichSelectorsStoreInto: 'x'
>>> #(#bitShiftPoint: #setR:degrees: #setX:setY: #fromSton:)
```

```
Point whichSelectorsReferTo: #+
>>> an OrderedCollection(#degrees #reflectedAbout: #grid: ...)
```

The following messages take inheritance into account:

whichClassIncludesSelector: returns the superclass that implements the given message

unreferencedInstanceVariables returns the list of instance variables that are neither used in the receiver class nor any of its subclasses

```
Rectangle whichClassIncludesSelector: #inspect
>>> Object
```

```
Rectangle unreferencedInstanceVariables
>>> #()
```

SystemNavigation is a facade that supports various useful methods for querying and browsing the source code of the system. SystemNavigation default returns an instance you can use to navigate the system. For example:

```
SystemNavigation default allClassesImplementing: #yourself
>>> {Object}
```

The following messages should also be self-explanatory:

```
SystemNavigation default allSentMessages size
>>>370
```

```
(SystemNavigation default allUnsentMessagesIn: Object selectors) size
>>> 31
```

```
SystemNavigation default allUnimplementedCalls size
>>> 521
```

Note that messages implemented but not sent are not necessarily useless, since they may be sent implicitly (*e.g.*, using perform:). Messages sent but not implemented, however, are more problematic, because the methods sending these messages will fail at runtime. They may be a sign of unfinished implementation, obsolete APIs, or missing libraries.

Point allCallsOn returns all messages sent explicitly to Point as a receiver.

All these features are integrated into the programming environment of Pharo, in particular the code browsers. As we mentioned before, there are convenient keyboard shortcuts for **browsing all implementors** (CMD-b CMD-m) and **browsing senders** (CMD-b CMD-n) of a given message. What is perhaps not so well known is that there are many such pre-packaged queries implemented

16.3 Classes, method dictionaries and methods

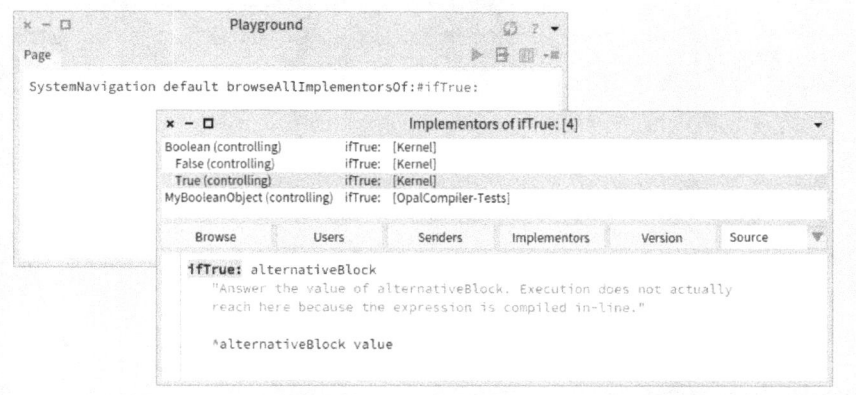

Figure 16.4: Browse all implementations of ifTrue:.

as methods of the SystemNavigation class in the browsing protocol. For example, you can programmatically browse all implementors of the message ifTrue: by evaluating:

```
SystemNavigation default browseAllImplementorsOf: #ifTrue:
```

Particularly useful are the methods browseAllSelect: and browseMethodsWithSourceString:matchCase:. Here are two different ways to browse all methods in the system that perform super sends (the first way is rather brute force, the second way is better and eliminates some false positives):

```
SystemNavigation default browseMethodsWithSourceString: 'super'
    matchCase: true.
SystemNavigation default browseAllSelect: [:method | method
    sendsToSuper ].
```

16.3 Classes, method dictionaries and methods

Since classes are objects, we can inspect or explore them just like any other object.

Evaluate Point inspect.

In Figure 16.5, the inspector shows the structure of class Point. You can see that the class stores its methods in a dictionary, indexing them by their selector. The selector #* points to the decompiled bytecode of Point>>*.

Let us consider the relationship between classes and methods. In Figure 16.6 we see that classes and metaclasses have the common superclass Behavior. This is where new is defined, amongst other key methods for classes. Every class has a method dictionary, which maps method selectors to compiled

Reflection

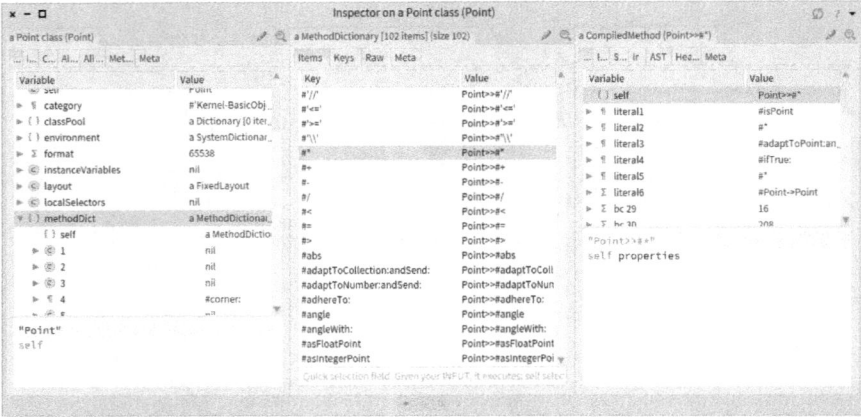

Figure 16.5: Inspector on class `Point` and the bytecode of its `#*` method.

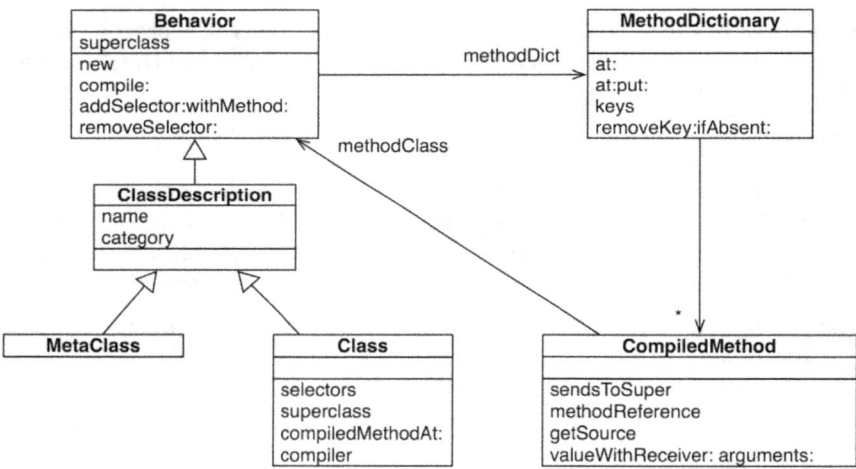

Figure 16.6: Classes, method dictionaries and compiled methods

methods. Each compiled method knows the class in which it is installed. In Figure 16.5 we can even see that this is stored in an association in `literal6`.

We can exploit the relationships between classes and methods to pose queries about the system. For example, to discover which methods are newly introduced in a given class, *i.e.*, do not override superclass methods, we can navigate from the class to the method dictionary as follows:

```
[:aClass| aClass methodDict keys select: [:aMethod |
    (aClass superclass canUnderstand: aMethod) not ]] value: SmallInteger
>>> an IdentitySet(#threeDigitName #printStringBase:nDigits: ...)
```

A compiled method does not simply store the bytecode of a method. It is also an object that provides numerous useful methods for querying the system. One such method is isAbstract (which tells if the method sends subclass-Responsibility). We can use it to identify all the abstract methods of an abstract class.

```
[:aClass| aClass methodDict keys select: [:aMethod |
    (aClass>>aMethod) isAbstract ]] value: Number
>>> an IdentitySet(#storeOn:base: #printOn:base: #+ #- #* #/ ...)
```

Note that this code sends the >> message to a class to obtain the compiled method for a given selector.

To browse the super-sends within a given hierarchy, for example within the Collections hierarchy, we can pose a more sophisticated query:

```
class := Collection.
SystemNavigation default
  browseMessageList: (class withAllSubclasses gather: [:each |
    each methodDict associations
      select: [:assoc | assoc value sendsToSuper]
      thenCollect: [:assoc | RGMethodDefinition realClass: each
          selector: assoc key]])
  name: 'Supersends of ', class name, ' and its subclasses'
```

Note how we navigate from classes to method dictionaries to compiled methods to identify the methods we are interested in. A RGMethodDefinition is a lightweight proxy for a compiled method that is used by many tools. There is a convenience method CompiledMethod>>methodReference to return the method reference for a compiled method.

```
(Object>>#=) methodReference selector
>>> #=
```

16.4 Browsing environments

Although SystemNavigation offers some useful ways to programmatically query and browse system code, there are more ways. The Browser, which is integrated into Pharo, allows us to restrict the environment in which a search is to perform.

Suppose we are interested to discover which classes refer to the class Point but only in its own package.

Open a browser on the class Point.

Action-click on the top level package Kernel in the package pane and select Browse scoped. A new browser opens, showing only the package Kernel and all classes within this package (and some classes which have extension methods from this package). Now, in this browser, select again the class Point,

313

Action-click on the class name and select Analyse > Class refs. This will show all methods that have references to the class Point but only those from the package Kernel. Compare this result with the search from a Browser without restricted scope.

This scope is what we call a *Browsing Environment* (class RBBrowserEnvironment). All other searches, like *senders of a method* or *implementors of a method* from within this browser are restricted to this environments too.

Browser environments can also be created programmatically. Here, for example, we create a new RBBrowserEnvironment for Collection and its subclasses, select the super-sending methods, and browse the resulting environment.

```
((RBBrowserEnvironment new forClasses: (Collection withAllSubclasses))
    selectMethods: [:method | method sendsToSuper])
    browse.
```

Note how this is considerably more compact than the earlier, equivalent example using SystemNavigation.

Finally, we can find just those methods that send a different super message programmatically as follows:

```
((RBBrowserEnvironment new forClasses: (Collection withAllSubclasses))
    selectMethods: [:method |
        method sendsToSuper
        and: [(method parseTree superMessages includes: method selector)
            not]])
    browse
```

Here we ask each compiled method for its (Refactoring Browser) parse tree, in order to find out whether the super messages differ from the method's selector. Have a look at the querying protocol of the class RBProgramNode to see some the things we can ask of parse trees.

Instead of browsing the environment in a System Browser, we can spawn a MessageBrower from the list of all methods in this environment.

```
MessageBrowser browse: ((RBBrowserEnvironment new forClasses:
    (Collection withAllSubclasses))
    selectMethods: [:method |
        method sendsToSuper
        and: [(method parseTree superMessages includes: method selector)
            not]]) methods
    title: 'Collection methods sending different super'
```

In Figure 16.7 we can see that 5 such methods have been found within the Collection hierarchy, including Collection>>printNameOn:, which sends super printOn:.

16.5 Accessing the run-time context

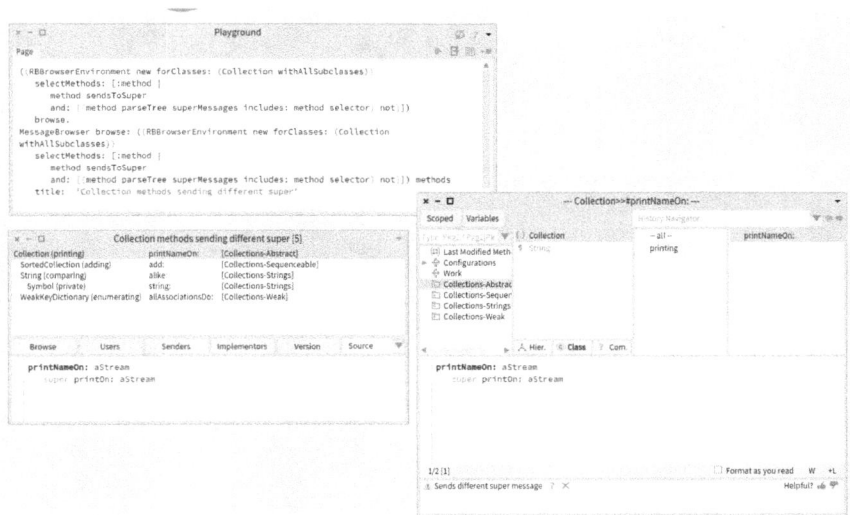

Figure 16.7: Finding methods

16.5 Accessing the run-time context

We have seen how Pharo's reflective capabilities let us query and explore objects, classes and methods. But what about the run-time environment?

Method contexts

In fact, the run-time context of an executing method is in the virtual machine — it is not in the image at all! On the other hand, the debugger obviously has access to this information, and we can happily explore the run-time context, just like any other object. How is this possible?

Actually, there is nothing magical about the debugger. The secret is the pseudo-variable thisContext, which we have encountered only in passing before. Whenever thisContext is referred to in a running method, the entire run-time context of that method is reified and made available to the image as a series of chained Context objects.

We can easily experiment with this mechanism ourselves.

Change the definition of Integer>>factorial by inserting the expression thisContext inspect. self halt. as shown below:

```
Integer>>factorial
    "Answer the factorial of the receiver."
    self = 0 ifTrue: [thisContext inspect. self halt. ^ 1].
    self > 0 ifTrue: [^ self * (self - 1) factorial].
    self error: 'Not valid for negative integers'
```

Reflection

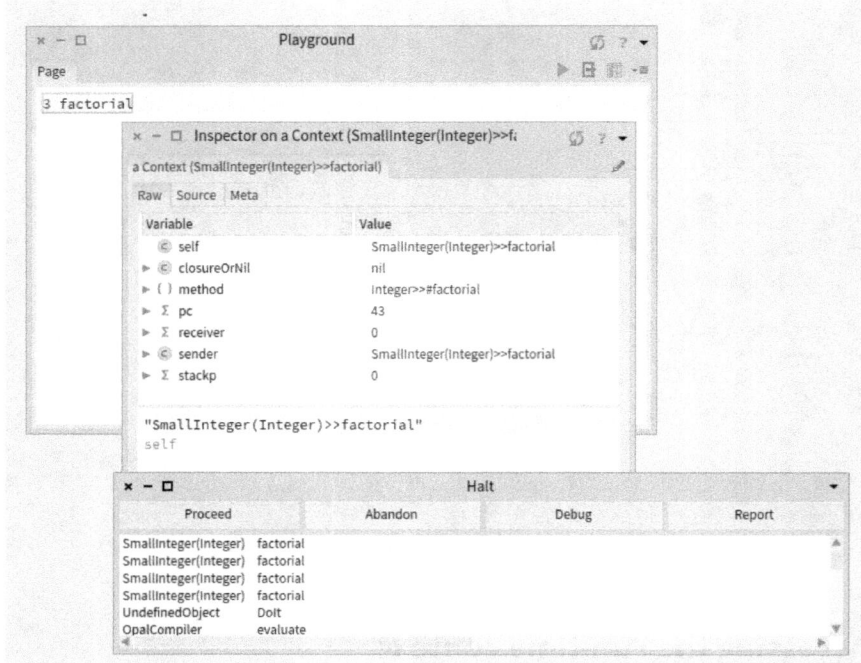

Figure 16.8: Inspecting `thisContext`.

Now evaluate `3 factorial` in a workspace. You should obtain both a debugger window and an inspector, as shown in Figure 16.8.

Inspecting thisContext gives you full access to the current execution context, the stack, the local tempories and arguments, the senders chain and the receiver. Welcome to the poor man's debugger! If you now browse the class of the explored object (*i.e.*, by evaluating `self browse` in the bottom pane of the inspector) you will discover that it is an instance of the class `Context`, as is each sender in the chain.

`thisContext` is not intended to be used for day-to-day programming, but it is essential for implementing tools like debuggers, and for accessing information about the call stack. You can evaluate the following expression to discover which methods make use of `thisContext`:

```
SystemNavigation default browseMethodsWithSourceString: 'thisContext'
    matchCase: true
```

As it turns out, one of the most common applications is to discover the sender of a message. Here is a typical application:

```
subclassResponsibility
    "This message sets up a framework for the behavior of the class'
```

16.5 Accessing the run-time context

```
        subclasses.
    Announce that the subclass should have implemented this message."

    SubclassResponsibility signalFor: thisContext sender selector
```

By convention, methods that send self subclassResponsibility are considered to be abstract. But how does Object>>subclassResponsibility provide a useful error message indicating which abstract method has been invoked? Very simply, by asking thisContext for the sender.

Intelligent breakpoints

The Pharo way to set a breakpoint is to evaluate self halt at an interesting point in a method. This will cause thisContext to be reified, and a debugger window will open at the breakpoint. Unfortunately this poses problems for methods that are intensively used in the system.

Suppose, for instance, that we want to explore the execution of Morph>>openInWorld. Setting a breakpoint in this method is problematic.

Pay attention the following experiment will break everything! Take a *fresh* image and set the following breakpoint:

```
Morph >> openInWorld
    "Add this morph to the world."
    self halt.
    self openInWorld: self currentWorld
```

Notice how your image immediately freezes as soon as you try to open any new Morph (Menu/Window/...)! We do not even get a debugger window. The problem is clear once we understand that 1) Morph>>openInWorld is used by many parts of the system, so the breakpoint is triggered very soon after we interact with the user interface, but 2) *the debugger itself* sends openInWorld as soon as it opens a window, preventing the debugger from opening! What we need is a way to *conditionally* halt only if we are in a context of interest. This is exactly what Object>>haltIf: offers.

Suppose now that we only want to halt if openInWorld is sent from, say, the context of MorphTest>>testOpenInWorld.

Fire up a fresh image again, and set the following breakpoint:

```
Morph>>openInWorld
    "Add this morph to the world."
    self haltIf: #testOpenInWorld.
    self openInWorld: self currentWorld
```

This time the image does not freeze. Try running the MorphTest.

```
MorphTest run:#testOpenInWorld.
```

How does this work? Let's have a look at `Object>>haltIf:`. It first calls `if:` with the condition to the Exception class `Halt`. This method itself will check if the condition is a symbol, which is true in this case and finally calls

```
Object >> haltIfCallChainContains: aSelector

    | cntxt |
    cntxt := thisContext.
        [cntxt sender isNil] whileFalse: [
            cntxt := cntxt sender.
            (cntxt selector = aSelector) ifTrue: [self signal]].
```

Starting from `thisContext`, `haltIfCallChainContains:` goes up through the execution stack, checking if the name of the calling method is the same as the one passed as parameter. If this is the case, then it signals itself, the exception which, by default, summons the debugger.

It is also possible to supply a boolean or a boolean block as an argument to `haltIf:`, but these cases are straightforward and do not make use of `thisContext`.

16.6 Intercepting messages not understood

So far we have used Pharo's reflective features mainly to query and explore objects, classes, methods and the run-time stack. Now we will look at how to use our knowledge of its system structure to intercept messages and modify behaviour at run time.

When an object receives a message, it first looks in the method dictionary of its class for a corresponding method to respond to the message. If no such method exists, it will continue looking up the class hierarchy, until it reaches `Object`. If still no method is found for that message, the object will *send itself* the message `doesNotUnderstand:` with the message selector as its argument. The process then starts all over again, until `Object>>doesNotUnderstand:` is found, and the debugger is launched.

But what if `doesNotUnderstand:` is overridden by one of the subclasses of Object in the lookup path? As it turns out, this is a convenient way of realizing certain kinds of very dynamic behaviour. An object that does not understand a message can, by overriding `doesNotUnderstand:`, fall back to an alternative strategy for responding to that message.

Two very common applications of this technique are 1) to implement lightweight proxies for objects, and 2) to dynamically compile or load missing code.

Lightweight proxies

In the first case, we introduce a *minimal object* to act as a proxy for an existing object. Since the proxy will implement virtually no methods of its own, any

16.6 Intercepting messages not understood

message sent to it will be trapped by doesNotUnderstand:. By implementing this message, the proxy can then take special action before delegating the message to the real subject it is the proxy for.

Let us have a look at how this may be implemented.

We define a LoggingProxy as follows:

```
ProtoObject subclass: #LoggingProxy
    instanceVariableNames: 'subject invocationCount'
    classVariableNames: ''
    package: 'PBE-Reflection'
```

Note that we subclass ProtoObject rather than Object because we do not want our proxy to inherit around 400 methods (!) from Object.

```
Object methodDict size
>>> 397
```

Our proxy has two instance variables: the subject it is a proxy for, and a count of the number of messages it has intercepted. We initialize the two instance variables and we provide an accessor for the message count. Initially the subject variable points to the proxy object itself.

```
LoggingProxy >> initialize
    invocationCount := 0.
    subject := self.

LoggingProxy >> invocationCount
    ^ invocationCount
```

We simply intercept all messages not understood, print them to the Transcript, update the message count, and forward the message to the real subject.

```
LoggingProxy >> doesNotUnderstand: aMessage
    Transcript show: 'performing ', aMessage printString; cr.
    invocationCount := invocationCount + 1.
    ^ aMessage sendTo: subject
```

Here comes a bit of magic. We create a new Point object and a new LoggingProxy object, and then we tell the proxy to become: the point object:

```
point := 1@2.
LoggingProxy new become: point.
```

This has the effect of swapping all references in the image to the point to now refer to the proxy, and vice versa. Most importantly, the proxy's subject instance variable will now refer to the point!

```
point invocationCount
>>> 0
point + (3@4)
>>> 4@6
```

```
point invocationCount
>>> 1
```

This works nicely in most cases, but there are some shortcomings:

```
point class
>>> LoggingProxy
```

Actually the method `class` is implemented in `ProtoObject`, but even if it were implemented in `Object`, which `LoggingProxy` does not inherit from, it isn't actually send to the LoggingProxy or its subject. The message is directly answered by the virtual machine. `yourself` is also never truly sent.

Other messages that may be directly interpreted by the VM, depending on the receiver, include:

```
+- < > <= >= = ~= * / \ == @ bitShift: // bitAnd: bitOr: at: at:put:
size next nextPut: atEnd blockCopy: value value: do: new new: x y.
```

Selectors that are never sent, because they are inlined by the compiler and transformed to comparison and jump bytecodes:

```
ifTrue: ifFalse: ifTrue:ifFalse: ifFalse:ifTrue: and: or: while-
False: whileTrue: whileFalse whileTrue to:do: to:by:do: caseOf:
caseOf:otherwise: ifNil: ifNotNil: ifNil:ifNotNil: ifNotNil:ifNil:
```

Attempts to send these messages to non-boolean normally results in an exception from the VM as it can not use the inlined dispatching for non-boolean receivers. You can intercept this and define the proper behavior by overriding `mustBeBoolean` in the receiver or by catching the `NonBooleanReceiver` exception.

Even if we can ignore such special message sends, there is another fundamental problem which cannot be overcome by this approach: self-sends cannot be intercepted:

```
point := 1@2.
LoggingProxy new become: point.
point invocationCount
>>> 0
point rectangle: (3@4)
>>> 1@2 corner: 3@4
point invocationCount
>>> 1
```

Our proxy has been cheated out of two self-sends in the `rect:` method:

```
Point >> rect: aPoint
    ^ Rectangle origin: (self min: aPoint) corner: (self max: aPoint)
```

Although messages can be intercepted by proxies using this technique, one should be aware of the inherent limitations of using a proxy. In Section 16.7 we will see another, more general approach for intercepting messages.

16.6 Intercepting messages not understood

Generating missing methods

The other most common application of intercepting not understood messages is to dynamically load or generate the missing methods. Consider a very large library of classes with many methods. Instead of loading the entire library, we could load a stub for each class in the library. The stubs know where to find the source code of all their methods. The stubs simply trap all messages not understood, and dynamically load the missing methods on demand. At some point, this behaviour can be deactivated, and the loaded code can be saved as the minimal necessary subset for the client application.

Let us look at a simple variant of this technique where we have a class that automatically adds accessors for its instance variables on demand:

```
DynamicAcccessors >> doesNotUnderstand: aMessage
    | messageName |
    messageName := aMessage selector asString.
    (self class instVarNames includes: messageName)
        ifTrue: [
            self class compile: messageName, String cr, ' ^ ', messageName.
            ^ aMessage sendTo: self ].
    ^ super doesNotUnderstand: aMessage
```

Any message not understood is trapped here. If an instance variable with the same name as the message sent exists, then we ask our class to compile an accessor for that instance variables and we re-send the message.

Suppose the class DynamicAccessors has an (uninitialized) instance variable x but no pre-defined accessor. Then the following will generate the accessor dynamically and retrieve the value:

```
myDA := DynamicAccessors new.
myDA x
>>> nil
```

Let us step through what happens the first time the message x is sent to our object (see Figure 16.9).

(1) We send x to myDA, (2) the message is looked up in the class, and (3) not found in the class hierarchy. (4) This causes self doesNotUnderstand: #x to be sent back to the object, (5) triggering a new lookup. This time doesNotUnderstand: is found immediately in DynamicAccessors, (6) which asks its class to compile the string 'x ^ x'. The compile method is looked up (7), and (8) finally found in Behavior, which (9-10) adds the new compiled method to the method dictionary of DynamicAccessors. Finally, (11-13) the message is resent, and this time it is found.

The same technique can be used to generate setters for instance variables, or other kinds of boilerplate code, such as visiting methods for a Visitor.

Note the use of Object>>perform: in step (12) which can be used to send messages that are composed at run-time:

Reflection

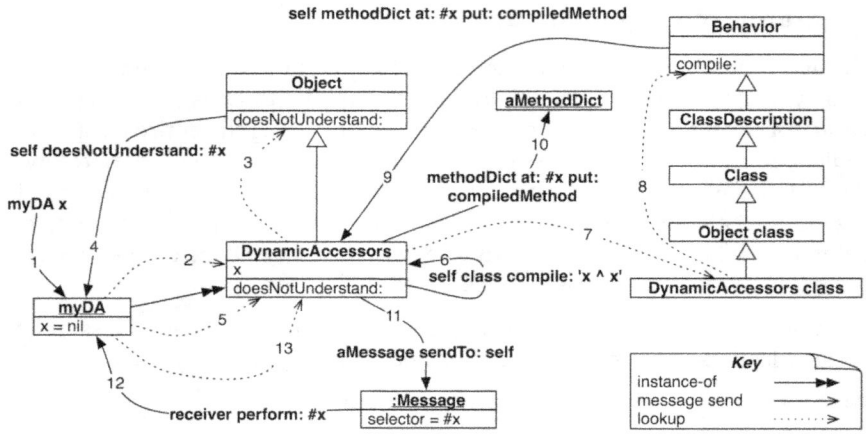

Figure 16.9: Dynamically creating accessors.

```
5 perform: #factorial
>>> 120
```

```
6 perform: ('fac', 'torial') asSymbol
>>> 720
```

```
4 perform: #max: withArguments: (Array with: 6)
>>> 6
```

16.7 Objects as method wrappers

We have already seen that compiled methods are ordinary objects in Pharo, and they support a number of methods that allow the programmer to query the runtime system. What is perhaps a bit more surprising, is that *any object* can play the role of a compiled method. All it has to do is respond to the method run:with:in: and a few other important messages.

Define an empty class Demo. Evaluate Demo new answer42 and notice how the usual *Message Not Understood* error is raised.

Now we will install a plain object in the method dictionary of our Demo class.

Evaluate Demo methodDict at: #answer42 put: ObjectsAsMethodsExample new.

Now try again to print the result of Demo new answer42. This time we get the answer 42.

If we take look at the class ObjectsAsMethodsExample we will find the following methods:

16.7 Objects as method wrappers

```
answer42
    ^42

run: oldSelector with: arguments in: aReceiver
    ^self perform: oldSelector withArguments: arguments
```

When our Demo instance receives the message answer42, method lookup proceeds as usual, however the virtual machine will detect that in place of a compiled method, an ordinary Pharo object is trying to play this role. The VM will then send this object a new message run:with:in: with the original method selector, arguments and receiver as arguments. Since ObjectsAsMethodsExample implements this method, it intercepts the message and delegates it to itself.

We can now remove the fake method as follows:

```
Demo methodDict removeKey: #answer42 ifAbsent: []
```

If we take a closer look at ObjectsAsMethodsExample, we will see that its superclass also implements some methods like flushcache, methodClass: and selector:, but they are all empty. These messages may be sent to a compiled method, so they need to be implemented by an object pretending to be a compiled method. (flushcache is the most important method to be implemented; others may be required by some tools and depending on whether the method is installed using Behavior>>addSelector:withMethod: or directly using MethodDictionary>>at:put:.)

Using method wrappers to perform test coverage

Method wrappers are a well-known technique for intercepting messages. In the original implementation(http://www.squeaksource.com/MethodWrappers.html), a method wrapper is an instance of a subclass of CompiledMethod. When installed, a method wrapper can perform special actions before or after invoking the original method. When uninstalled, the original method is returned to its rightful position in the method dictionary.

In Pharo, method wrappers can be implemented more easily by implementing run:with:in: instead of by subclassing CompiledMethod. In fact, there exists a lightweight implementation of objects as method wrappers(http://www.squeaksource.com/ObjectsAsMethodsWrap.html), but it is not part of standard Pharo at the time of this writing.

Nevertheless, the Pharo Test Runner uses precisely this technique to evaluate test coverage. Let's have a quick look at how it works.

The entry point for test coverage is the method TestRunner>>runCoverage:

```
TestRunner >> runCoverage
    | packages methods |
    ... "identify methods to check for coverage"
    self collectCoverageFor: methods
```

The method `TestRunner>>collectCoverageFor:` clearly illustrates the coverage checking algorithm:

```
TestRunner >> collectCoverageFor: methods
  | wrappers suite |
  wrappers := methods collect: [ :each | TestCoverage on: each ].
  suite := self
    resetResult;
    suiteForAllSelected.

  [ wrappers do: [ :each | each install ].
  [ self runSuite: suite ] ensure: [ wrappers do: [ :each | each
      uninstall ] ] ] valueUnpreemptively.

  wrappers := wrappers reject: [:each | each hasRun].
  wrappers := wrappers collect: [:each | each reference].
  wrappers isEmpty
    ifTrue: [ UIManager default inform: 'Congratulations. Your tests
        cover all code under analysis.' ]
    ifFalse: ...
```

A wrapper is created for each method to be checked, and each wrapper is installed. The tests are run, and all wrappers are uninstalled. Finally the user obtains feedback concerning the methods that have not been covered.

How does the wrapper itself work? The `TestCoverage` wrapper has three instance variables, `hasRun`, `reference` and `method`. They are initialized as follows:

```
TestCoverage class >> on: aMethodReference
  ^ self new initializeOn: aMethodReference

TestCoverage >> initializeOn: aMethodReference
  hasRun := false.
  reference := aMethodReference.
  method := reference compiledMethod
```

The install and uninstall methods simply update the method dictionary in the obvious way:

```
TestCoverage >> install
  reference actualClass methodDict
    at: reference selector
    put: self

TestCoverage >> uninstall
  reference actualClass methodDict
    at: reference selector
    put: method
```

The `run:with:in:` method simply updates the `hasRun` variable, uninstalls the wrapper (since coverage has been verified), and resends the message to the

16.8 Pragmas

original method.

```
run: aSelector with: anArray in: aReceiver
    self mark; uninstall.
    ^ aReceiver withArgs: anArray executeMethod: method

mark
    hasRun := true
```

Take a look at ProtoObject>>withArgs:executeMethod: to see how a method displaced from its method dictionary can be invoked.

That's all there is to it!

Method wrappers can be used to perform any kind of suitable behaviour before or after the normal operation of a method. Typical applications are instrumentation (collecting statistics about the calling patterns of methods), checking optional pre- and post-conditions, and memoization (optionally cacheing computed values of methods).

16.8 Pragmas

A *pragma* is an annotation that specifies data about a program, but is not involved in the execution of the program. Pragmas have no direct effect on the operation of the method they annotate. Pragmas have a number of uses, among them:

Information for the compiler: pragmas can be used by the compiler to make a method call a primitive function. This function has to be defined by the virtual machine or by an external plug-in.

Runtime processing: Some pragmas are available to be examined at runtime.

Pragmas can be applied to a program's method declarations only. A method may declare one or more pragmas, and the pragmas have to be declared prior any Smalltalk statement. Each pragma is in effect a static message send with literal arguments.

We briefly saw pragmas when we introduced primitives earlier in this chapter. A primitive is nothing more than a pragma declaration. Consider <primitive: 173 error:ec> as contained in instVarAt:. The pragma's selector is primitive:error: and its arguments is an immediate literal value, 173. The variable ec is an error code, filled by the VM in case the execution of the implementation on the VM side failed.

The compiler is probably the bigger user of pragmas. SUnit is another tool that makes use of annotations. SUnit is able to estimate the coverage of an application from a test unit. One may want to exclude some methods from the coverage. This is the case of the documentation method in SplitJointTest class:

```
SplitJointTest class >> documentation
    <ignoreForCoverage>
    "self showDocumentation"

    ^ 'This package provides function.... "
```

By simply annotating a method with the pragma <ignoreForCoverage> one can control the scope of the coverage.

As instances of the class Pragma, pragmas are first class objects. A compiled method answers to the message pragmas. This method returns an array of pragmas.

```
(SplitJointTest class >> #showDocumentation) pragmas.
>>> an Array(<ignoreForCoverage>)
(Float>>#+) pragmas
>>> an Array(<primitive: 41>)
```

Methods defining a particular query may be retrieved from a class. The class side of SplitJointTest contains some methods annotated with <ignoreForCoverage>:

```
Pragma allNamed: #ignoreForCoverage in: SplitJointTest class
>>> an Array(<ignoreForCoverage> <ignoreForCoverage>
    <ignoreForCoverage>)
```

A variant of allNamed:in: may be found on the class side of Pragma.

A pragma knows in which method it is defined (using method), the name of the method (selector), the class that contains the method (methodClass), its number of arguments (numArgs), about the literals the pragma has for arguments (hasLiteral: and hasLiteralSuchThat:).

16.9 Chapter summary

Reflection refers to the ability to query, examine and even modify the metaobjects of the runtime system as ordinary objects.

- The Inspector uses instVarAt: and related methods to view *private* instance variables of objects.
- Send Behavior>>allInstances to query instances of a class.
- The messages class, isKindOf:, respondsTo: etc. are useful for gathering metrics or building development tools, but they should be avoided in regular applications: they violate the encapsulation of objects and make your code harder to understand and maintain.
- SystemNavigation is a utility class holding many useful queries for navigation and browsing the class hierarchy. For example, use SystemNavigation default browseMethodsWithSourceString: 'pharo'

- `matchCase: true.` to find and browse all methods with a given source string. (Slow, but thorough!)
- Every Pharo class points to an instance of `MethodDictionary` which maps selectors to instances of `CompiledMethod`. A compiled method knows its class, closing the loop.
- `RGMethodDefinition` is a leightweight proxy for a compiled method, providing additional convenience methods, and used by many Pharo tools.
- `RBBrowserEnvironment`, part of the Refactoring Browser infrastructure, offers a more refined interface than `SystemNavigation` for querying the system, since the result of a query can be used as a the scope of a new query. Both GUI and programmatic interfaces are available.
- `thisContext` is a pseudo-variable that reifies the runtime stack of the virtual machine. It is mainly used by the debugger to dynamically construct an interactive view of the stack. It is also especially useful for dynamically determining the sender of a message.
- Intelligent breakpoints can be set using `haltIf:`, taking a method selector as its argument. `haltIf:` halts only if the named method occurs as a sender in the run-time stack.
- A common way to intercept messages sent to a given target is to use a *minimal object* as a proxy for that target. The proxy implements as few methods as possible, and traps all message sends by implementing `doesNotunderstand:`. It can then perform some additional action and then forward the message to the original target.
- Send `become:` to swap the references of two objects, such as a proxy and its target.
- Beware, some messages, like `class` and `yourself` are never really sent, but are interpreted by the VM. Others, like +, - and `ifTrue:` may be directly interpreted or inlined by the VM depending on the receiver.
- Another typical use for overriding `doesNotUnderstand:` is to lazily load or compile missing methods.
- `doesNotUnderstand:` cannot trap `self`-sends.
- A more rigorous way to intercept messages is to use an object as a method wrapper. Such an object is installed in a method dictionary in place of a compiled method. It should implement `run:with:in:` which is sent by the VM when it detects an ordinary object instead of a compiled method in the method dictionary. This technique is used by the SUnit Test Runner to collect coverage data.

CHAPTER 17

Regular expressions in Pharo

Regular expressions are widely used in many scripting languages such as Perl, Python and Ruby. They are useful to identify strings that match a certain pattern, to check that input conforms to an expected format, and to rewrite strings to new formats. Pharo also supports regular expressions due to the Regex package contributed by Vassili Bykov. Regex is installed by default in Pharo. If you are using an older image that does not include Regex the Regex package, you can install it yourself from SqueakSource (http://www.squeaksource.com/Regex.html).

A regular expression[1] is a pattern that matches a set of strings. For example, the regular expression 'h.*o' will match the strings 'ho', 'hiho' and 'hello', but it will not match 'hi' or 'yo'. We can see this in Pharo as follows:

```
'ho' matchesRegex: 'h.*o'
>>> true
```

```
'hiho' matchesRegex: 'h.*o'
>>> true
```

```
'hello' matchesRegex: 'h.*o'
>>> true
```

```
'hi' matchesRegex: 'h.*o'
>>> false
```

```
'yo' matchesRegex: 'h.*o'
>>> false
```

---
[1] http://en.wikipedia.org/wiki/Regular_expression

In this chapter we will start with a small tutorial example in which we will develop a couple of classes to generate a very simple site map for a web site. We will use regular expressions

1. to identify HTML files,
2. to strip the full path name of a file down to just the file name,
3. to extract the title of each web page for the site map, and
4. to generate a relative path from the root directory of the web site to the HTML files it contains.

After we complete the tutorial example, we will provide a more complete description of the Regex package, based largely on Vassili Bykov's documentation provided in the package. (The original documentation can be found on the class side of RxParser.)

17.1 Tutorial example — generating a site map

Our job is to write a simple application that will generate a site map for a web site that we have stored locally on our hard drive. The site map will contain links to each of the HTML files in the web site, using the title of the document as the text of the link. Furthermore, links will be indented to reflect the directory structure of the web site.

Accessing the web directory

> To do   If you do not have a web site on your machine, copy a few HTML files to a local directory to serve as a test bed.

We will develop two classes, WebDir and WebPage, to represent directories and web pages. The idea is to create an instance of WebDir which will point to the root directory containing our web site. When we send it the message makeToc, it will walk through the files and directories inside it to build up the site map. It will then create a new file, called toc.html, containing links to all the pages in the web site.

One thing we will have to watch out for: each WebDir and WebPage must remember the path to the root of the web site, so it can properly generate links relative to the root.

> To do   Define the class WebDir with instance variables webDir and home-Path, and define the appropriate initialization method.

Also define class-side methods to prompt the user for the location of the web site on your computer, as follows:

17.1 Tutorial example — generating a site map

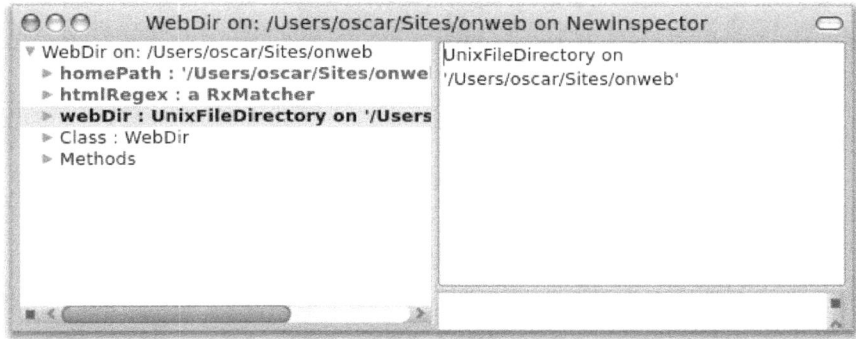

Figure 17.1: A WebDir instance.

```
WebDir >> setDir: dir home: path
    webDir := dir.
    homePath := path

WebDir class >> onDir: dir
    ^ self new setDir: dir home: dir pathString

WebDir class >> selectHome
    ^ self onDir: UIManager default chooseDirectory
```

The last method opens a browser to select the directory to open. Now, if you inspect the result of WebDir selectHome, you will be prompted for the directory containing your web pages, and you will be able to verify that webDir and homePath are properly initialized to the directory holding your web site and the full path name of this directory.

It would be nice to be able to programmatically instantiate a WebDir, so let's add another creation method.

> **To do** Add the following methods and try it out by inspecting the result of WebDir onPath: 'path to your web site'.

```
WebDir class>>onPath: homePath
    ^ self onPath: homePath home: homePath

WebDir class>>onPath: path home: homePath
    ^ self new setDir: path asFileReference home: homePath
```

Pattern matching HTML files

So far so good. Now we would like to use regexes to find out which HTML files this web site contains.

331

If we browse the `FileDirectory` class, we find that the method `fileNames` will list all the files in a directory. We want to select just those with the file extension `.html`. The regex that we need is `'.*\.html'`. The first dot will match any character except a newline:

```
'x' matchesRegex: '.'
>>> true
```

```
' ' matchesRegex: '.'
>>> true
```

```
Character cr asString matchesRegex: '.'
>>> true
```

The `*` (known as the *Kleene star*, after Stephen Kleene, who invented it) is a regex operator that will match the preceding regex any number of times (including zero).

```
'' matchesRegex: 'x*'
>>> true
```

```
'x' matchesRegex: 'x*'
>>> true
```

```
'xx' matchesRegex: 'x*'
>>> true
```

```
'y' matchesRegex: 'x*'
>>> false
```

Since the dot is a special character in regexes, if we want to literally match a dot, then we must escape it.

```
'.' matchesRegex: '.'
>>> true
```

```
'x' matchesRegex: '.'
>>> true
```

```
'.' matchesRegex: '\.'
>>> true
```

```
'x' matchesRegex: '\.'
>>> false
```

Now let's check our regex to find HTML files works as expected.

```
'index.html' matchesRegex: '.*\.html'
>>> true
```

```
'foo.html' matchesRegex: '.*\.html'
>>> true
```

```
'style.css' matchesRegex: '.*\.html'
>>> false
```

17.1 Tutorial example — generating a site map

```
'index.htm' matchesRegex: '.*\.html'
>>> false
```

Looks good. Now let's try it out in our application.

> **To do** Add the following method to `WebDir` and try it out on your test web site.

```
WebDir >> htmlFiles
    ^ webDir fileNames select: [ :each | each matchesRegex: '.*\.html' ]
```

If you send `htmlFiles` to a `WebDir` instance and `print` it, you should see something like this:

```
(WebDir onPath: '...') htmlFiles
>>> #('index.html' ...)
```

Caching the regex

Now, if you browse `matchesRegex:`, you will discover that it is an extension method of `String` that creates a fresh instance of `RxParser` every time it is sent. That is fine for ad hoc queries, but if we are applying the same regex to every file in a web site, it is smarter to create just one instance of `RxParser` and reuse it. Let's do that.

> **To do** Add a new instance variable `htmlRegex` to `WebDir` and initialize it by sending `asRegex` to our regex string. Modify `WebDir>>htmlFiles` to use the same regex each time as follows:

```
WebDir >> initialize
    htmlRegex := '.*\.html' asRegex

WebDir >> htmlFiles
    ^ webDir fileNames select: [ :each | htmlRegex matches: each ]
```

Now listing the HTML files should work just as it did before, except that we reuse the same regex object many times.

Accessing web pages

Accessing the details of individual web pages should be the responsibility of a separate class, so let's define it, and let the `WebDir` class create the instances.

> **To do** Define a class `WebPage` with instance variables `path`, to identify the HTML file, and `homePath`, to identify the root directory of the web site. (We will need this to correctly generate links from the root of the web site to the files it contains.) Define an initialization method on the instance side and a creation method on the class side.

```
WebPage >> initializePath: filePath homePath: dirPath
    path := filePath.
    homePath := dirPath

WebPage class >> on: filePath forHome: homePath
    ^ self new initializePath: filePath homePath: homePath
```

A WebDir instance should be able to return a list of all the web pages it contains.

> **To do**   Add the following method to WebDir, and inspect the return value to verify that it works correctly.

```
WebDir >> webPages
    ^ self htmlFiles collect:
        [ :each | WebPage
            on: webDir pathString, '/', each
            forHome: homePath ]
```

You should see something like this:

```
(WebDir onPath: '...') webPages
>>> an Array(a WebPage a WebPage ...)
```

String substitutions

That's not very informative, so let's use a regex to get the actual file name for each web page. To do this, we want to strip away all the characters from the path name up to the last directory. On a Unix file system directories end with a slash (/), so we need to delete everything up to the last slash in the file path.

The String extension method copyWithRegex:matchesReplacedWith: does what we want:

```
'hello' copyWithRegex: '[elo]+' matchesReplacedWith: 'i'
>>> 'hi'
```

In this example the regex [elo] matches any of the characters e, l or o. The operator + is like the Kleene star, but it matches exactly *one* or more instances of the regex preceding it. Here it will match the entire substring 'ello' and replay it in a fresh string with the letter i.

> **To do**   Add the following method and verify that it works as expected.

```
WebPage >> fileName
    ^ path copyWithRegex: '.*/' matchesReplacedWith: ''
```

Now you should see something like this on your test web site:

```
(WebDir onPath: '...') webPages collect: [:each | each fileName ]
>>> #('index.html' ...)
```

17.1 Tutorial example — generating a site map

Extracting regex matches

Our next task is to extract the title of each HTML page. First we need a way to get at the contents of each page. This is straightforward.

▌ **To do**   Add the following method and try it out.

```
WebPage >> contents
    ^ (FileStream oldFileOrNoneNamed: path) contents
```

Actually, you might have problems if your web pages contain non-ascii characters, in which case you might be better off with the following code:

```
WebPage >> contents
    ^ (FileStream oldFileOrNoneNamed: path)
        converter: Latin1TextConverter new;
        contents
```

You should now be able to see something like this:

```
(WebDir onPath: '...') webPages first contents
>>> '<head>
<title>Home Page</title>
...
'
```

Now let's extract the title. In this case we are looking for the text that occurs *between* the HTML tags <title> and </title>.

What we need is a way to extract *part* of the match of a regular expression. Subexpressions of regexes are delimited by parentheses. Consider the regex ([CARETaeiou]+)([aeiou]+); it consists of two subexpressions, the first of which will match a sequence of one or more non-vowels, and the second of which will match one or more vowels: the operator CARET at the start of a bracketed set of characters negates the set. (NB: In Pharo the caret is also the return keyword, which we write as ^. To avoid confusion, we will write CARET when we are using the caret within regular expressions to negate sets of characters, but you should not forget, they are actually the same thing.) Now we will try to match a *prefix* of the string 'pharo' and extract the submatches:

```
| re |
re := '([CARETaeiou]+)([aeiou]+)' asRegex.
re matchesPrefix: 'pharo'
>>> true
re subexpression: 1
>>> 'pha'
re subexpression: 2
>>> 'ph'
re subexpression: 3
>>> 'a'
```

335

After successfully matching a regex against a string, you can always send it the message subexpression: 1 to extract the entire match. You can also send subexpression: n where n-1 is the number of subexpressions in the regex. The regex above has two subexpressions, numbered 2 and 3.

We will use the same trick to extract the title from an HTML file.

▎ **To do**   Define the following method:

```
WebPage >> title
    | re |
    re := '[\w\W]*<title>(.*)</title>' asRegexIgnoringCase.
    ^ (re matchesPrefix: self contents)
        ifTrue: [ re subexpression: 2 ]
        ifFalse: [ '(', self fileName, ' -- untitled)' ]
```

There are a couple of subtle points to notice here. First, HTML does not care whether tags are upper or lower case, so we must make our regex case insensitive by instantiating it with asRegexIgnoringCase.

Second, since dot matches any character *except a newline*, the regex .*<title>(.*)</title> will not work as expected if multiple lines appear before the title. The regex \w matches any alphanumeric, and \W will match any non-alphanumeric, so [\w\W] will match any character *including newlines.* (If we expect titles to possible contain newlines, we should play the same trick with the subexpression.)

Now we can test our title extractor, and we should see something like this:

```
(WebDir onPath: '...') webPages first title
>>> 'Home page'
```

More string substitutions

In order to generate our site map, we need to generate links to the individual web pages. We can use the document title as the name of the link. We just need to generate the right path to the web page from the root of the web site. Luckily this is trivial — it is simple the full path to the web page minus the full path to the root directory of the web site.

We must only watch out for one thing. Since the homePath variable does not end in a /, we must append one, so that relative path does not include a leading /. Notice the difference between the following two results:

```
'/home/testweb/index.html' copyWithRegex: '/home/testweb'
    matchesReplacedWith: ''
>>> '/index.html'
```

```
'/home/testweb/index.html' copyWithRegex: '/home/testweb/'
    matchesReplacedWith: ''
>>> 'index.html'
```

17.1 Tutorial example — generating a site map

The first result would give us an absolute path, which is probably not what we want.

To do Define the following methods:

```
WebPage >> relativePath
   ^ path
      copyWithRegex: homePath, '/'
      matchesReplacedWith: ''

WebPage >> link
   ^ '<a href="', self relativePath, '">', self title, '</a>'
```

You should now be able to see something like this:

```
(WebDir onPath: '...') webPages first link
>>> '<a href="index.html">Home Page</a>'
```

Generating the site map

Actually, we are now done with the regular expressions we need to generate the site map. We just need a few more methods to complete the application.

To do If you want to see the site map generation, just add the following methods.

If our web site has subdirectories, we need a way to access them:

```
WebDir >> webDirs
   ^ webDir directoryNames
      collect: [ :each | WebDir onPath: webDir pathString, '/', each
            home: homePath ]
```

We need to generate HTML bullet lists containing links for each web page of a web directory. Subdirectories should be indented in their own bullet list.

```
WebDir >> printTocOn: aStream
   self htmlFiles
      ifNotEmpty: [
         aStream nextPutAll: '<ul>'; cr.
         self webPages
            do: [:each | aStream nextPutAll: '<li>';
               nextPutAll: each link;
               nextPutAll: '</li>'; cr].
         self webDirs
            do: [:each | each printTocOn: aStream].
         aStream nextPutAll: '</ul>'; cr]
```

We create a file called *toc.html* in the root web directory and dump the site map there.

Figure 17.2: A small site map.

```
WebDir >> tocFileName
    ^ 'toc.html'

WebDir >> makeToc
    | tocStream |
    tocStream := (webDir / self tocFileName) writeStream.
    self printTocOn: tocStream.
    tocStream close.
```

Now we can generate a table of contents for an arbitrary web directory!

```
WebDir selectHome makeToc
```

17.2 Regex syntax

We will now have a closer look at the syntax of regular expressions as supported by the Regex package.

The simplest regular expression is a single character. It matches exactly that character. A sequence of characters matches a string with exactly the same sequence of characters:

```
'a' matchesRegex: 'a'
>>> true
```

```
'foobar' matchesRegex: 'foobar'
>>> true
```

```
'blorple' matchesRegex: 'foobar'
>>> false
```

Operators are applied to regular expressions to produce more complex regular expressions. Sequencing (placing expressions one after another) as an operator is, in a certain sense, *invisible* — yet it is arguably the most common.

17.2 Regex syntax

We have already seen the Kleene star (*) and the + operator. A regular expression followed by an asterisk matches any number (including 0) of matches of the original expression. For example:

```
'ab' matchesRegex: 'a*b'
>>> true
```

```
'aaaaab' matchesRegex: 'a*b'
>>> true
```

```
'b' matchesRegex: 'a*b'
>>> true
```

```
'aac' matchesRegex: 'a*b'
>>> false "b does not match"
```

The Kleene star has higher precedence than sequencing. A star applies to the shortest possible subexpression that precedes it. For example, ab* means a followed by zero or more occurrences of b, not *zero or more occurrences of* ab:

```
'abbb' matchesRegex: 'ab*'
>>> true
```

```
'abab' matchesRegex: 'ab*'
>>> false
```

To obtain a regex that matches *zero or more occurrences of* ab, we must enclose ab in parentheses:

```
'abab' matchesRegex: '(ab)*'
>>> true
```

```
'abcab' matchesRegex: '(ab)*'
>>> false "c spoils the fun"
```

Two other useful operators similar to * are + and ?. + matches one or more instances of the regex it modifies, and ? will match zero or one instance.

```
'ac' matchesRegex: 'ab*c'
>>> true
```

```
'ac' matchesRegex: 'ab+c'
>>> false "need at least one b"
```

```
'abbc' matchesRegex: 'ab+c'
>>> true
```

```
'abbc' matchesRegex: 'ab?c'
>>> false "too many b's"
```

As we have seen, the characters *, +, ?, (, and) have special meaning within regular expressions. If we need to match any of them literally, it should be escaped by preceding it with a backslash \ . Thus, backslash is also special character, and needs to be escaped for a literal match. The same holds for all further special characters we will see.

```
'ab*' matchesRegex: 'ab*'
>>> false "star in the right string is special"
```

```
'ab*' matchesRegex: 'ab\*'
>>> true
```

```
'a\c' matchesRegex: 'a\\c'
>>> true
```

The last operator is |, which expresses choice between two subexpressions. It matches a string if either of the two subexpressions matches the string. It has the lowest precedence — even lower than sequencing. For example, ab*|ba* means *a followed by any number of b's, or b followed by any number of a's*:

```
'abb' matchesRegex: 'ab*|ba*'
>>> true
```

```
'baa' matchesRegex: 'ab*|ba*'
>>> true
```

```
'baab' matchesRegex: 'ab*|ba*'
>>> false
```

A bit more complex example is the expression c(a|d)+r, which matches the name of any of the Lisp-style car, cdr, caar, cadr, ... functions:

```
'car' matchesRegex: 'c(a|d)+r'
>>> true
```

```
'cdr' matchesRegex: 'c(a|d)+r'
>>> true
```

```
'cadr' matchesRegex: 'c(a|d)+r'
>>> true
```

It is possible to write an expression that matches an empty string, for example the expression a| matches an empty string. However, it is an error to apply *, +, or ? to such an expression: (a|)* is invalid.

So far, we have used only characters as the *smallest* components of regular expressions. There are other, more interesting, components. A character set is a string of characters enclosed in square brackets. It matches any single character if it appears between the brackets. For example, [01] matches either 0 or 1:

```
'0' matchesRegex: '[01]'
>>> true
```

```
'3' matchesRegex: '[01]'
>>> false
```

```
'11' matchesRegex: '[01]'
>>> false "a set matches only one character"
```

Using plus operator, we can build the following binary number recognizer:

17.2 Regex syntax

```
'10010100' matchesRegex: '[01]+'
>>> true
```
```
'10001210' matchesRegex: '[01]+'
>>> false
```

If the first character after the opening bracket is CARET, the set is inverted: it matches any single character *not* appearing between the brackets:

```
'0' matchesRegex: '[CARET01]'
>>> false
```
```
'3' matchesRegex: '[CARET01]'
>>> true
```

For convenience, a set may include ranges: pairs of characters separated by a hyphen (-). This is equivalent to listing all characters in between: '[0-9]' is the same as '[0123456789]'. Special characters within a set are CARET, -, and], which closes the set. Below are examples how to literally match them in a set:

```
'CARET' matchesRegex: '[01CARET]'
>>> true   "put the caret anywhere except the start"
```
```
'-' matchesRegex: '[01-]'
>>> true   "put the hyphen at the end"
```
```
']' matchesRegex: '[]01]'
>>> true   "put the closing bracket at the start"
```

Thus, empty and universal sets cannot be specified.

Character classes

Regular expressions can also include the following backquote escapes to refer to popular classes of characters: \w to match alphanumeric characters, \d to match digits, and \s to match whitespace. Their upper-case variants, \W, \D and \S, match the complementary characters (non-alphanumerics, non-digits and non-whitespace). Here is a summary of the syntax seen so far:

341

Syntax	What it represents
a	literal match of character a
.	match any char (except newline)
(...)	group subexpression
\x	escape the following special character where 'x' can be 'w','s','d','W','S','D'
*	Kleene star — match previous regex zero or more times
+	match previous regex one or more times
?	match previous regex zero times or once
|	match choice of left and right regex
[abcd]	match choice of characters abcd
[^abcd]	match negated choice of characters
[0-9]	match range of characters 0 to 9
\w	match alphanumeric
\W	match non-alphanumeric
\d	match digit
\D	match non-digit
\s	match space
\S	match non-space

As mentioned in the introduction, regular expressions are especially useful for validating user input, and character classes turn out to be especially useful for defining such regexes. For example, non-negative numbers can be matched with the regex \d+:

```
'42' matchesRegex: '\d+'
>>> true
```

```
'-1' matchesRegex: '\d+'
>>> false
```

Better yet, we might want to specify that non-zero numbers should not start with the digit 0:

```
'0' matchesRegex: '0|([1-9]\d*)'
>>> true
```

```
'1' matchesRegex: '0|([1-9]\d*)'
>>> true
```

```
'42' matchesRegex: '0|([1-9]\d*)'
>>> true
```

```
'099' matchesRegex: '0|([1-9]\d*)'
>>> false "leading 0"
```

We can check for negative and positive numbers as well:

```
'0' matchesRegex: '(0|((\+|-)?[1-9]\d*))'
>>> true
```

17.2 Regex syntax

```
'-1' matchesRegex: '(0|((\+|-)?[1-9]\d*))'
>>> true
```

```
'42' matchesRegex: '(0|((\+|-)?[1-9]\d*))'
>>> true
```

```
'+99' matchesRegex: '(0|((\+|-)?[1-9]\d*))'
>>> true
```

```
'-0' matchesRegex: '(0|((\+|-)?[1-9]\d*))'
>>> false "negative zero"
```

```
'01' matchesRegex: '(0|((\+|-)?[1-9]\d*))'
>>> false "leading zero"
```

Floating point numbers should require at least one digit after the dot:

```
'0' matchesRegex: '(0|((\+|-)?[1-9]\d*))(\.\d+)?'
>>> true
```

```
'0.9' matchesRegex: '(0|((\+|-)?[1-9]\d*))(\.\d+)?'
>>> true
```

```
'3.14' matchesRegex: '(0|((\+|-)?[1-9]\d*))(\.\d+)?'
>>> true
```

```
'-42' matchesRegex: '(0|((\+|-)?[1-9]\d*))(\.\d+)?'
>>> true
```

```
'2.' matchesRegex: '(0|((\+|-)?[1-9]\d*))(\.\d+)?'
>>> false "need digits after ."
```

For dessert, here is a recognizer for a general number format: anything like 999, or 999.999, or -999.999e+21.

```
'-999.999e+21' matchesRegex: '(\+|-)?\d+(\.\d*)?((e|E)(\+|-)?\d+)?'
>>> true
```

Character classes can also include the following grep(1)-compatible elements:

Syntax	What it represents
[:alnum:]	any alphanumeric
[:alpha:]	any alphabetic character
[:cntrl:]	any control character (ascii code below 32)
[:digit:]	any decimal digit
[:graph:]	any graphical character (ascii code above 32)
[:lower:]	any lowercase character
[:print:]	any printable character (here, the same as [:graph:])
[:punct:]	any punctuation character
[:space:]	any whitespace character
[:upper:]	any uppercase character
[:xdigit:]	any hexadecimal character

Note that these elements are components of the character classes, *i.e.*, they have to be enclosed in an extra set of square brackets to form a valid regular expression. For example, a non-empty string of digits would be represented as [[:digit:]]+. The above primitive expressions and operators are common to many implementations of regular expressions.

```
'42' matchesRegex: '[[:digit:]]+'
>>> true
```

Special character classes

The next primitive expression is unique to this Smalltalk implementation. A sequence of characters between colons is treated as a unary selector which is supposed to be understood by characters. A character matches such an expression if it answers true to a message with that selector. This allows a more readable and efficient way of specifying character classes. For example, [0-9] is equivalent to :isDigit:, but the latter is more efficient. Analogously to character sets, character classes can be negated: :CARETisDigit: matches a character that answers false to isDigit, and is therefore equivalent to [CARET0-9].

So far we have seen the following equivalent ways to write a regular expression that matches a non-empty string of digits: [0-9]+, \d+, [\d]+, [[:digit:]]+, :isDigit:+.

```
'42' matchesRegex: '[0-9]+'
>>> true
```

```
'42' matchesRegex: '\d+'
>>> true
```

```
'42' matchesRegex: '[\d]+'
>>> true
```

```
'42' matchesRegex: '[[:digit:]]+'
>>> true
```

```
'42' matchesRegex: ':isDigit:+'
>>> true
```

Matching boundaries

The last group of special primitive expressions shown next is used to match boundaries of strings.

Syntax	What it represents
CARET	match an empty string at the beginning of a line
\$	match an empty string at the end of a line
\b	match an empty string at a word boundary
\B	match an empty string not at a word boundary
\<	match an empty string at the beginning of a word
\>	match an empty string at the end of a word

```
'hello world' matchesRegex: '.*\bw.*'
>>> true "word boundary before w"
```

```
'hello world' matchesRegex: '.*\bo.*'
>>> false "no boundary before o"
```

17.3 Regex API

Up to now we have focussed mainly on the syntax of regexes. Now we will have a closer look at the different messages understood by strings and regexes.

Matching prefixes and ignoring case

So far most of our examples have used the String extension method matchesRegex:.

Strings also understand the following messages: prefixMatchesRegex:, matchesRegexIgnoringCase: and prefixMatchesRegexIgnoringCase:.

The message prefixMatchesRegex: is just like matchesRegex, except that the whole receiver is not expected to match the regular expression passed as the argument; matching just a prefix of it is enough.

```
'abacus' matchesRegex: '(a|b)+'
>>> false
```

```
'abacus' prefixMatchesRegex: '(a|b)+'
>>> true
```

```
'ABBA' matchesRegexIgnoringCase: '(a|b)+'
>>> true
```

```
'Abacus' matchesRegexIgnoringCase: '(a|b)+'
>>> false
```

```
'Abacus' prefixMatchesRegexIgnoringCase: '(a|b)+'
>>> true
```

Enumeration interface

Some applications need to access *all* matches of a certain regular expression within a string. The matches are accessible using a protocol modeled after the familiar Collection-like enumeration protocol.

regex:matchesDo: evaluates a one-argument aBlock for every match of the regular expression within the receiver string.

```
| list |
list := OrderedCollection new.
'Jack meet Jill' regex: '\w+' matchesDo: [:word | list add: word].
list
>>> an OrderedCollection('Jack' 'meet' 'Jill')
```

regex:matchesCollect: evaluates a one-argument aBlock for every match of the regular expression within the receiver string. It then collects the results and answers them as a SequenceableCollection.

```
'Jack meet Jill' regex: '\w+' matchesCollect: [:word | word size]
>>> an OrderedCollection(4 4 4)
```

allRegexMatches: returns a collection of all matches (substrings of the receiver string) of the regular expression.

```
'Jack and Jill went up the hill' allRegexMatches: '\w+'
>>> an OrderedCollection('Jack' 'and' 'Jill' 'went' 'up' 'the' 'hill')
```

Replacement and translation

It is possible to replace all matches of a regular expression with a certain string using the message copyWithRegex:matchesReplacedWith:.

```
'Krazy hates Ignatz' copyWithRegex: '\<[[:lower:]]+\>'
    matchesReplacedWith: 'loves'
>>> 'Krazy loves Ignatz'
```

A more general substitution is match translation. This message evaluates a block passing it each match of the regular expression in the receiver string and answers a copy of the receiver with the block results spliced into it in place of the respective matches.

```
'Krazy loves Ignatz' copyWithRegex: '\b[a-z]+\b'
    matchesTranslatedUsing: [:each | each asUppercase]
>>> 'Krazy LOVES Ignatz'
```

All messages of enumeration and replacement protocols perform a case-sensitive match. Case-insensitive versions are not provided as part of a String protocol. Instead, they are accessible using the lower-level matching interface presented in the following section.

Lower-level interface

When you send the message `matchesRegex:` to a string, the following happens:

- A fresh instance of `RxParser` is created, and the regular expression string is passed to it, yielding the expression's syntax tree.
- The syntax tree is passed as an initialization parameter to an instance of `RxMatcher`. The instance sets up some data structure that will work as a recognizer for the regular expression described by the tree.
- The original string is passed to the matcher, and the matcher checks for a match.

The Matcher

If you repeatedly match a number of strings against the same regular expression using one of the messages defined in `String`, the regular expression string is parsed and a new matcher is created for every match. You can avoid this overhead by building a matcher for the regular expression, and then reusing the matcher over and over again. You can, for example, create a matcher at a class or instance initialization stage, and store it in a variable for future use. You can create a matcher using one of the following methods:

- You can send `asRegex` or `asRegexIgnoringCase` to the string.
- You can directly invoke the `RxMatcher` constructor methods `forString:` or `forString:ignoreCase:` (which is what the convenience methods above will do).

Here we send `matchesIn:` to collect all the matches found in a string:

```
| octal |
octal := '8r[0-9A-F]+' asRegex.
octal matchesIn: '8r52 = 16r2A'
>>> an OrderedCollection('8r52')
```

```
| hex |
hex := '16r[0-9A-F]+' asRegexIgnoringCase.
hex matchesIn: '8r52 = 16r2A'
>>> an OrderedCollection('16r2A')
```

```
| hex |
hex := RxMatcher forString: '16r[0-9A-Fa-f]+' ignoreCase: true.
hex matchesIn: '8r52 = 16r2A'
>>> an OrderedCollection('16r2A')
```

Matching

A matcher understands these messages (all of them return `true` to indicate successful match or search, and `false` otherwise):

matches: aString — true if the whole argument string (aString) matches.

```
'\w+' asRegex matches: 'Krazy'
>>> true
```

matchesPrefix: aString — true if some prefix of the argument string (not necessarily the whole string) matches.

```
'\w+' asRegex matchesPrefix: 'Ignatz hates Krazy'
>>> true
```

search: aString — Search the string for the first occurrence of a matching substring. Note that the first two methods only try matching from the very beginning of the string. Using the above example with a matcher for a+, this method would answer success given a string 'baaa', while the previous two would fail.

```
'\b[a-z]+\b' asRegex search: 'Ignatz hates Krazy'
>>> true  "finds 'hates'"
```

The matcher also stores the outcome of the last match attempt and can report it: `lastResult` answers a Boolean: the outcome of the most recent match attempt. If no matches were attempted, the answer is unspecified.

```
| number |
number := '\d+' asRegex.
number search: 'Ignatz throws 5 bricks'.
number lastResult
>>> true
```

`matchesStream:`, `matchesStreamPrefix:` and `searchStream:` are analogous to the above three messages, but takes streams as their argument.

```
| ignatz names |
ignatz := ReadStream on: 'Ignatz throws bricks at Krazy'.
names := '\<[A-Z][a-z]+\>' asRegex.
names matchesStreamPrefix: ignatz
>>> true
```

Subexpression matches

After a successful match attempt, you can query which part of the original string has matched which part of the regex. A subexpression is a parenthesized part of a regular expression, or the whole expression. When a regular expression is compiled, its subexpressions are assigned indices starting from 1, depth-first, left-to-right.

For example, the regex `((\d+)\s*(\w+))` has four subexpressions, including itself.

```
1: ((\d+)\s*(\w+)) "the complete expression"
2: (\d+)\s*(\w+) "top parenthesized subexpression"
```

17.3 Regex API

```
3: \d+ "first leaf subexpression"
4: \w+ "second leaf subexpression"
```

The highest valid index is equal to 1 plus the number of matching parentheses. (So, 1 is always a valid index, even if there are no parenthesized subexpressions.)

After a successful match, the matcher can report what part of the original string matched what subexpression. It understands these messages:

subexpressionCount answers the total number of subexpressions: the highest value that can be used as a subexpression index with this matcher. This value is available immediately after initialization and never changes.

subexpression: takes a valid index as its argument, and may be sent only after a successful match attempt. The method answers a substring of the original string the corresponding subexpression has matched to.

subBeginning: and subEnd: answer the positions within the argument string or stream where the given subexpression match has started and ended, respectively.

```
| items |
items := '((\d+)\s*(\w+))' asRegex.
items search: 'Ignatz throws 1 brick at Krazy'.
items subexpressionCount
>>> 4
items subexpression: 1
>>> '1 brick' "complete expression"
items subexpression: 2
>>> '1 brick' "top subexpression"
items subexpression: 3
>>> '1' "first leaf subexpression"
items subexpression: 4
>>> 'brick' "second leaf subexpression"
items subBeginning: 3
>>> 14
items subEnd: 3
>>> 15
items subBeginning: 4
>>> 16
items subEnd: 4
>>> 21
```

As a more elaborate example, the following piece of code uses a MMM DD, YYYY date format recognizer to convert a date to a three-element array with year, month, and day strings:

```
| date result |
date :=
    '(Jan|Feb|Mar|Apr|May|Jun|Jul|Aug|Sep|Oct|Nov|Dec)\s+(\d\d?)\s*,\s*19(\d\d)'
    asRegex.
```

```
result := (date matches: 'Aug 6, 1996')
        ifTrue: [{ (date subexpression: 4) .
            (date subexpression: 2) .
            (date subexpression: 3) } ]
        ifFalse: ['no match'].
result
>>> #('96' 'Aug' '6')
```

Enumeration and Replacement

The String enumeration and replacement protocols that we saw earlier in this section are actually implemented by the matcher. RxMatcher implements the following methods for iterating over matches within strings: matchesIn:, matchesIn:do:, matchesIn:collect:, copy:replacingMatchesWith: and copy:translatingMatchesUsing:.

```
| seuss aWords |
seuss := 'The cat in the hat is back'.
aWords := '\<([^aeiou]|[a])+\>' asRegex. "match words with 'a' in them"
aWords matchesIn: seuss
>>> an OrderedCollection('cat' 'hat' 'back')
aWords matchesIn: seuss collect: [:each | each asUppercase ]
>>> an OrderedCollection('CAT' 'HAT' 'BACK')
aWords copy: seuss replacingMatchesWith: 'grinch'
>>> 'The grinch in the grinch is grinch'
aWords copy: seuss translatingMatchesUsing: [ :each | each asUppercase ]
>>> 'The CAT in the HAT is BACK'
```

There are also the following methods for iterating over matches within streams: matchesOnStream:, matchesOnStream:do:, matchesOnStream:collect:, copyStream:to:replacingMatchesWith: and copyStream:to:translatingMatchesUsing:.

Error Handling

Several exceptions may be raised by RxParser when building regexes. The exceptions have the common parent RegexError. You may use the usual Smalltalk exception handling mechanism to catch and handle them.

- RegexSyntaxError is raised if a syntax error is detected while parsing a
- regex RegexCompilationError is raised if an error is detected while
- building a matcher RegexMatchingError is raised if an error occurs while
- matching (for example, if a bad selector was specified using ':<selector>:'
- syntax, or because of the matcher's internal error).

```
[' +' asRegex] on: RegexError do: [:ex | ^ ex printString ]
>>> 'RegexSyntaxError: nullable closure'
```

17.4 Implementation Notes by Vassili Bykov

What to look at first.   In 90% of the cases, the method String>>matchesRegex: is all you need to access the package.

RxParser accepts a string or a stream of characters with a regular expression, and produces a syntax tree corresponding to the expression. The tree is made of instances of Rxs* classes.

RxMatcher accepts a syntax tree of a regular expression built by the parser and compiles it into a matcher: a structure made of instances of Rxm* classes. The RxMatcher instance can test whether a string or a positionable stream of characters matches the original regular expression, or it can search a string or a stream for substrings matching the expression. After a match is found, the matcher can report a specific string that matched the whole expression, or any parenthesized subexpression of it. All other classes support the same functionality and are used by RxParser, RxMatcher, or both.

Caveats   The matcher is similar in spirit, but *not* in design to Henry Spencer's original regular expression implementation in C. The focus is on simplicity, not on efficiency. I didn't optimize or profile anything. The matcher passes H. Spencer's test suite (see *test suite* protocol), with quite a few extra tests added, so chances are good there are not too many bugs. But watch out anyway.

Acknowledgments   Since the first release of the matcher, thanks to the input from several fellow Smalltalkers, I became convinced a native Smalltalk regular expression matcher was worth the effort to keep it alive. For the advice and encouragement that made this release possible, I want to thank: Felix Hack, Eliot Miranda, Robb Shecter, David N. Smith, Francis Wolinski and anyone whom I haven't yet met or heard from, but who agrees this has not been a complete waste of time.

17.5 Chapter Summary

Regular expressions are an essential tool for manipulating strings in a trivial way. This chapter presented the Regex package for Pharo. The essential points of this chapter are:

- For simple matching, just send matchesRegex: to a string
- When performance matters, send asRegex to the string representing the regex, and reuse the resulting matcher for multiple matches

- Subexpression of a matching regex may be easily retrieved to an arbitrary depth
- A matching regex can also replace or translate subexpressions in a new copy of the string matched
- An enumeration interface is provided to access all matches of a certain regular expression
- Regexes work with streams as well as with strings.

www.ingramcontent.com/pod-product-compliance
Lightning Source LLC
Chambersburg PA
CBHW060821170526
45158CB00001B/43